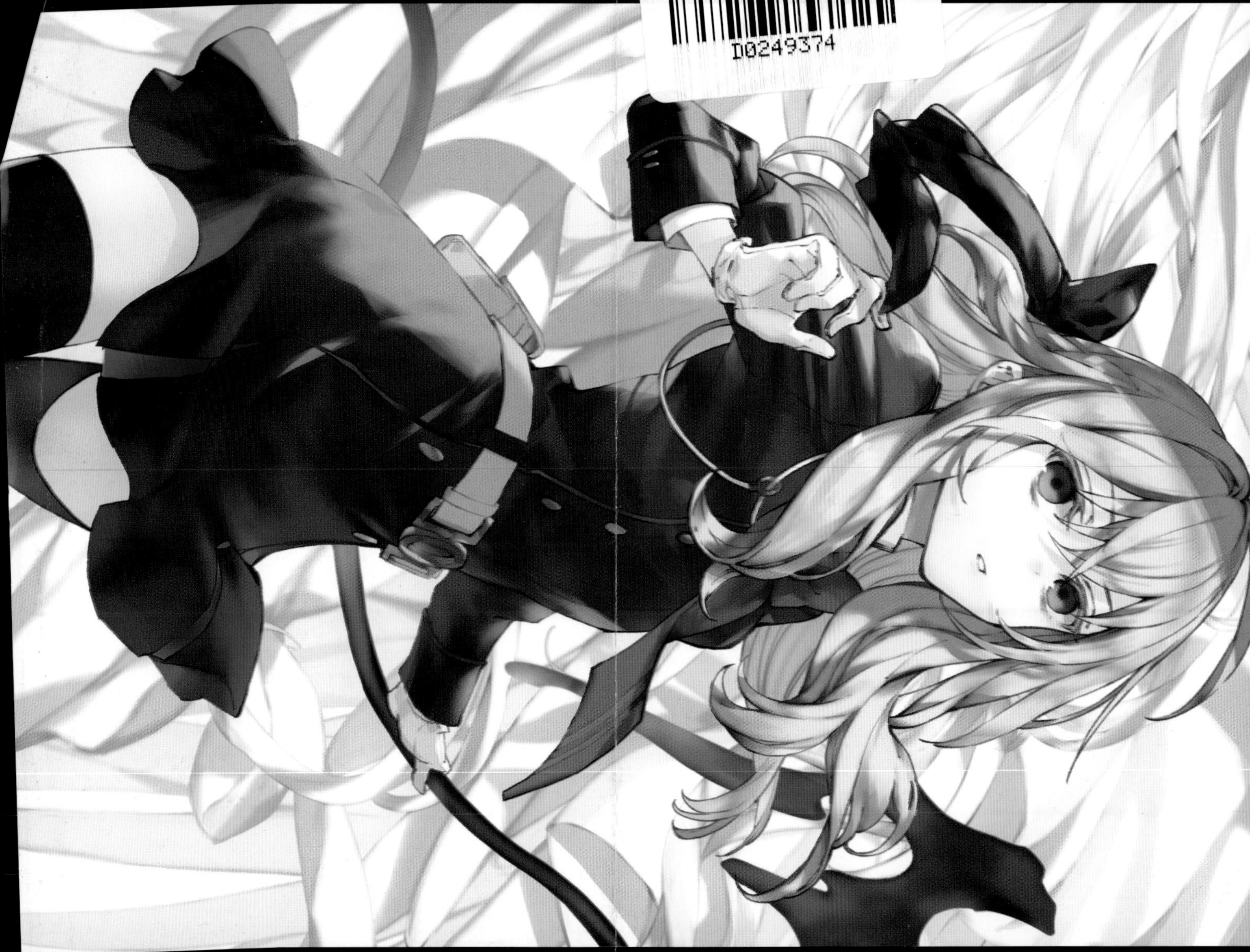

Seraph of the End

—VAMPIRE REIGN—

17

STORY BY **Takaya Kagami**

ART BY **Yamato Yamamoto**

STORYBOARDS BY **Daisuke Furuya**

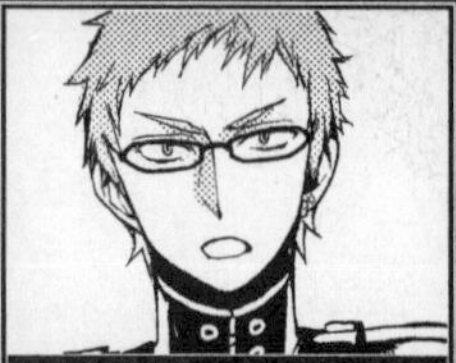

SHIHO KIMIZUKI

Yuichiro's friend. Smart but abrasive. His Cursed Gear is Kiseki-o, twin blades.

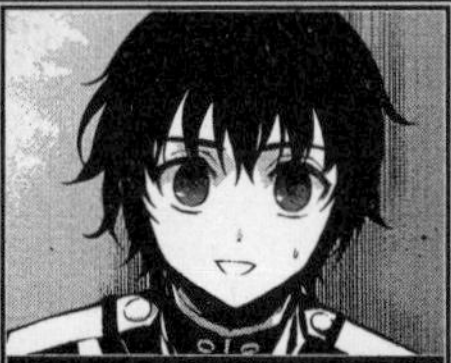

YOICHI SAOTOME

Yuichiro's friend. His sister was killed by a vampire. His Cursed Gear is Gekkouin, a bow.

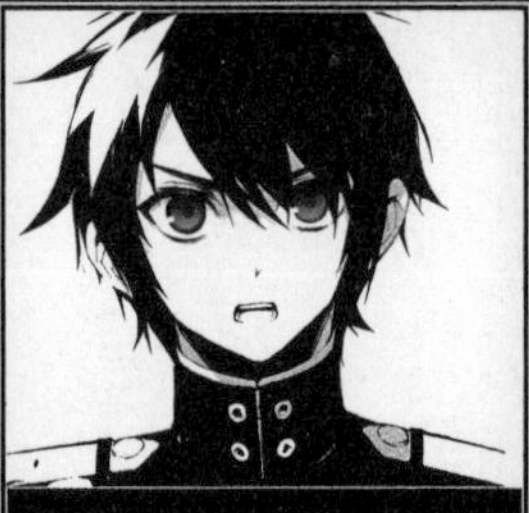

YUICHIRO HYAKUYA

A boy who escaped from the vampire capital, he has both great kindness and a great desire for revenge. Lone wolf. His Cursed Gear is Asuramaru, a katana.

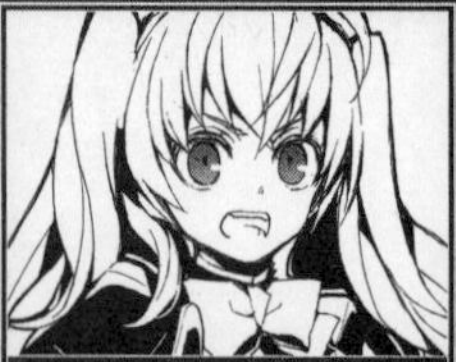

MITSUBA SANGU

An elite soldier who has been part of the Moon Demon Company since age 13. Bossy. Her Cursed Gear is Tenjiryu, a giant axe.

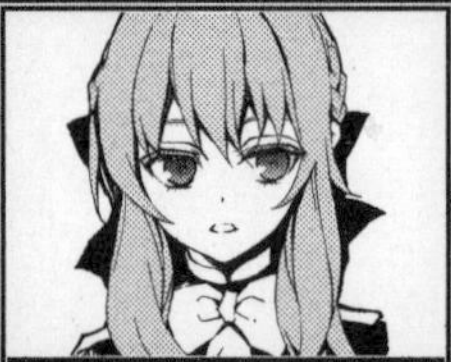

SHINOA HIRAGI

Guren's subordinate and Yuichiro's surveillance officer. Member of the illustrious Hiragi family. Her Cursed Gear is Shikama Doji, a scythe.

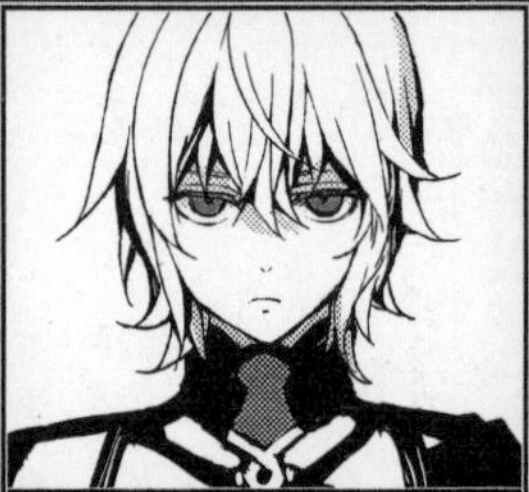

MIKAELA HYAKUYA

Yuichiro's best friend. He was supposedly killed but has come back to life as a vampire. Currently working with Shinoa Squad.

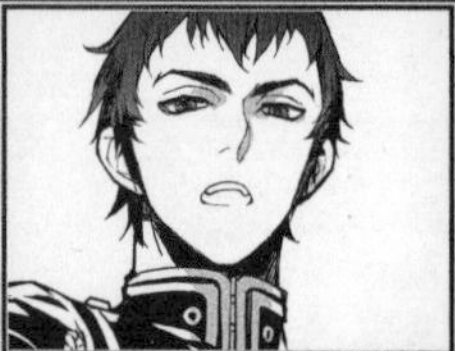

KURETO HIRAGI

A Lieutenant General in the Demon Army. Heir apparent to the Hiragi family, he is cold, cruel and ruthless.

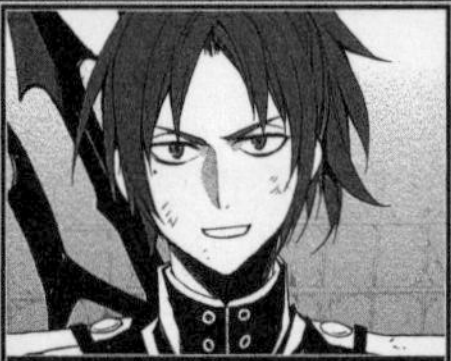

MAKOTO NARUMI

Former leader of Narumi Squad. After his entire squad died during the battle of Nagoya, he deserted the Demon Army with Shinoa Squad.

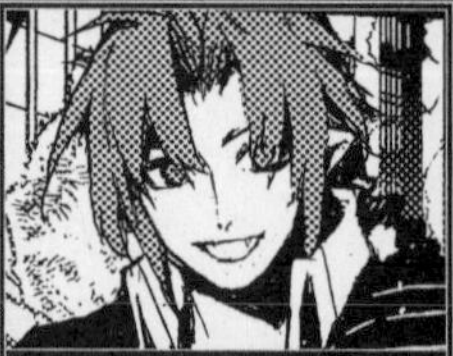

CROWLEY EUSFORD

A Thirteenth Progenitor vampire. Part of Ferid's faction.

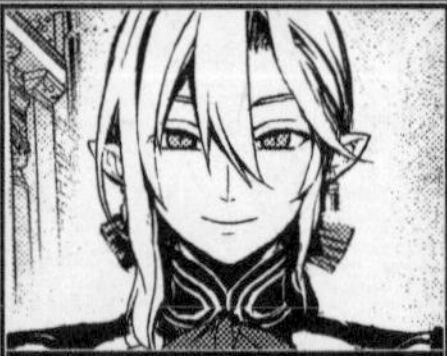

FERID BATHORY

A Seventh Progenitor vampire, he killed Mikaela.

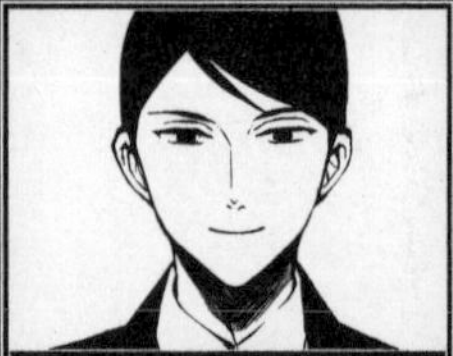

SAITO

A mysterious man somehow connected with the Hyakuya Sect. He was once a Second Progenitor vampire.

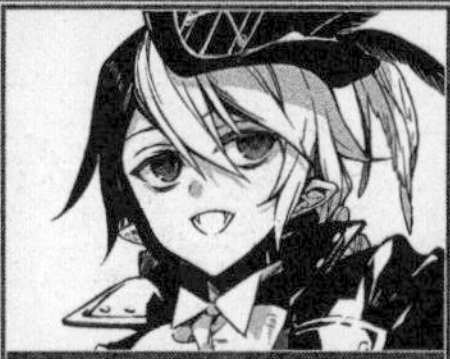

LEST KARR

Third Progenitor and ruler over the parts of Europe that used to be Germany.

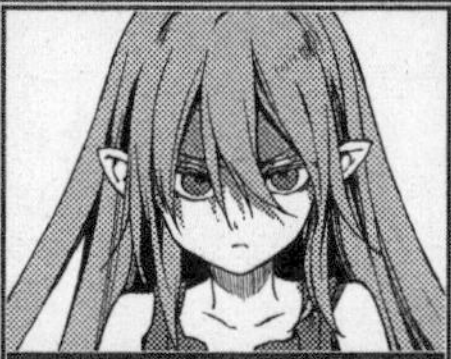

KRUL TEPES

Third Progenitor and Queen of the Vampires. She is currently being held prisoner by Urd Geales.

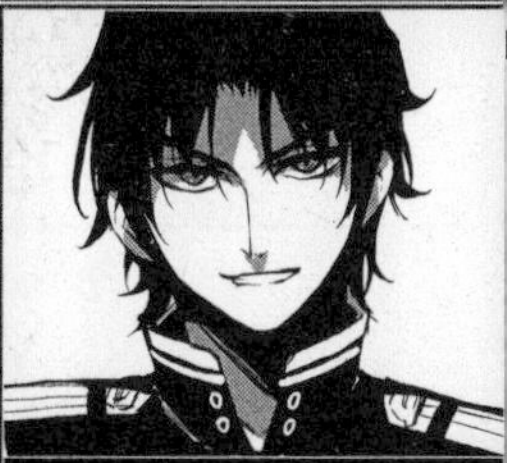

GUREN ICHINOSE

Lt. Colonel of the Moon Demon Company. He recruited Yuichiro into the Demon Army. During the battle in Nagoya, he began acting strangely... His Cursed Gear is Mahiru-no-yo, a katana.

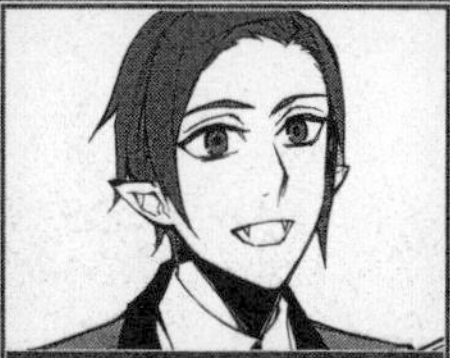

KY LUC

A Fifth Progenitor Vampire who follows Second Progenitor Urd Geales. Guarded Krul and Ferid when they were undergoing Exposure Torture.

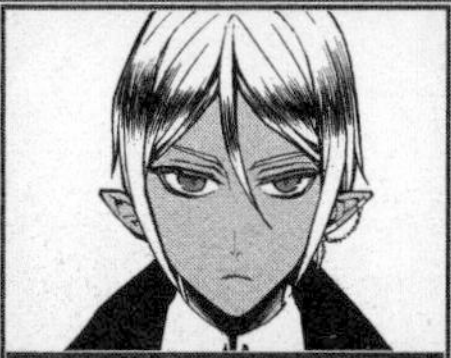

URD GEALES

Second Progenitor and ruler over the parts of Europe that used to be Russia.

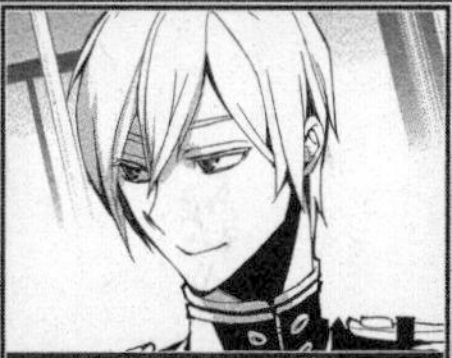

SHINYA HIRAGI

A Major General and adoptee into the Hiragi Family. He was Mahiru Hiragi's fiancé.

STORY

A mysterious virus decimates the human population, and vampires claim dominion over the world. Yuichiro and his adopted family of orphans are kept as vampire fodder in an underground city until the day Mikaela, Yuichiro's best friend, plots an ill-fated escape for the orphans. Only Yuichiro survives and reaches the surface.

Four years later, Yuichiro enters into the Moon Demon Company, a Vampire Extermination Unit in the Japanese Imperial Demon Army, to enact his revenge. There he gains Asuramaru, a demon-possessed weapon capable of killing vampires, and a squad of trusted friends—Shinoa, Yoichi, Kimizuki and Mitsuba.

In his battles against the vampires, Yuichiro discovers that not only is Mikaela alive, but he also has been turned into a vampire. After misunderstandings and near-misses, Yuichiro and Mikaela finally rejoin each other in Nagoya.

After the chaos and confusion of the Seraph of the End experiment and Guren's betrayal in Nagoya, Shinoa Squad deserts the Demon Army and accompanies Ferid to Osaka. There, Ferid and Krul are sentenced to exposure torture by Second Progenitor Urd Geales.

Meanwhile, Kureto carries out a successful coup d'état, taking control of the Demon Army from his father, Tenri. However, the godlike being Shikama Doji, which had been possessing Tenri, possesses him.

Back in Osaka, Yuichiro and the others battle Ky Luc and manage to rescue Ferid, while Ky runs off with Krul. Taking it as a small victory, the group moves to Guren's childhood home in Nagoya, where they find the Sixth Trumpeter...

Seraph of the End
VAMPIRE REIGN

17

CONTENTS

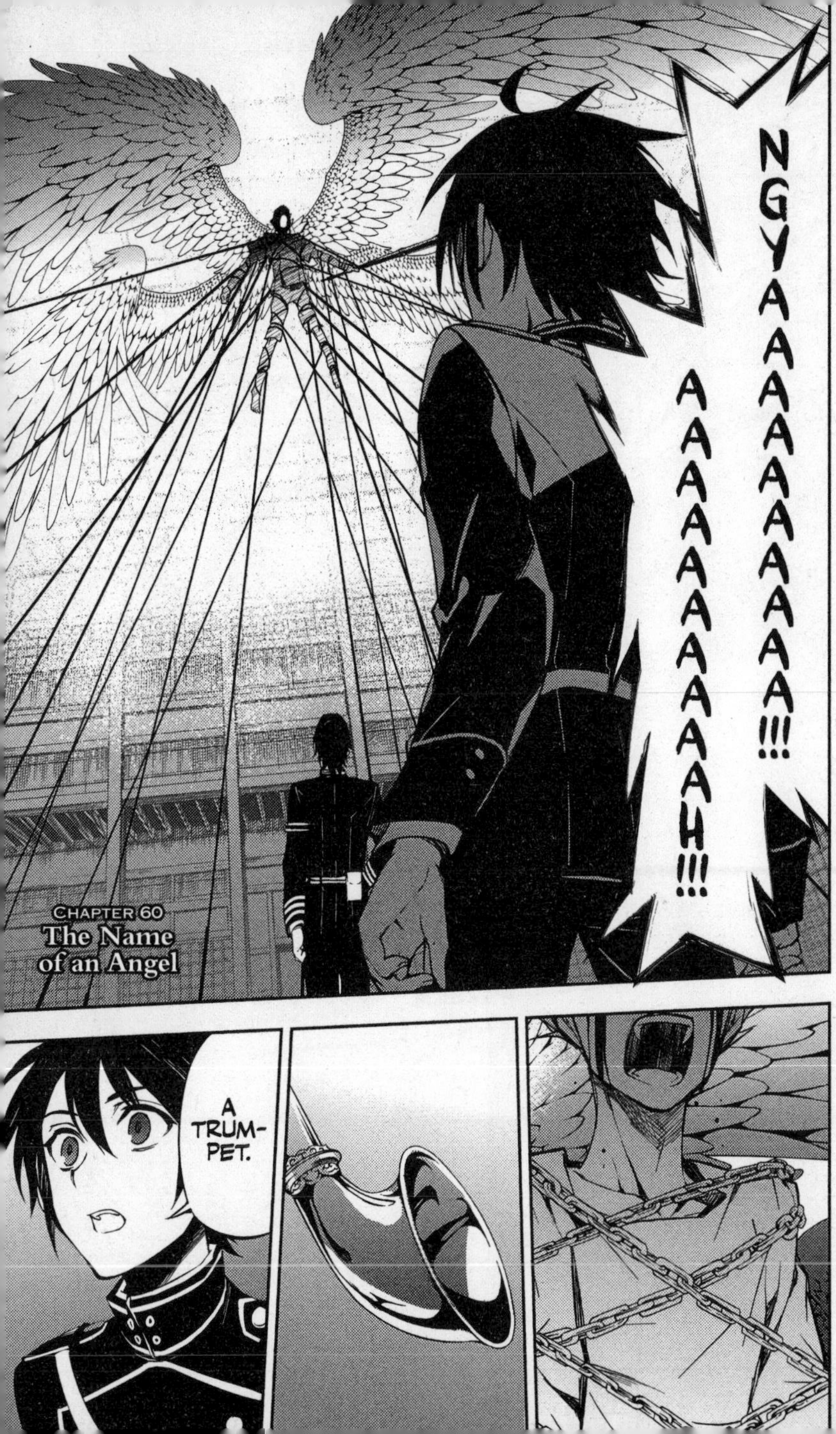
NGYAAAAAAAAAAA!!! AAAAAAAAAAAH!!!
CHAPTER 60
The Name of an Angel
A TRUMPET.

Chapter 60
The Name of an Angel

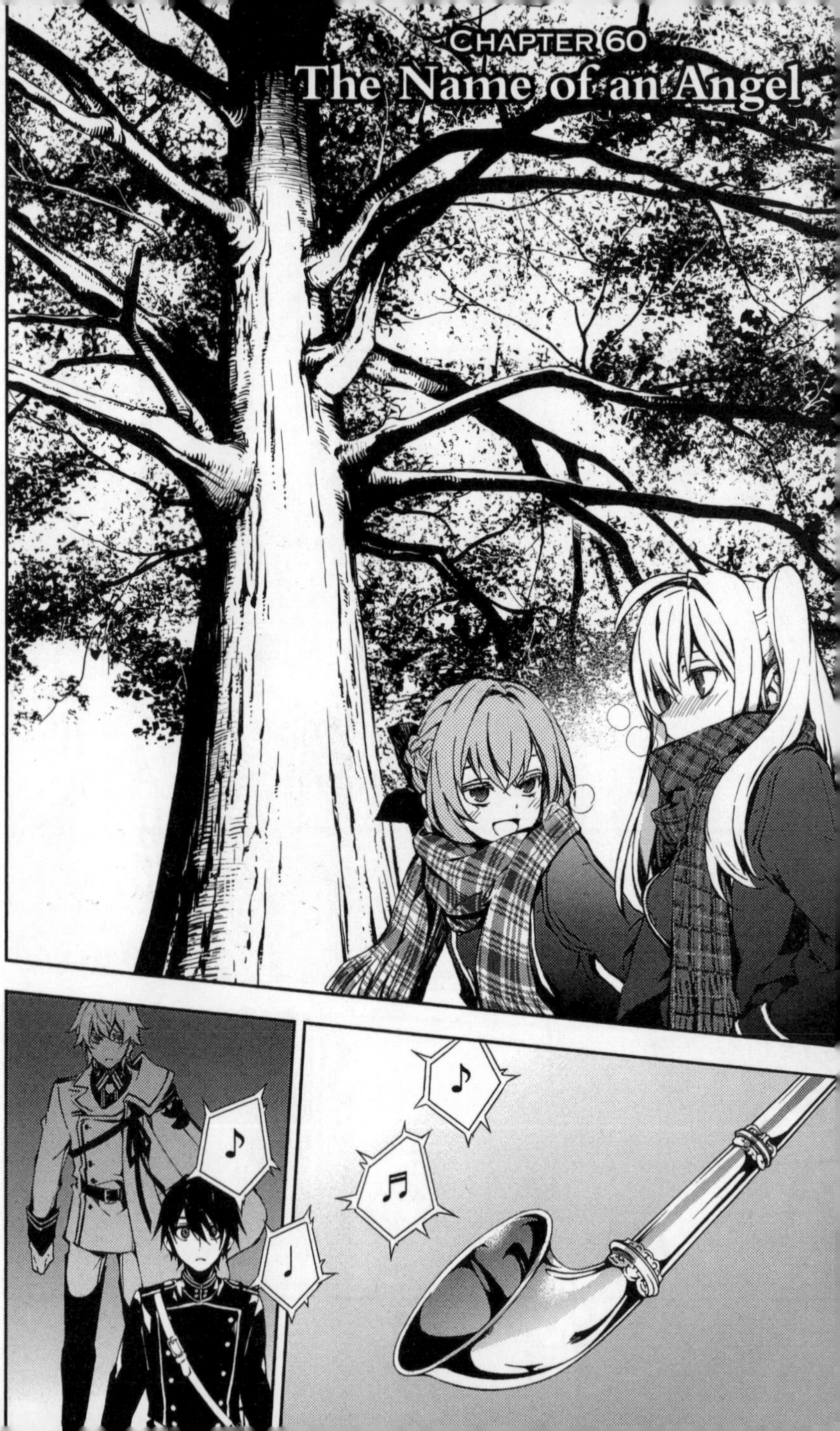

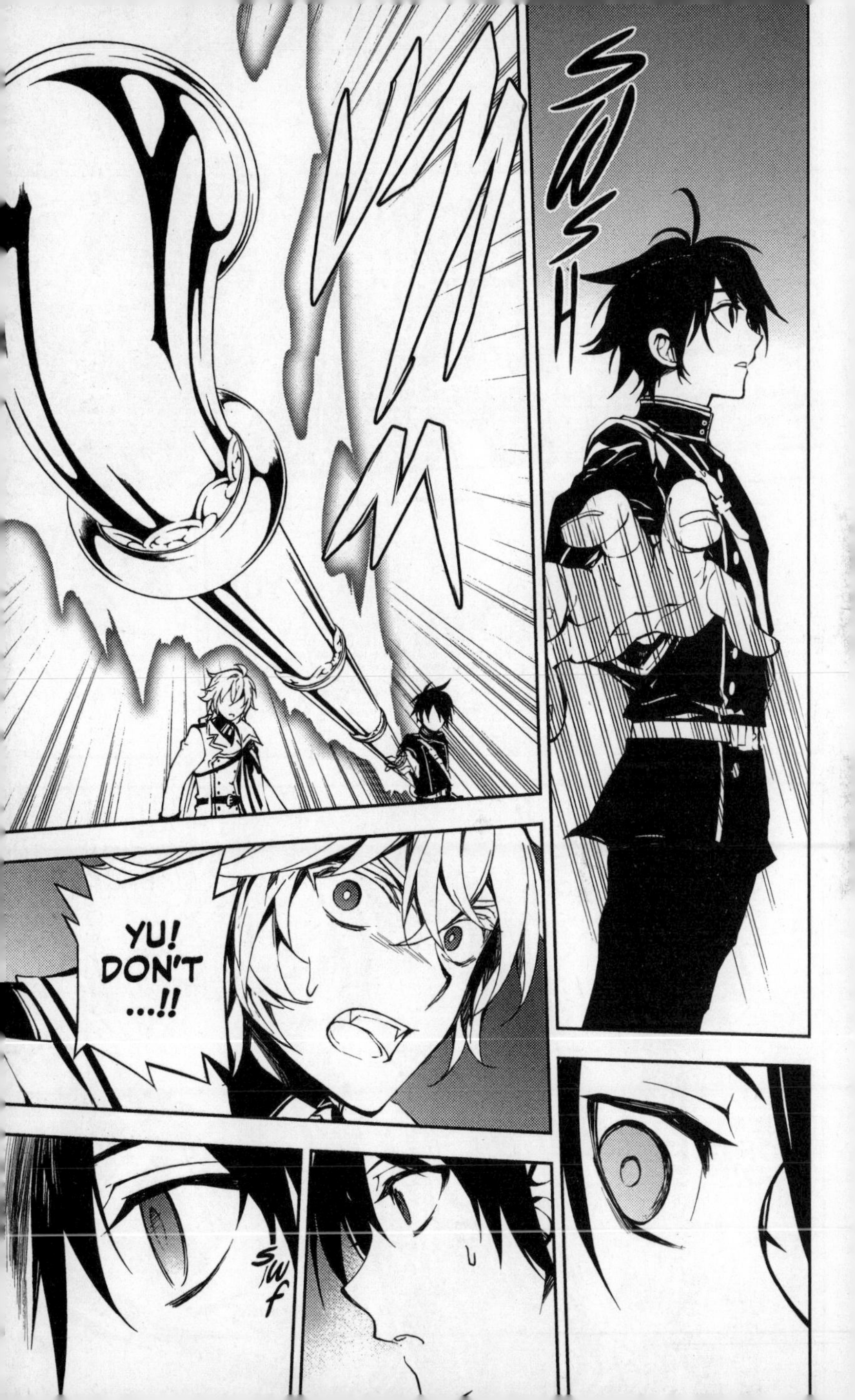
SWASH
VWM
YU! DON'T ...!!
SWF

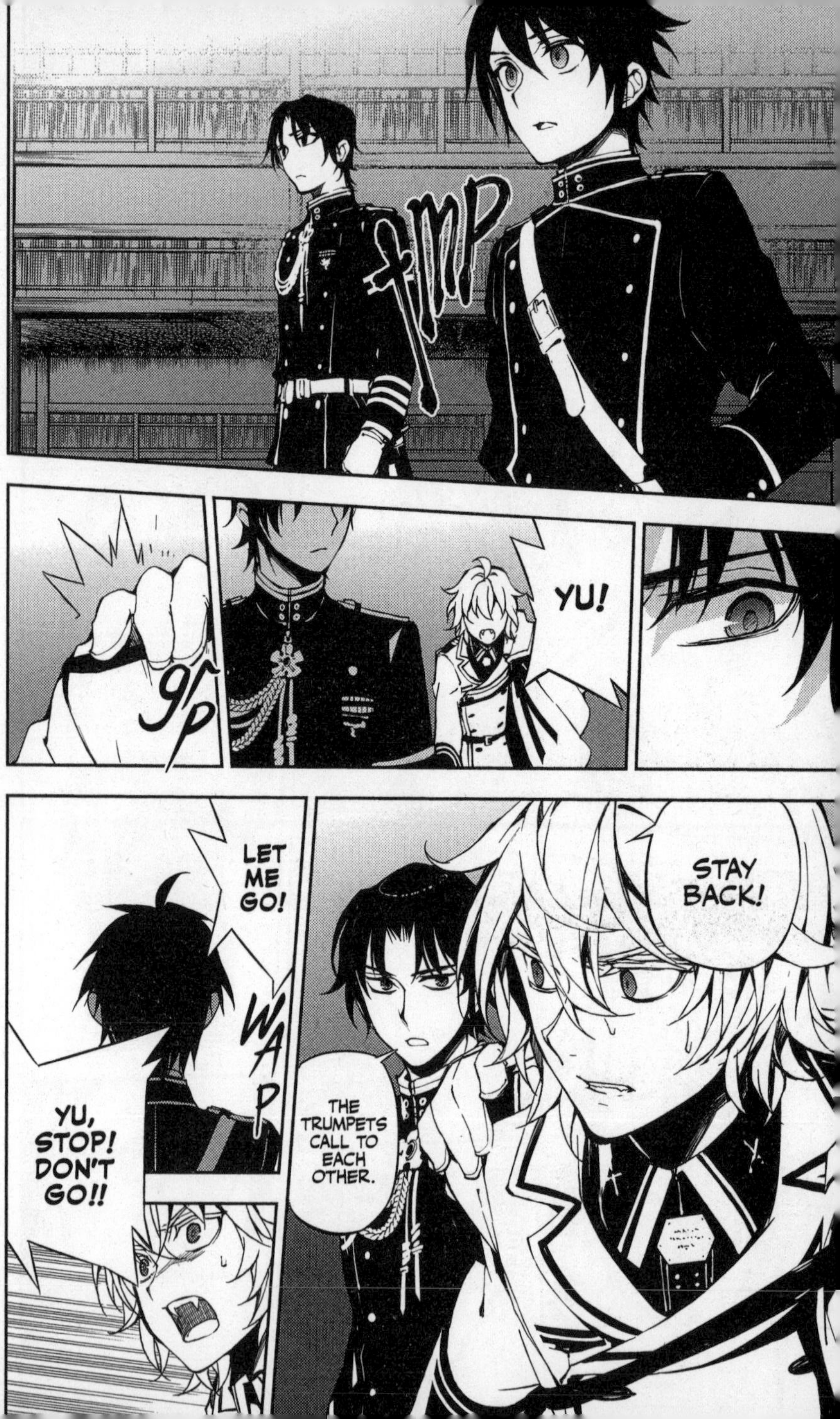
TMP
YU!
STAY BACK!
THE TRUMPETS CALL TO EACH OTHER.
LET ME GO!
WAP
YU, STOP! DON'T GO!!

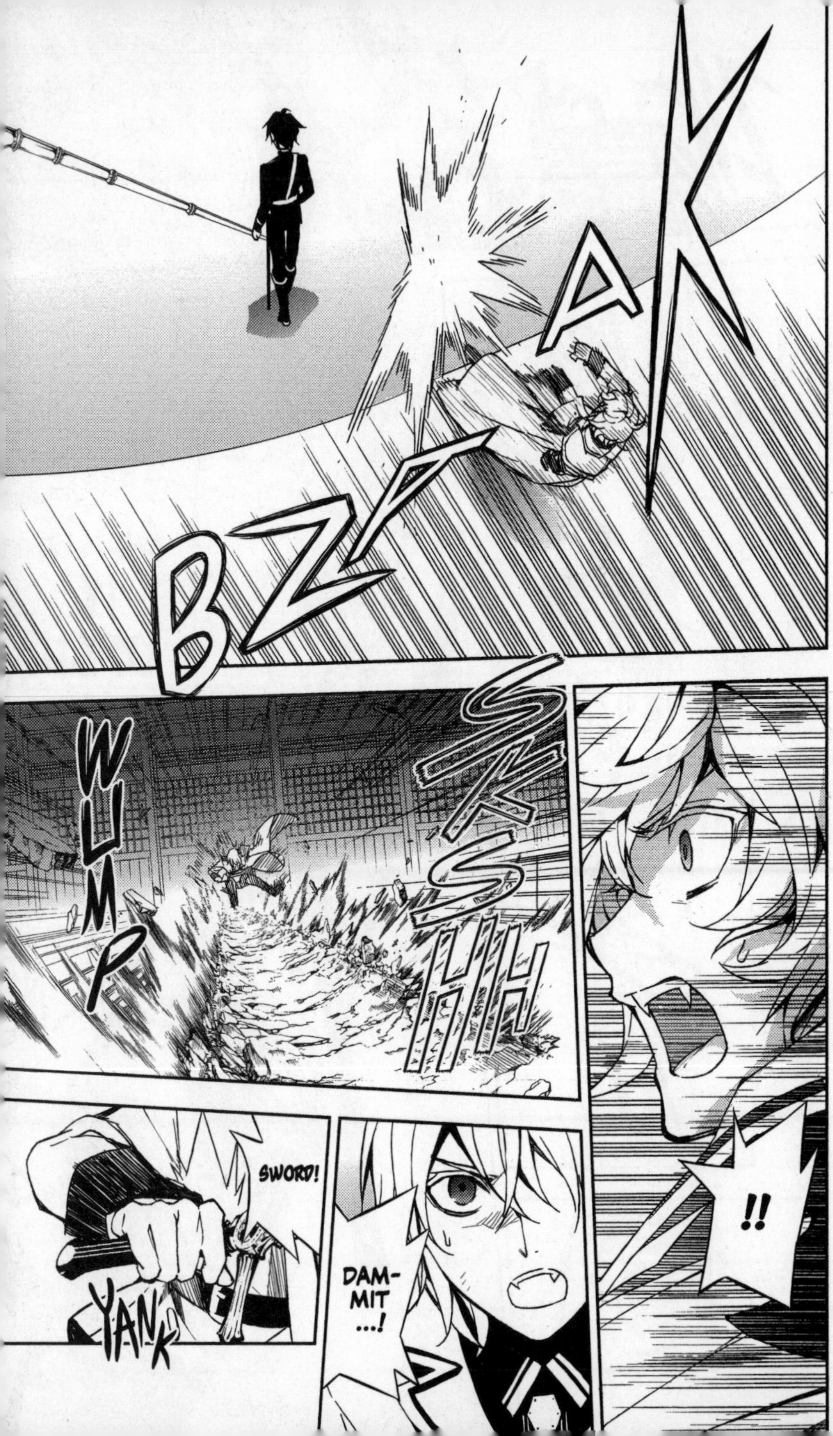
BZZAK
!!
WUMP
SKSHH
DAM-
MIT
...!
SWORD!
YANK

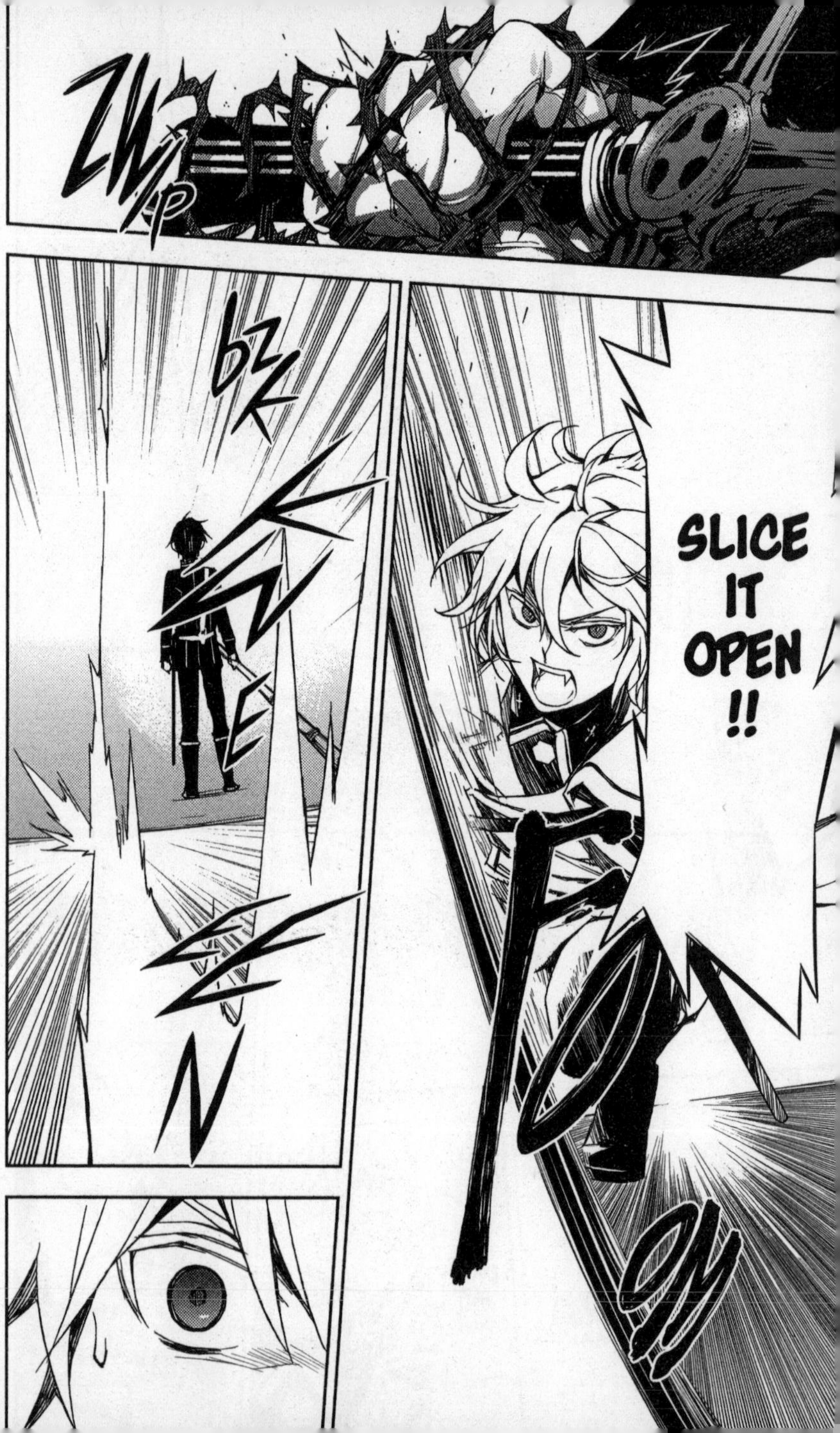
ZWIP
SLICE IT OPEN!!
BZZK

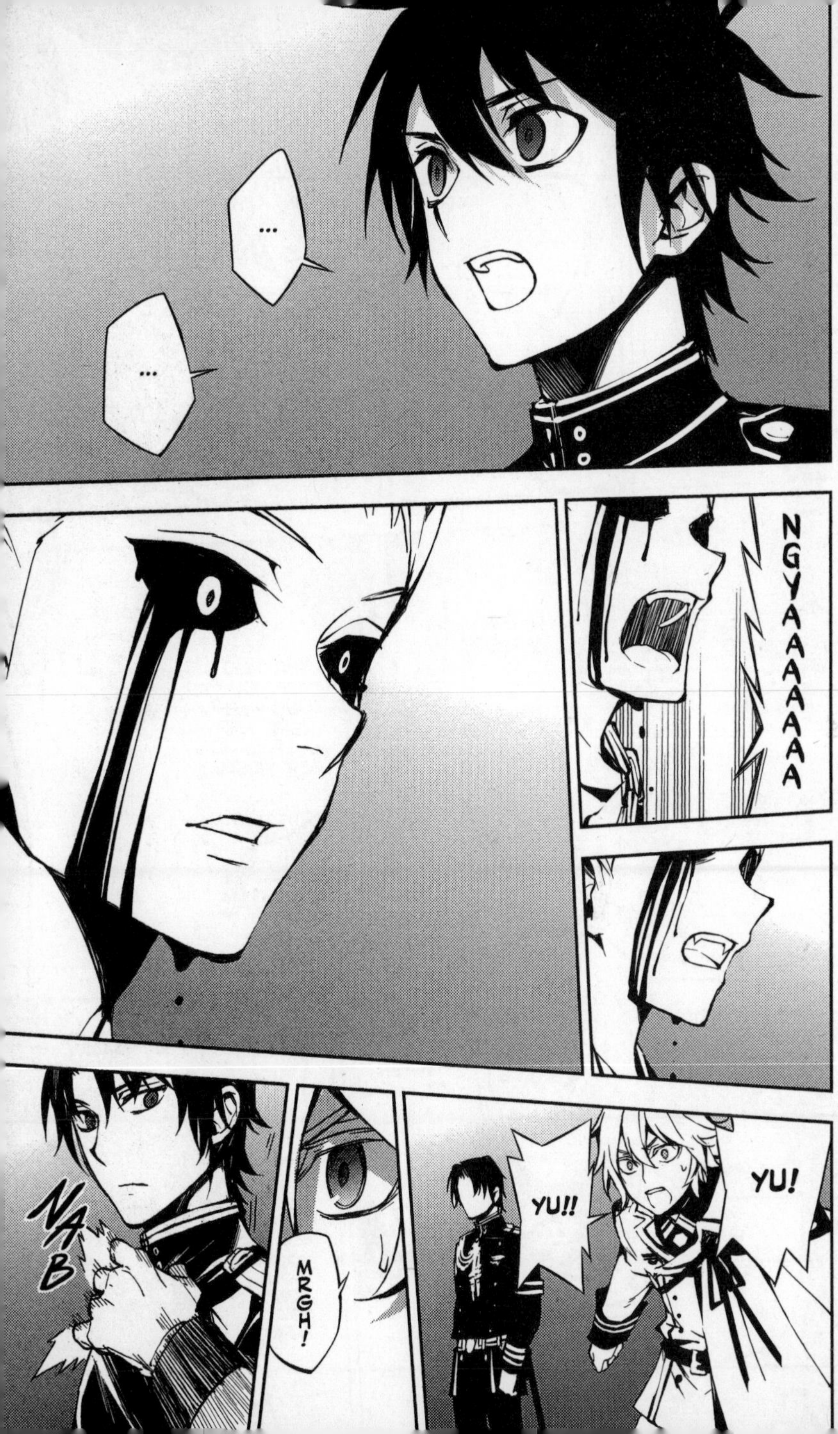
...
...
NGYAAAAAAA
YU!
YU!!
MRGH!
NAB

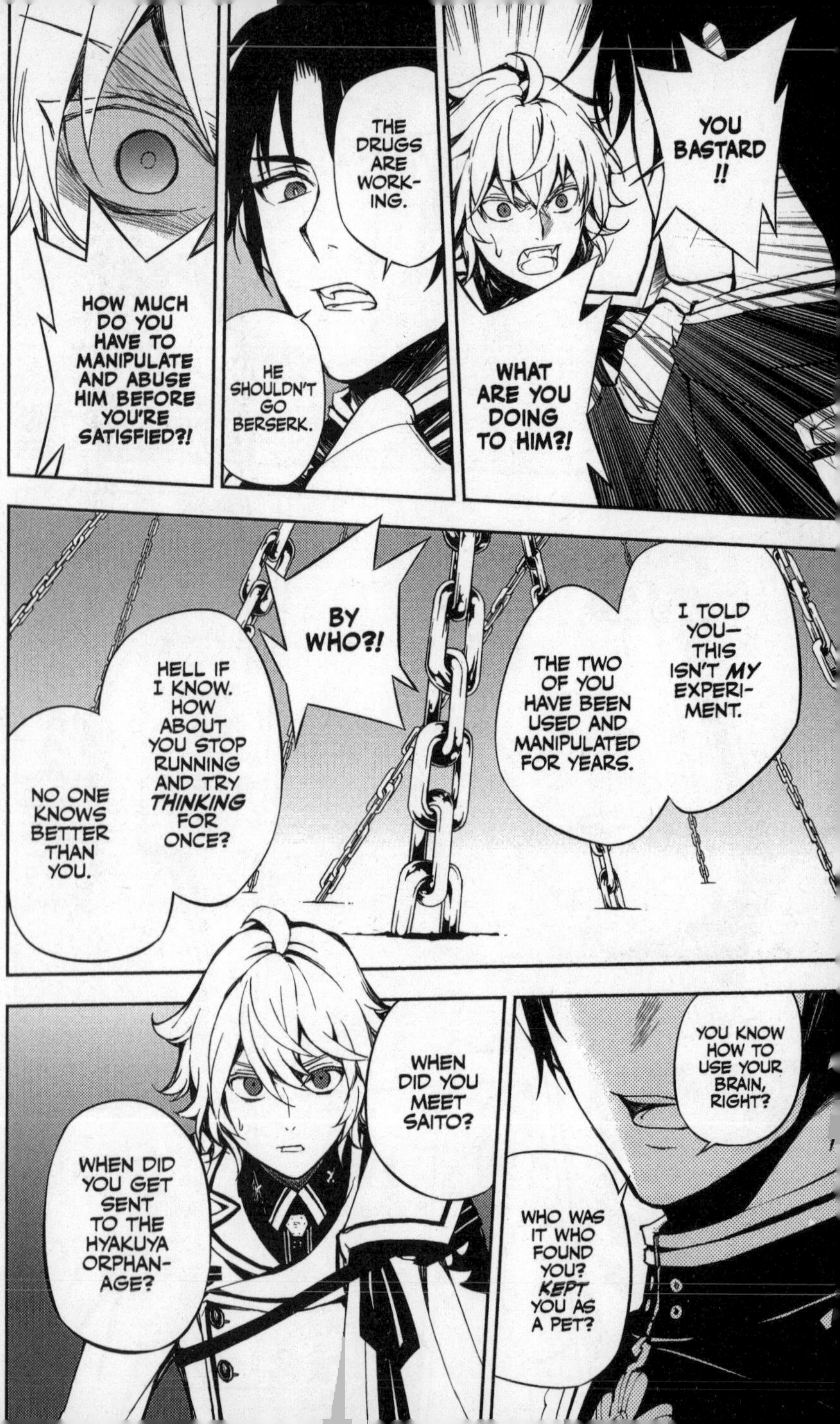
YOU BASTARD !!
WHAT ARE YOU DOING TO HIM?!
THE DRUGS ARE WORKING.
HE SHOULDN'T GO BERSERK.
HOW MUCH DO YOU HAVE TO MANIPULATE AND ABUSE HIM BEFORE YOU'RE SATISFIED?!
I TOLD YOU— THIS ISN'T *MY* EXPERIMENT.
THE TWO OF YOU HAVE BEEN USED AND MANIPULATED FOR YEARS.
BY WHO?!
HELL IF I KNOW. HOW ABOUT YOU STOP RUNNING AND TRY *THINKING* FOR ONCE?
NO ONE KNOWS BETTER THAN YOU.
YOU KNOW HOW TO USE YOUR BRAIN, RIGHT?
WHO WAS IT WHO FOUND YOU? *KEPT* YOU AS A PET?
WHEN DID YOU MEET SAITO?
WHEN DID YOU GET SENT TO THE HYAKUYA ORPHANAGE?

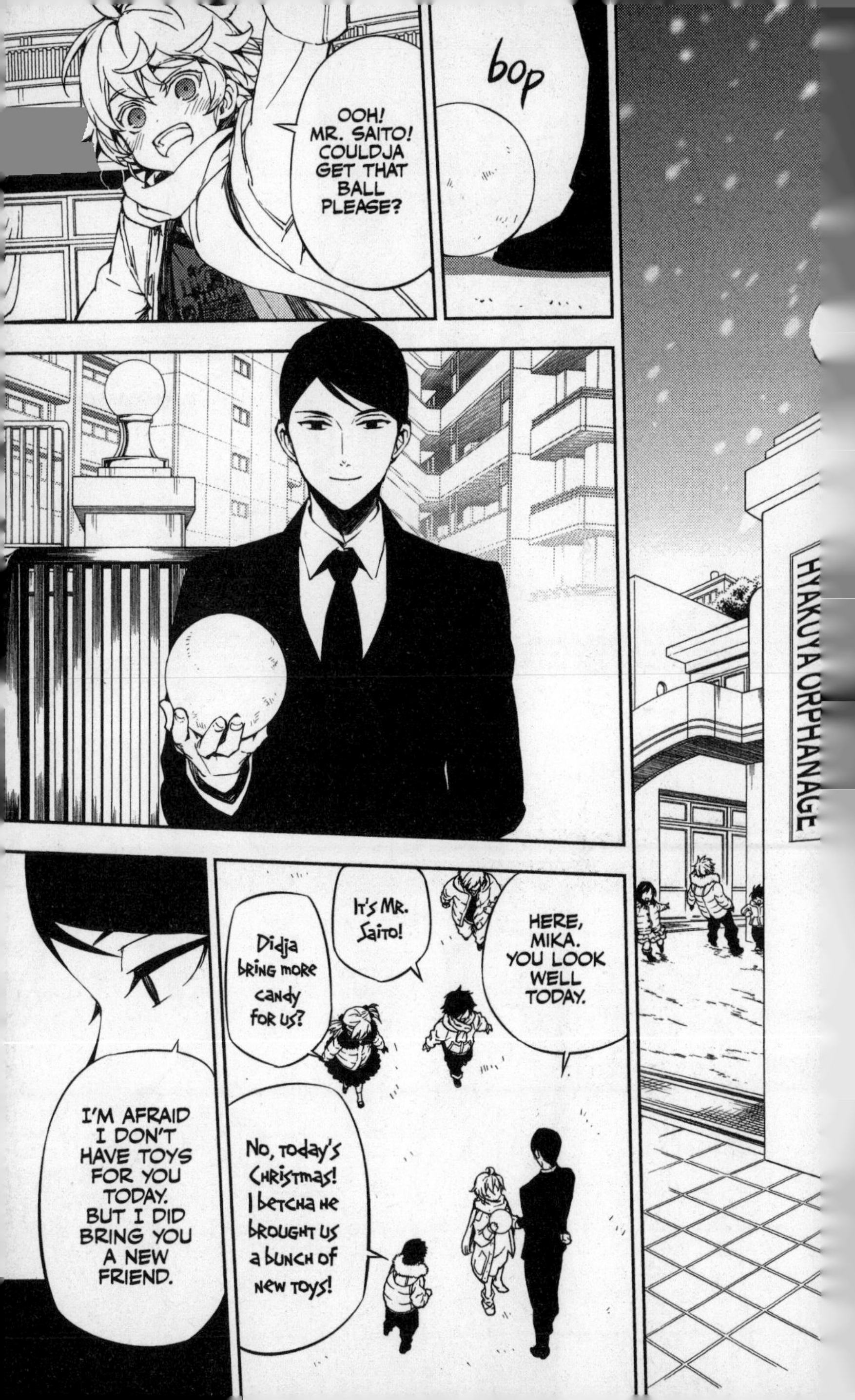
HYAKUYA ORPHANAGE
bop
OOH! MR. SAITO! COULDJA GET THAT BALL PLEASE?
HERE, MIKA. YOU LOOK WELL TODAY.
It's Mr. Saito!
Didja bring more candy for us?
No, today's Christmas! I betcha he brought us a bunch of new toys!
I'M AFRAID I DON'T HAVE TOYS FOR YOU TODAY. BUT I DID BRING YOU A NEW FRIEND.

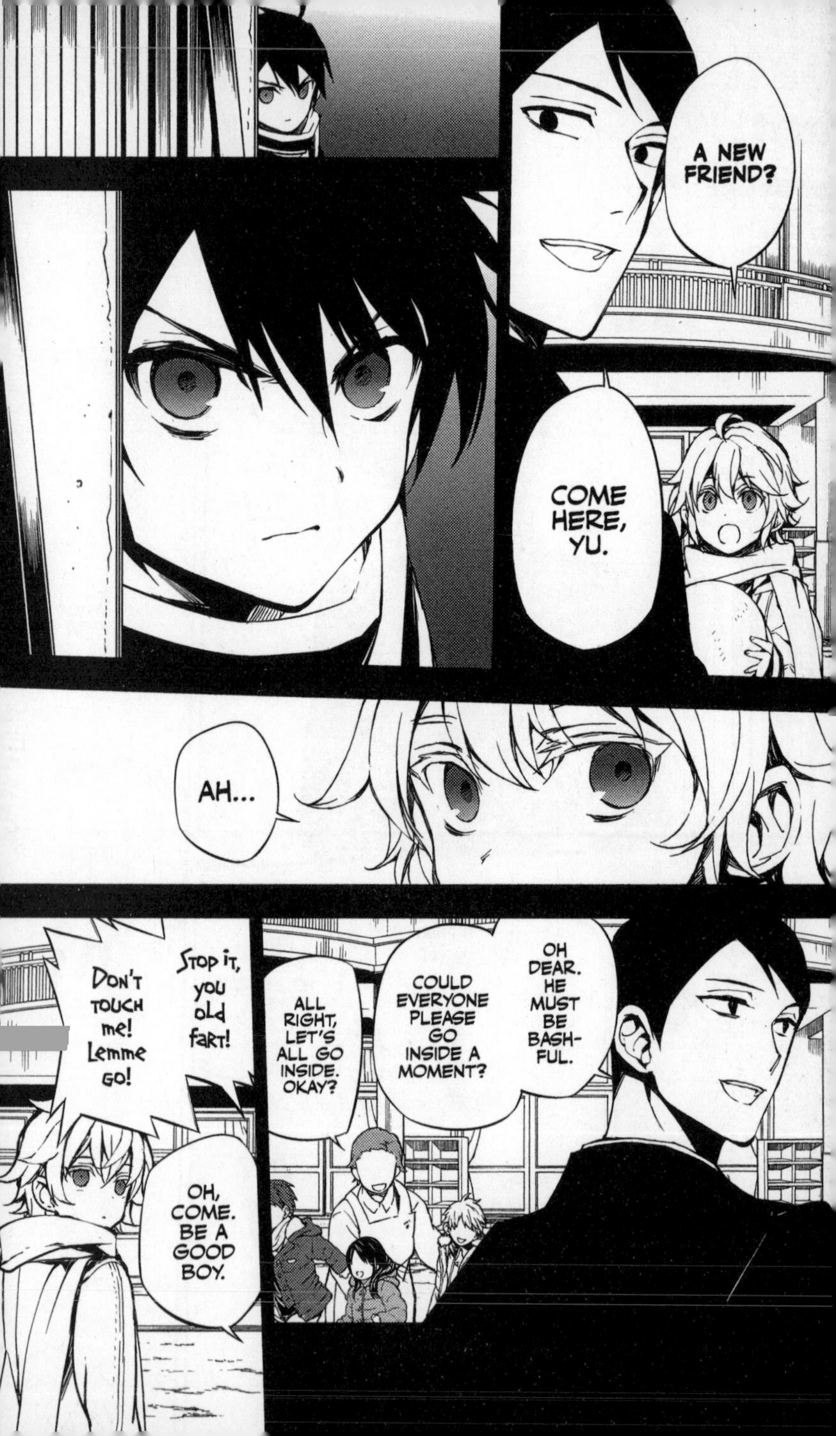
A NEW FRIEND?
COME HERE, YU.
AH...
OH DEAR. HE MUST BE BASH-FUL.
COULD EVERYONE PLEASE GO INSIDE A MOMENT?
ALL RIGHT, LET'S ALL GO INSIDE. OKAY?
Stop it, you old fart!
Don't touch me! Lemme go!
OH, COME. BE A GOOD BOY.

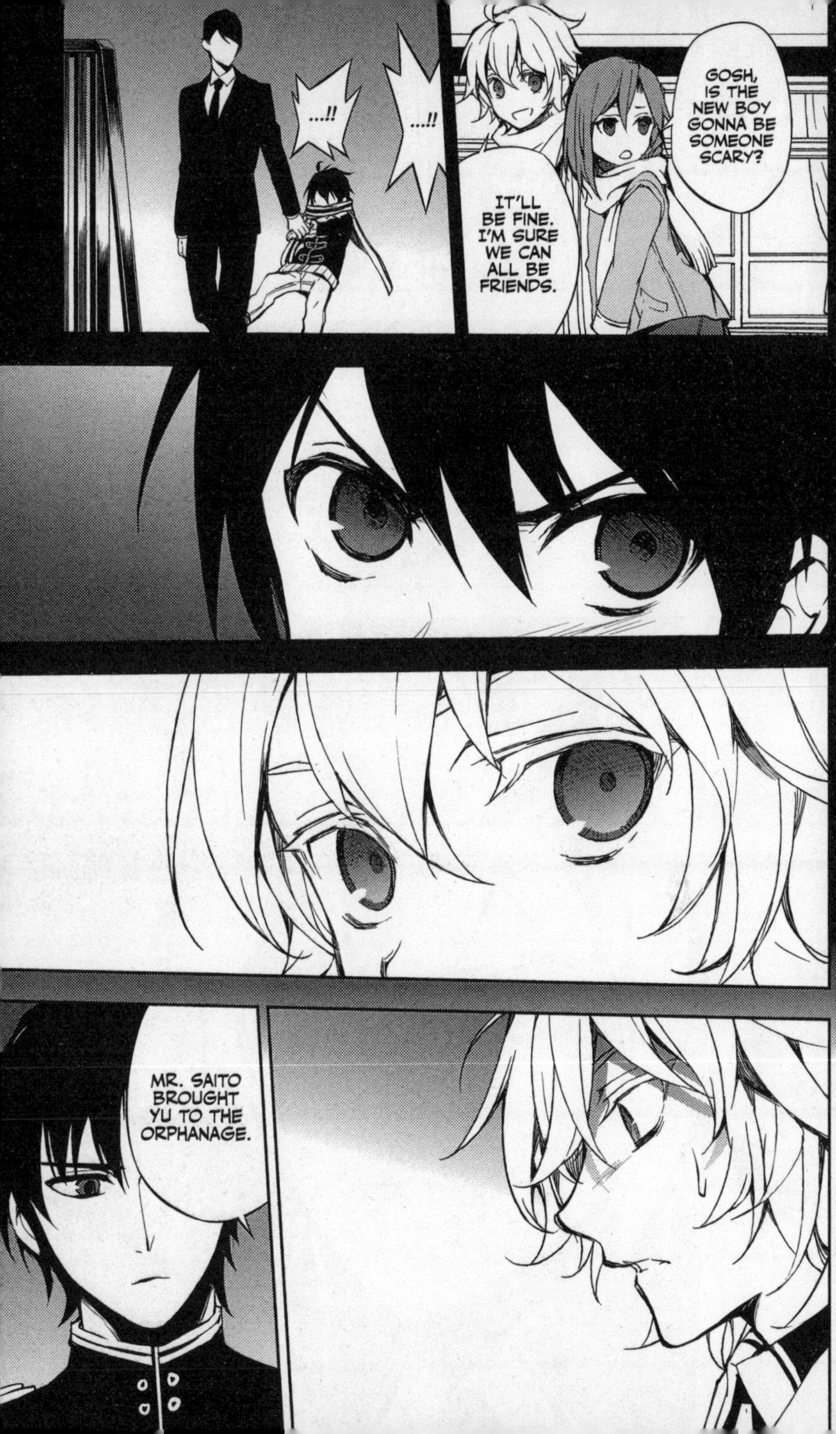
GOSH, IS THE NEW BOY GONNA BE SOMEONE SCARY?
IT'LL BE FINE. I'M SURE WE CAN ALL BE FRIENDS.
...!!
...!!
MR. SAITO BROUGHT YU TO THE ORPHANAGE.

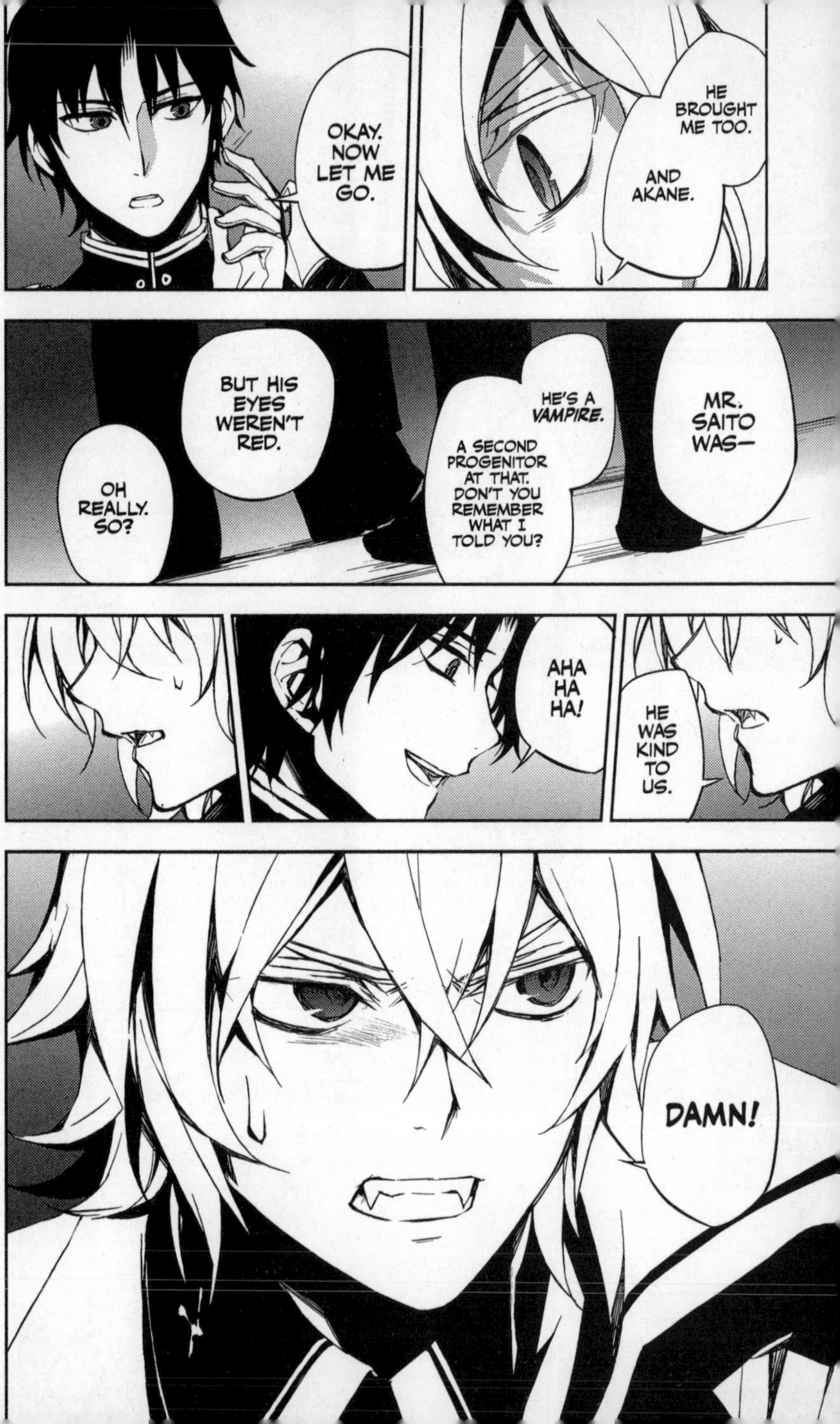
HE BROUGHT ME TOO.
AND AKANE.
OKAY. NOW LET ME GO.
MR. SAITO WAS—
HE'S A *VAMPIRE*.
A SECOND PROGENITOR AT THAT. DON'T YOU REMEMBER WHAT I TOLD YOU?
BUT HIS EYES WEREN'T RED.
OH REALLY. SO?
HE WAS KIND TO US.
AHA HA HA!
DAMN!

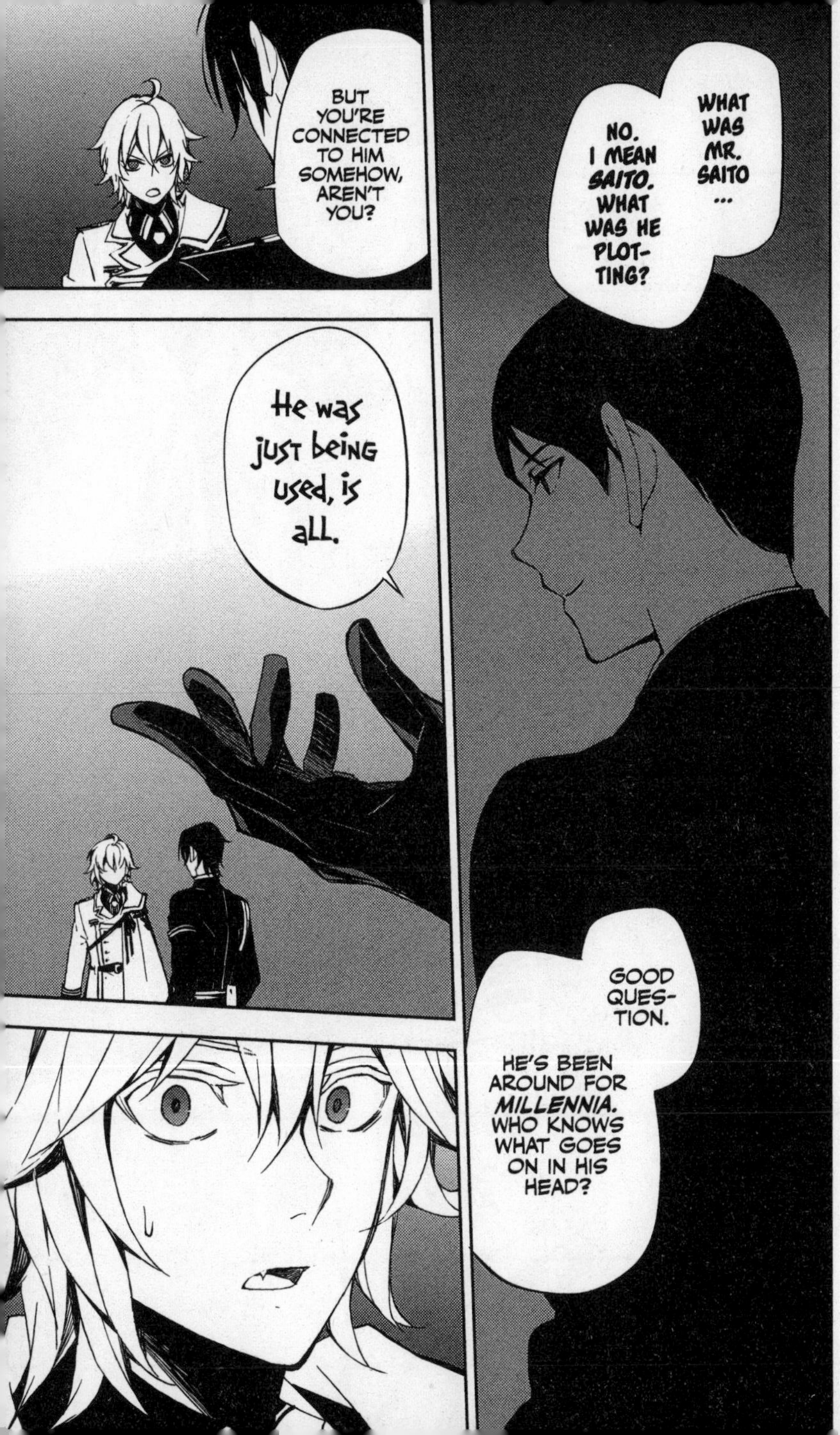
WHAT WAS MR. SAITO...
NO. I MEAN *SAITO.* WHAT WAS HE PLOTTING?
GOOD QUESTION.
HE'S BEEN AROUND FOR *MILLENNIA.* WHO KNOWS WHAT GOES ON IN HIS HEAD?
BUT YOU'RE CONNECTED TO HIM SOMEHOW, AREN'T YOU?
He was just being used, is all.

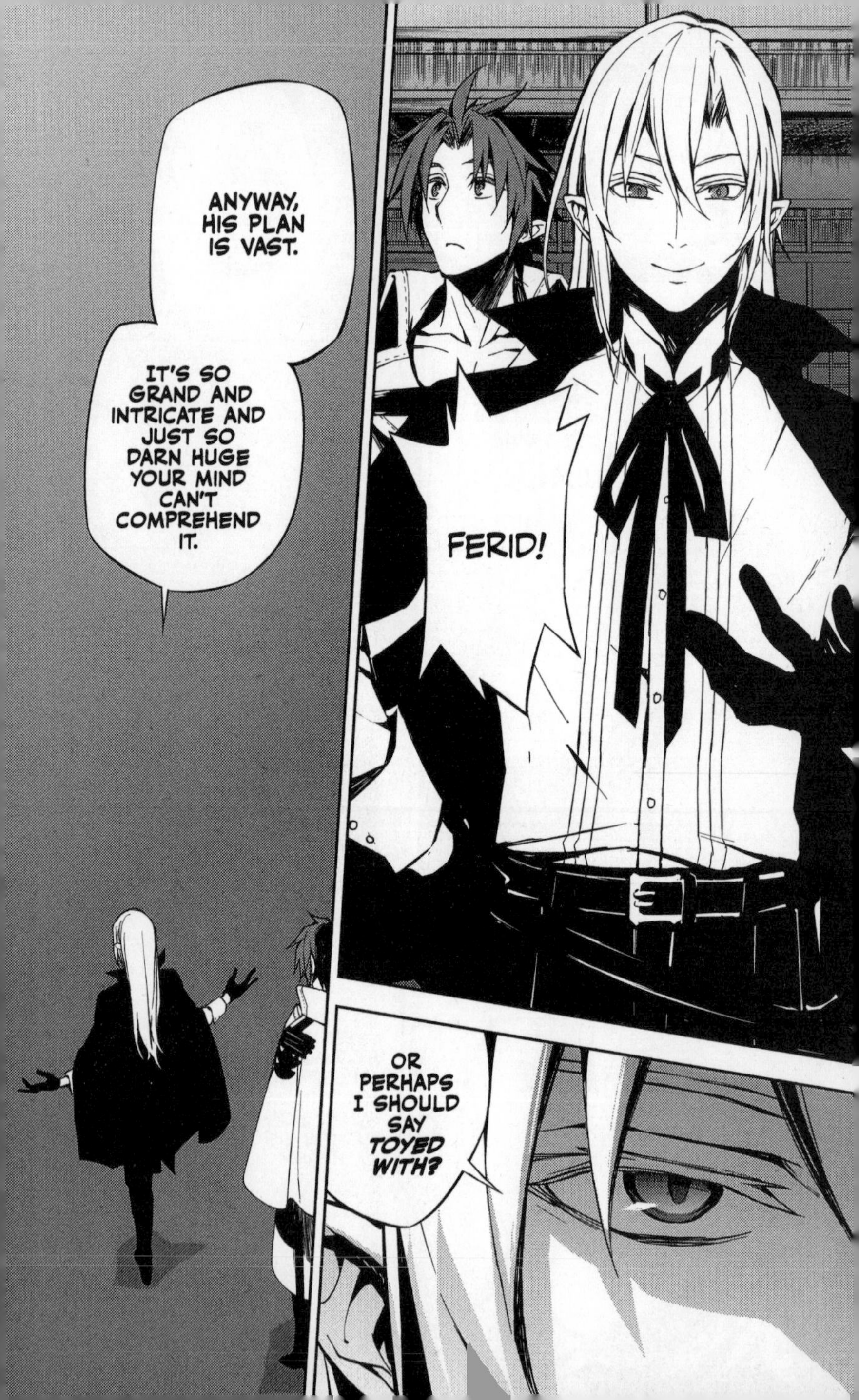
FERID!
OR PERHAPS I SHOULD SAY *TOYED WITH?*
ANYWAY, HIS PLAN IS VAST.
IT'S SO GRAND AND INTRICATE AND JUST SO DARN HUGE YOUR MIND CAN'T COMPREHEND IT.

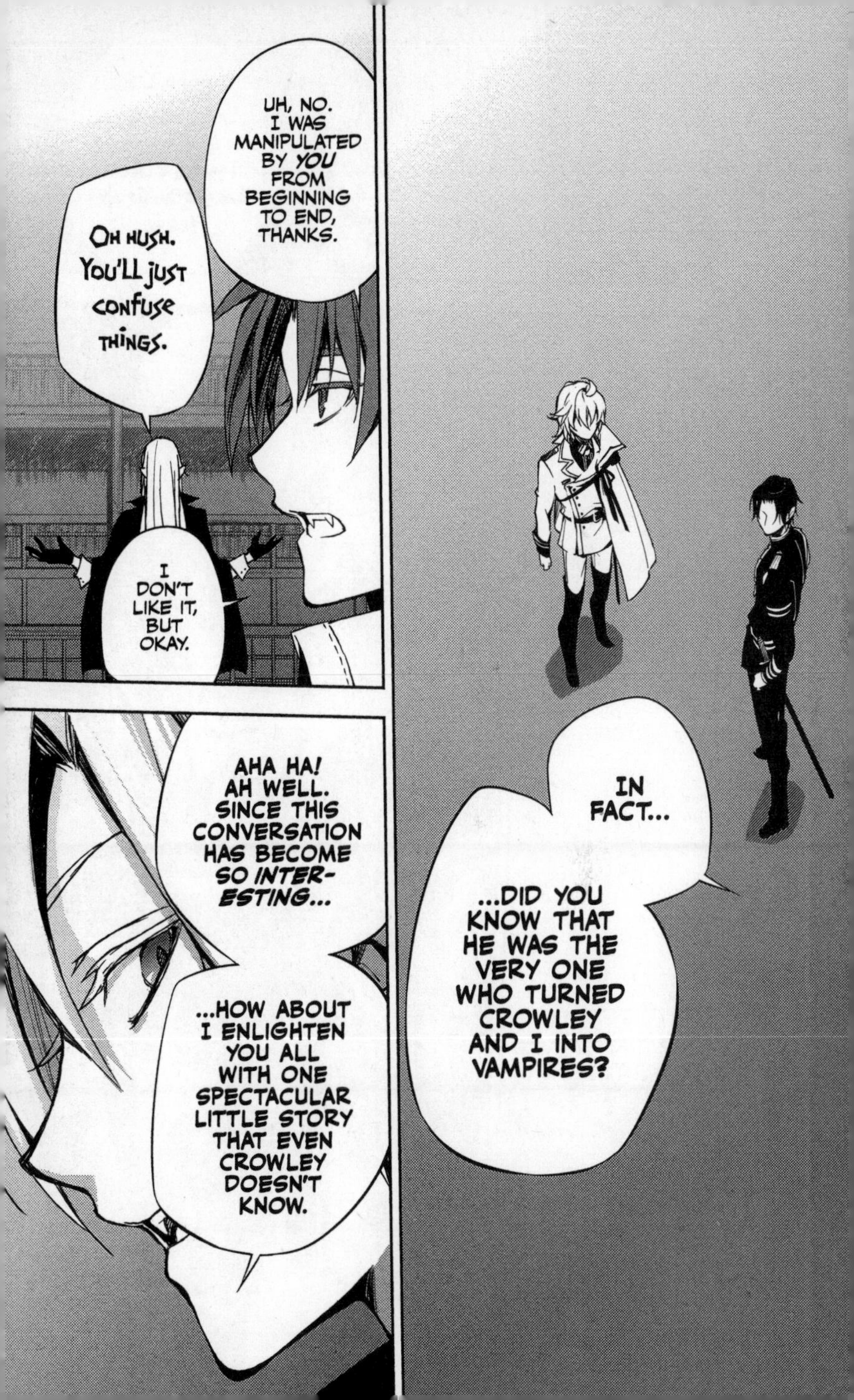
IN FACT...
...DID YOU KNOW THAT HE WAS THE VERY ONE WHO TURNED CROWLEY AND I INTO VAMPIRES?
UH, NO. I WAS MANIPULATED BY *YOU* FROM BEGINNING TO END, THANKS.
OH HUSH. YOU'LL JUST CONFUSE THINGS.
I DON'T LIKE IT, BUT OKAY.
AHA HA! AH WELL. SINCE THIS CONVERSATION HAS BECOME SO *INTERESTING*...
...HOW ABOUT I ENLIGHTEN YOU ALL WITH ONE SPECTACULAR LITTLE STORY THAT EVEN CROWLEY DOESN'T KNOW.

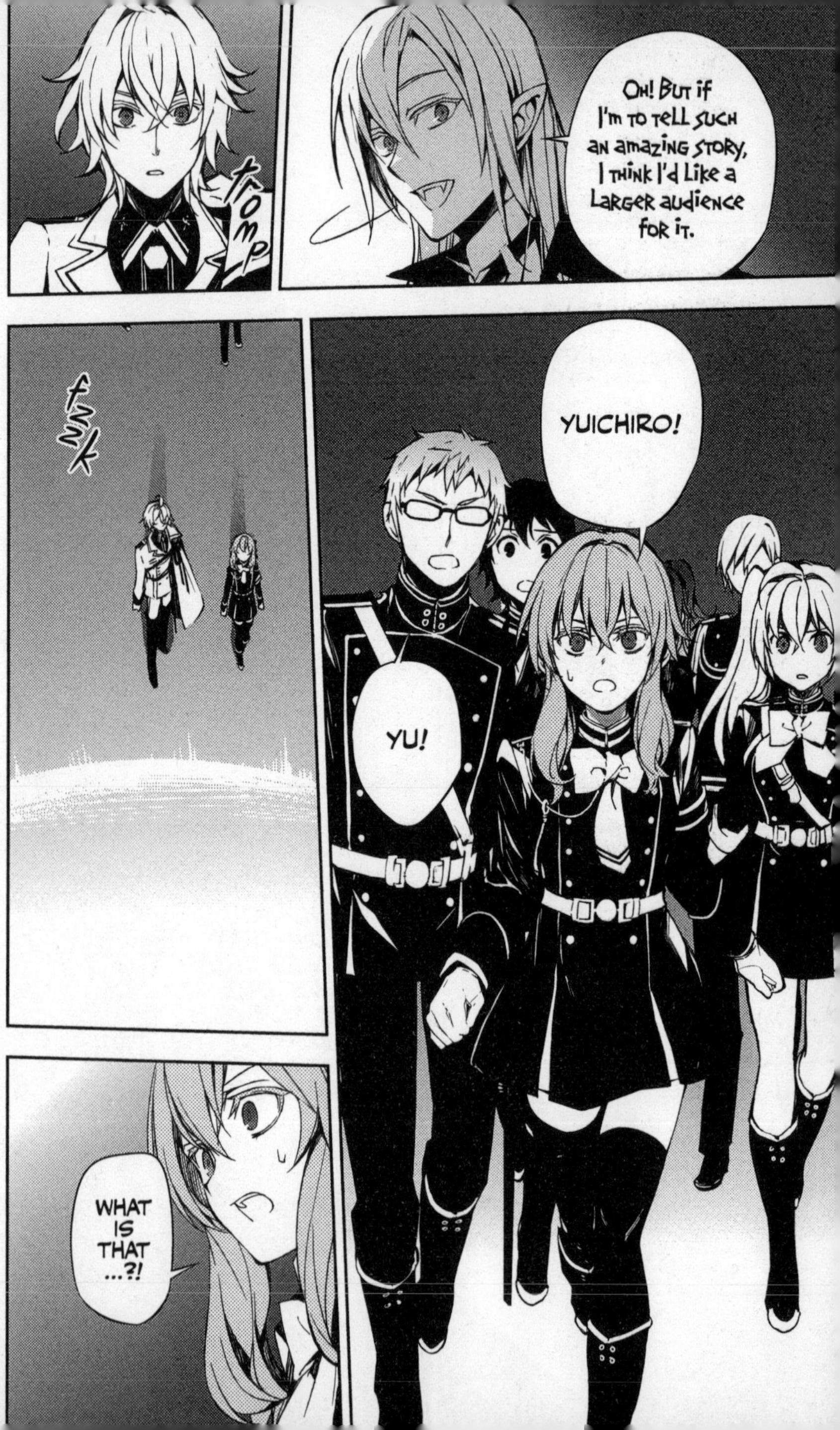
Oh! But if I'm to tell such an amazing story, I think I'd like a larger audience for it.
tromp
YUICHIRO!
YU!
fzzk
WHAT IS THAT ...?!

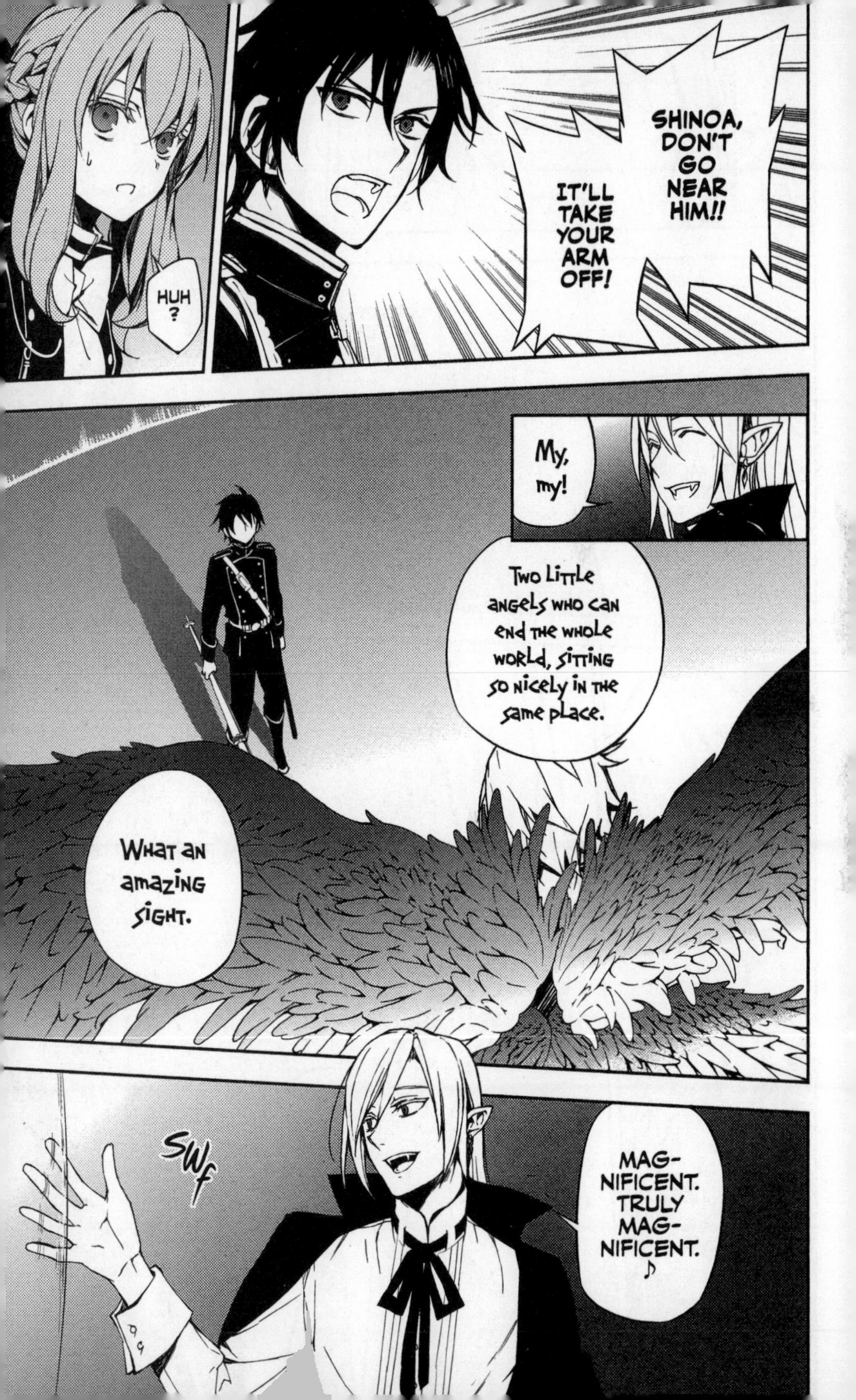
SHINOA, DON'T GO NEAR HIM!!
IT'LL TAKE YOUR ARM OFF!
HUH?
My, my!
Two little angels who can end the whole world, sitting so nicely in the same place.
What an amazing sight.
MAGNIFICENT. TRULY MAGNIFICENT. ♪
SWF

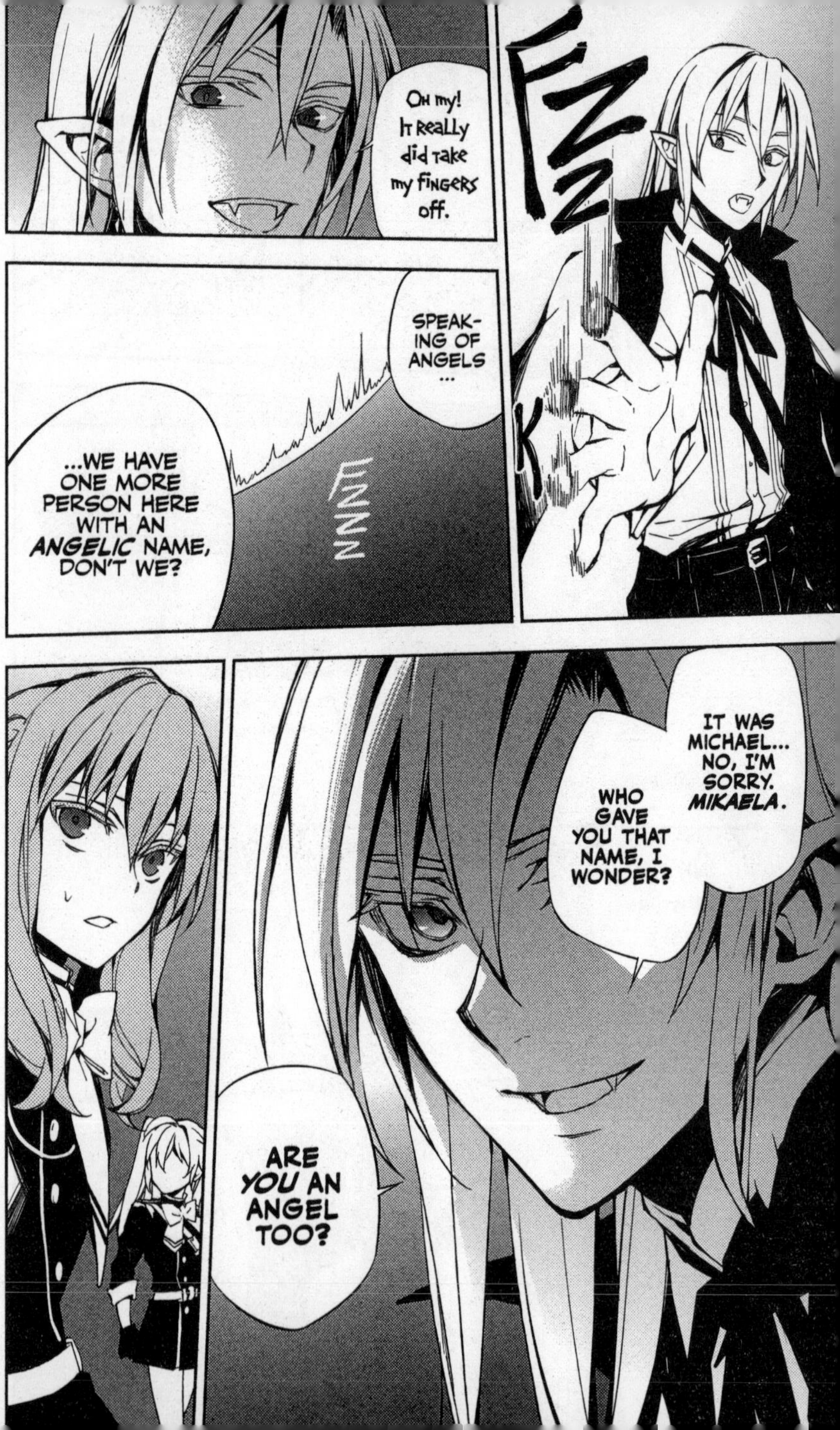
FZZ
K
Oh my! It really did take my fingers off.
SPEAKING OF ANGELS...
...WE HAVE ONE MORE PERSON HERE WITH AN *ANGELIC* NAME, DON'T WE?
FZZZ
IT WAS MICHAEL... NO, I'M SORRY. *MIKAELA*.
WHO GAVE YOU THAT NAME, I WONDER?
ARE *YOU* AN ANGEL TOO?

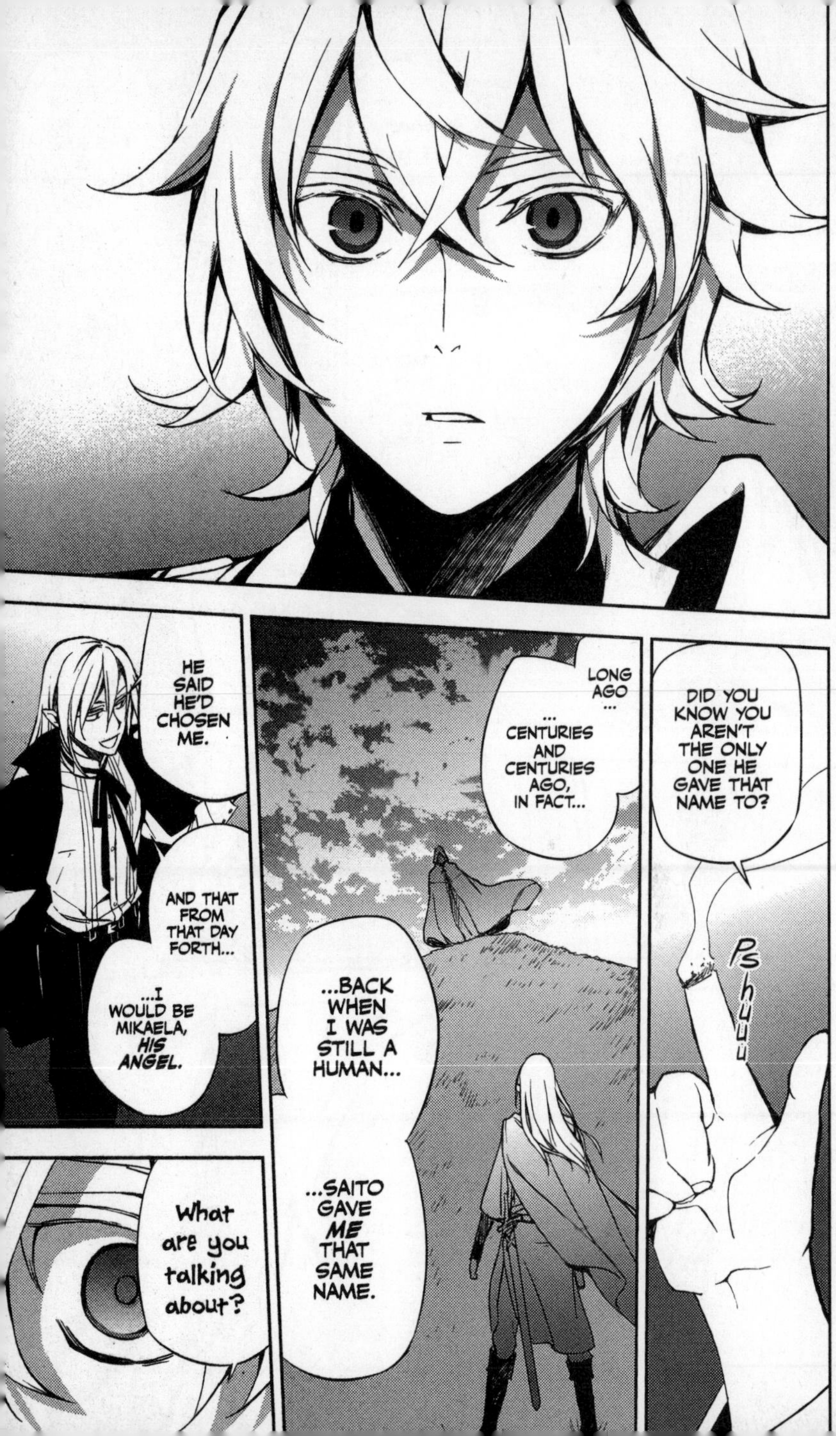
DID YOU KNOW YOU AREN'T THE ONLY ONE HE GAVE THAT NAME TO?
Pshuuu
LONG AGO ...
... CENTURIES AND CENTURIES AGO, IN FACT...
...BACK WHEN I WAS STILL A HUMAN...
...SAITO GAVE *ME* THAT SAME NAME.
HE SAID HE'D CHOSEN ME.
AND THAT FROM THAT DAY FORTH...
...I WOULD BE MIKAELA, *HIS ANGEL*.
What are you talking about?

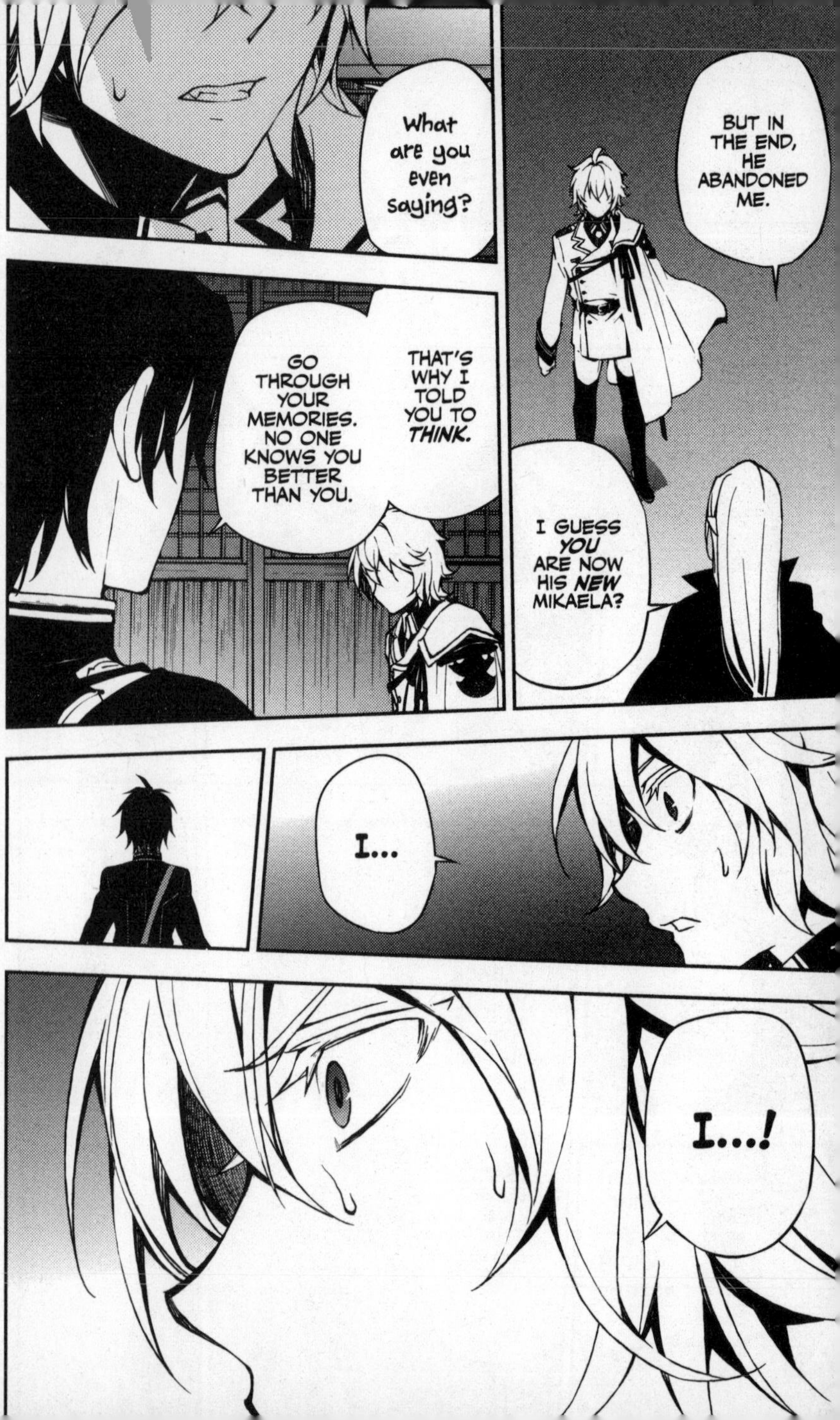
BUT IN THE END, HE ABANDONED ME.
I GUESS *YOU* ARE NOW HIS *NEW* MIKAELA?
What are you even saying?
THAT'S WHY I TOLD YOU TO ***THINK.***
GO THROUGH YOUR MEMORIES. NO ONE KNOWS YOU BETTER THAN YOU.
I...
I...!

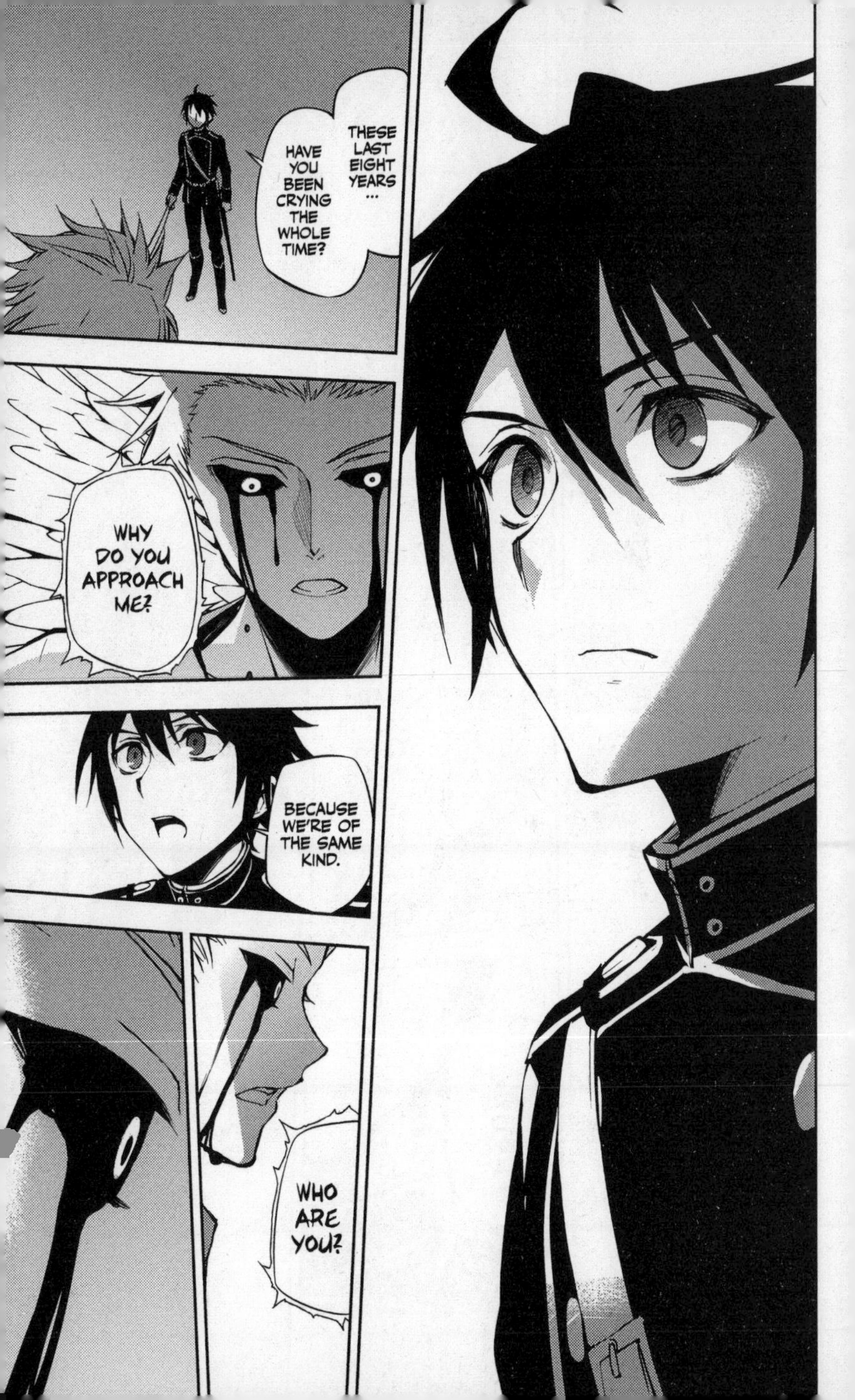
THESE LAST EIGHT YEARS...
HAVE YOU BEEN CRYING THE WHOLE TIME?
WHY DO YOU APPROACH ME?
BECAUSE WE'RE OF THE SAME KIND.
WHO ARE YOU?

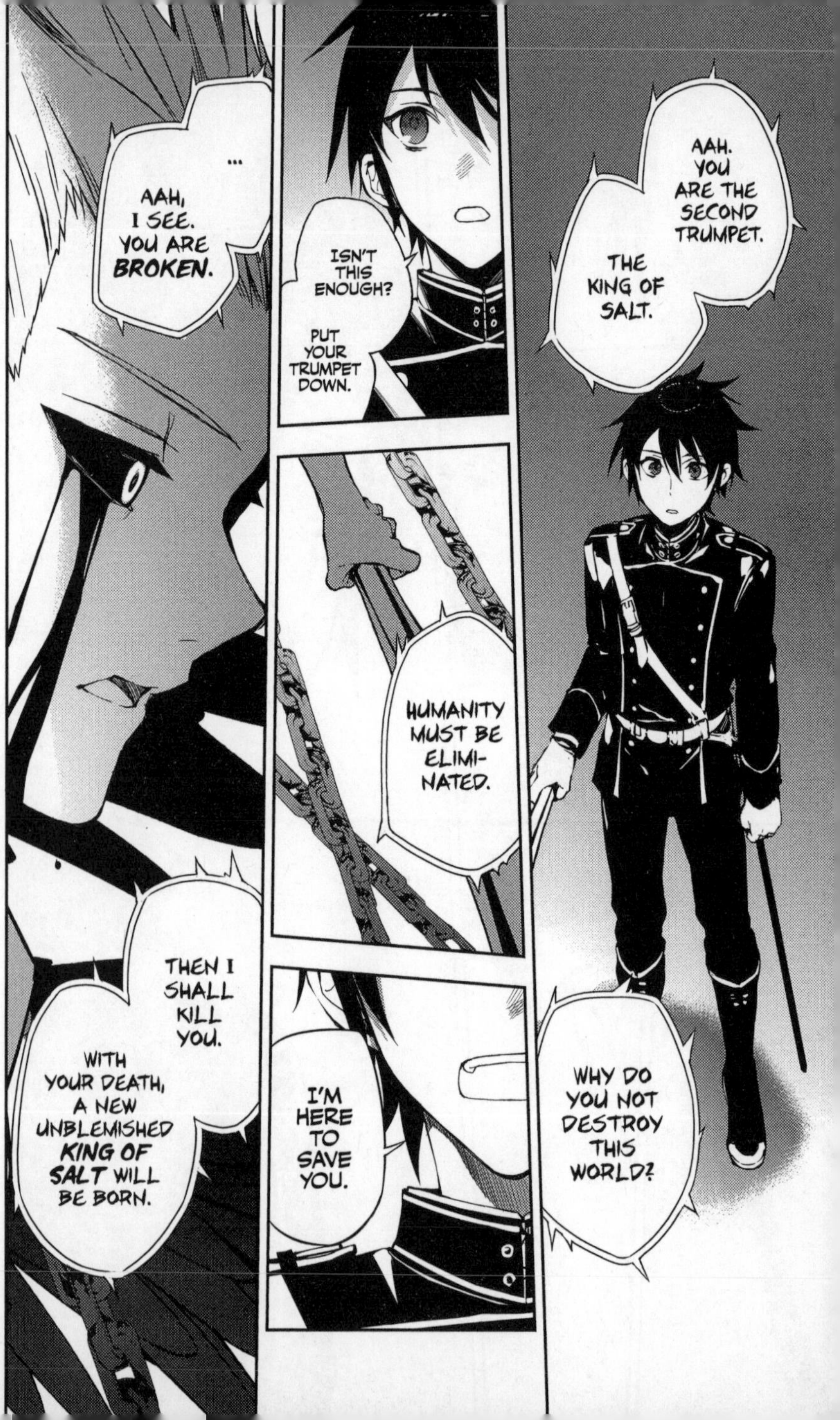
AAH. YOU ARE THE SECOND TRUMPET.
THE KING OF SALT.
WHY DO YOU NOT DESTROY THIS WORLD?
ISN'T THIS ENOUGH?
PUT YOUR TRUMPET DOWN.
HUMANITY MUST BE ELIMI-NATED.
I'M HERE TO SAVE YOU.
...
AAH, I SEE. YOU ARE BROKEN.
THEN I SHALL KILL YOU.
WITH YOUR DEATH, A NEW UNBLEMISHED KING OF SALT WILL BE BORN.

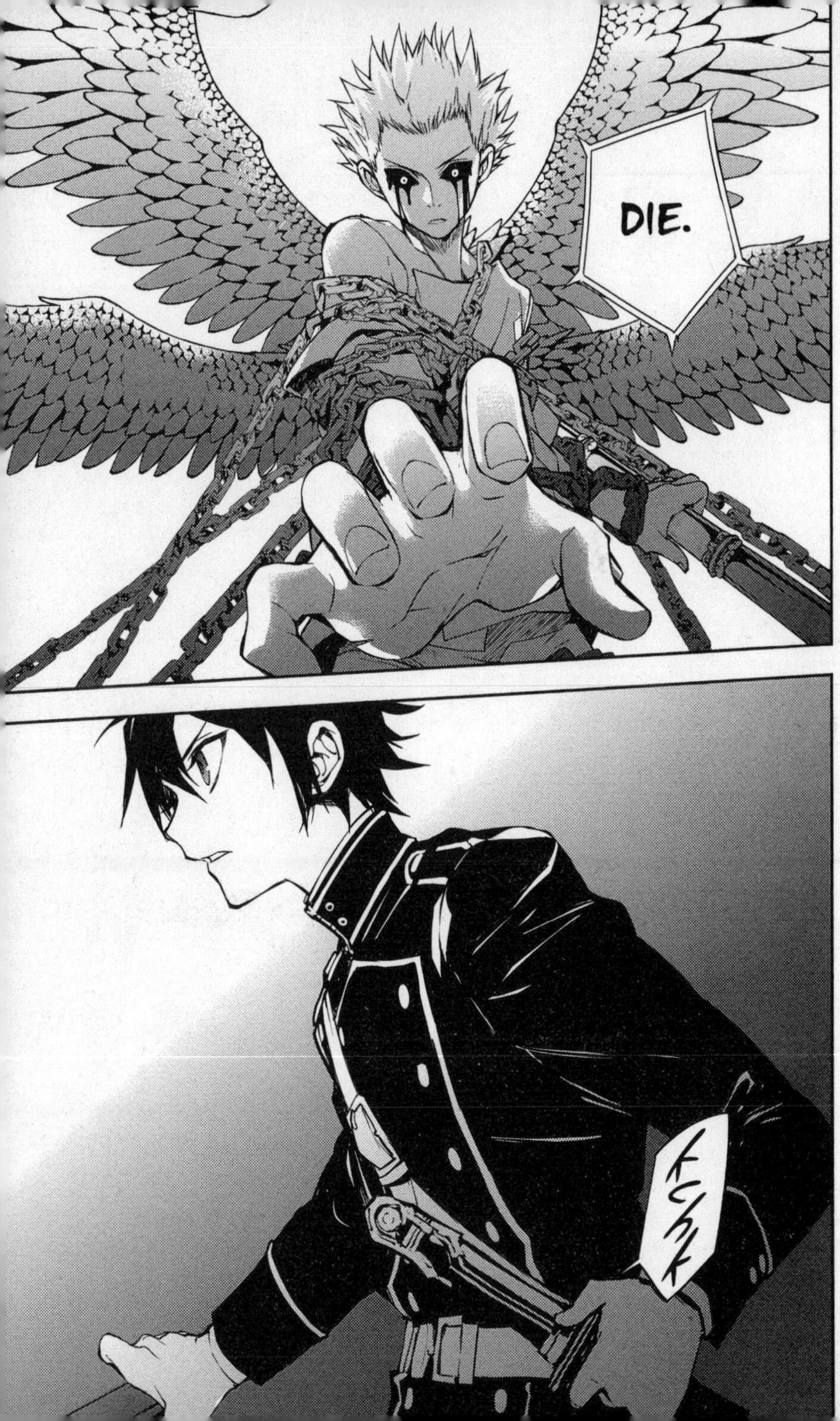
DIE.
KCHK

Seraph of the End

VAMPIRE REIGN

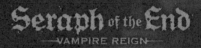

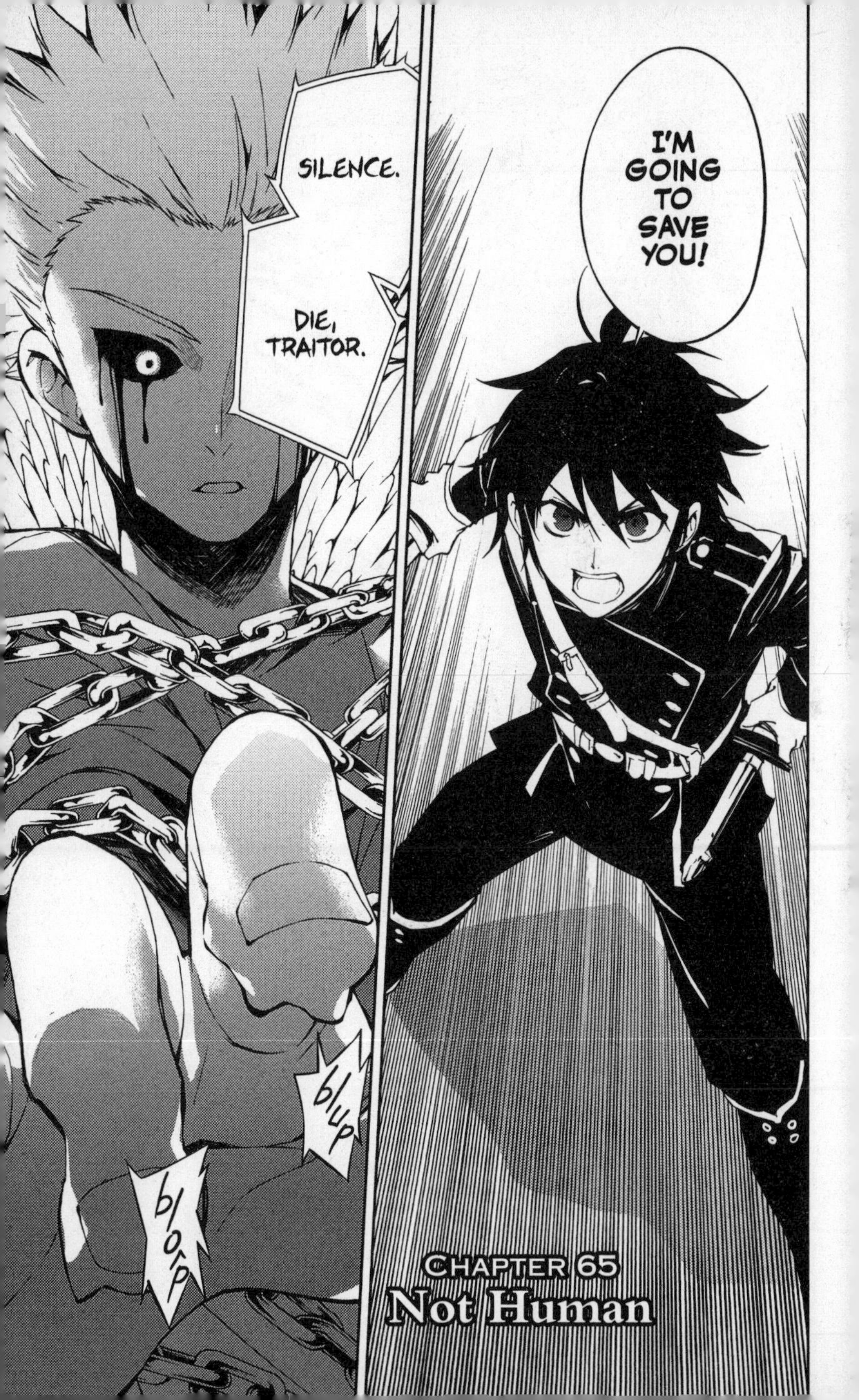
I'M GOING TO SAVE YOU!
CHAPTER 65
Not Human
SILENCE.
DIE, TRAITOR.
blup
bloop

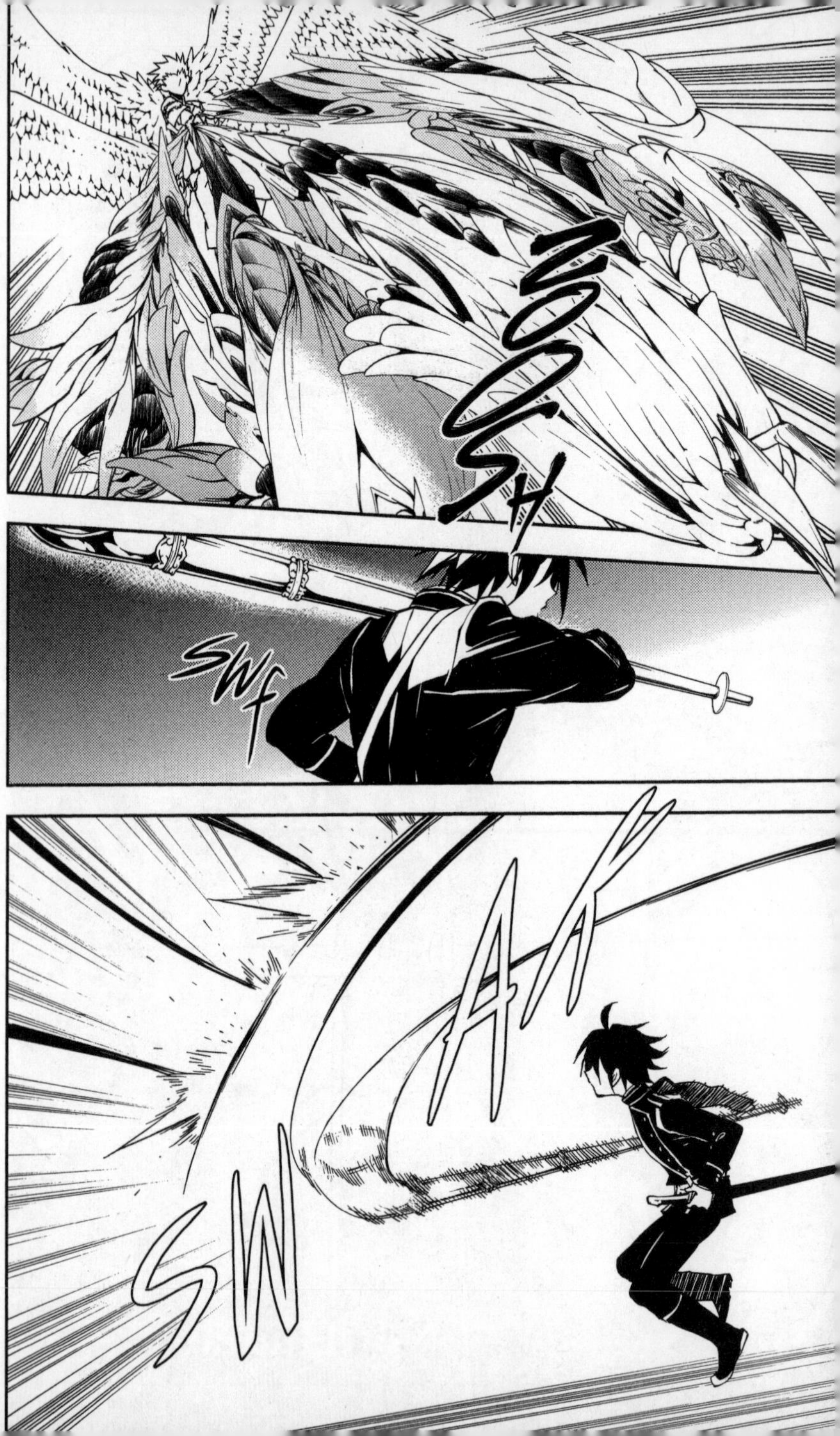
WOOSH
SWF
SWAAK

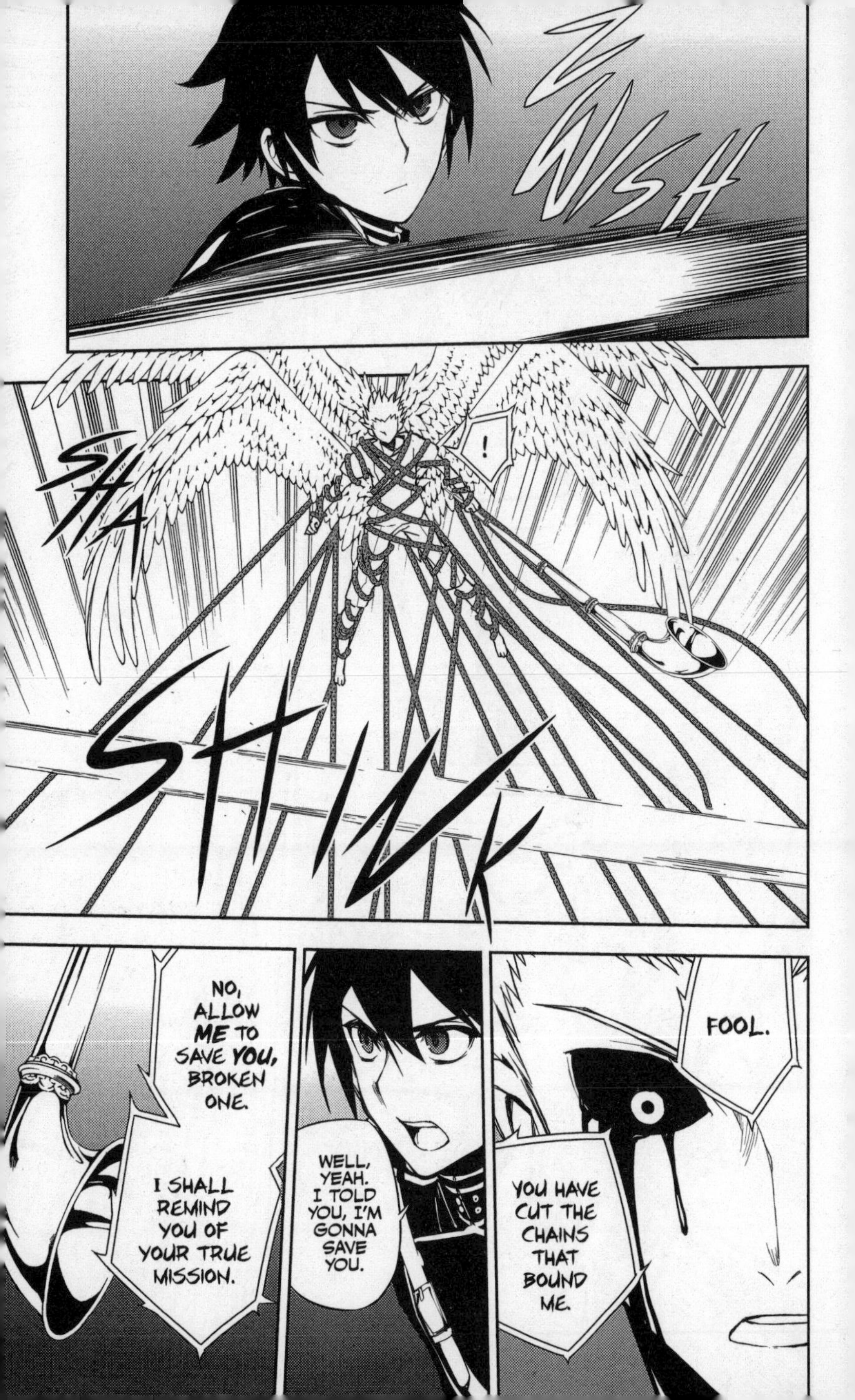
ZWISH
SHA
!
SHINK
FOOL.
YOU HAVE CUT THE CHAINS THAT BOUND ME.
WELL, YEAH. I TOLD YOU, I'M GONNA SAVE YOU.
NO, ALLOW ME TO SAVE YOU, BROKEN ONE.
I SHALL REMIND YOU OF YOUR TRUE MISSION.

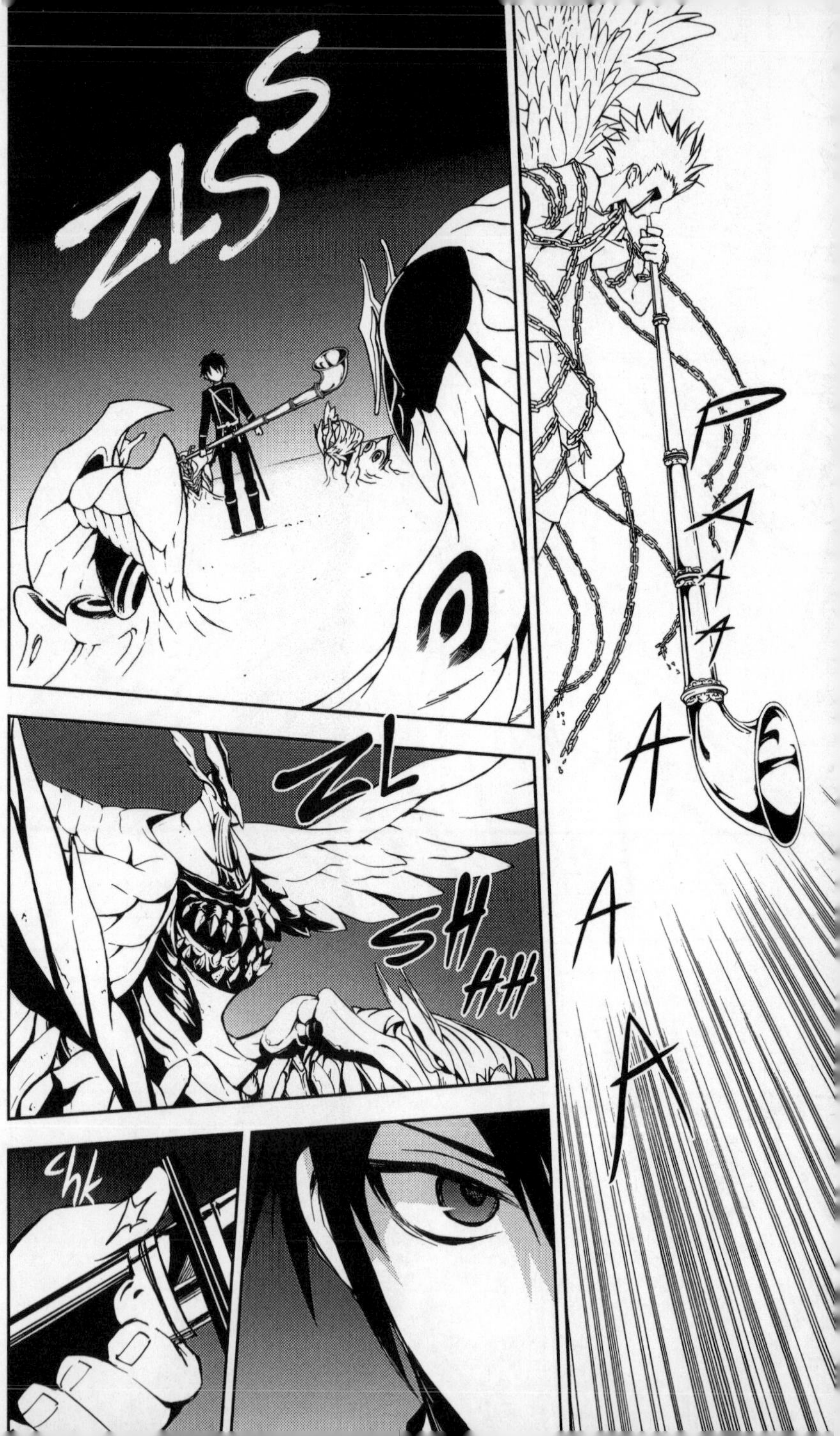
PAAAAAA
ZLSS
ZL
SHHH
chk

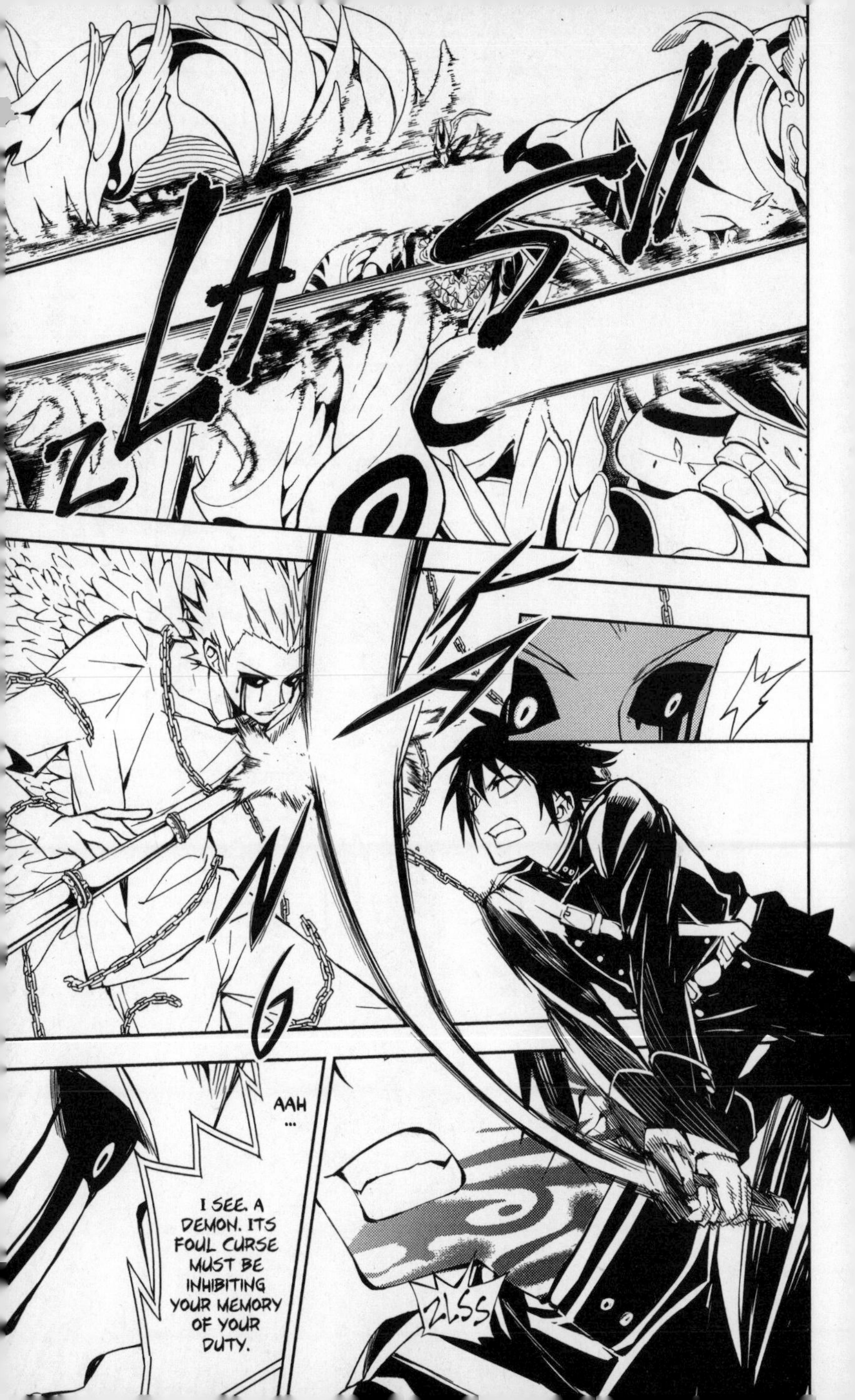

SLASH
KLANG
ZLSS
AAH ...
I SEE. A DEMON. ITS FOUL CURSE MUST BE INHIBITING YOUR MEMORY OF YOUR DUTY.

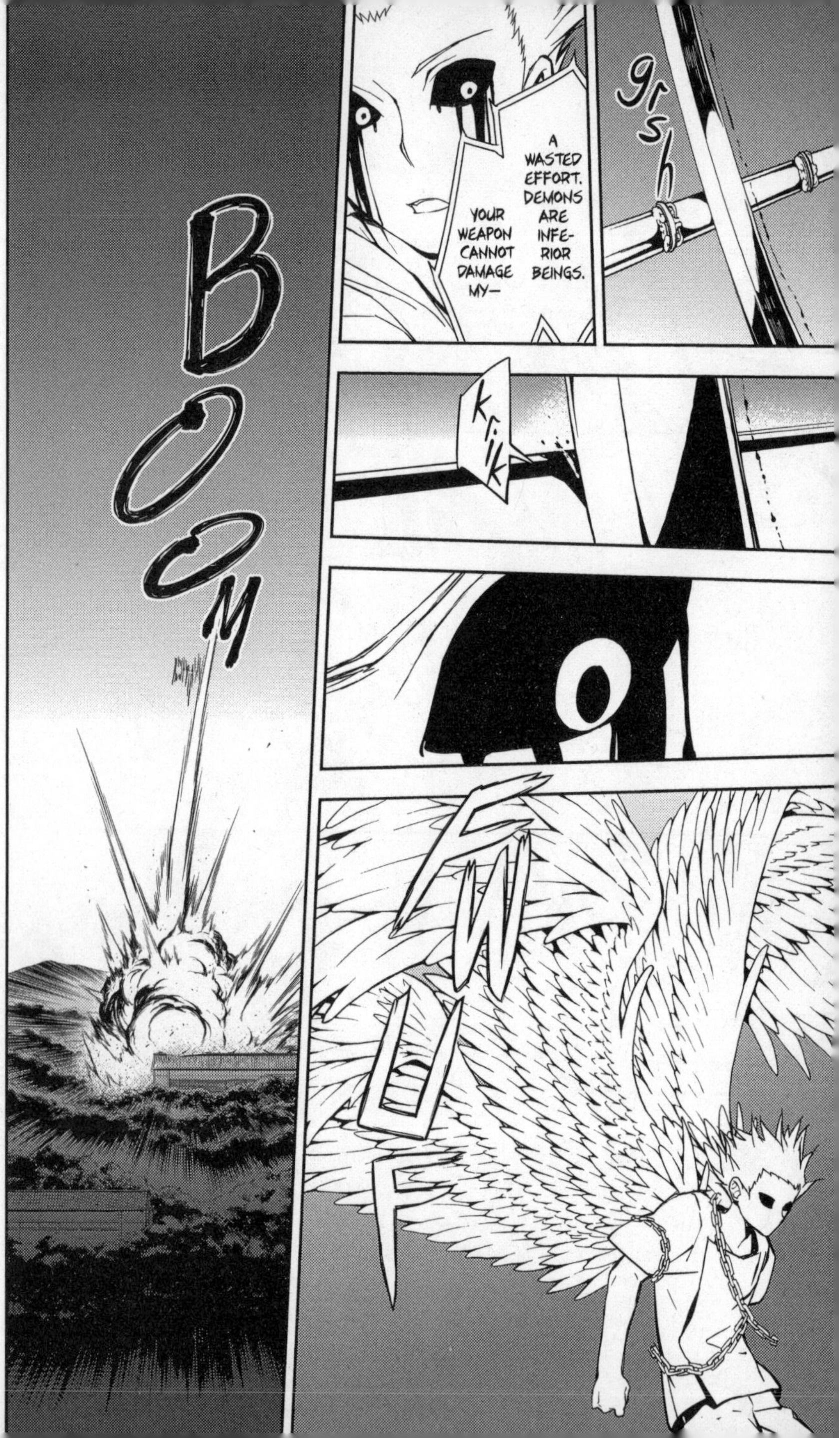
grsh
A WASTED EFFORT. DEMONS ARE INFE-RIOR BEINGS.
YOUR WEAPON CANNOT DAMAGE MY—
krik
FWUF
BOOM

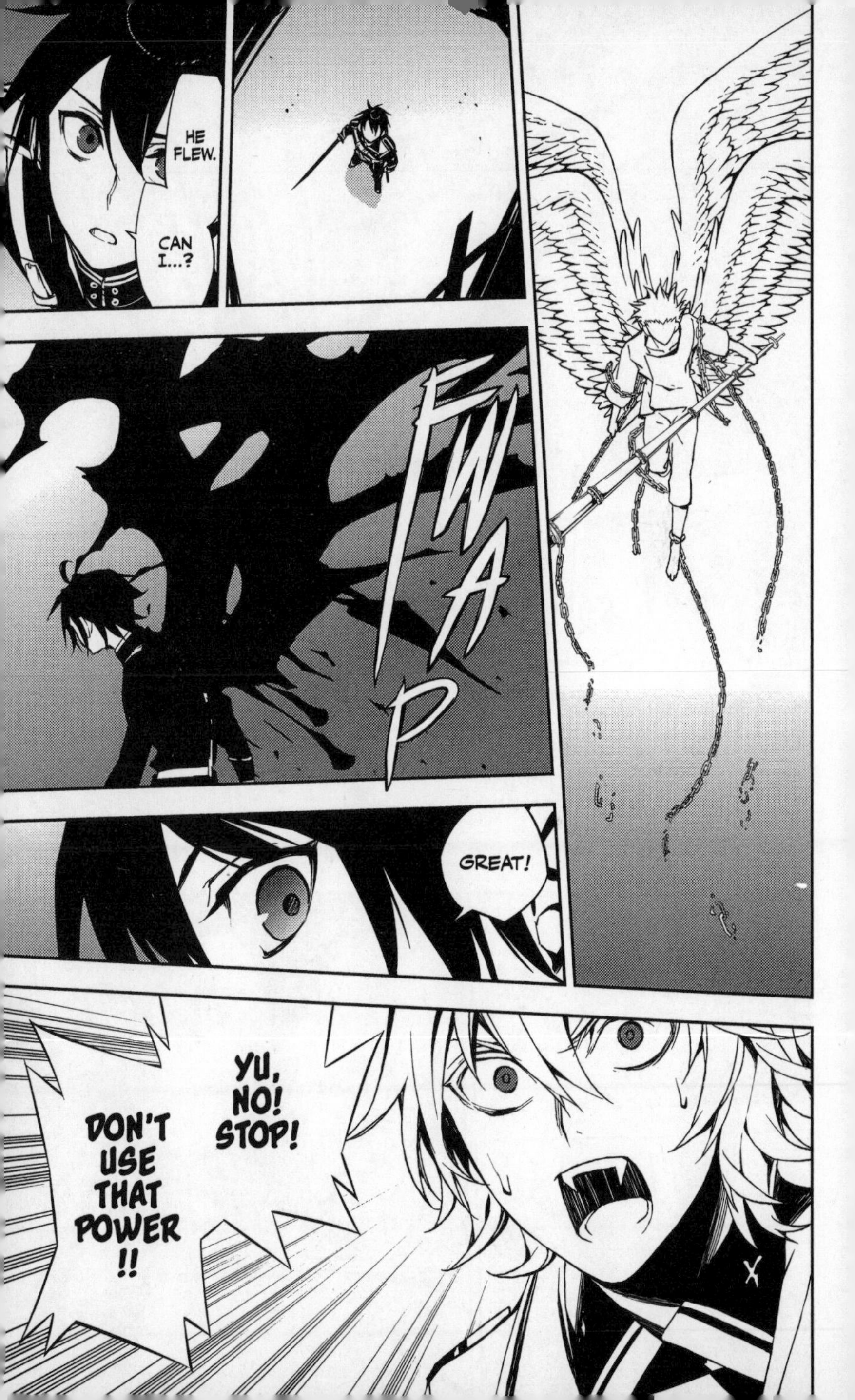
HE FLEW.
CAN I...?
FWAP
GREAT!
YU, NO! STOP!
DON'T USE THAT POWER!!

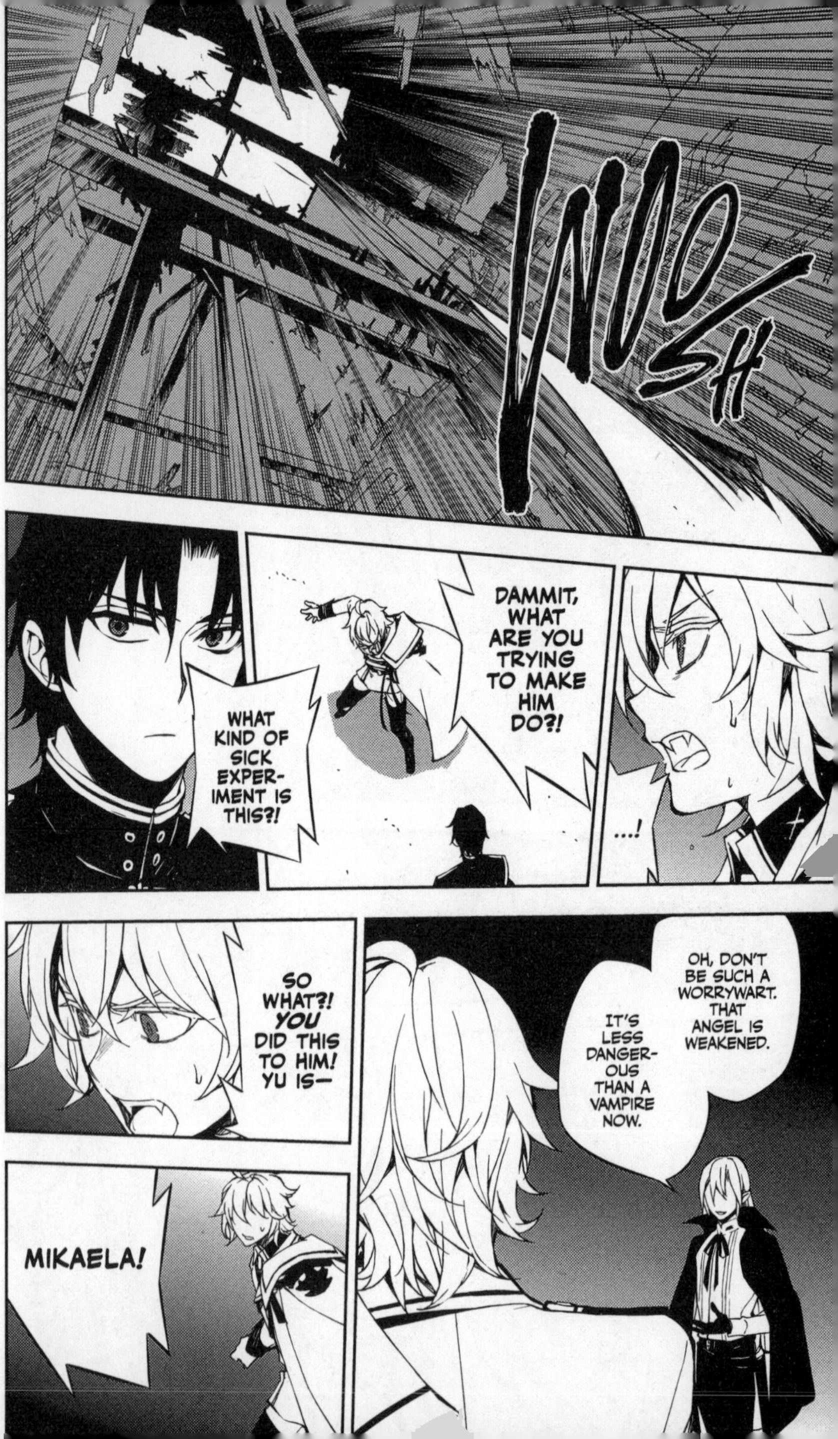
WHOOSH
...!
DAMMIT, WHAT ARE YOU TRYING TO MAKE HIM DO?!
WHAT KIND OF SICK EXPERIMENT IS THIS?!
OH, DON'T BE SUCH A WORRYWART. THAT ANGEL IS WEAKENED.
IT'S LESS DANGEROUS THAN A VAMPIRE NOW.
SO WHAT?! *YOU* DID THIS TO HIM! YU IS—
MIKAELA!

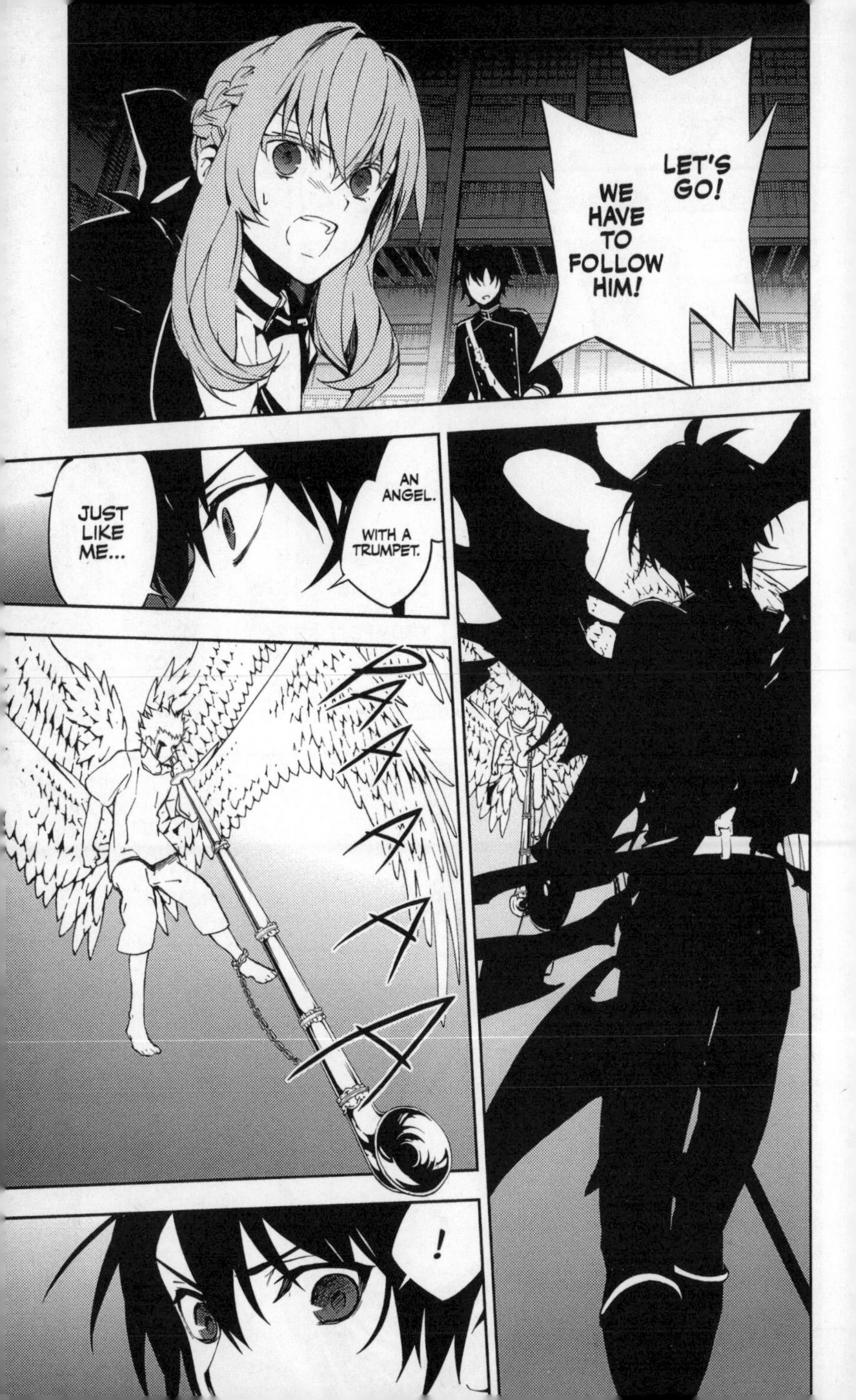
LET'S GO!
WE HAVE TO FOLLOW HIM!
AN ANGEL.
WITH A TRUMPET.
JUST LIKE ME...
PAAAAAA
!

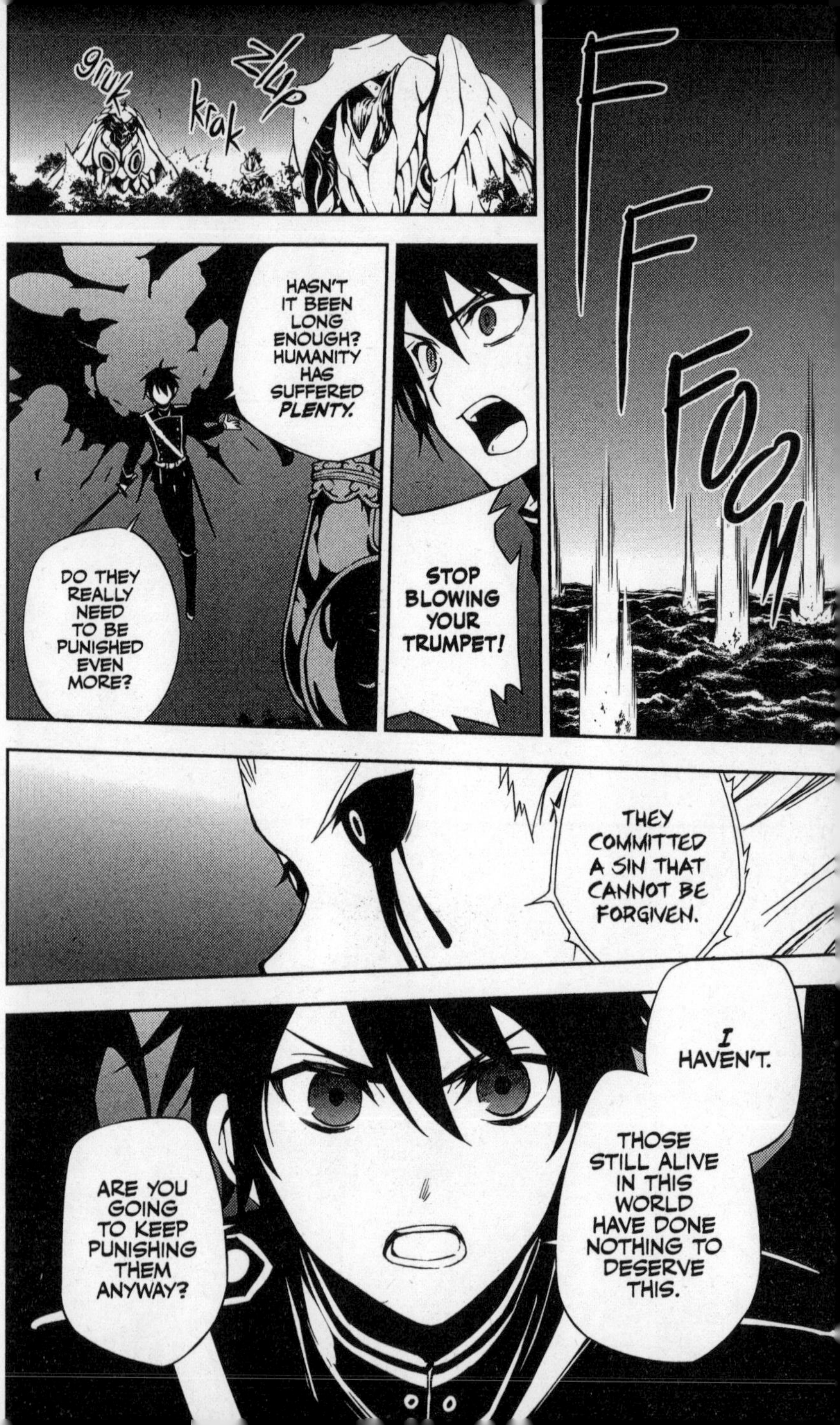
FFFOOM
zlup
krak
gruk
STOP BLOWING YOUR TRUMPET!
HASN'T IT BEEN LONG ENOUGH? HUMANITY HAS SUFFERED *PLENTY.*
DO THEY REALLY NEED TO BE PUNISHED EVEN MORE?
THEY COMMITTED A SIN THAT CANNOT BE FORGIVEN.
I HAVEN'T.
THOSE STILL ALIVE IN THIS WORLD HAVE DONE NOTHING TO DESERVE THIS.
ARE YOU GOING TO KEEP PUNISHING THEM ANYWAY?

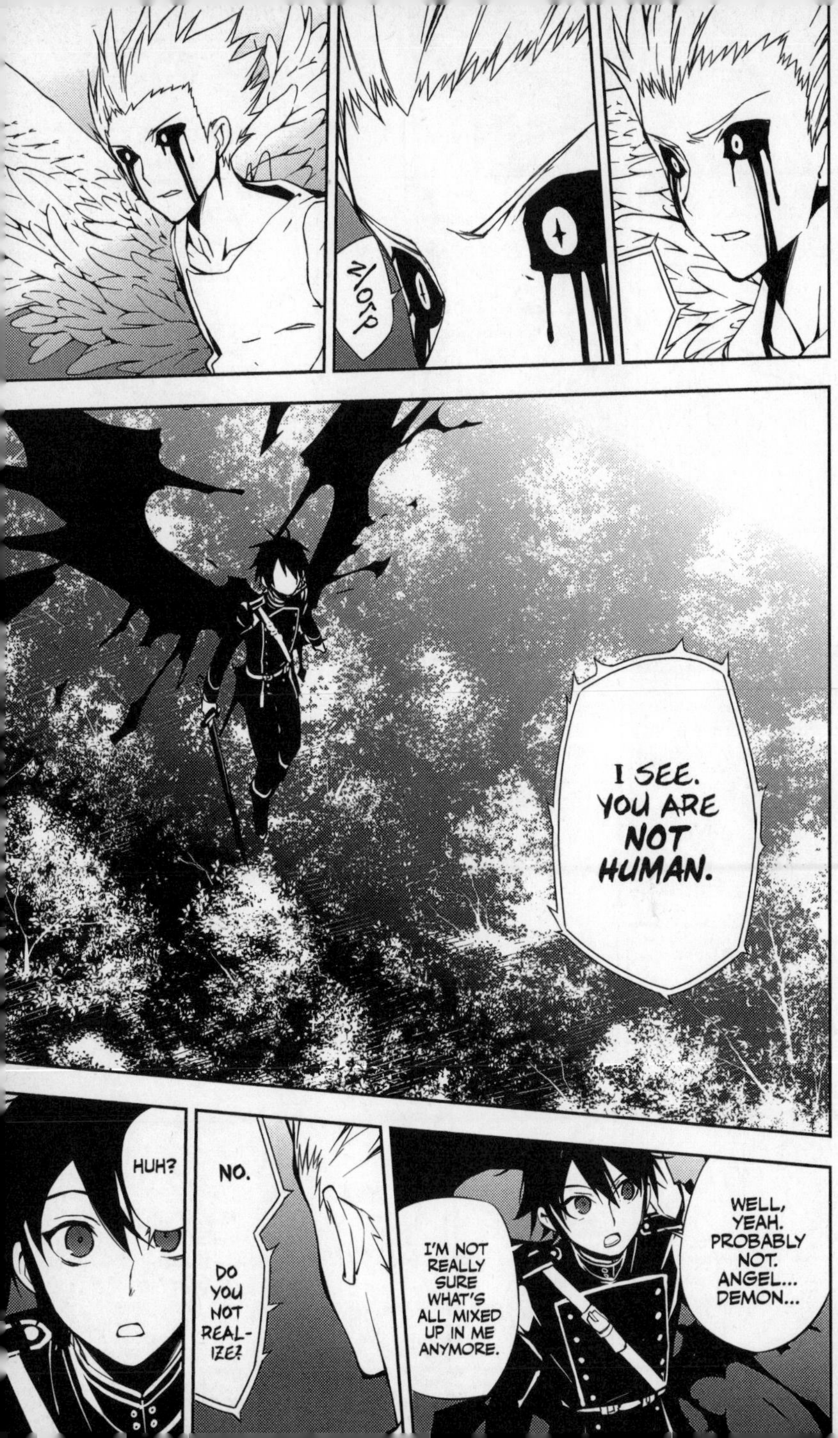
I SEE. YOU ARE NOT HUMAN.
WELL, YEAH. PROBABLY NOT. ANGEL... DEMON...
I'M NOT REALLY SURE WHAT'S ALL MIXED UP IN ME ANYMORE.
NO.
DO YOU NOT REAL-IZE?
HUH?

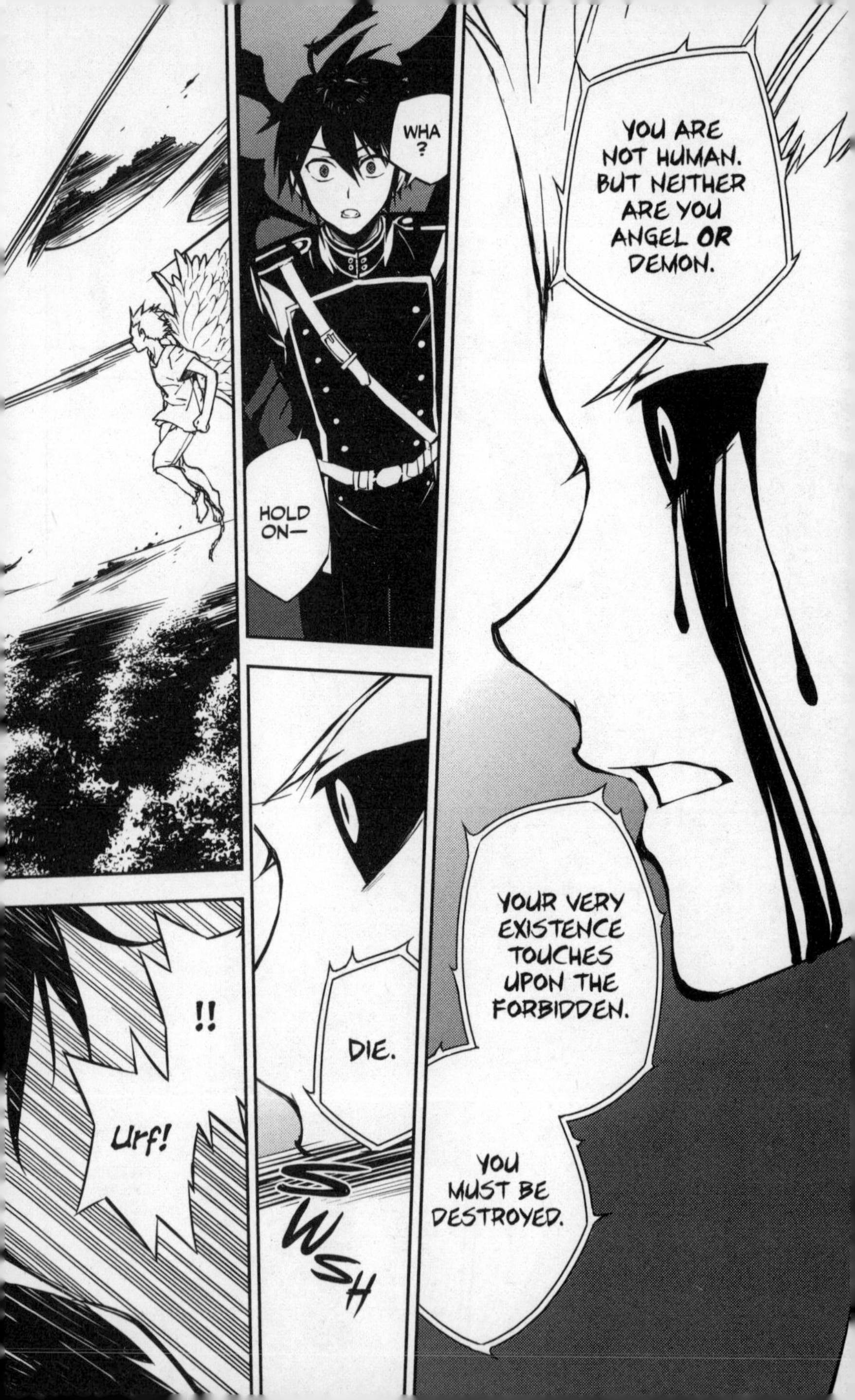
YOU ARE NOT HUMAN. BUT NEITHER ARE YOU ANGEL OR DEMON.
YOUR VERY EXISTENCE TOUCHES UPON THE FORBIDDEN.
YOU MUST BE DESTROYED.
WHA ?
HOLD ON—
DIE.
SWSH
!!
Urf!

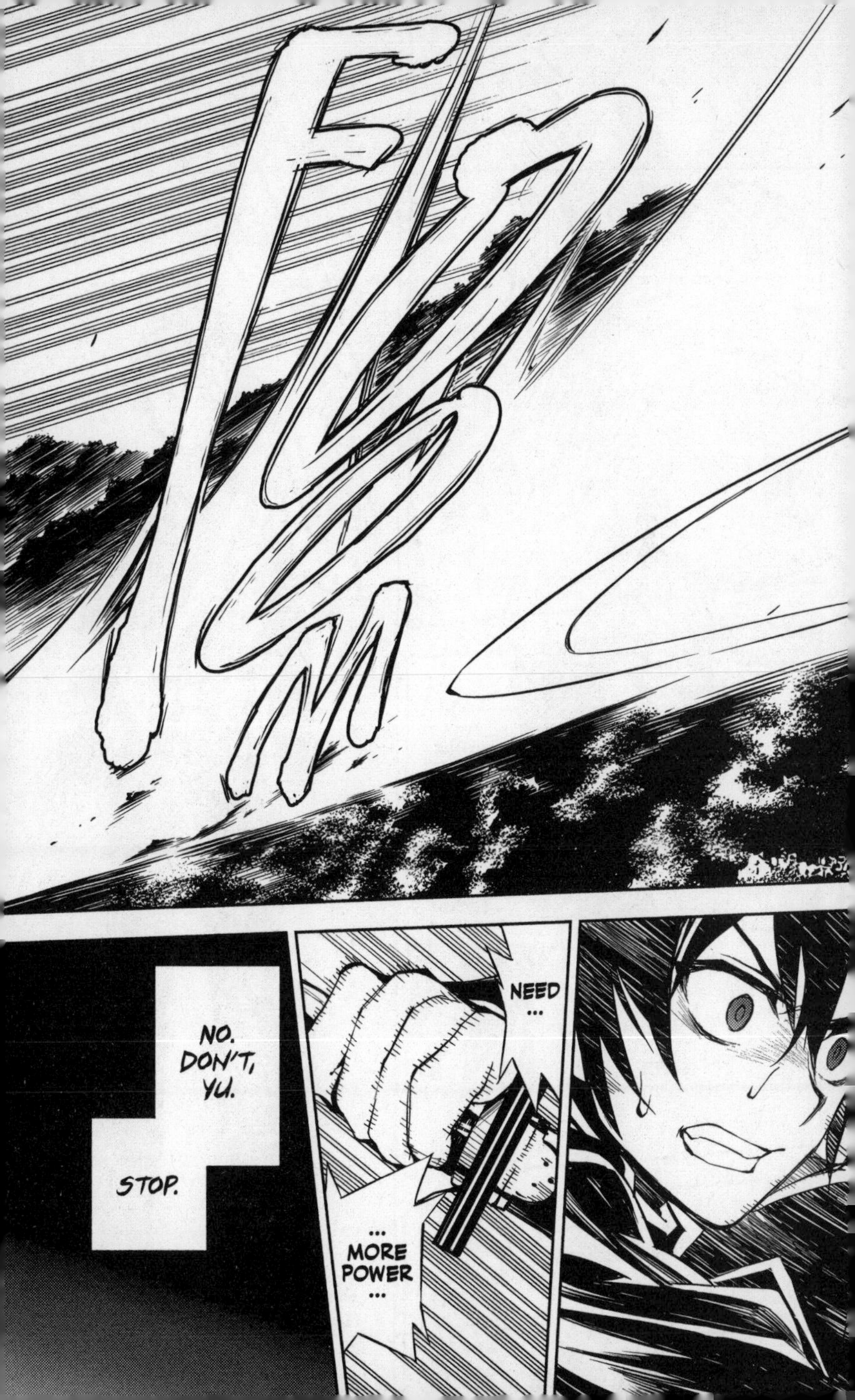
NEED ...
... MORE POWER ...
NO. DON'T, YU.
STOP.

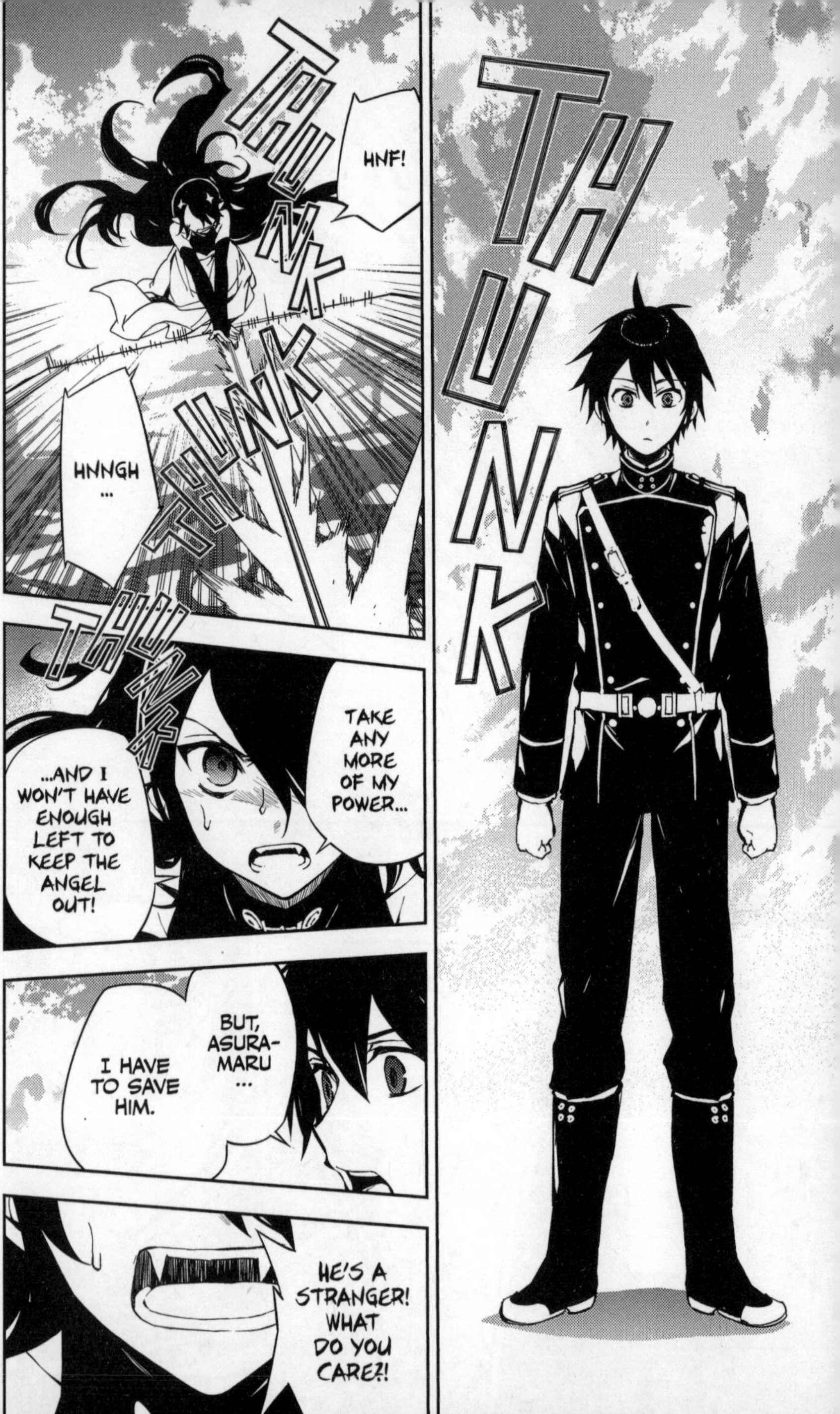
THUNK
THUNK
HNF!
THUNK
HNNGH ...
THUNK
TAKE ANY MORE OF MY POWER...
...AND I WON'T HAVE ENOUGH LEFT TO KEEP THE ANGEL OUT!
BUT, ASURA-MARU ...
I HAVE TO SAVE HIM.
HE'S A STRANGER! WHAT DO YOU CARE?!

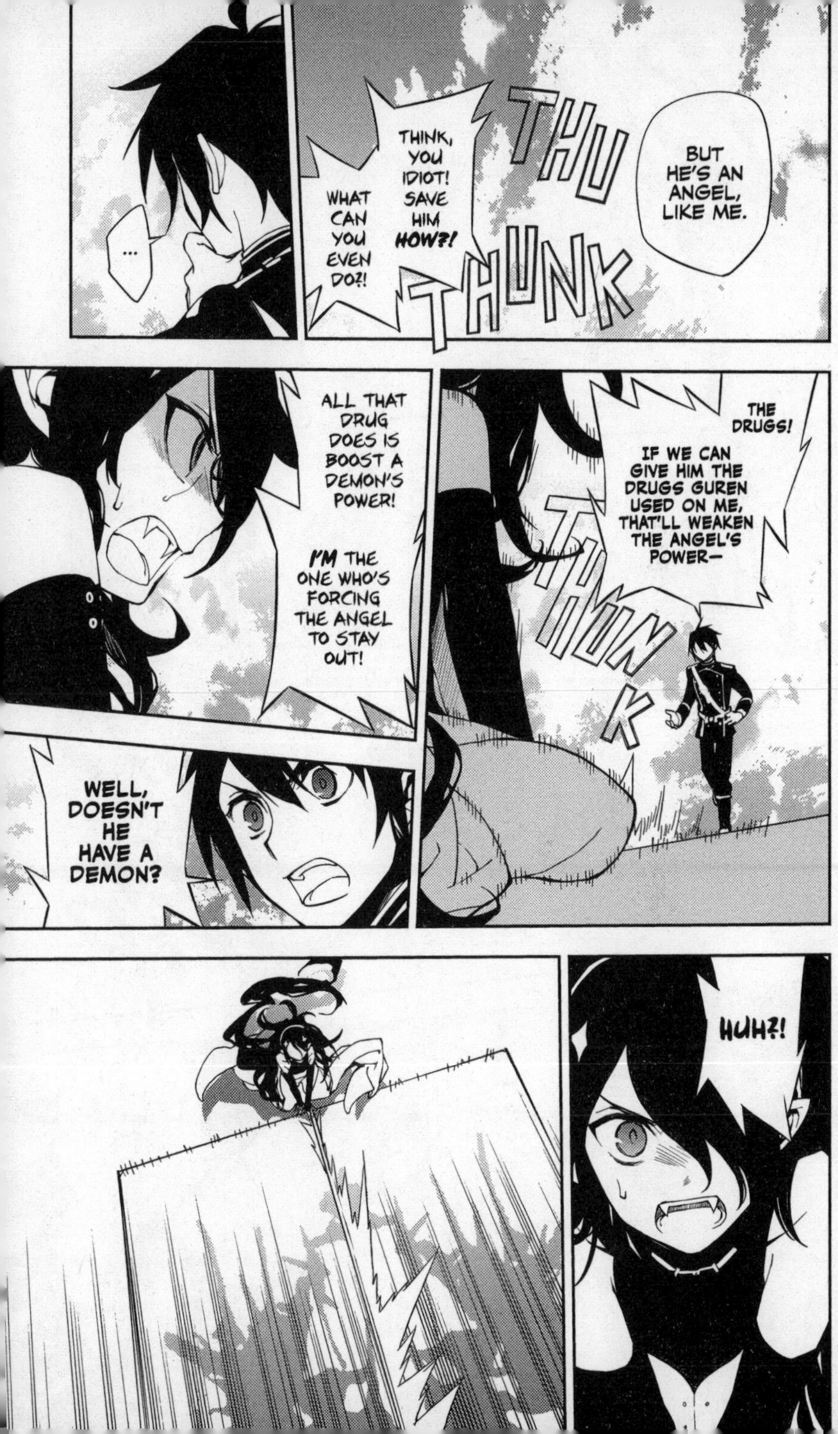
BUT HE'S AN ANGEL, LIKE ME.
THUNK
THINK, YOU IDIOT! SAVE HIM *HOW?!*
WHAT CAN YOU EVEN DO?!
...
THE DRUGS!
IF WE CAN GIVE HIM THE DRUGS GUREN USED ON ME, THAT'LL WEAKEN THE ANGEL'S POWER—
THUNK
ALL THAT DRUG DOES IS BOOST A DEMON'S POWER!
I'M THE ONE WHO'S FORCING THE ANGEL TO STAY OUT!
WELL, DOESN'T HE HAVE A DEMON?
HUH?!

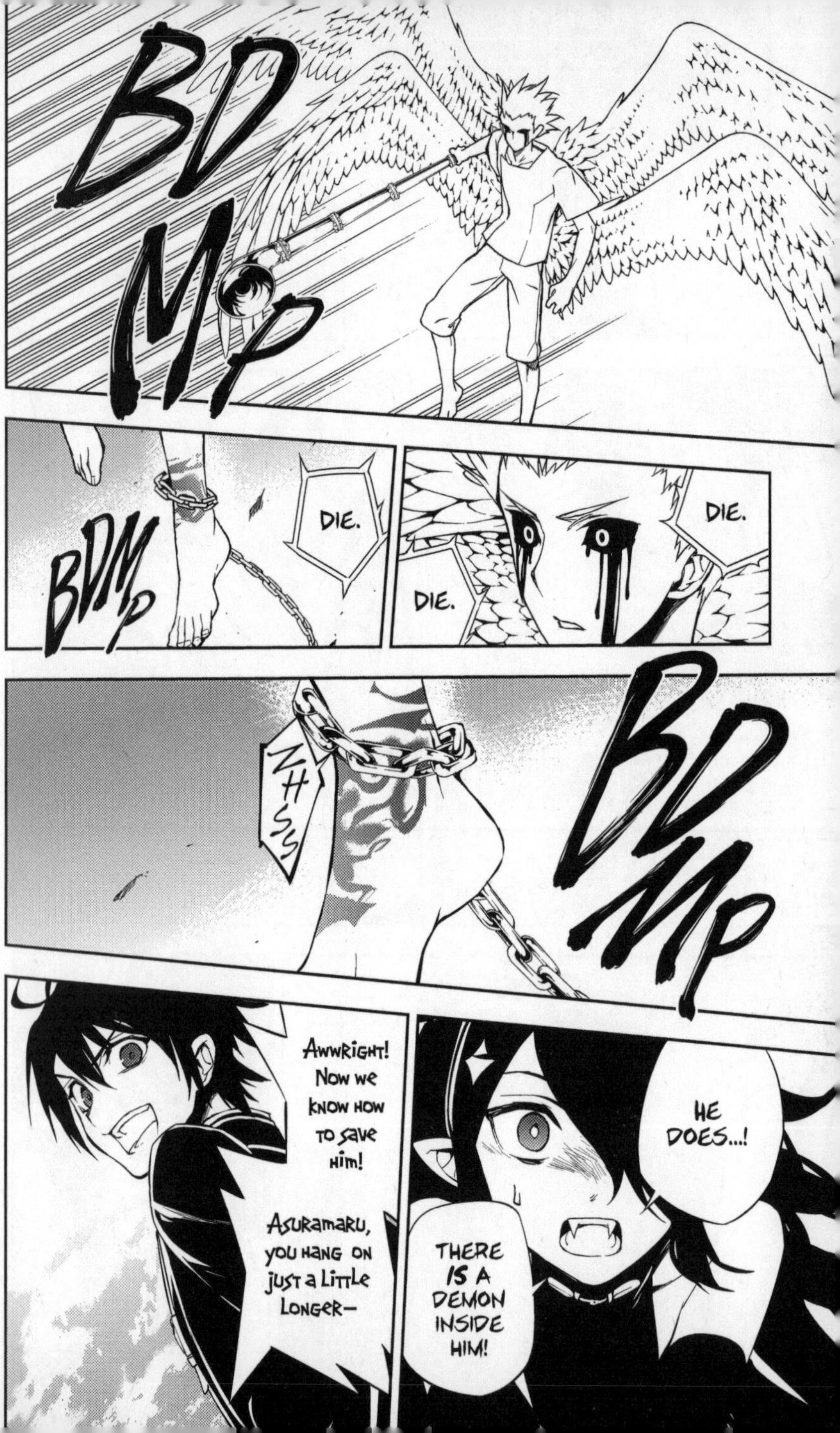
BDMP
DIE.
DIE.
DIE.
BDMP
BDMP
ZHSS
HE DOES...!
THERE IS A DEMON INSIDE HIM!
Awwright! Now we know how to save him!
Asuramaru, you hang on just a little longer—

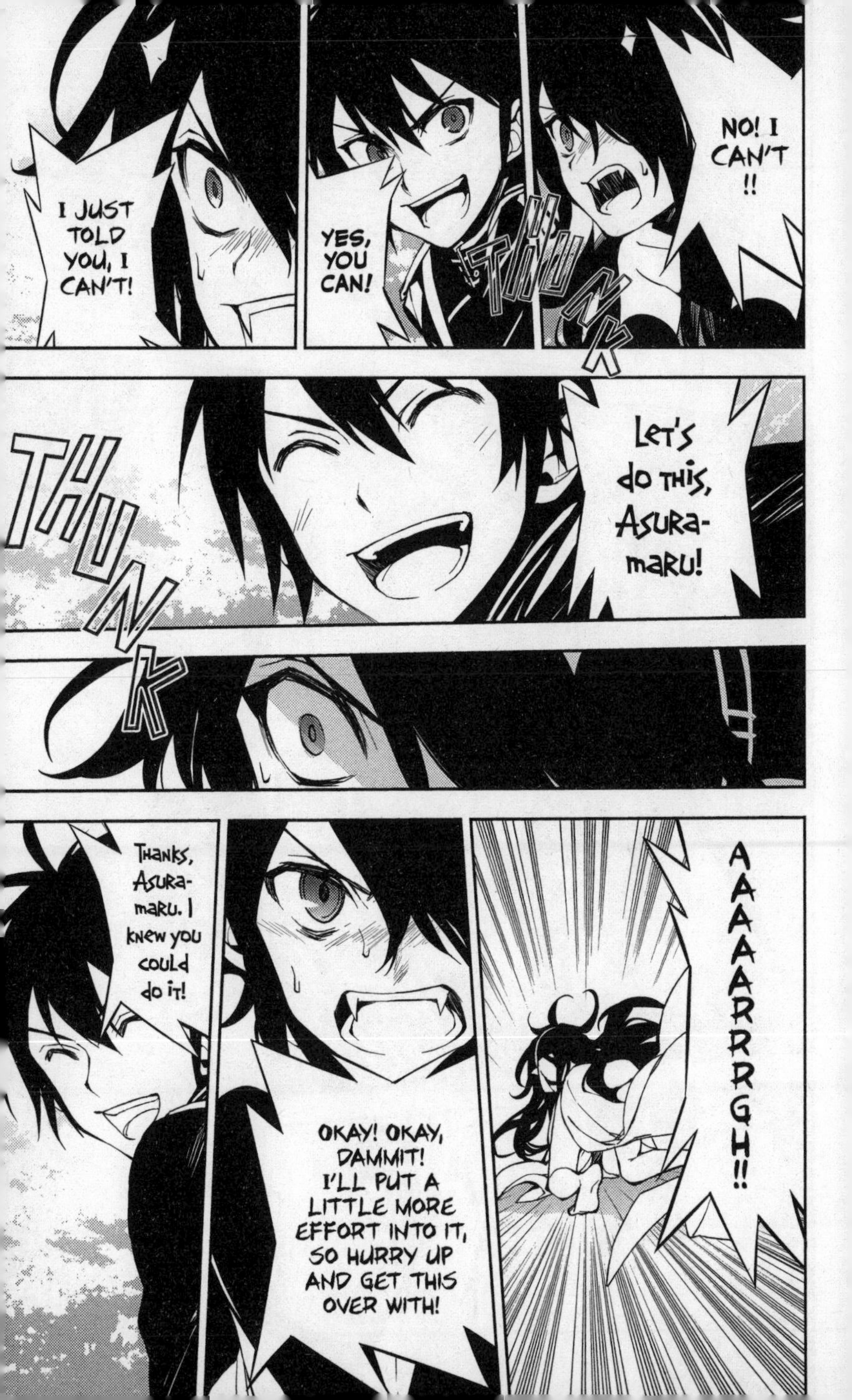
NO! I CAN'T !!
YES, YOU CAN!
THUNK
I JUST TOLD YOU, I CAN'T!
Let's do this, Asura-maru!
THUNK
AAAAARRRGH!!
OKAY! OKAY, DAMMIT! I'LL PUT A LITTLE MORE EFFORT INTO IT, SO HURRY UP AND GET THIS OVER WITH!
Thanks, Asura-maru. I knew you could do it!

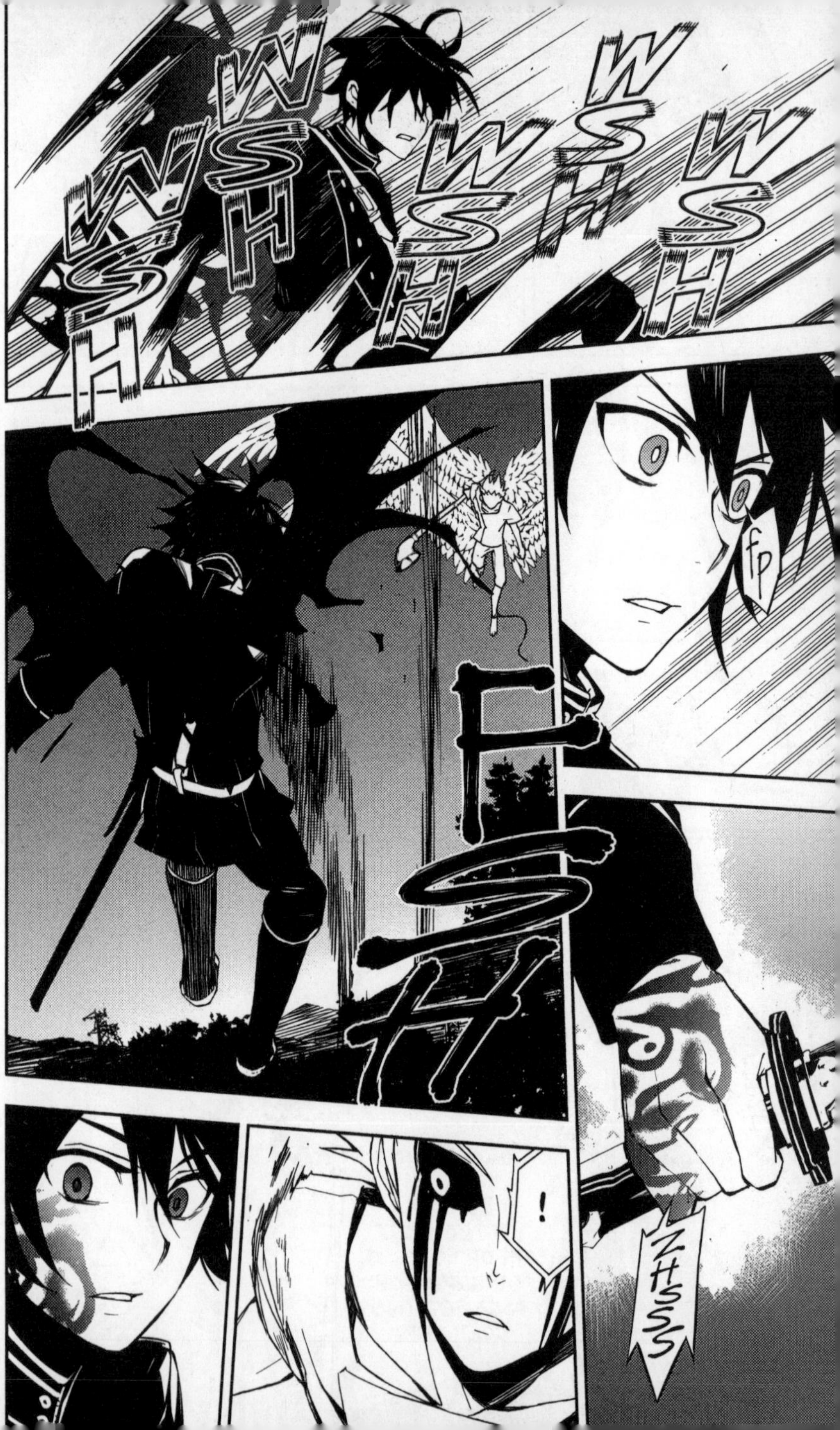
WSH
WSH
WSH
WSH
WSH
fp
FSH
ZHSSS
!

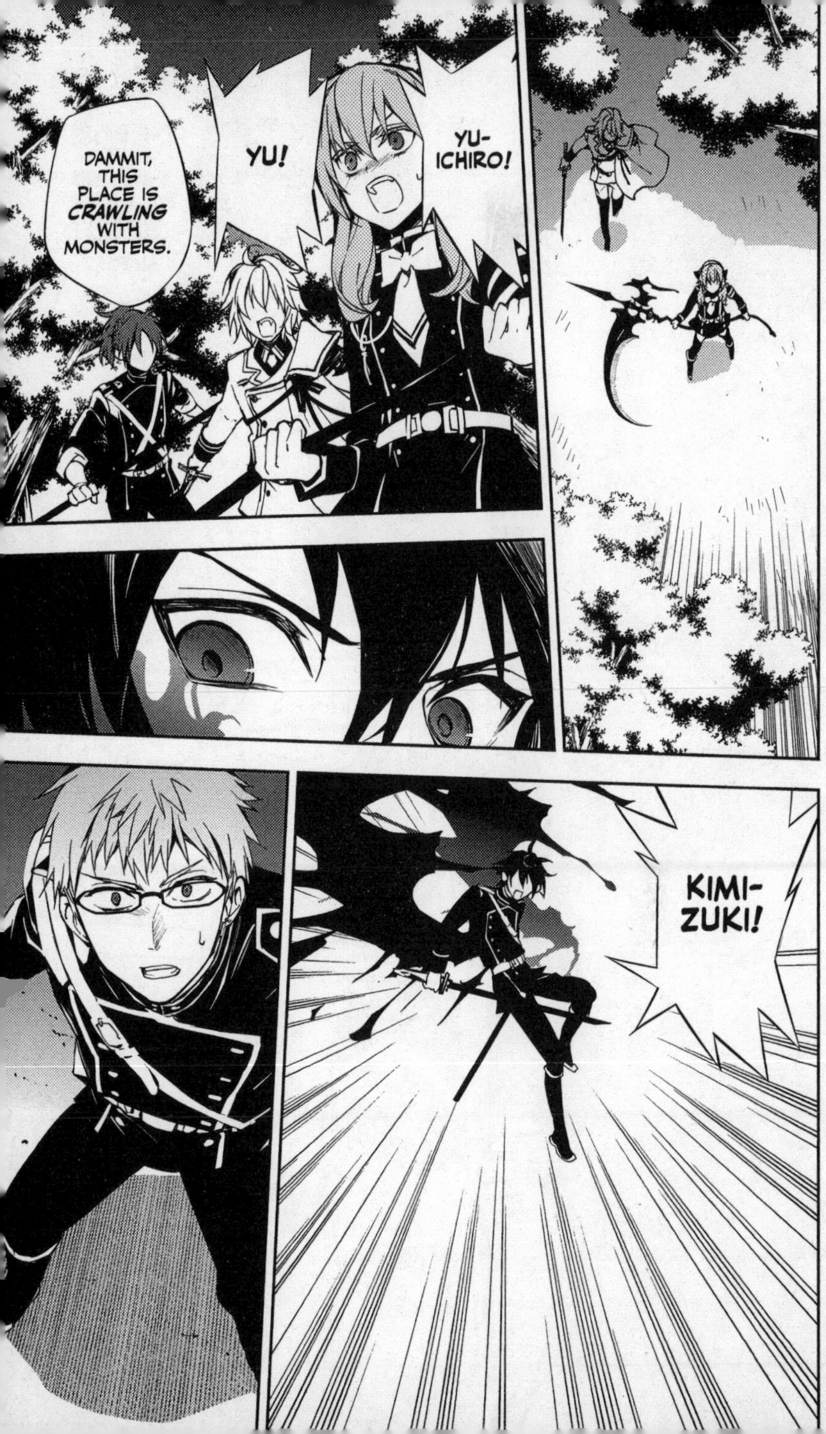
YU-ICHIRO!
YU!
DAMMIT, THIS PLACE IS *CRAWLING* WITH MONSTERS.
KIMI-ZUKI!

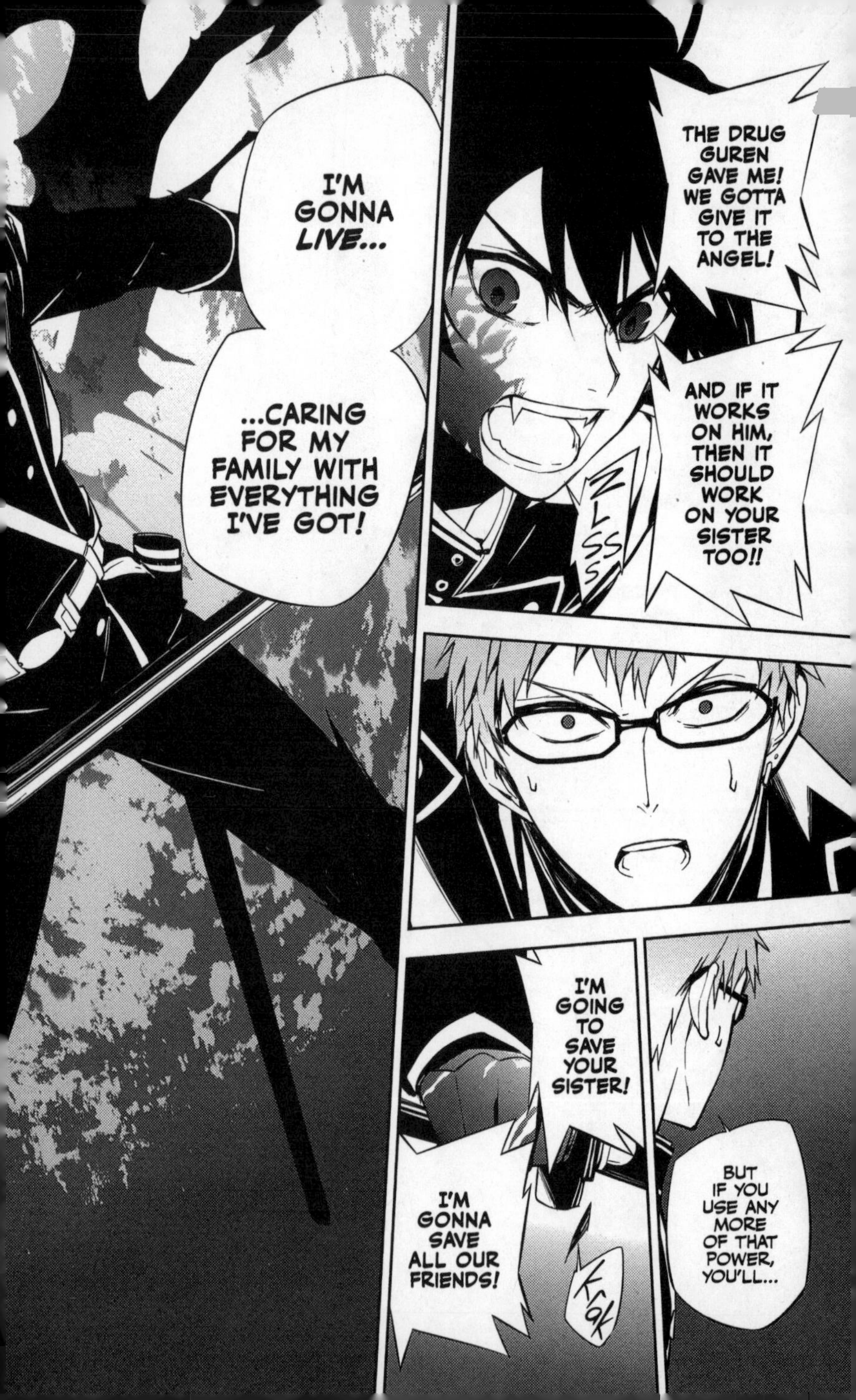
THE DRUG GUREN GAVE ME! WE GOTTA GIVE IT TO THE ANGEL!
AND IF IT WORKS ON HIM, THEN IT SHOULD WORK ON YOUR SISTER TOO!!
ZLSSS
I'M GOING TO SAVE YOUR SISTER!
BUT IF YOU USE ANY MORE OF THAT POWER, YOU'LL...
I'M GONNA SAVE ALL OUR FRIENDS!
KRAK
I'M GONNA *LIVE*...
...CARING FOR MY FAMILY WITH EVERYTHING I'VE GOT!

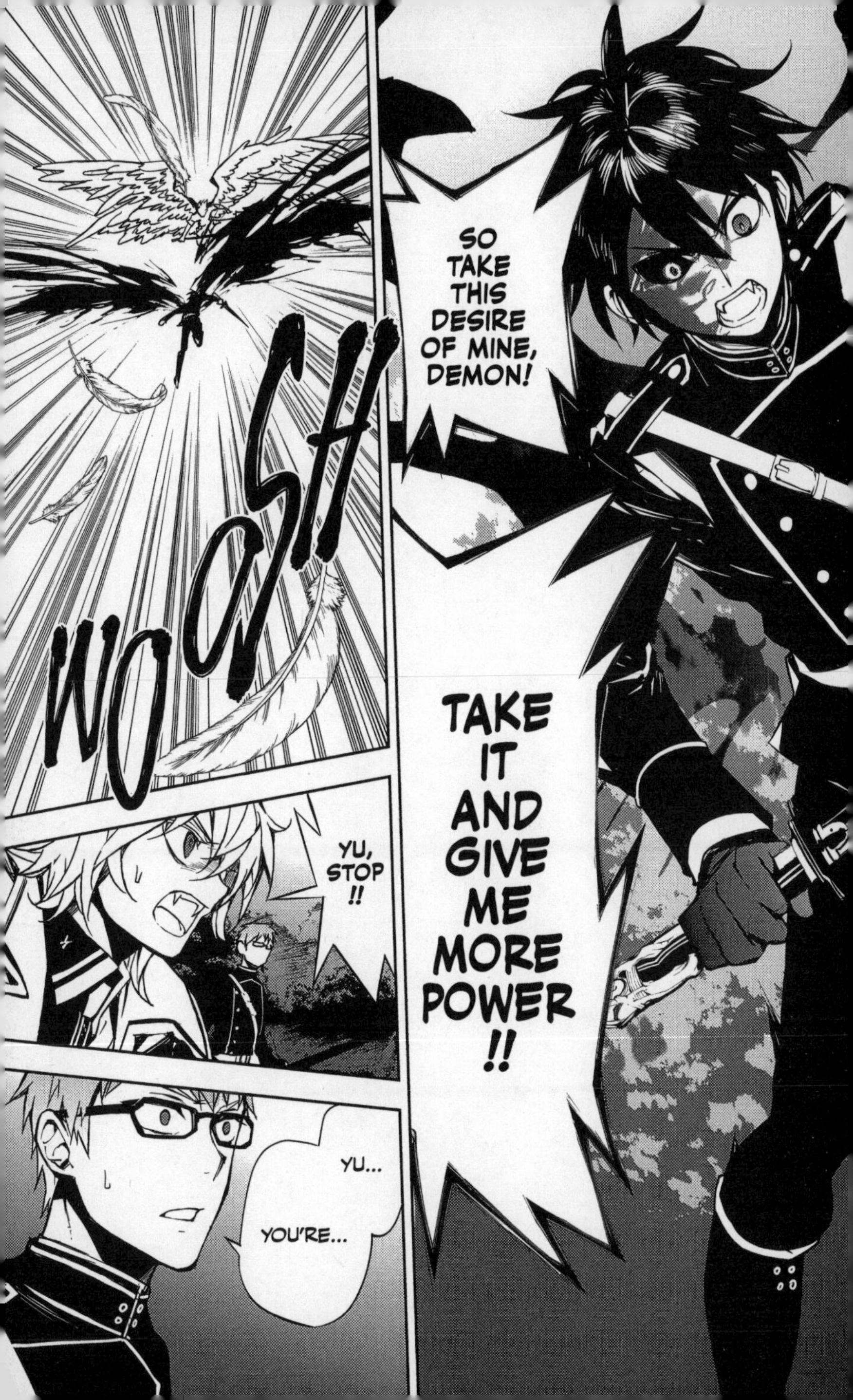
SO TAKE THIS DESIRE OF MINE, DEMON!
TAKE IT AND GIVE ME MORE POWER!!
WOOSH
YU, STOP!!
YU...
YOU'RE...

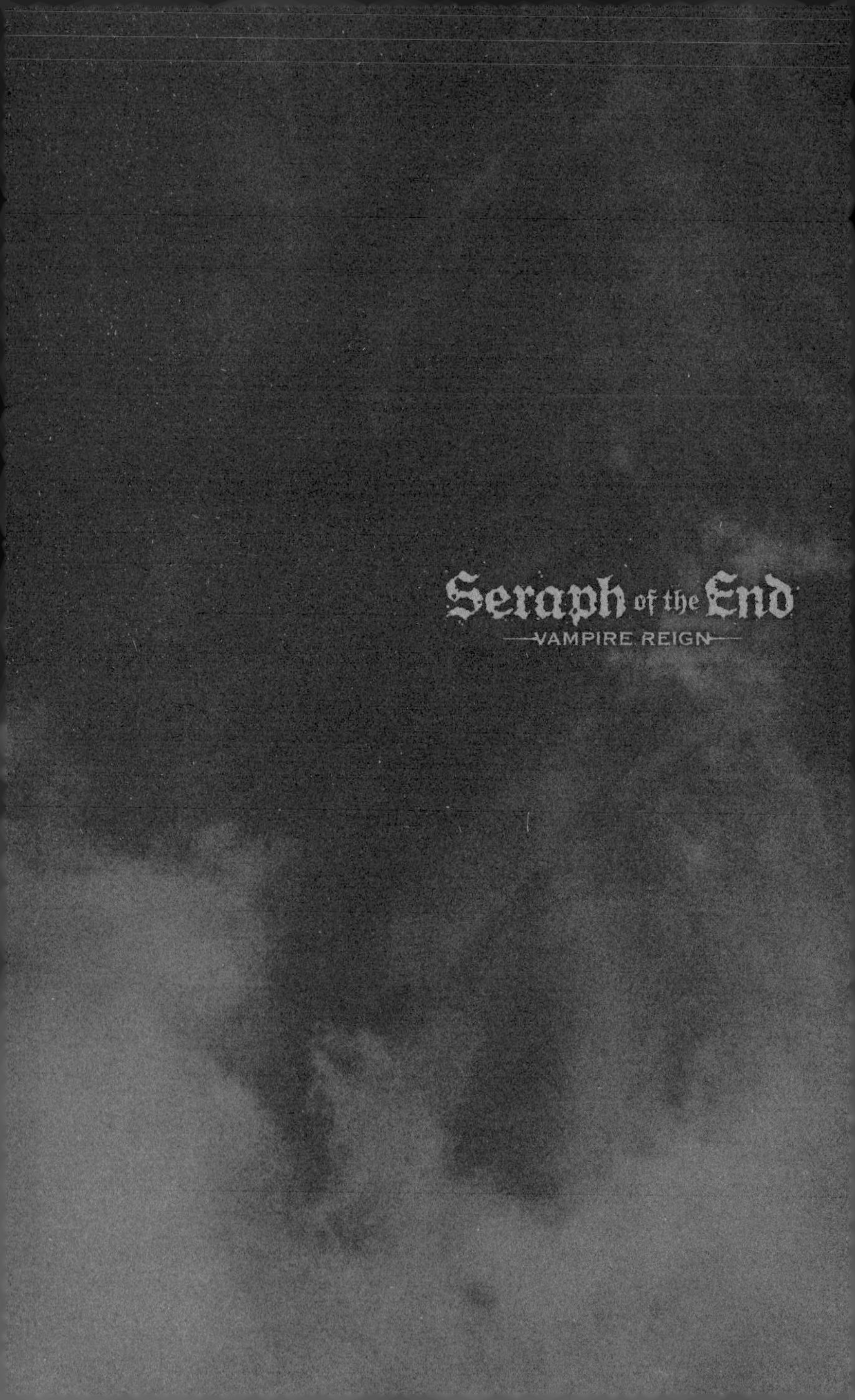
Seraph of the End
VAMPIRE REIGN

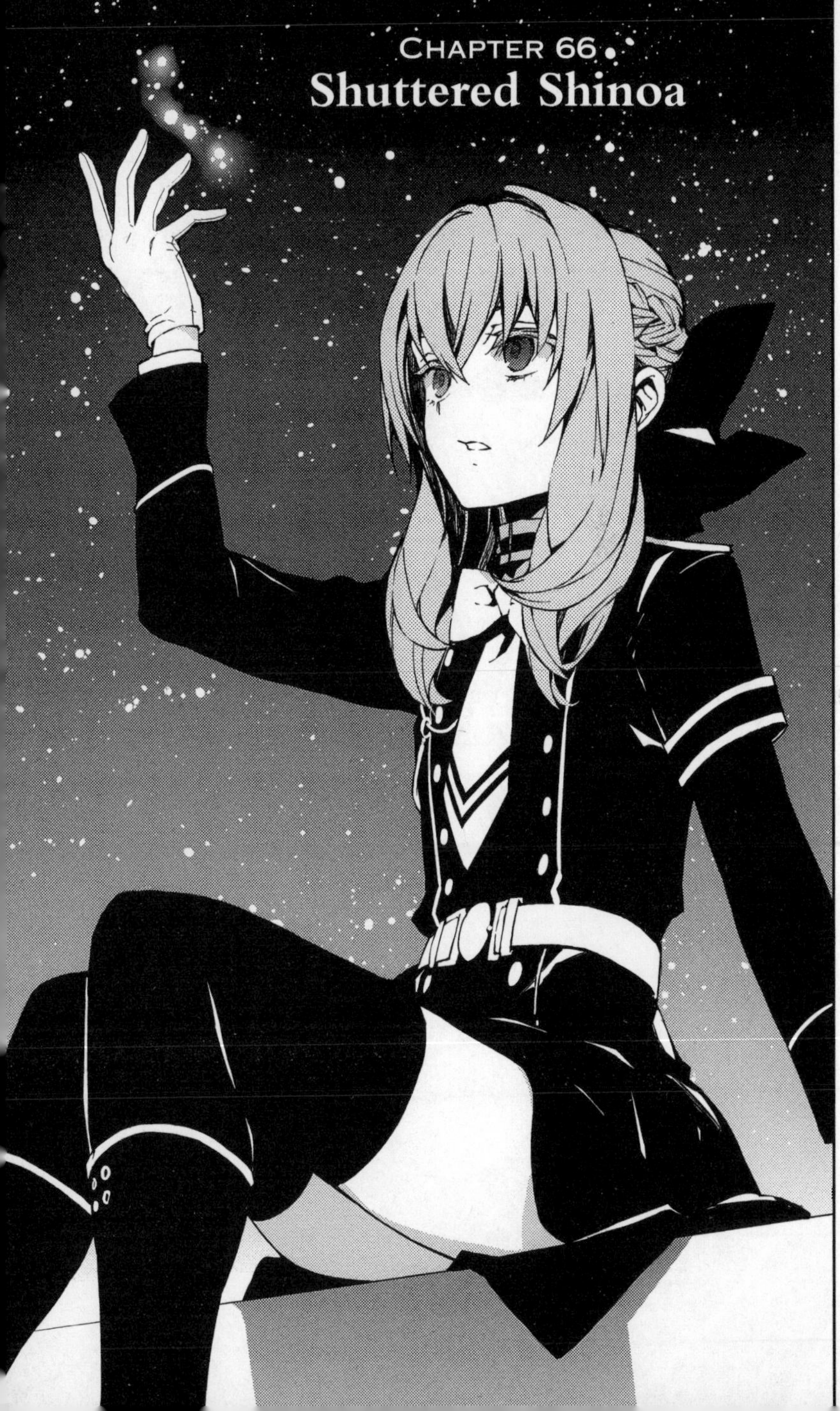
CHAPTER 66
Shuttered Shinoa

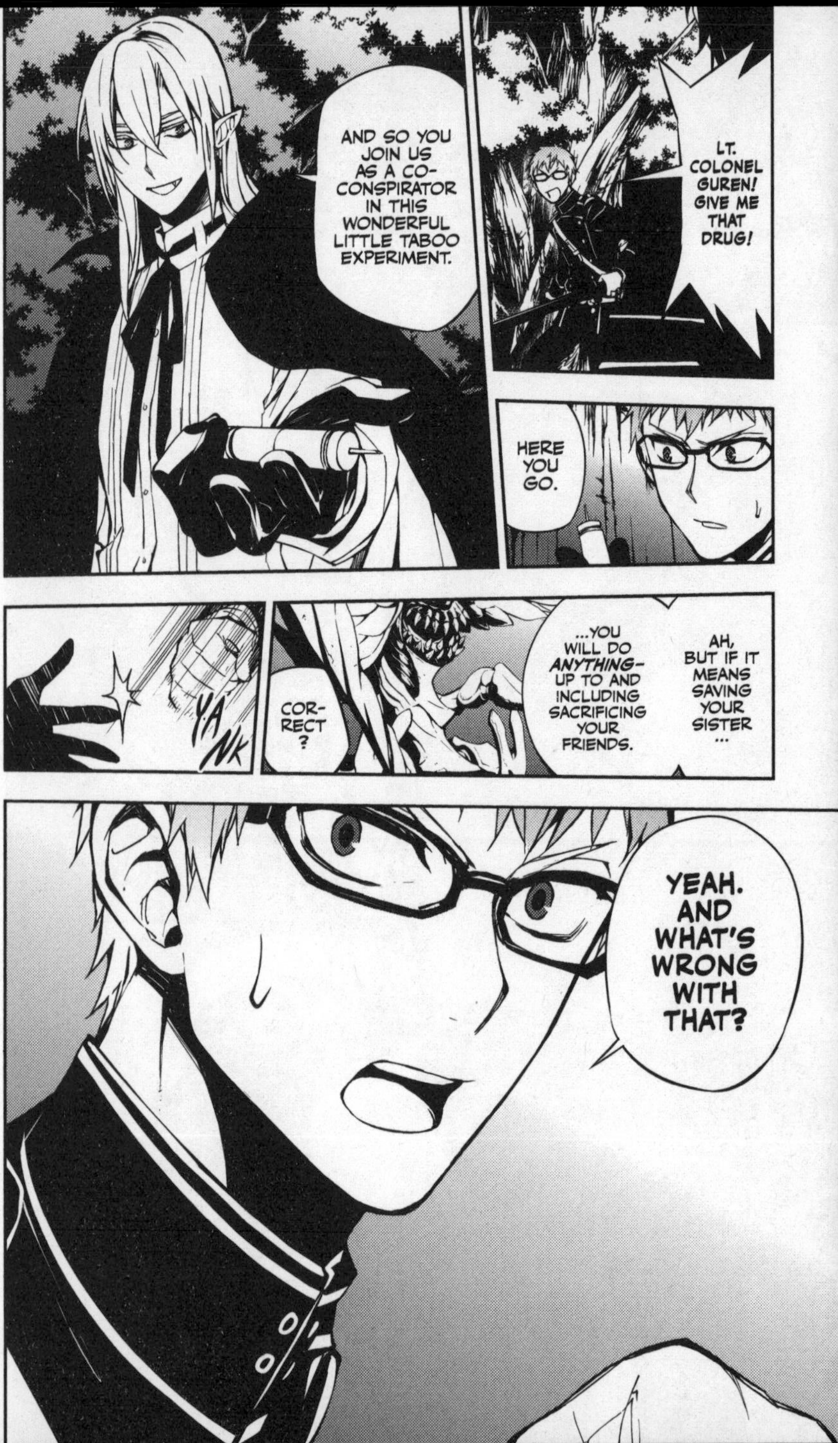
LT. COLONEL GUREN! GIVE ME THAT DRUG!
HERE YOU GO.
AND SO YOU JOIN US AS A CO-CONSPIRATOR IN THIS WONDERFUL LITTLE TABOO EXPERIMENT.
AH, BUT IF IT MEANS SAVING YOUR SISTER...
...YOU WILL DO *ANYTHING*—UP TO AND INCLUDING SACRIFICING YOUR FRIENDS.
CORRECT?
YANK
YEAH. AND WHAT'S WRONG WITH THAT?

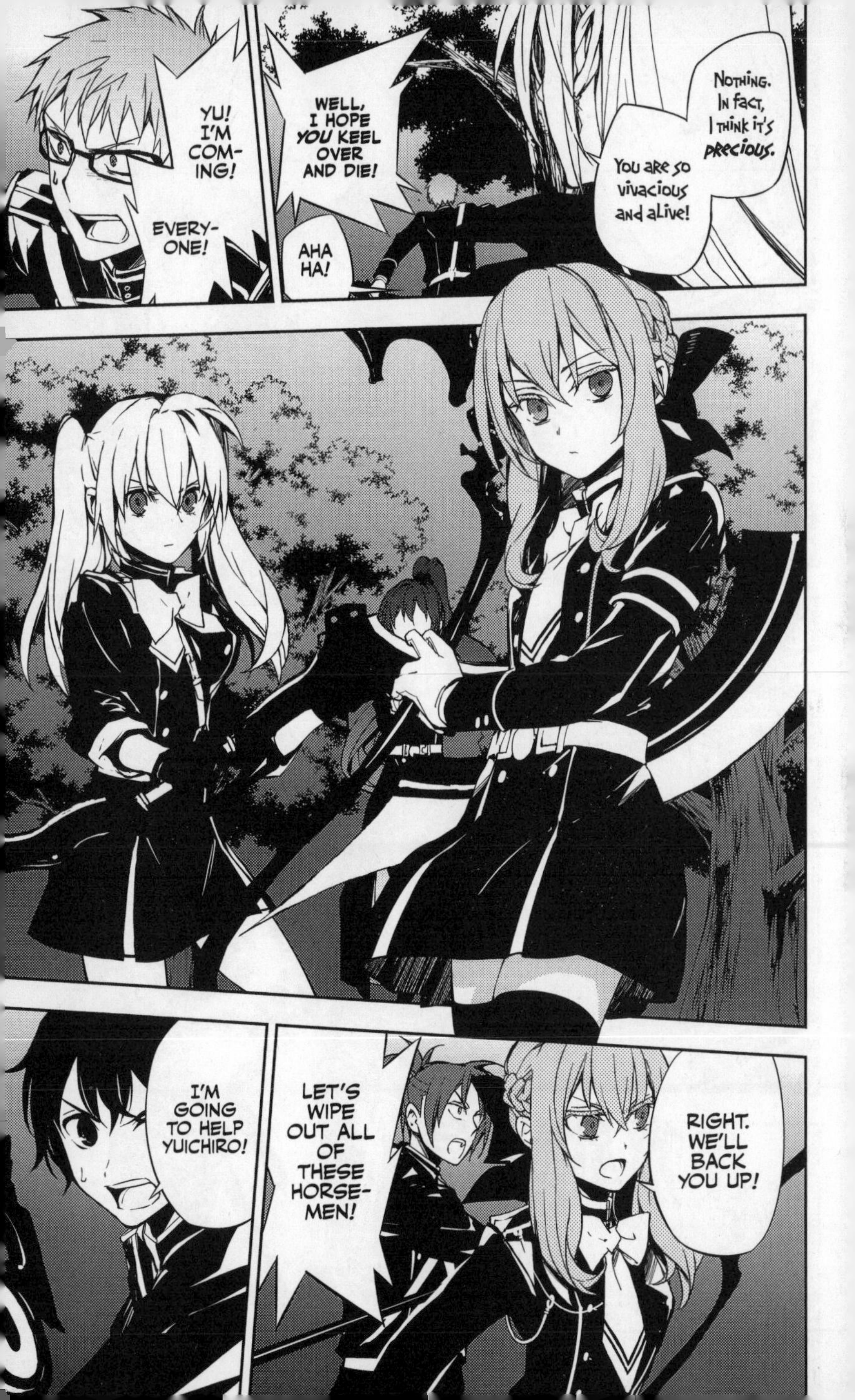
NOTHING. IN FACT, I THINK IT'S PRECIOUS.
YOU ARE SO VIVACIOUS AND ALIVE!
WELL, I HOPE YOU KEEL OVER AND DIE!
AHA HA!
YU! I'M COM-ING!
EVERY-ONE!
RIGHT. WE'LL BACK YOU UP!
LET'S WIPE OUT ALL OF THESE HORSE-MEN!
I'M GOING TO HELP YUICHIRO!

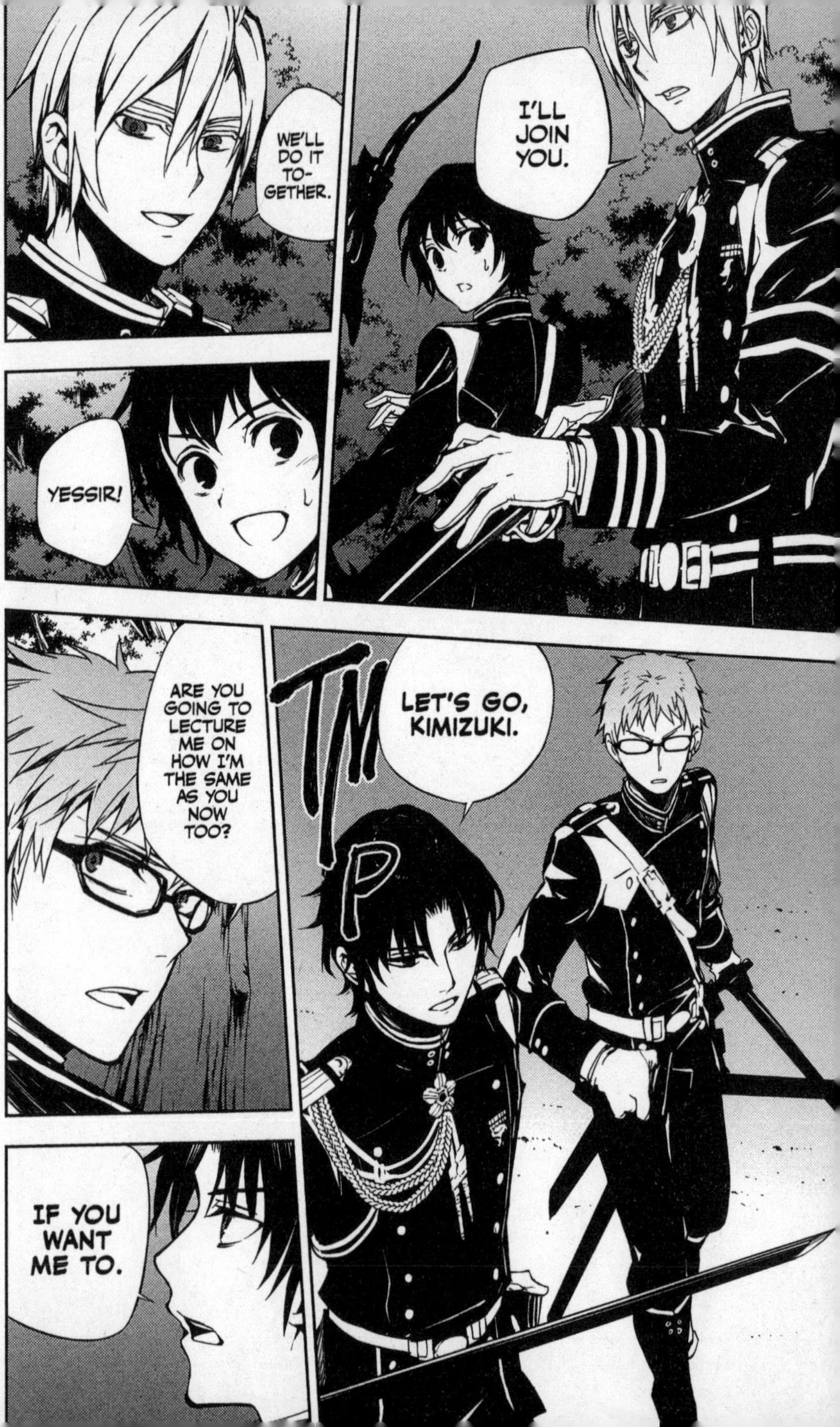
I'LL JOIN YOU.
WE'LL DO IT TO-GETHER.
YESSIR!
LET'S GO, KIMIZUKI.
TMP
ARE YOU GOING TO LECTURE ME ON HOW I'M THE SAME AS YOU NOW TOO?
IF YOU WANT ME TO.

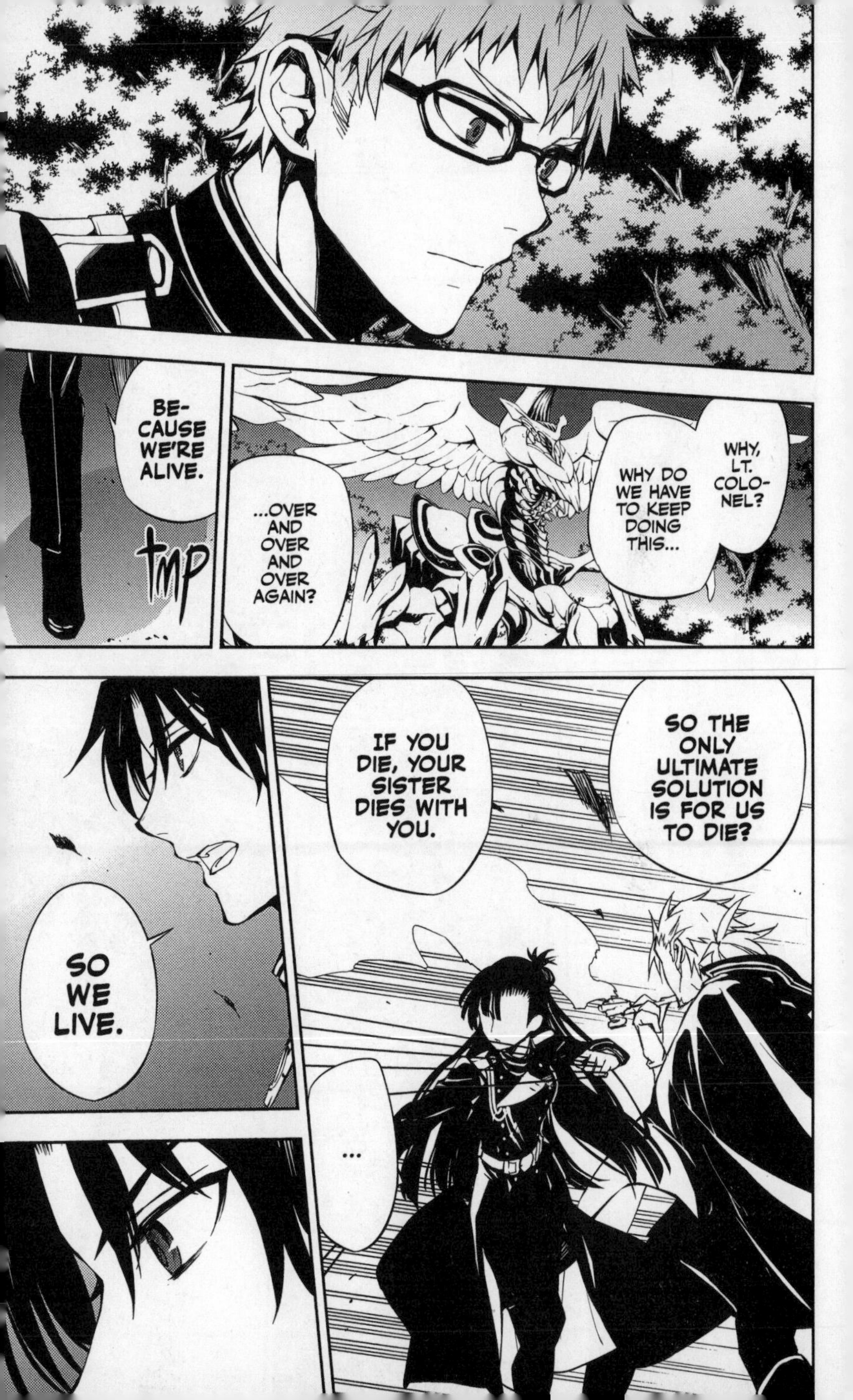
WHY, LT. COLONEL?
WHY DO WE HAVE TO KEEP DOING THIS...
...OVER AND OVER AND OVER AGAIN?
BECAUSE WE'RE ALIVE.
tmp
SO THE ONLY ULTIMATE SOLUTION IS FOR US TO DIE?
IF YOU DIE, YOUR SISTER DIES WITH YOU.
...
SO WE LIVE.

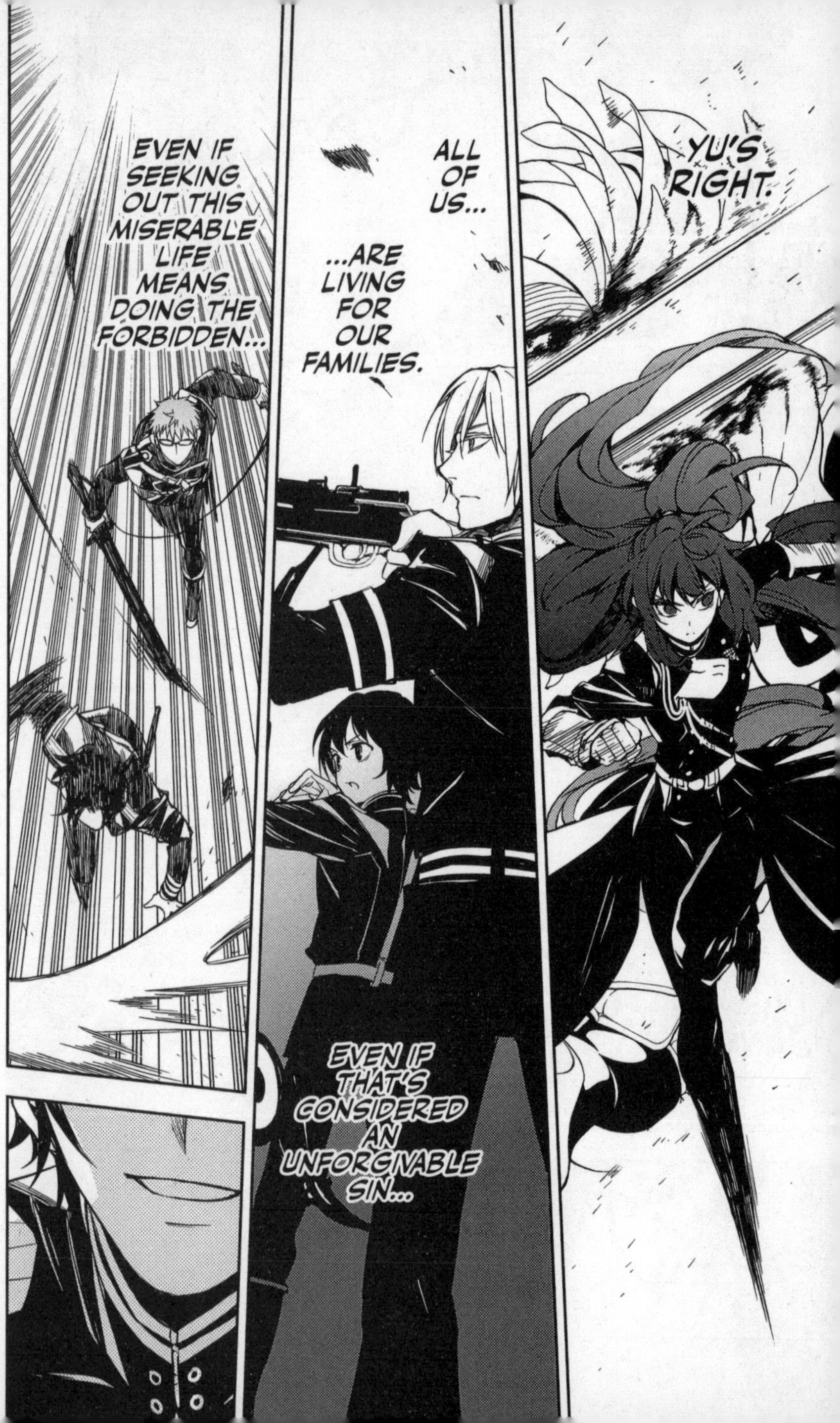
YU'S RIGHT.
ALL OF US...
...ARE LIVING FOR OUR FAMILIES.
EVEN IF THAT'S CONSIDERED AN UNFORGIVABLE SIN...
EVEN IF SEEKING OUT THIS MISERABLE LIFE MEANS DOING THE FORBIDDEN...

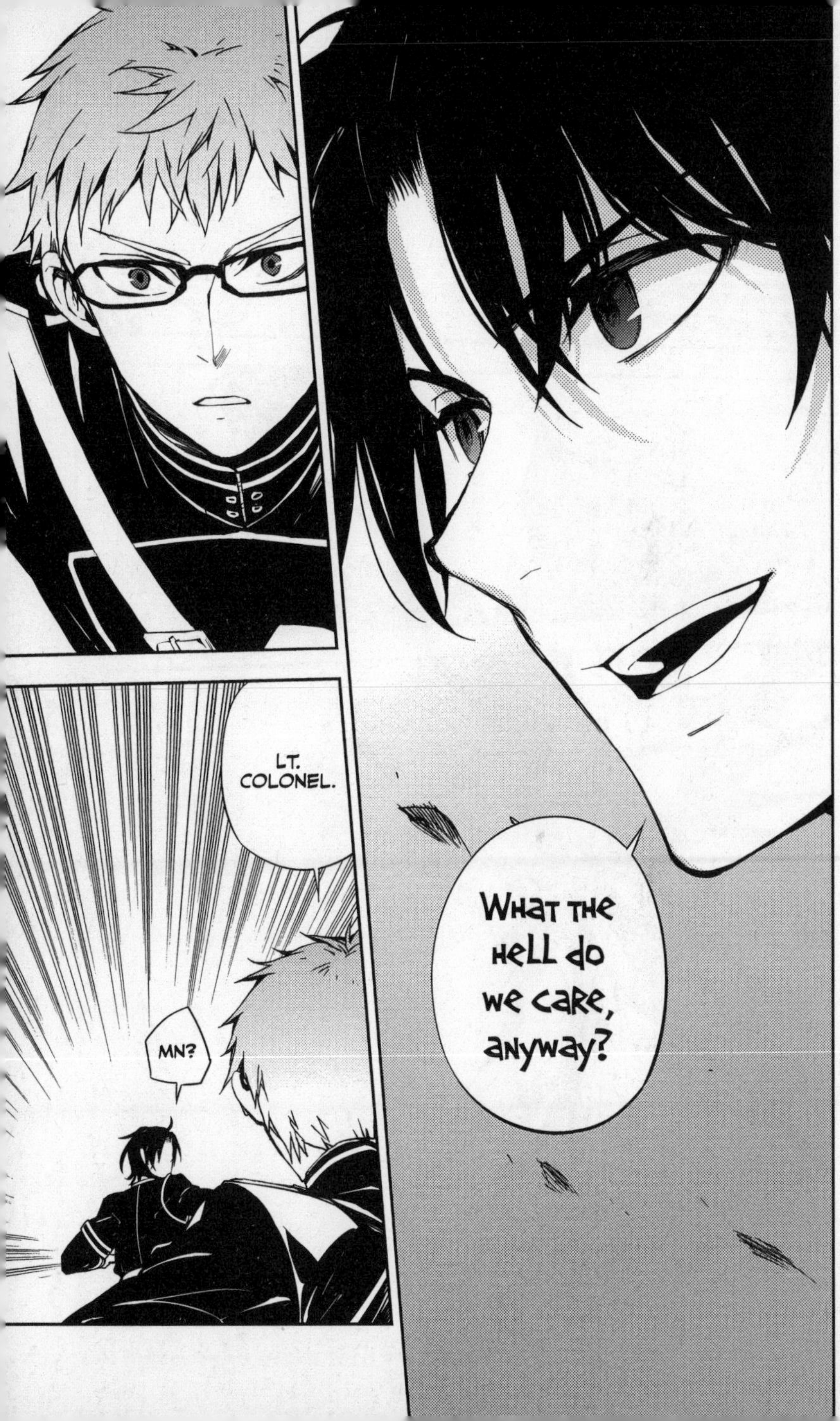
What the hell do we care, anyway?
LT. COLONEL.
MN?

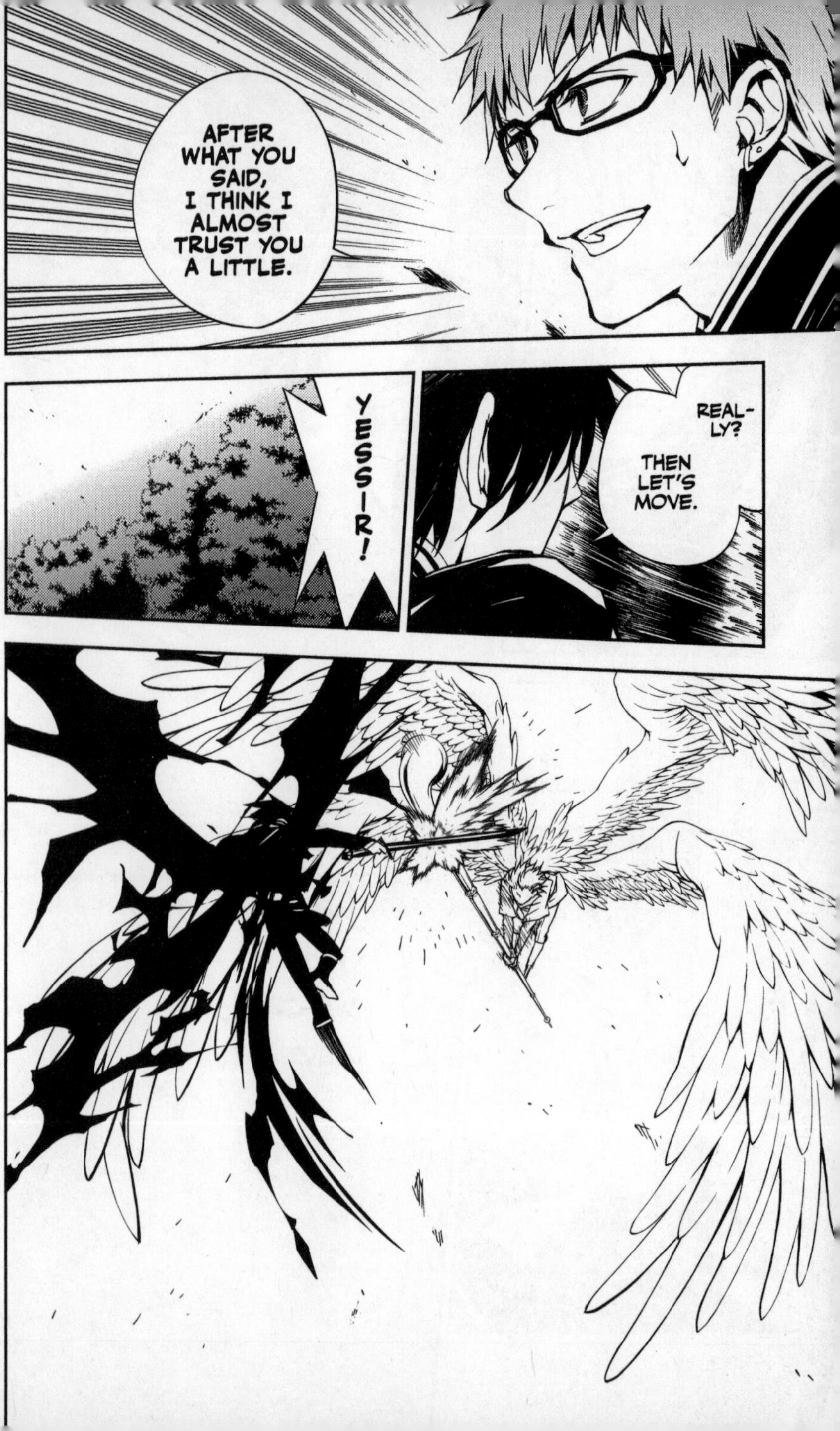
AFTER WHAT YOU SAID, I THINK I ALMOST TRUST YOU A LITTLE.
REAL-LY?
THEN LET'S MOVE.
YESSIR!

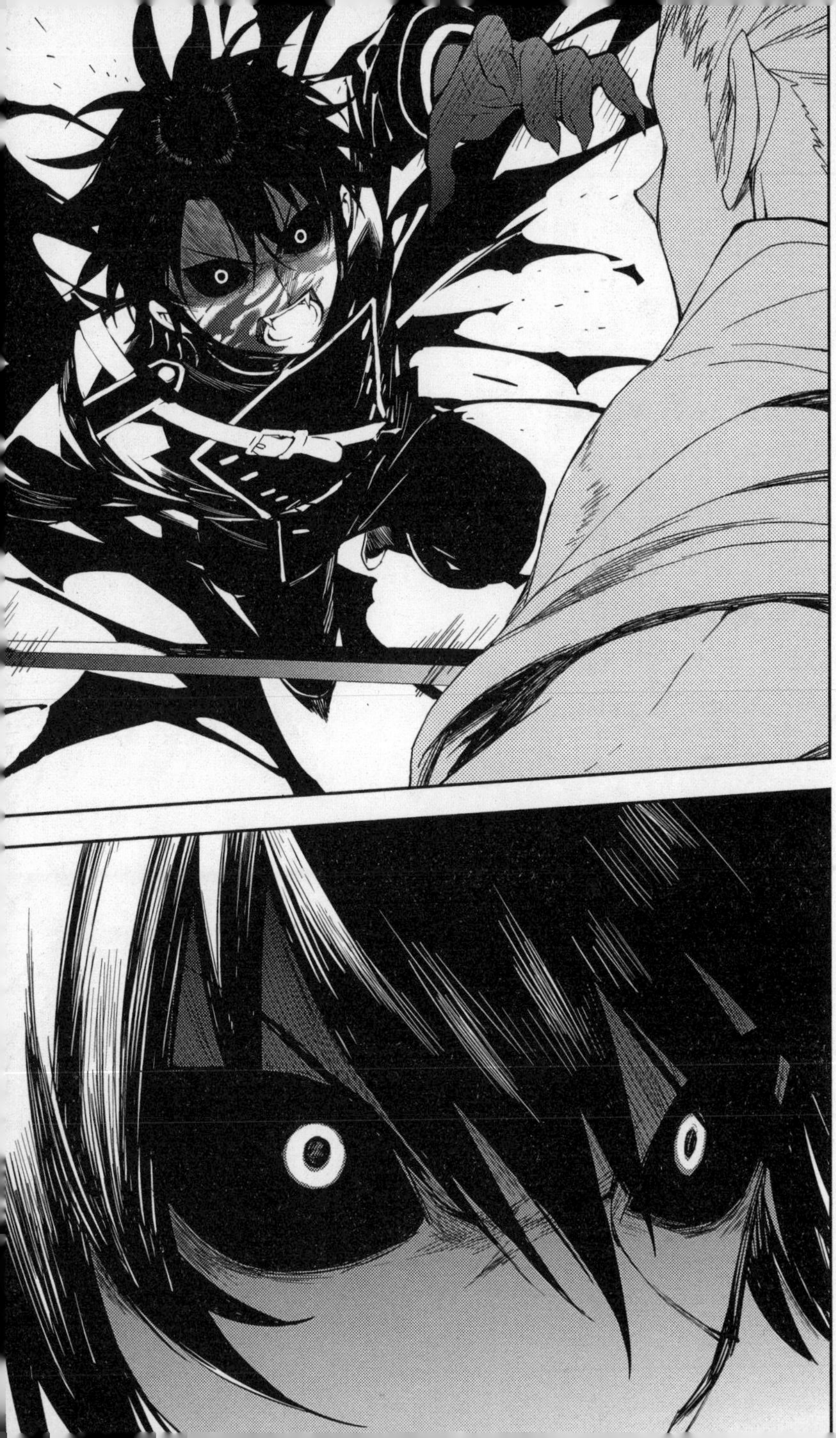

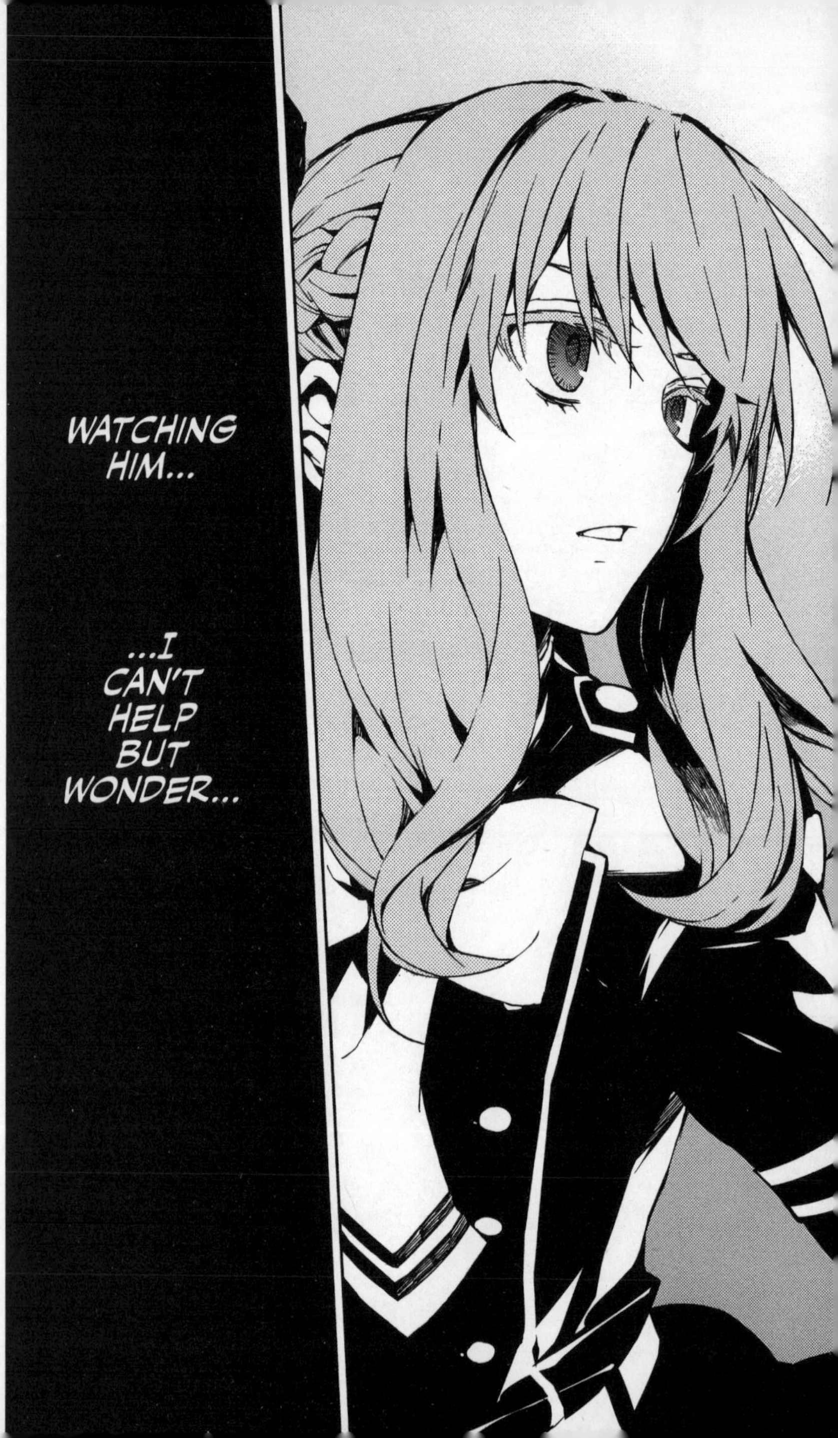
WATCHING HIM...
...I CAN'T HELP BUT WONDER...

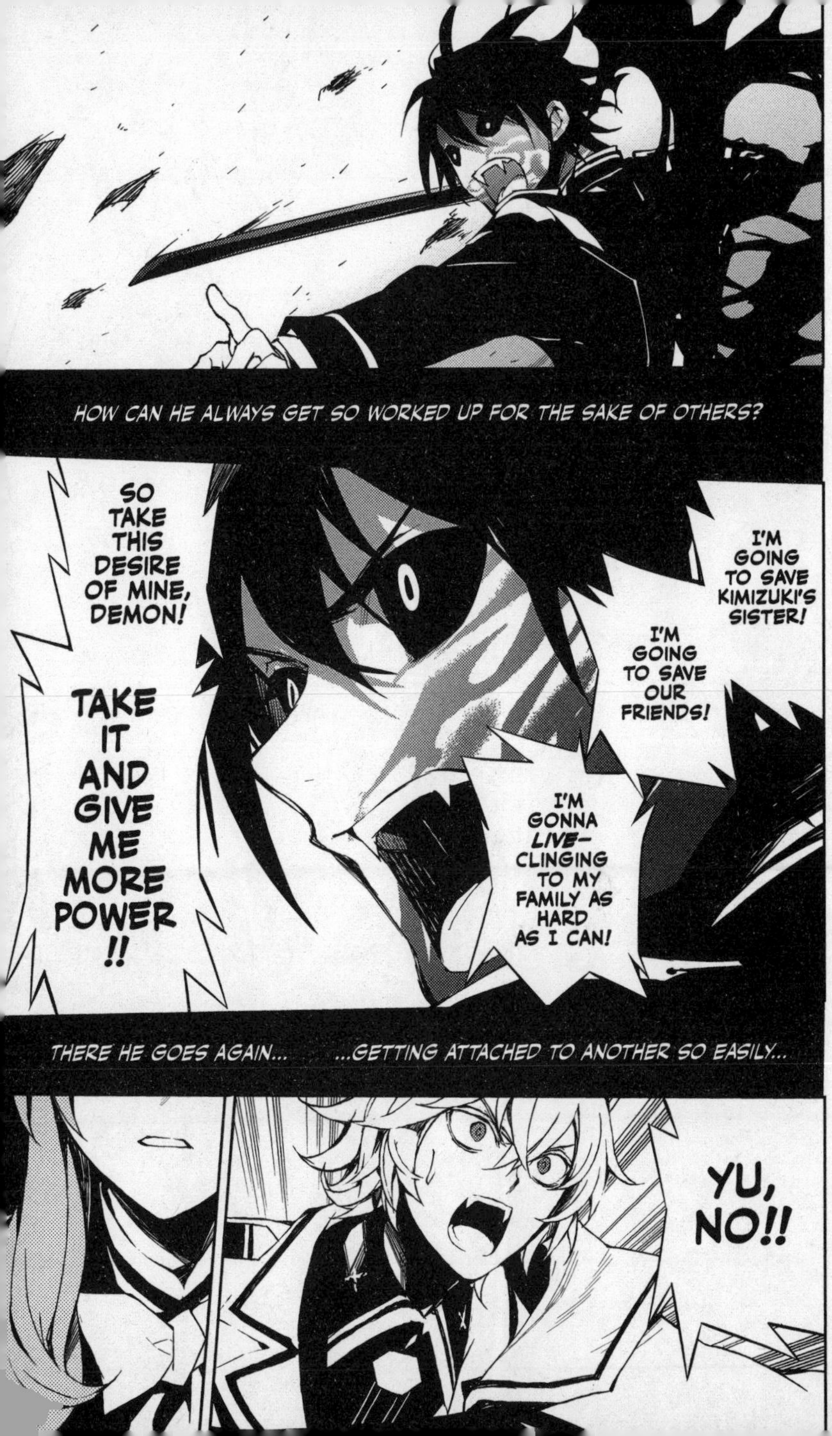
HOW CAN HE ALWAYS GET SO WORKED UP FOR THE SAKE OF OTHERS?
I'M GOING TO SAVE KIMIZUKI'S SISTER!
I'M GOING TO SAVE OUR FRIENDS!
I'M GONNA *LIVE*—CLINGING TO MY FAMILY AS HARD AS I CAN!
SO TAKE THIS DESIRE OF MINE, DEMON!
TAKE IT AND GIVE ME MORE POWER!!
THERE HE GOES AGAIN...
...GETTING ATTACHED TO ANOTHER SO EASILY...
YU, NO!!

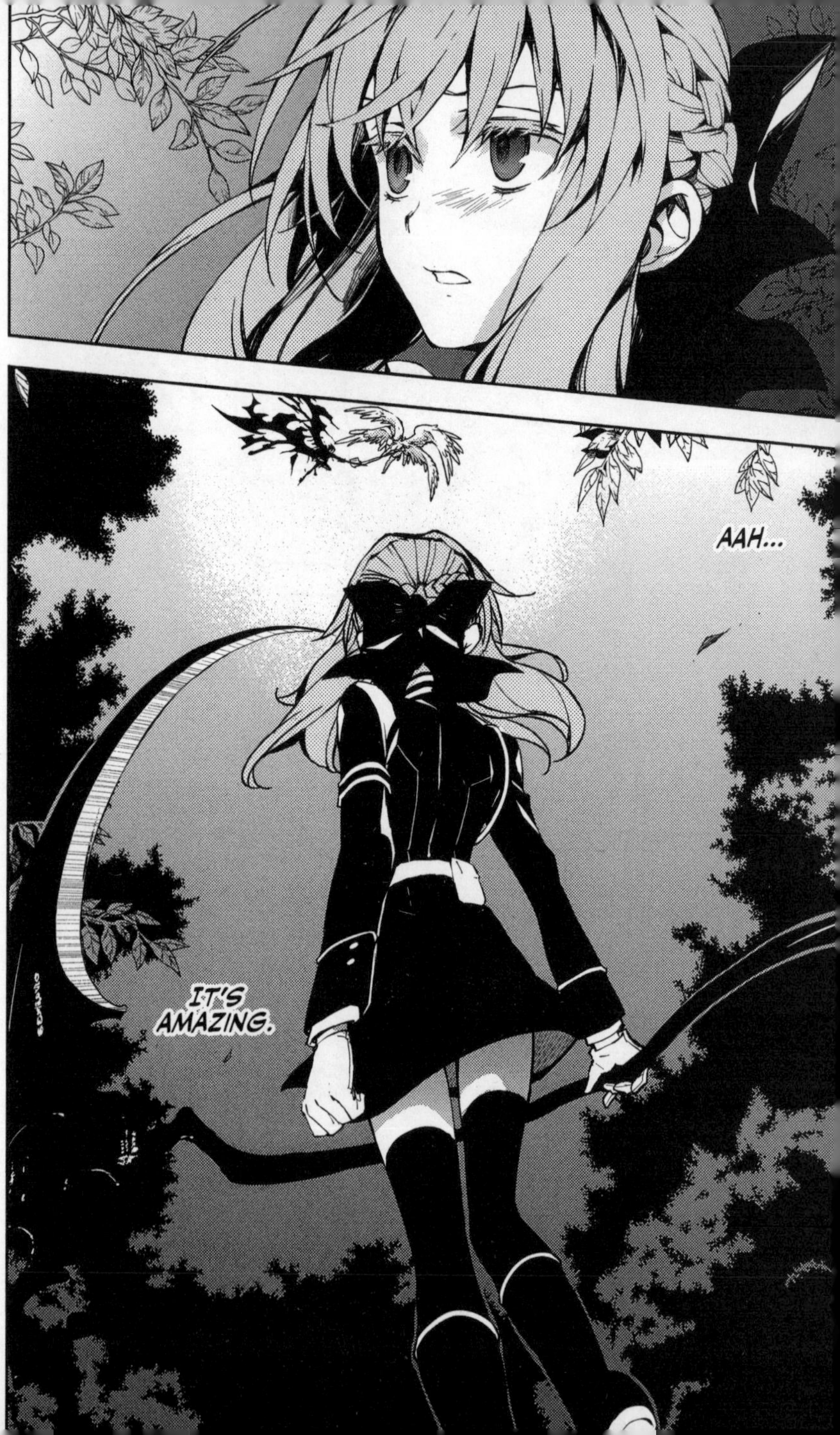
AAH...
IT'S AMAZING.

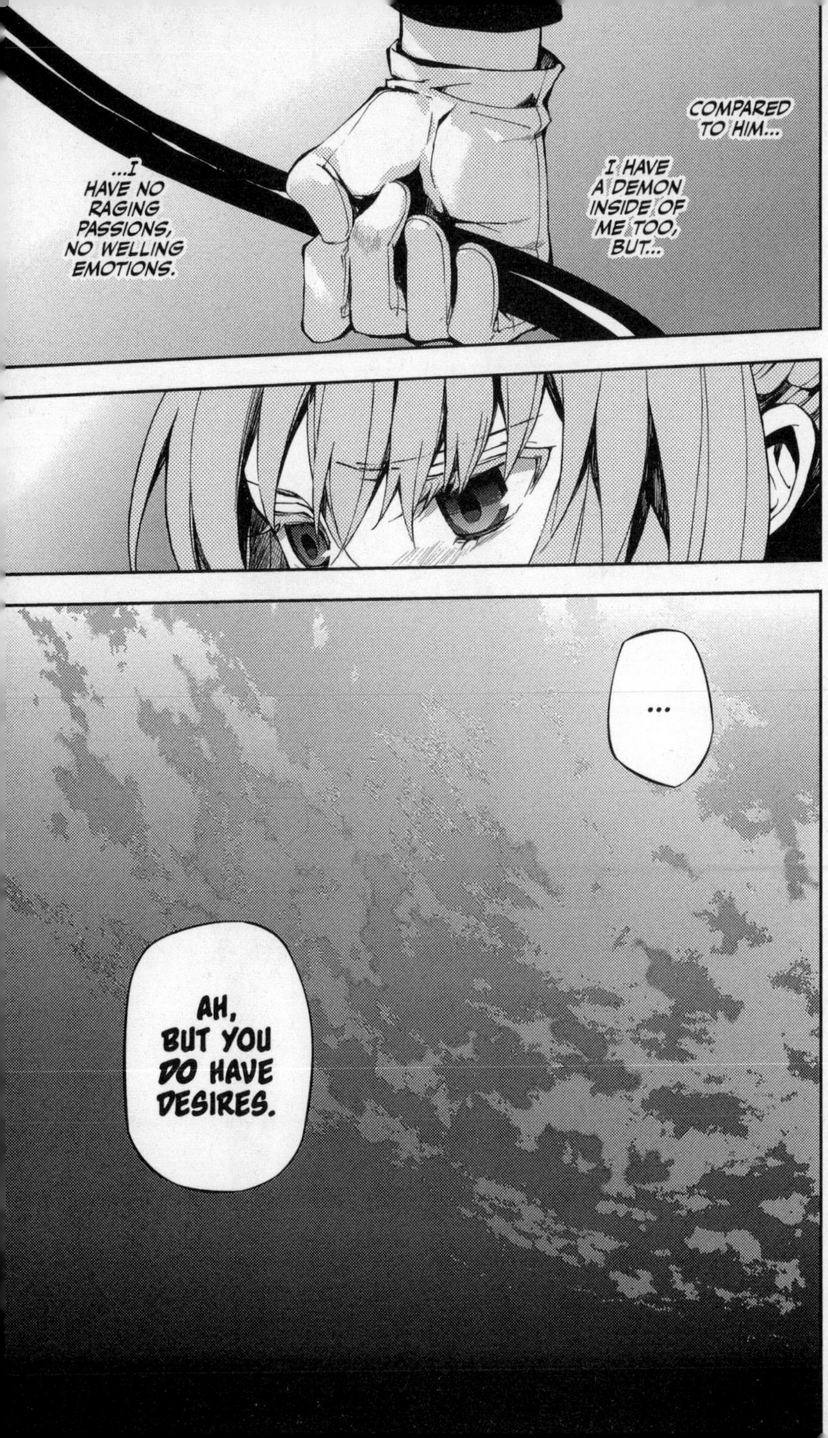
COMPARED TO HIM...
I HAVE A DEMON INSIDE OF ME TOO, BUT...
...I HAVE NO RAGING PASSIONS, NO WELLING EMOTIONS.
...
AH, BUT YOU DO HAVE DESIRES.

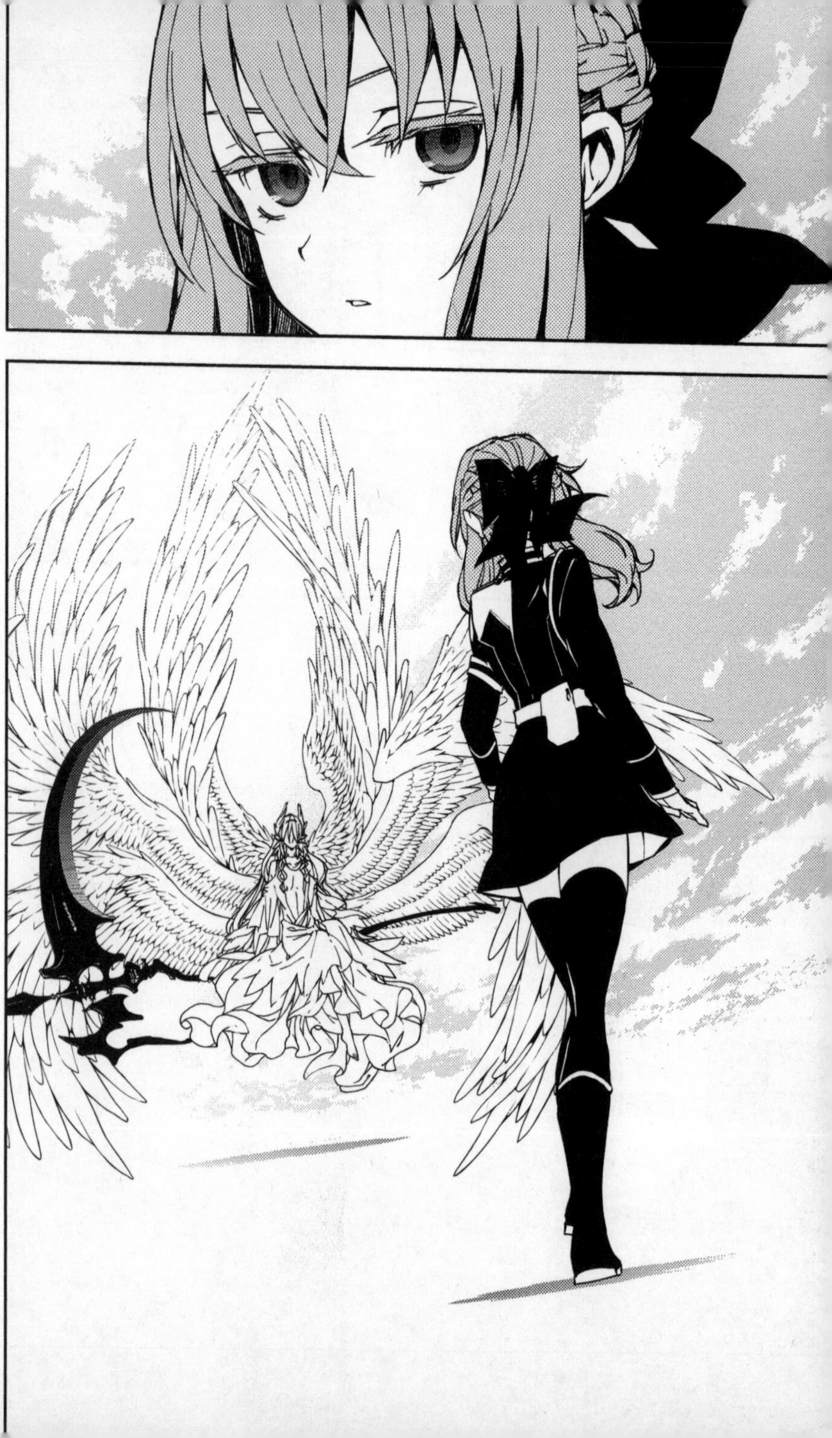

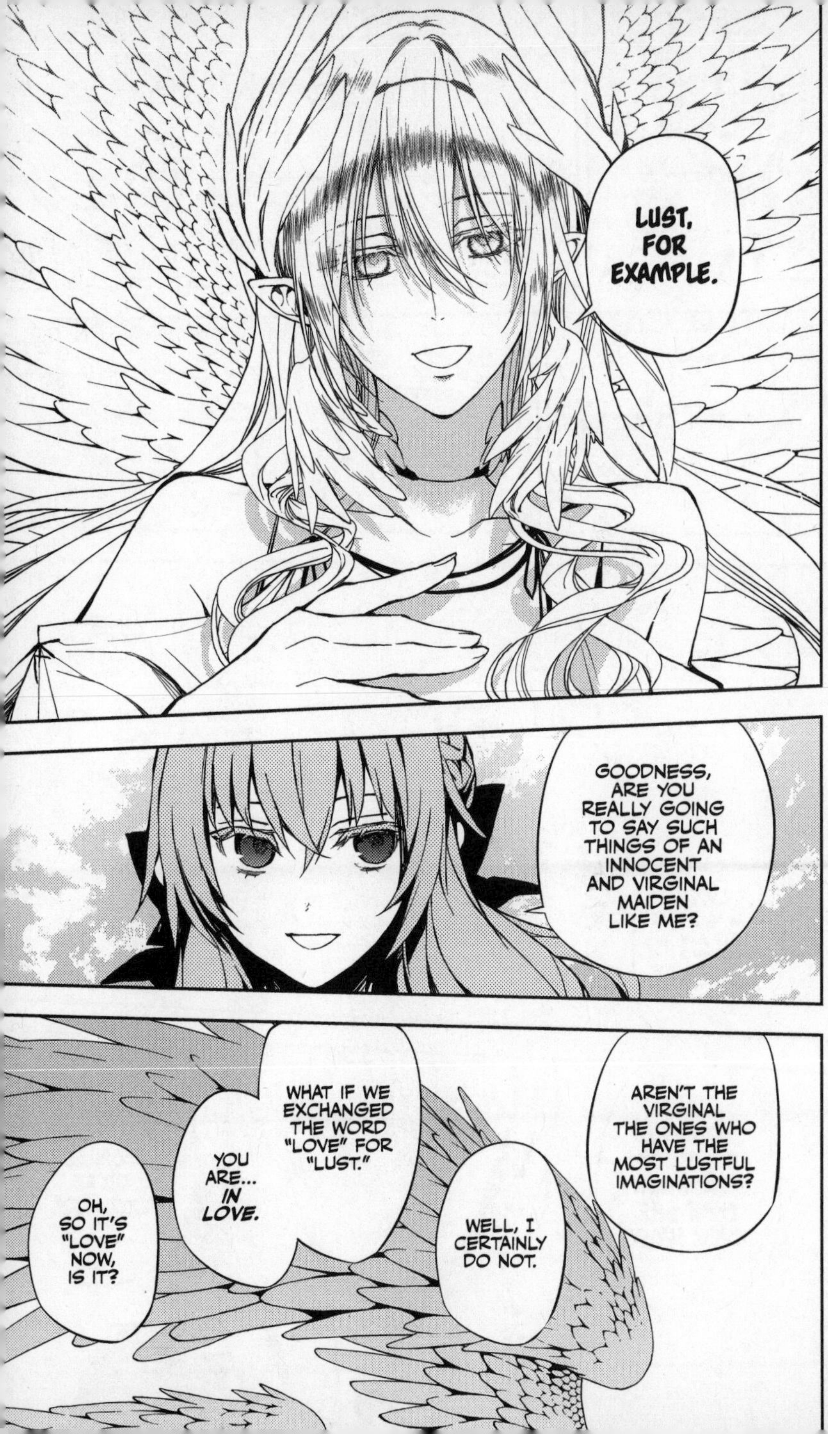
LUST, FOR EXAMPLE.
GOODNESS, ARE YOU REALLY GOING TO SAY SUCH THINGS OF AN INNOCENT AND VIRGINAL MAIDEN LIKE ME?
AREN'T THE VIRGINAL THE ONES WHO HAVE THE MOST LUSTFUL IMAGINATIONS?
WELL, I CERTAINLY DO NOT.
WHAT IF WE EXCHANGED THE WORD "LOVE" FOR "LUST."
YOU ARE... *IN LOVE.*
OH, SO IT'S "LOVE" NOW, IS IT?

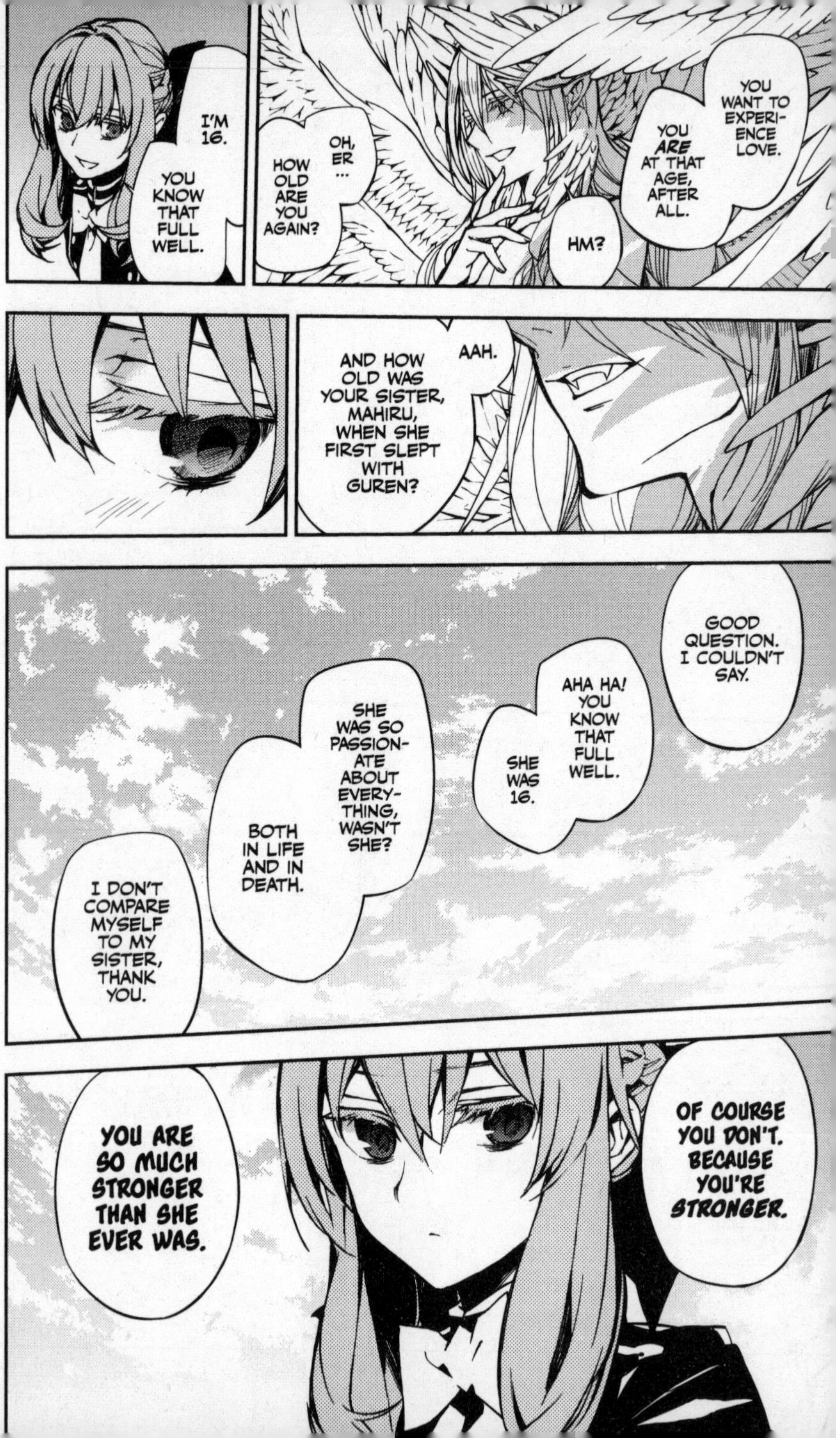
YOU WANT TO EXPERIENCE LOVE.
YOU ARE AT THAT AGE, AFTER ALL.
HM?
OH, ER... HOW OLD ARE YOU AGAIN?
I'M 16.
YOU KNOW THAT FULL WELL.
AAH.
AND HOW OLD WAS YOUR SISTER, MAHIRU, WHEN SHE FIRST SLEPT WITH GUREN?
GOOD QUESTION. I COULDN'T SAY.
AHA HA! YOU KNOW THAT FULL WELL.
SHE WAS 16.
SHE WAS SO PASSIONATE ABOUT EVERYTHING, WASN'T SHE?
BOTH IN LIFE AND IN DEATH.
I DON'T COMPARE MYSELF TO MY SISTER, THANK YOU.
OF COURSE YOU DON'T. BECAUSE YOU'RE STRONGER.
YOU ARE SO MUCH STRONGER THAN SHE EVER WAS.

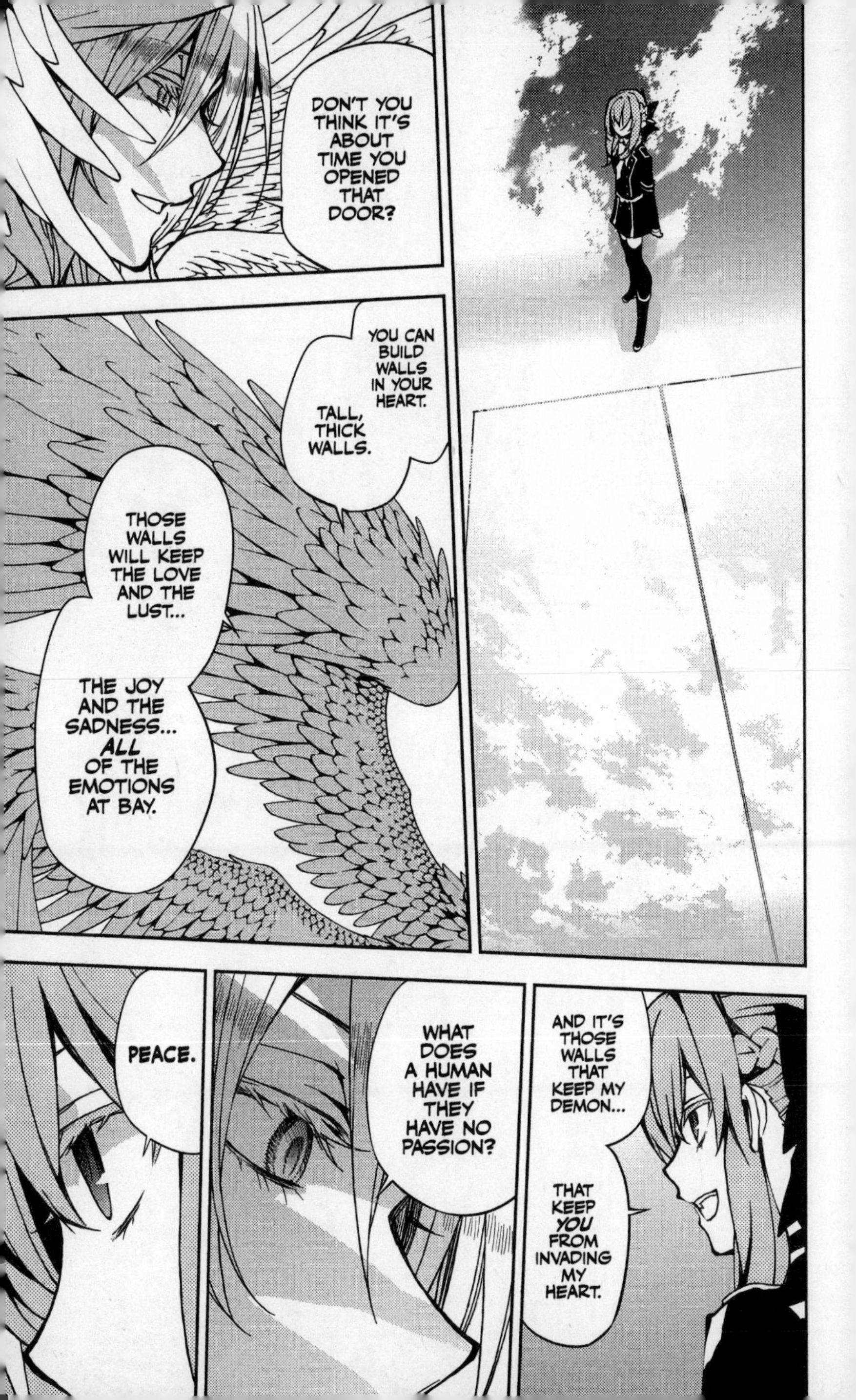
DON'T YOU THINK IT'S ABOUT TIME YOU OPENED THAT DOOR?
YOU CAN BUILD WALLS IN YOUR HEART.
TALL, THICK WALLS.
THOSE WALLS WILL KEEP THE LOVE AND THE LUST...
THE JOY AND THE SADNESS... *ALL* OF THE EMOTIONS AT BAY.
AND IT'S THOSE WALLS THAT KEEP MY DEMON...
THAT KEEP *YOU* FROM INVADING MY HEART.
WHAT DOES A HUMAN HAVE IF THEY HAVE NO PASSION?
PEACE.

YOU LIE.
YOU WANT TO EXPERIENCE LOVE.
WHEN YOU WATCH YUICHIRO HYAKUYA, YOU FEEL YOUR HEART RACE.
WHY DON'T I GET THIS BALL ROLLING BY OPENING THAT DOOR.
SWF

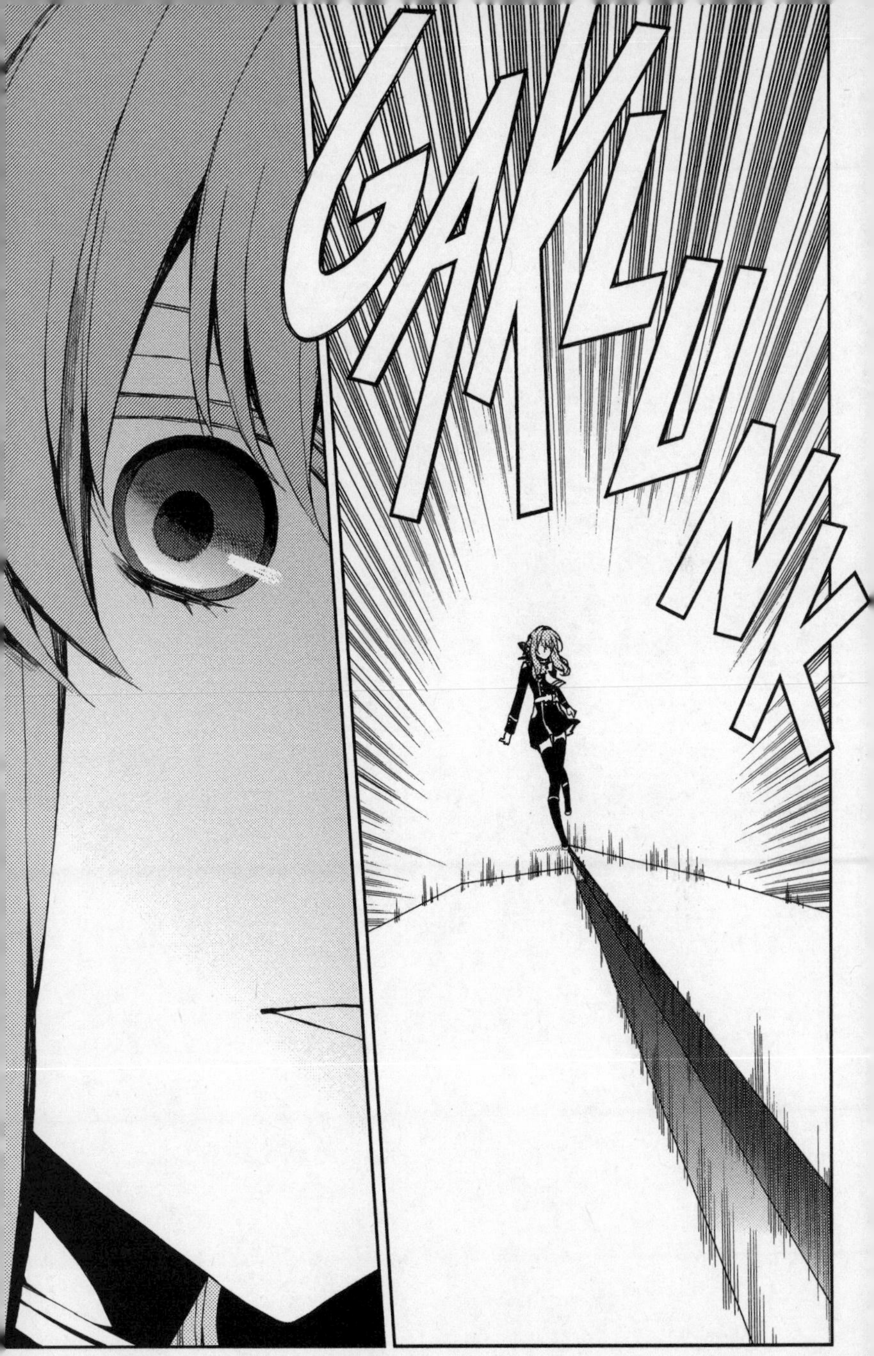
GAKLUNK

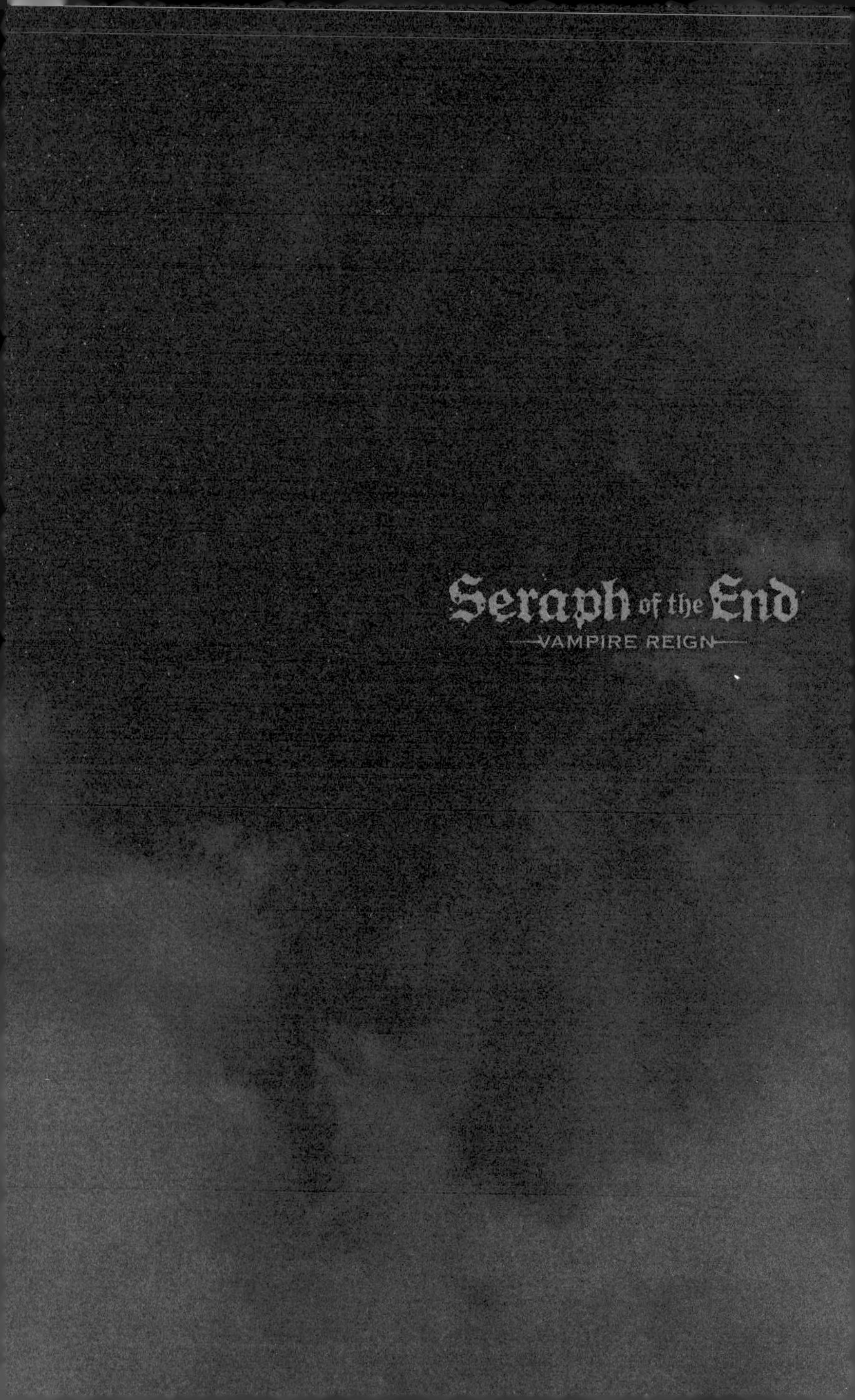
Seraph of the End
VAMPIRE REIGN

CHAPTER 67

The Door into Puberty

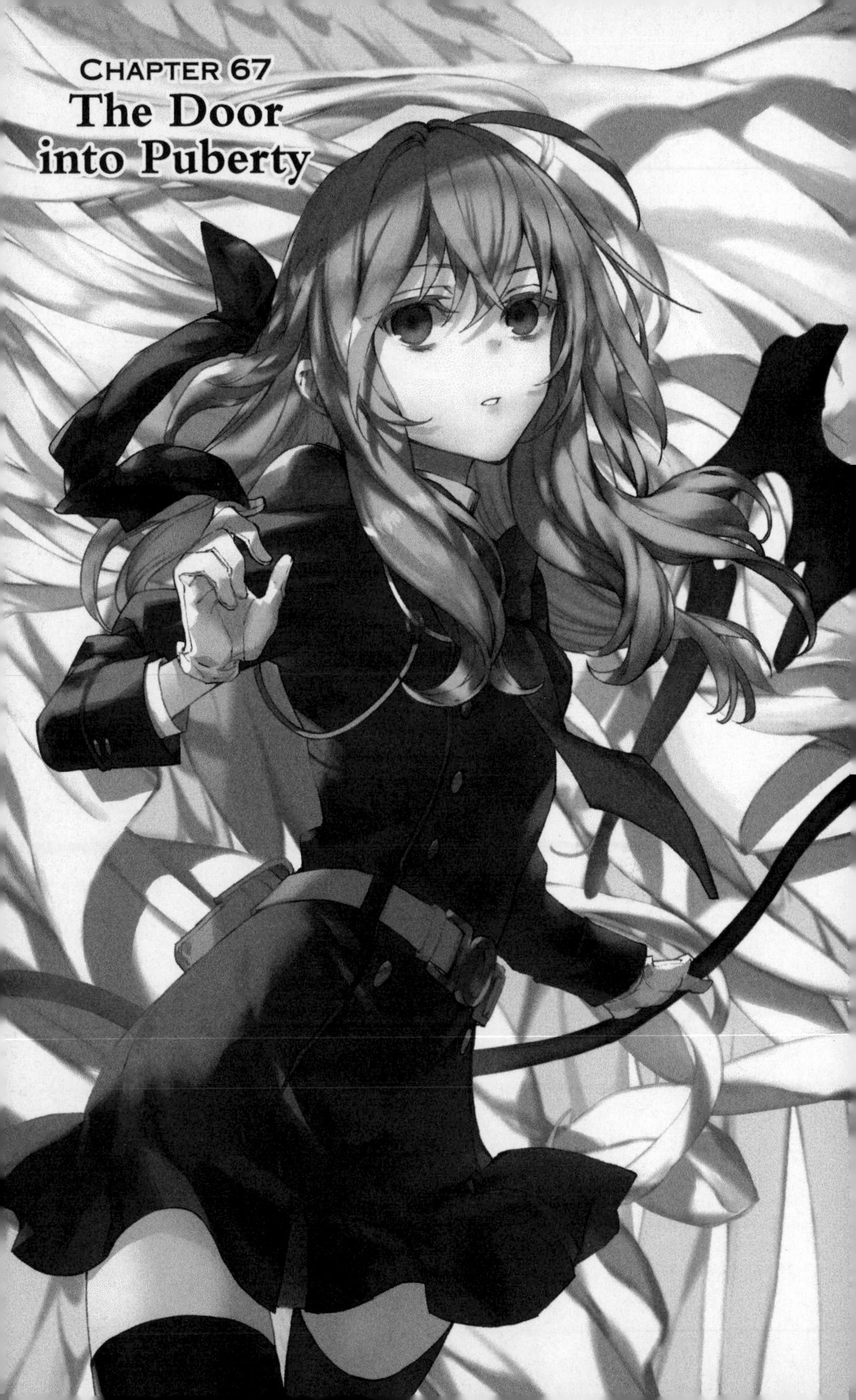

Seraph of the End
VAMPIRE REIGN

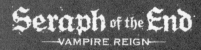

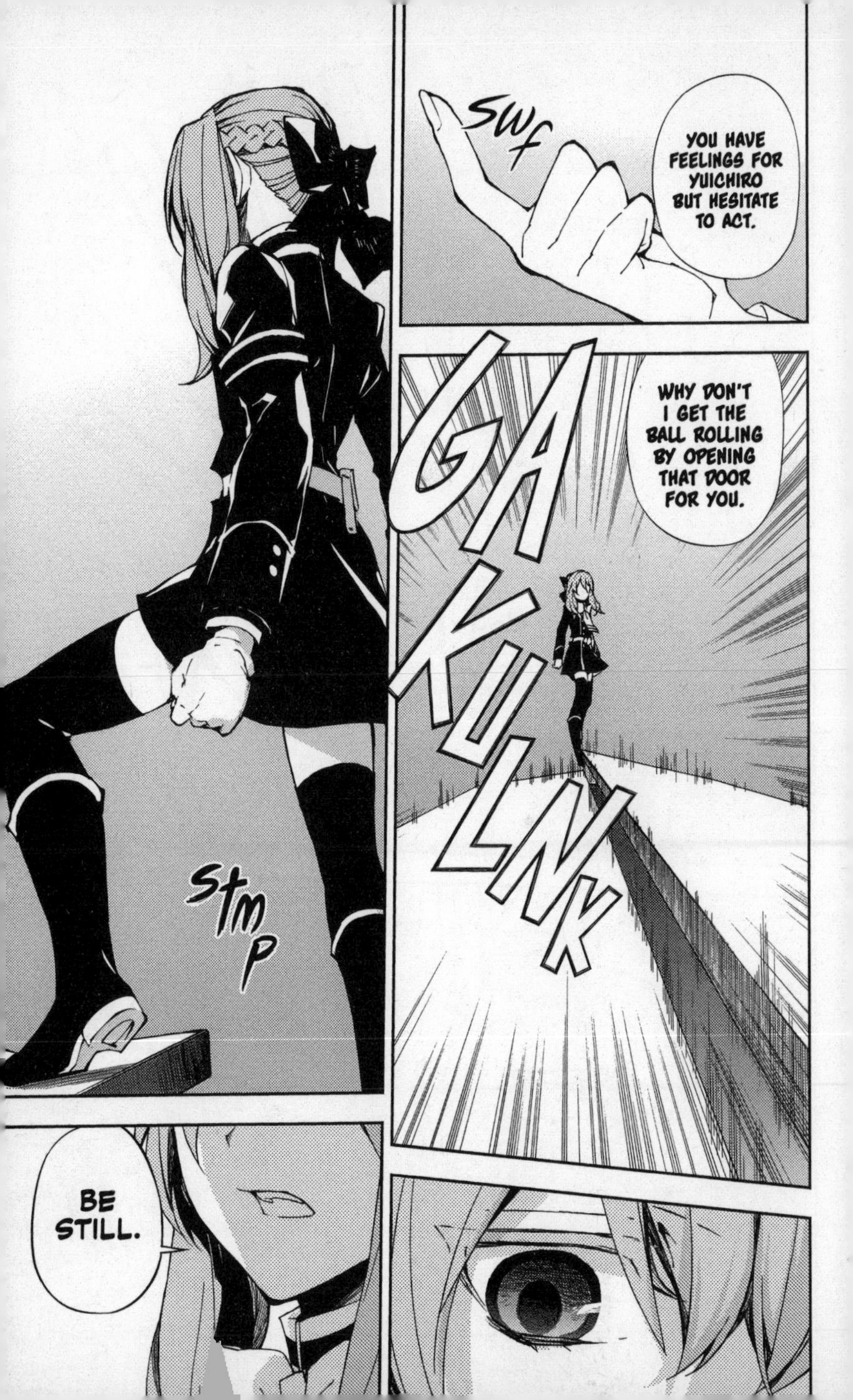
SWf
YOU HAVE FEELINGS FOR YUICHIRO BUT HESITATE TO ACT.
GAKULNK
WHY DON'T I GET THE BALL ROLLING BY OPENING THAT DOOR FOR YOU.
Stmp
BE STILL.

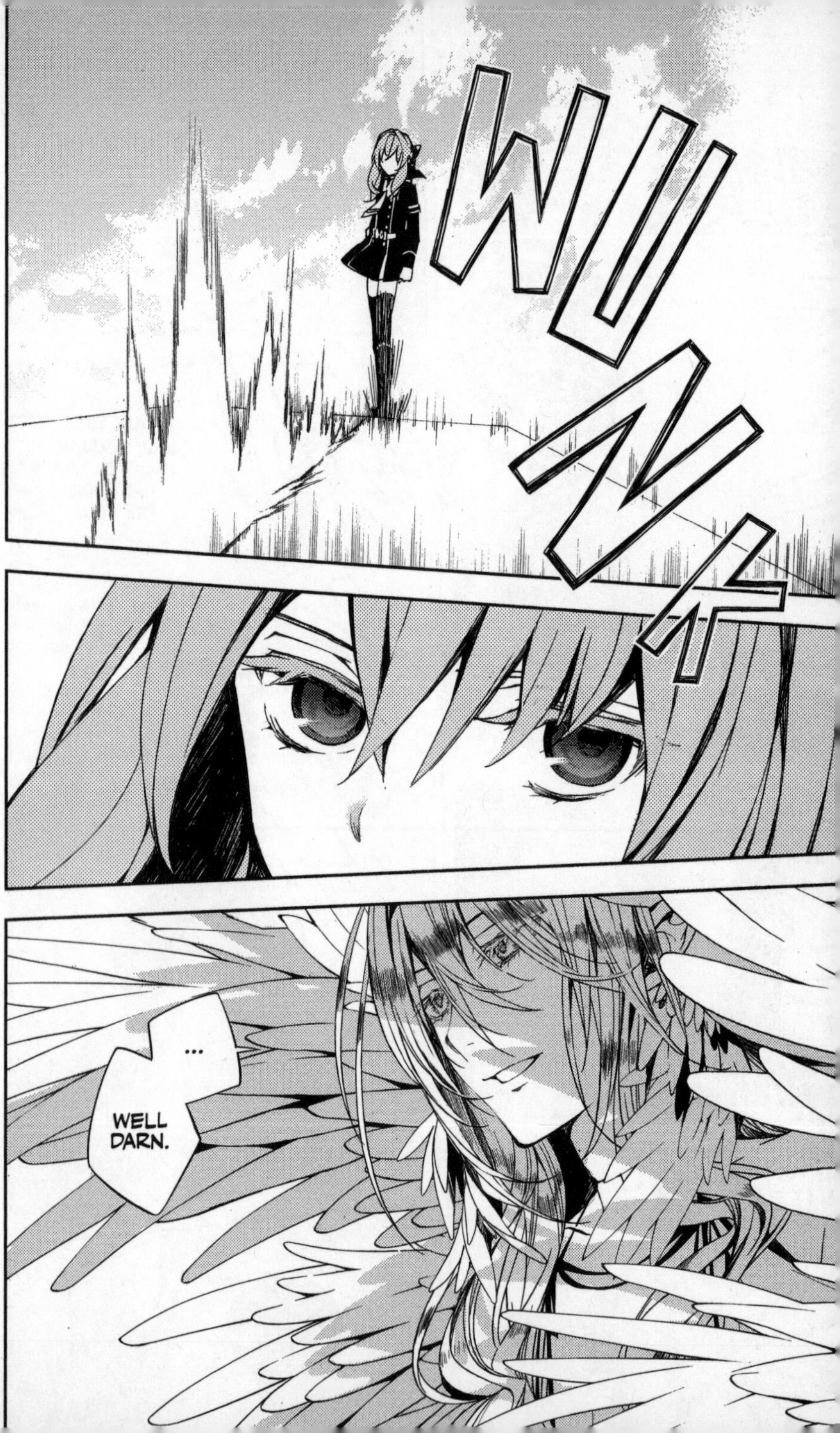
WHIN
...
WELL DARN.

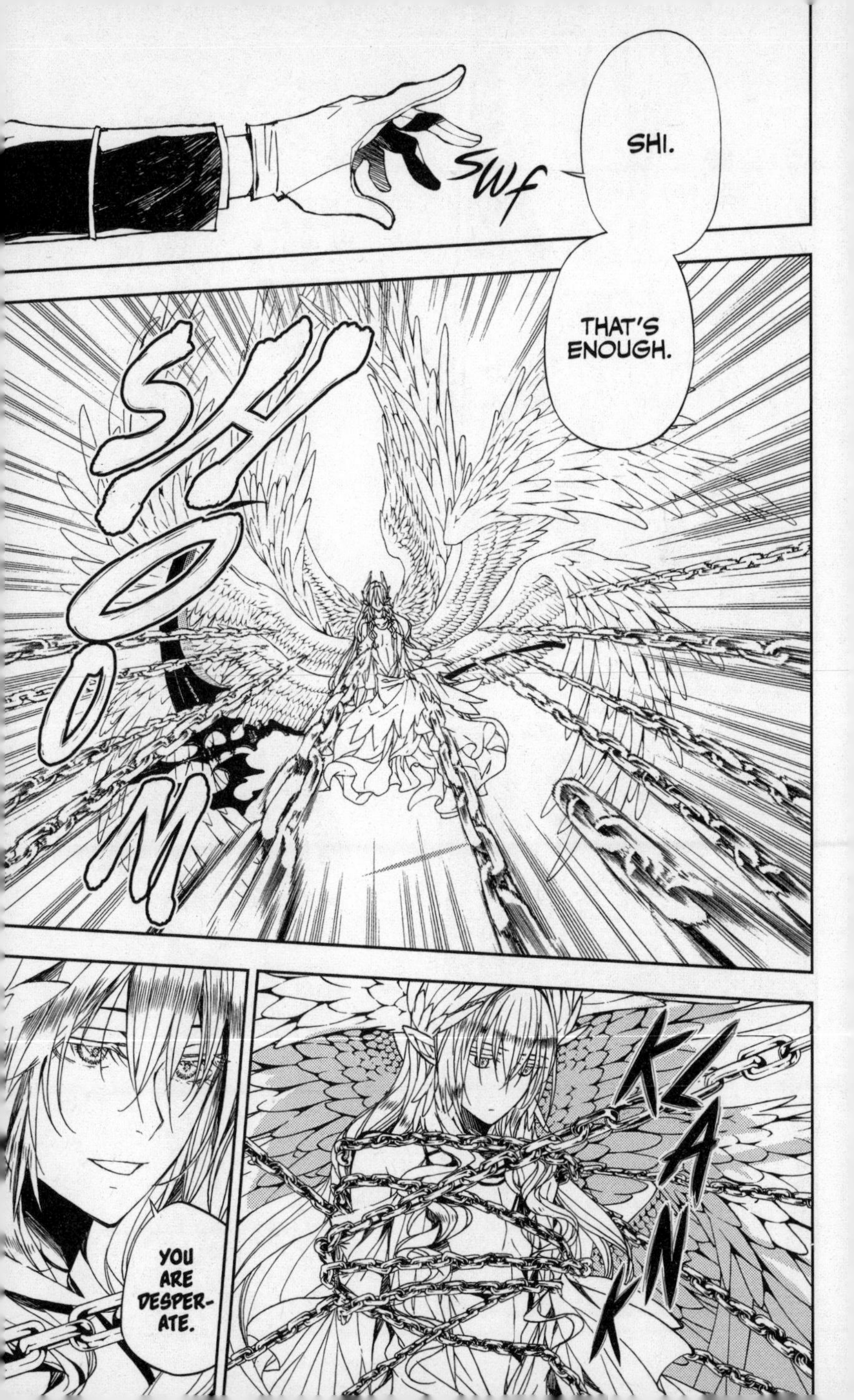
SHI.
SWF
THAT'S ENOUGH.
SHOOM
KLANK
YOU ARE DESPERATE.

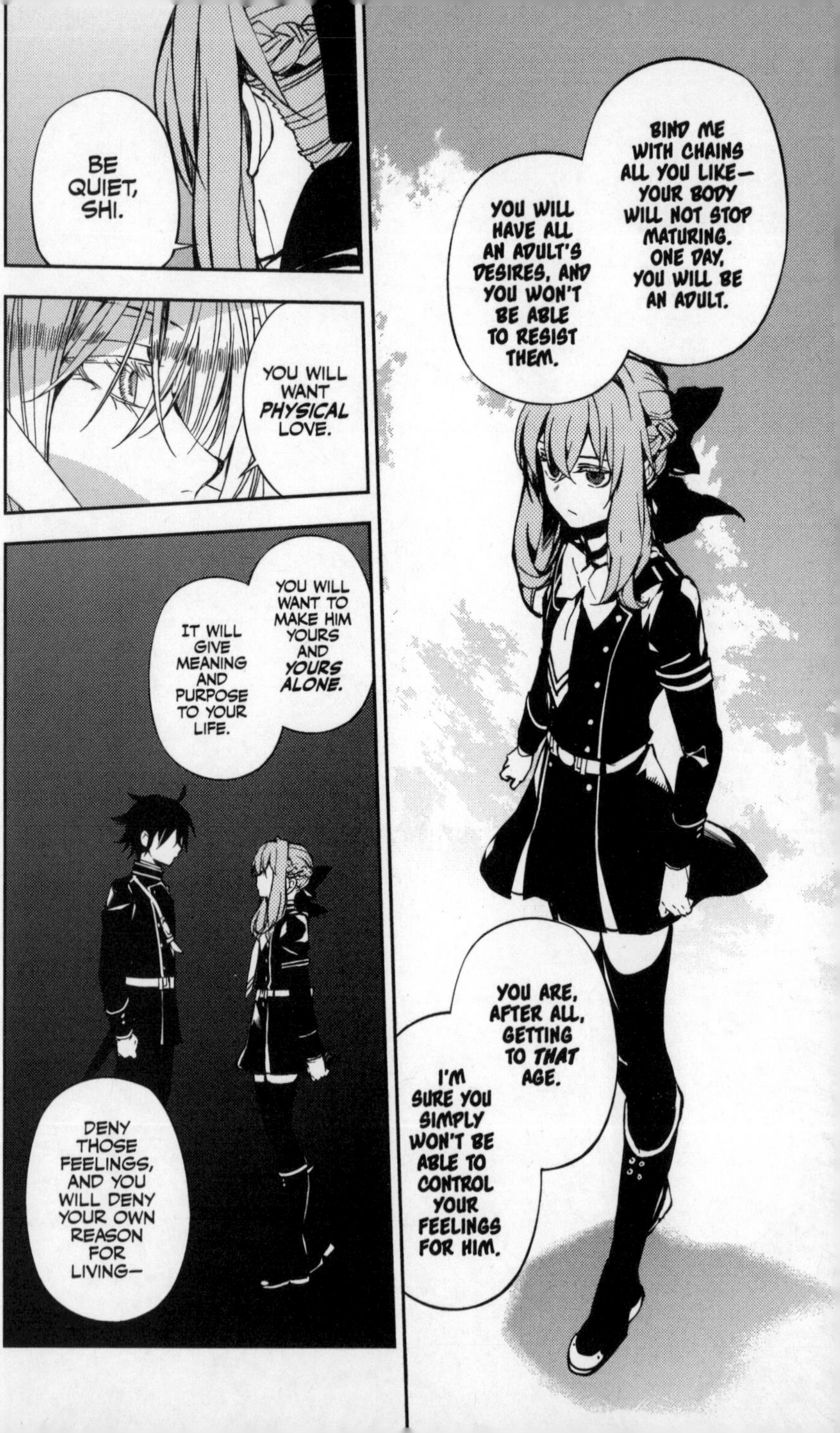
BIND ME WITH CHAINS ALL YOU LIKE— YOUR BODY WILL NOT STOP MATURING. ONE DAY, YOU WILL BE AN ADULT.
YOU WILL HAVE ALL AN ADULT'S DESIRES, AND YOU WON'T BE ABLE TO RESIST THEM.
YOU ARE, AFTER ALL, GETTING TO *THAT* AGE.
I'M SURE YOU SIMPLY WON'T BE ABLE TO CONTROL YOUR FEELINGS FOR HIM.
BE QUIET, SHI.
YOU WILL WANT *PHYSICAL* LOVE.
YOU WILL WANT TO MAKE HIM YOURS AND *YOURS ALONE.*
IT WILL GIVE MEANING AND PURPOSE TO YOUR LIFE.
DENY THOSE FEELINGS, AND YOU WILL DENY YOUR OWN REASON FOR LIVING—

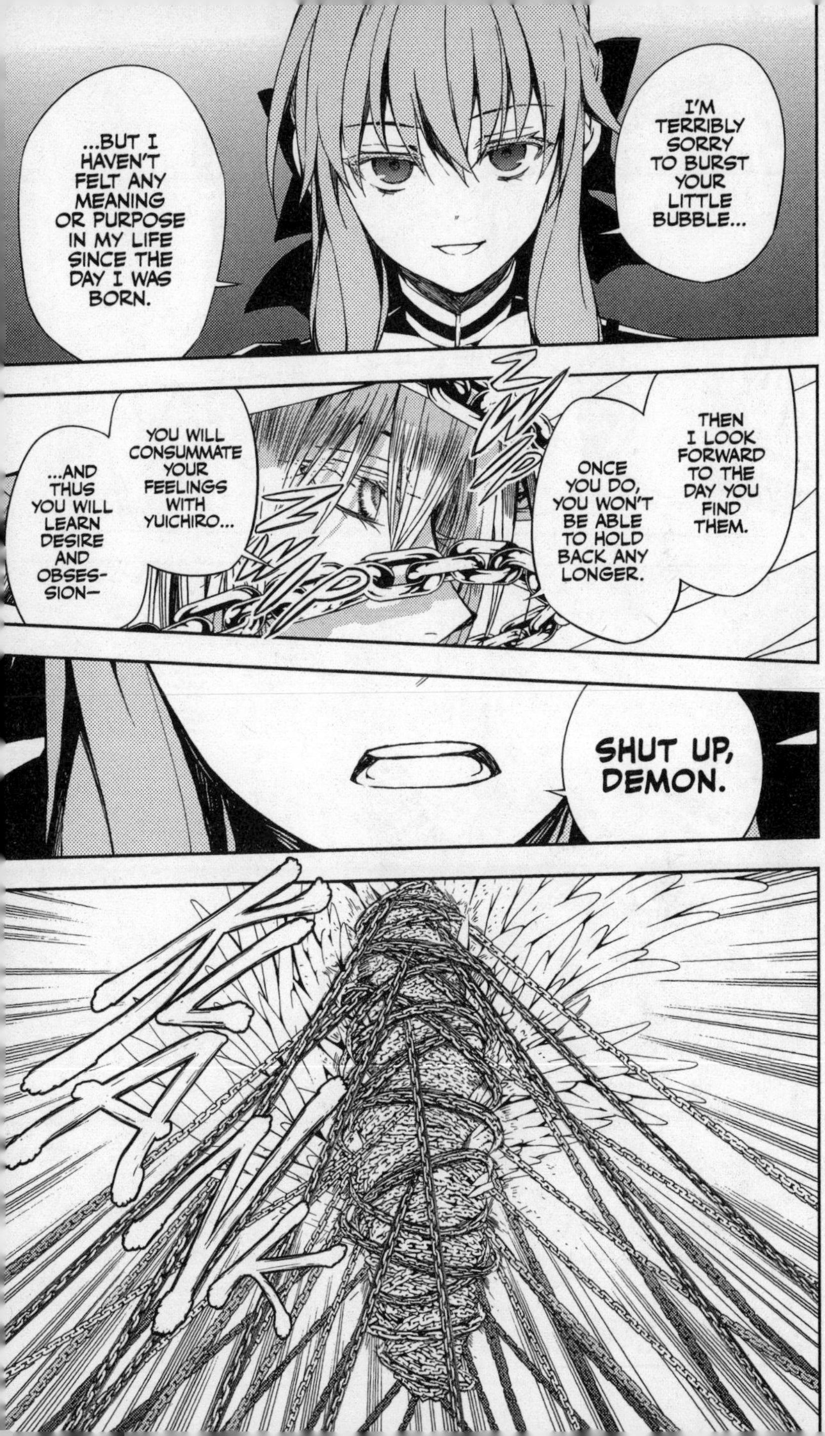
I'M TERRIBLY SORRY TO BURST YOUR LITTLE BUBBLE...
...BUT I HAVEN'T FELT ANY MEANING OR PURPOSE IN MY LIFE SINCE THE DAY I WAS BORN.
THEN I LOOK FORWARD TO THE DAY YOU FIND THEM.
ONCE YOU DO, YOU WON'T BE ABLE TO HOLD BACK ANY LONGER.
YOU WILL CONSUMMATE YOUR FEELINGS WITH YUICHIRO...
...AND THUS YOU WILL LEARN DESIRE AND OBSES-SION—
SHUT UP, DEMON.

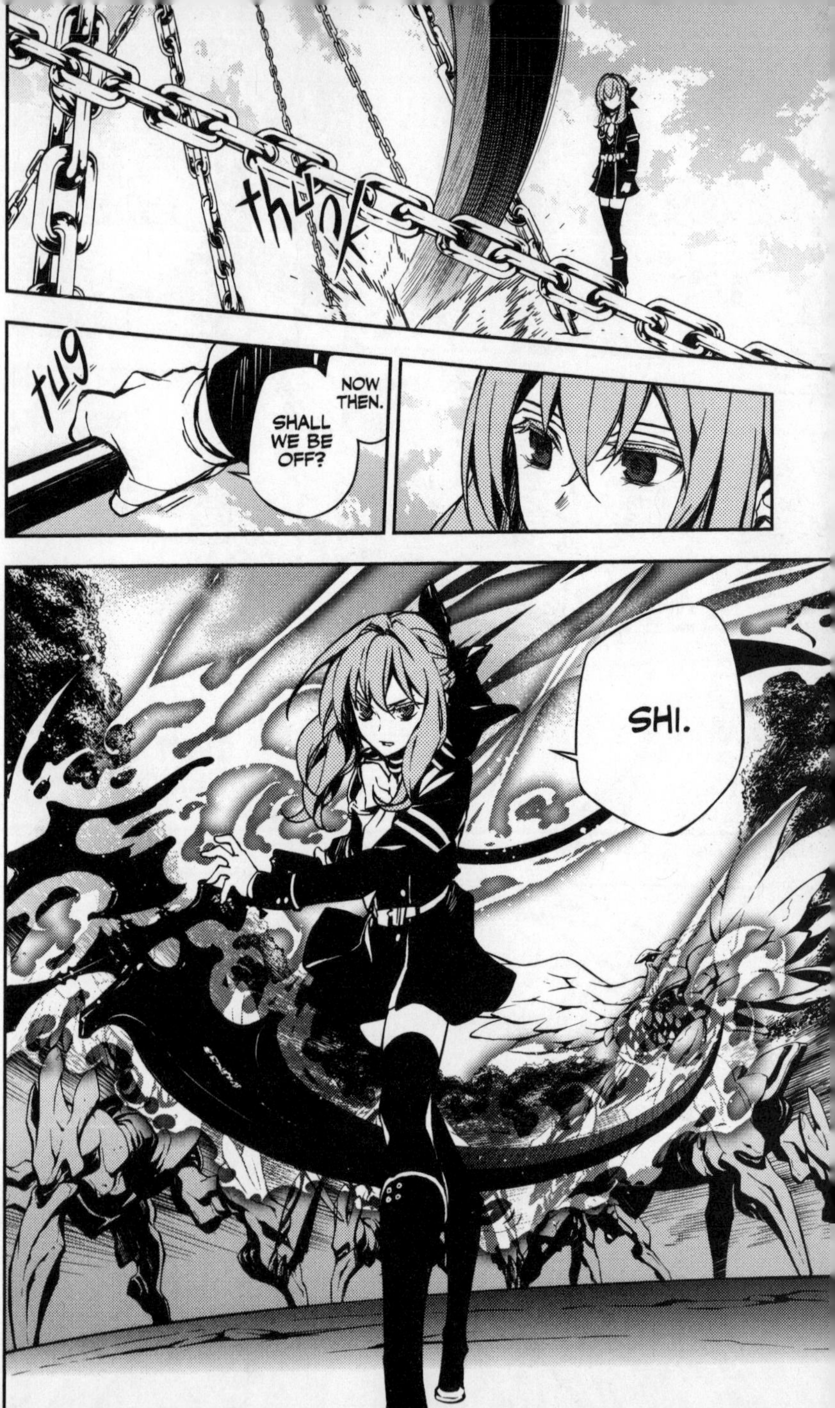
thunk
NOW THEN.
SHALL WE BE OFF?
tug
SHI.

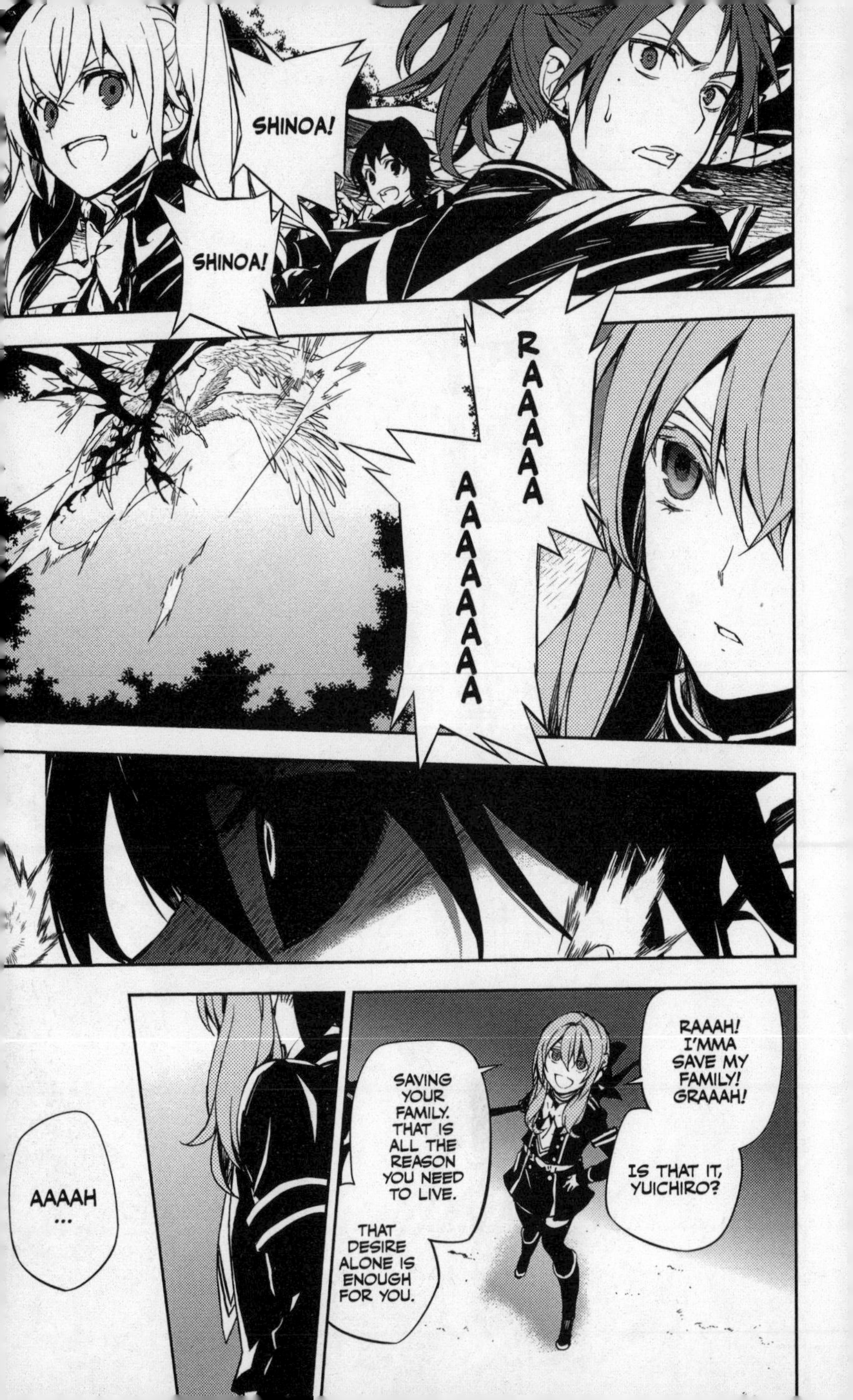
SHINOA!
SHINOA!
RAAAAA
AAAAAAAA
RAAAH! I'MMA SAVE MY FAMILY! GRAAAH!
IS THAT IT, YUICHIRO?
SAVING YOUR FAMILY. THAT IS ALL THE REASON YOU NEED TO LIVE.
THAT DESIRE ALONE IS ENOUGH FOR YOU.
AAAAH ...

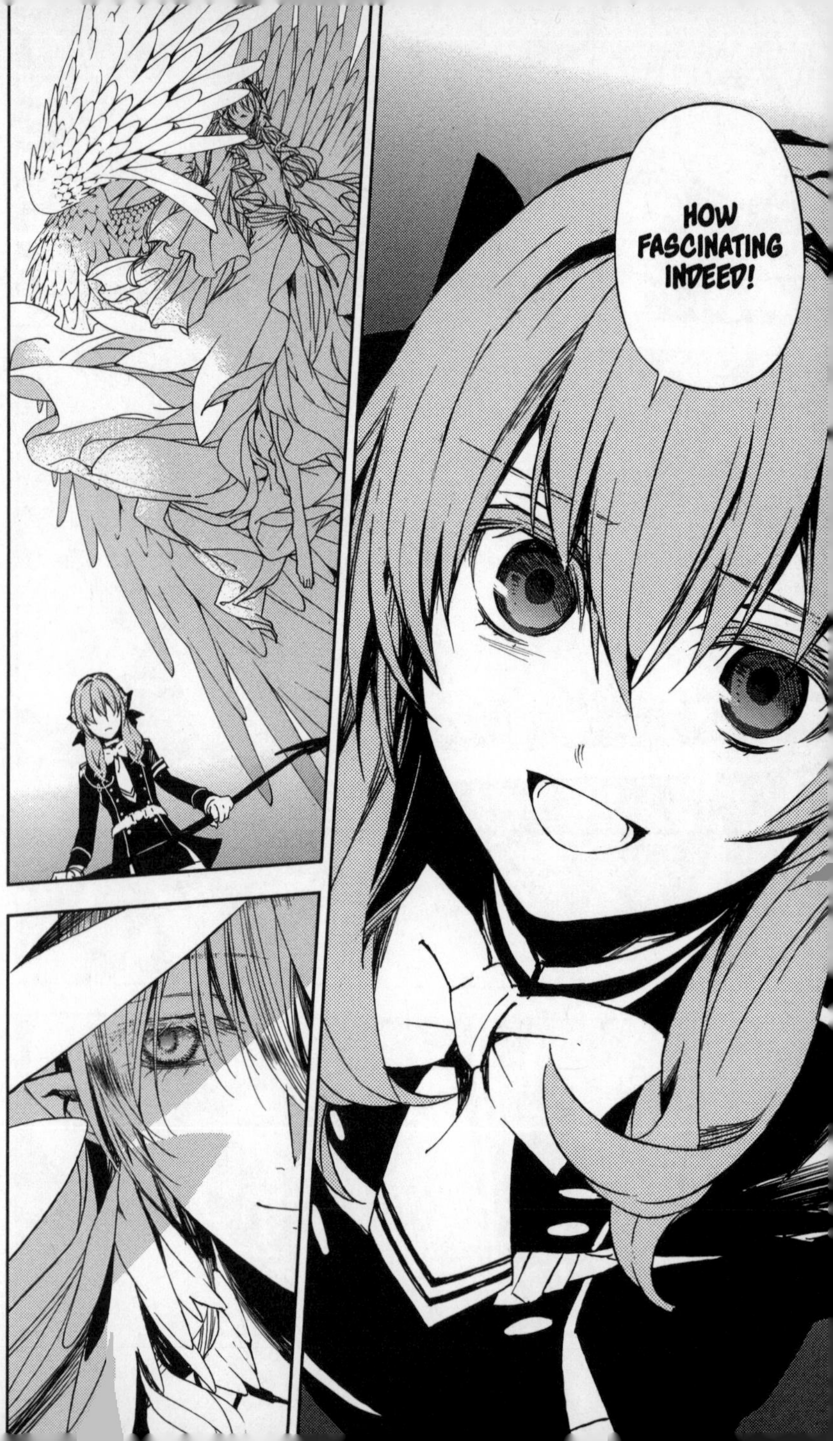
HOW FASCINATING INDEED!

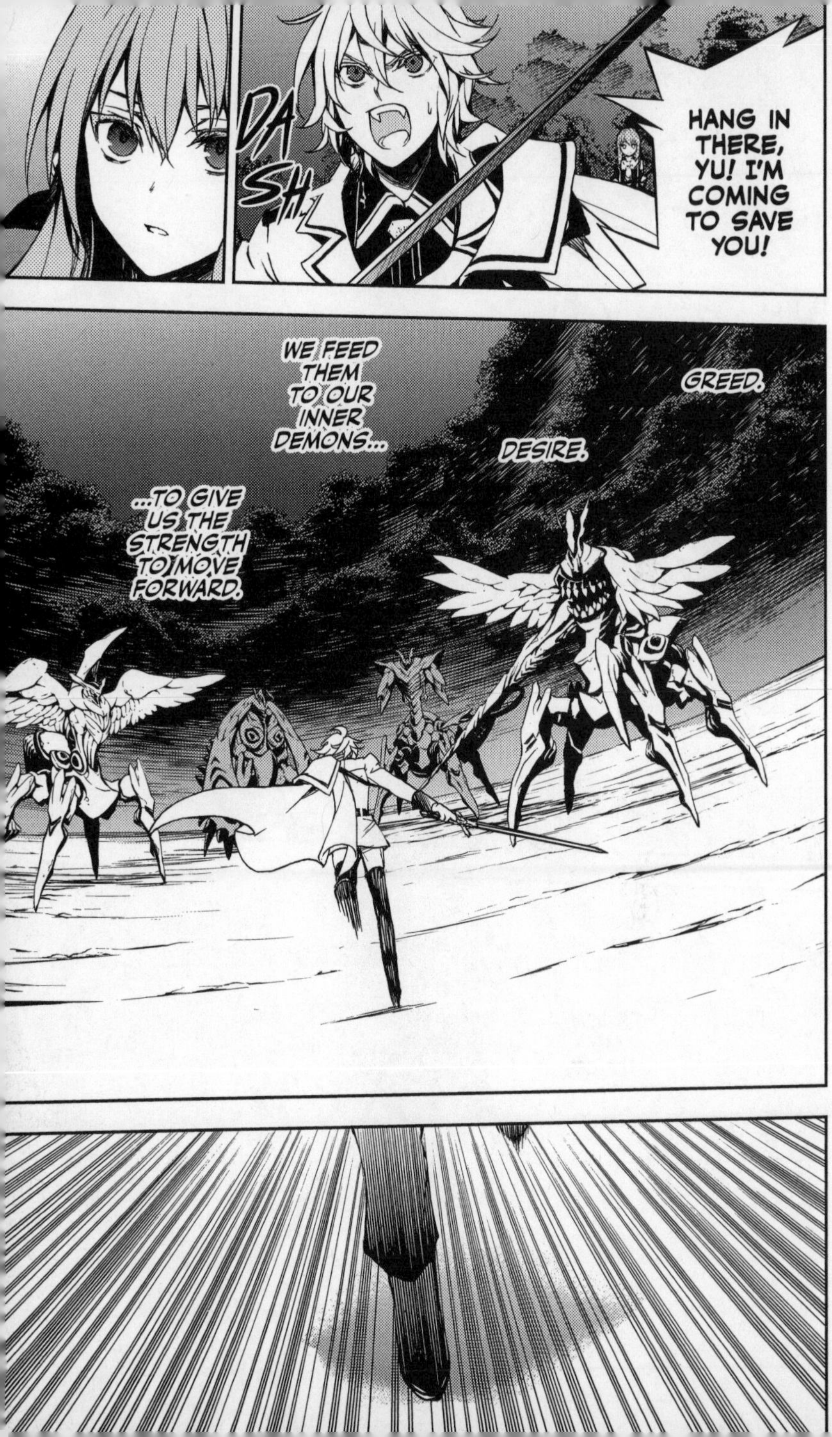
HANG IN THERE, YU! I'M COMING TO SAVE YOU!
DASH
GREED.
DESIRE.
WE FEED THEM TO OUR INNER DEMONS...
...TO GIVE US THE STRENGTH TO MOVE FORWARD.

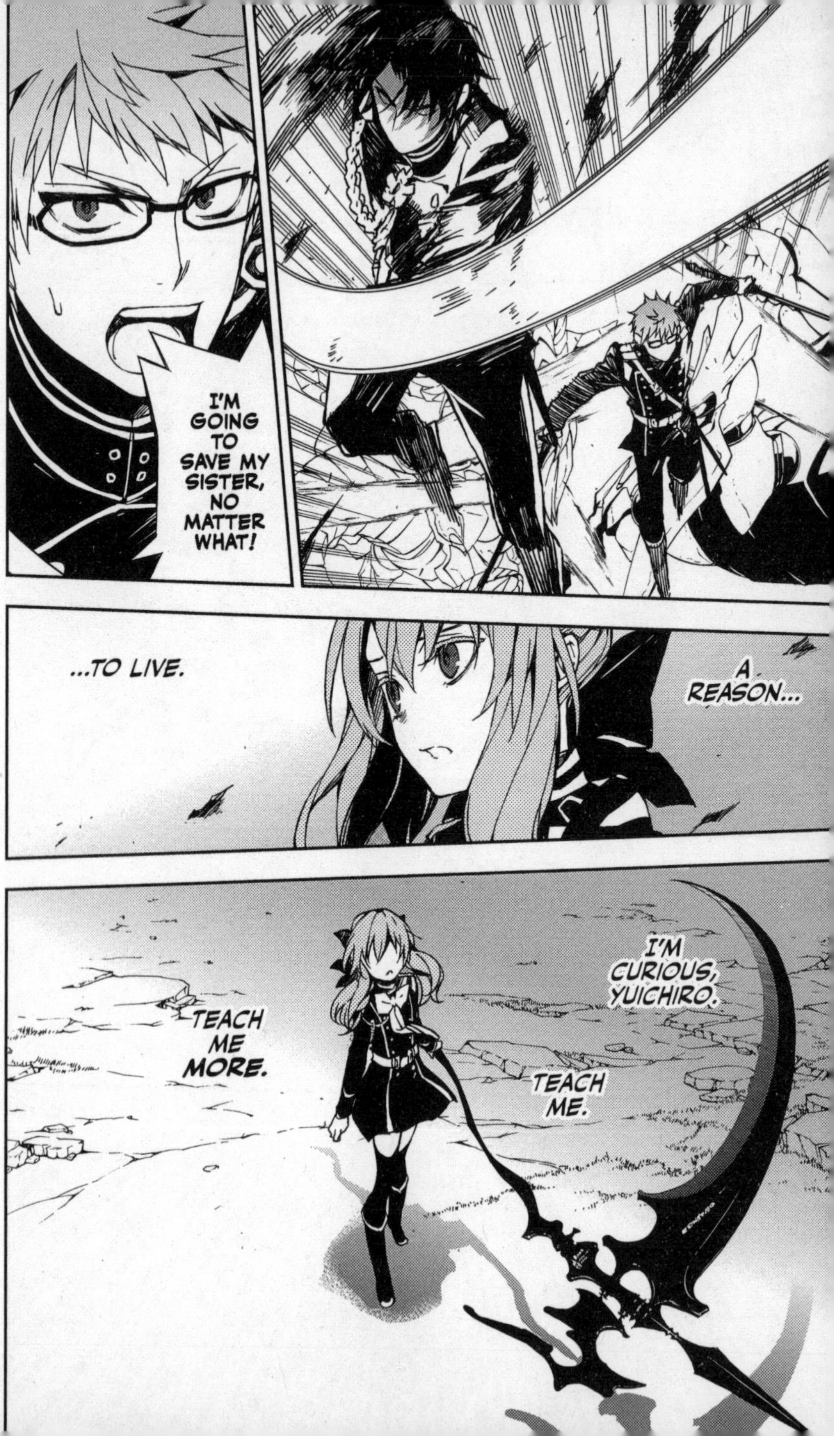
I'M GOING TO SAVE MY SISTER, NO MATTER WHAT!
A REASON...
...TO LIVE.
I'M CURIOUS, YUICHIRO.
TEACH ME.
TEACH ME MORE.

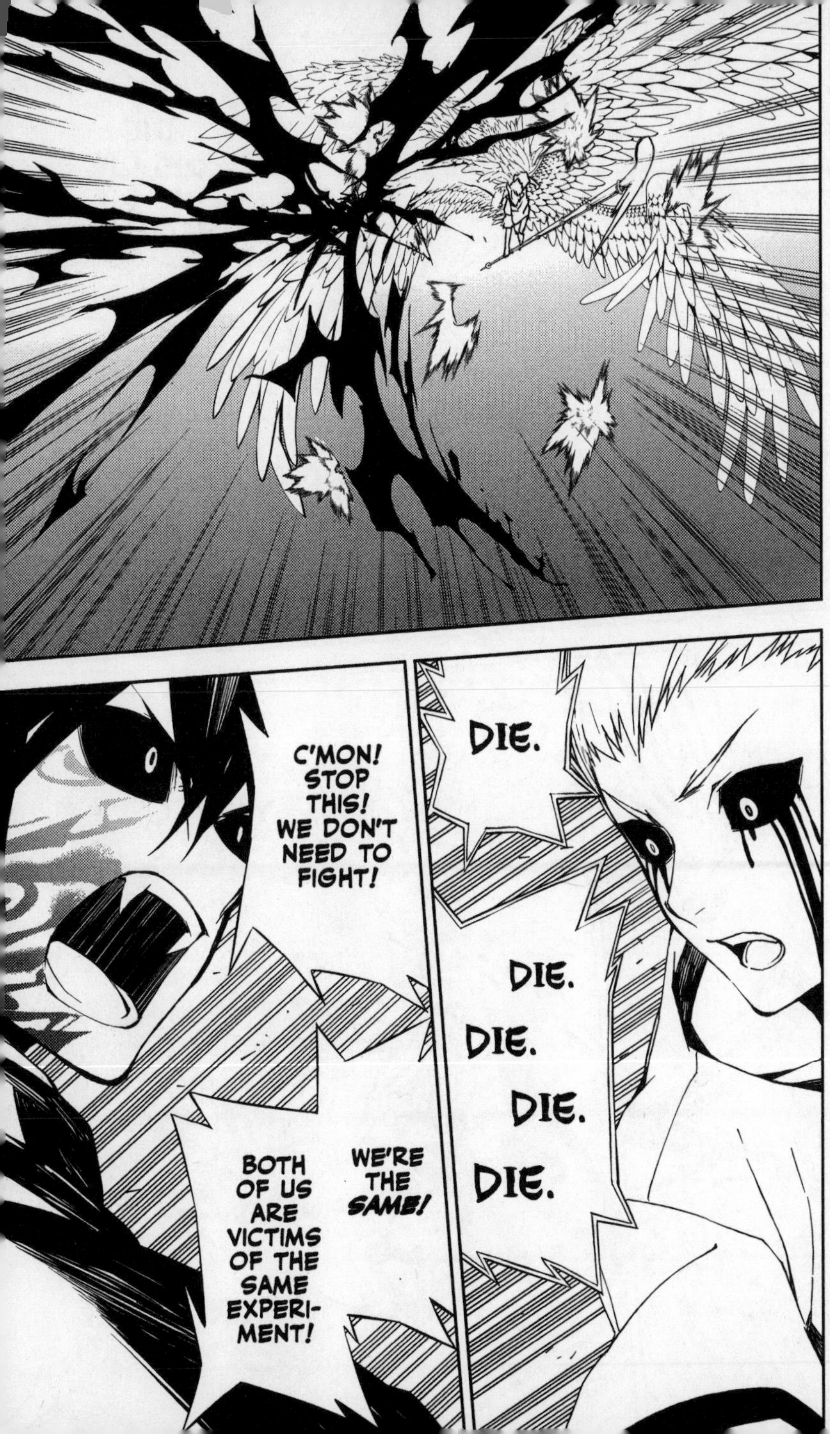
DIE.
DIE.
DIE.
DIE.
DIE.
C'MON! STOP THIS! WE DON'T NEED TO FIGHT!
WE'RE THE *SAME!*
BOTH OF US ARE VICTIMS OF THE SAME EXPERIMENT!

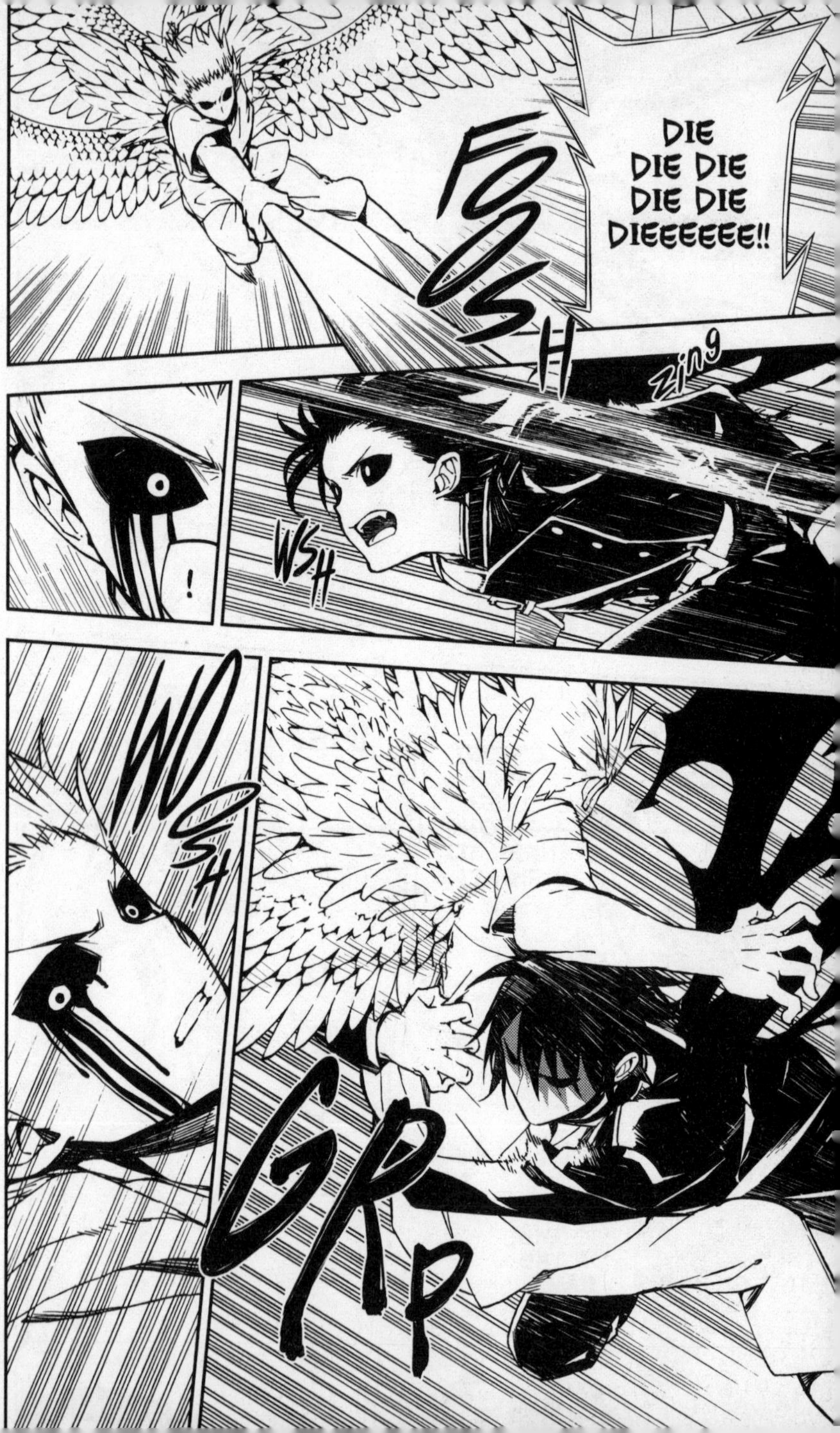
DIE DIE DIE DIE DIE DIEEEEEEE!!
FOSH
zing
WSH
!
GRP
WOOSH

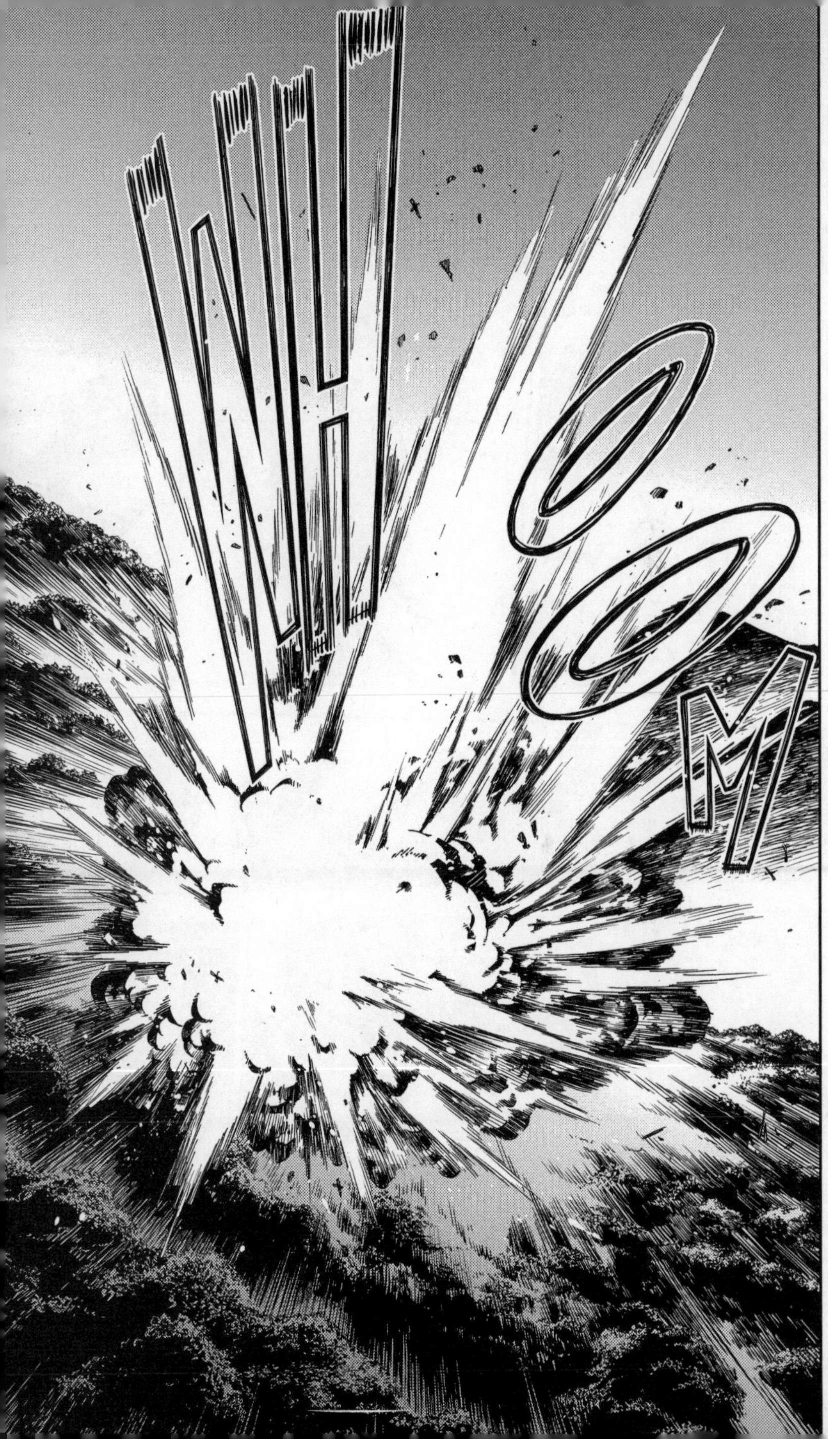
WHOOM

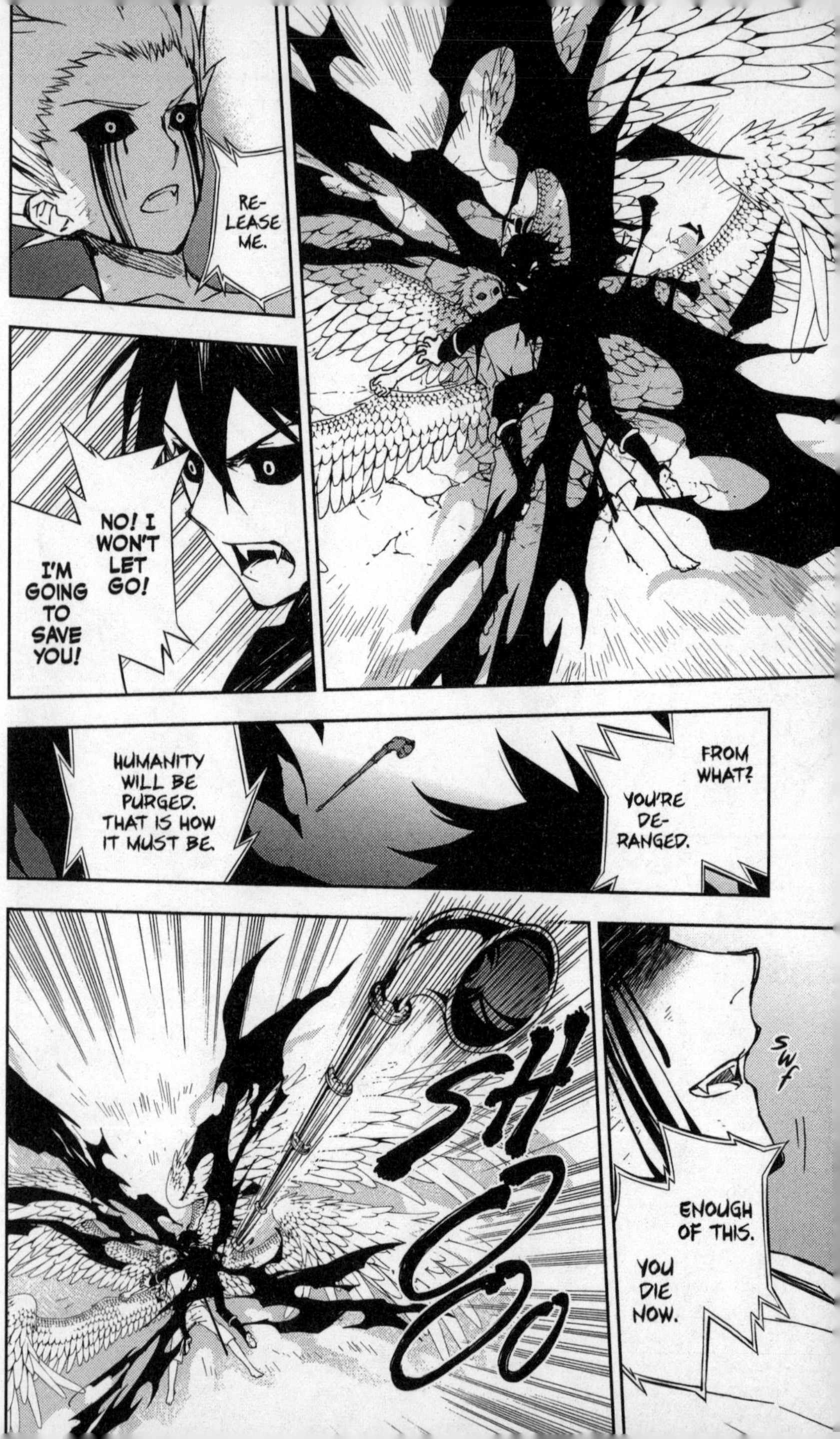
RE-LEASE ME.
NO! I WON'T LET GO!
I'M GOING TO SAVE YOU!
FROM WHAT?
YOU'RE DE-RANGED.
HUMANITY WILL BE PURGED. THAT IS HOW IT MUST BE.
SWF
ENOUGH OF THIS.
YOU DIE NOW.
SHOOO

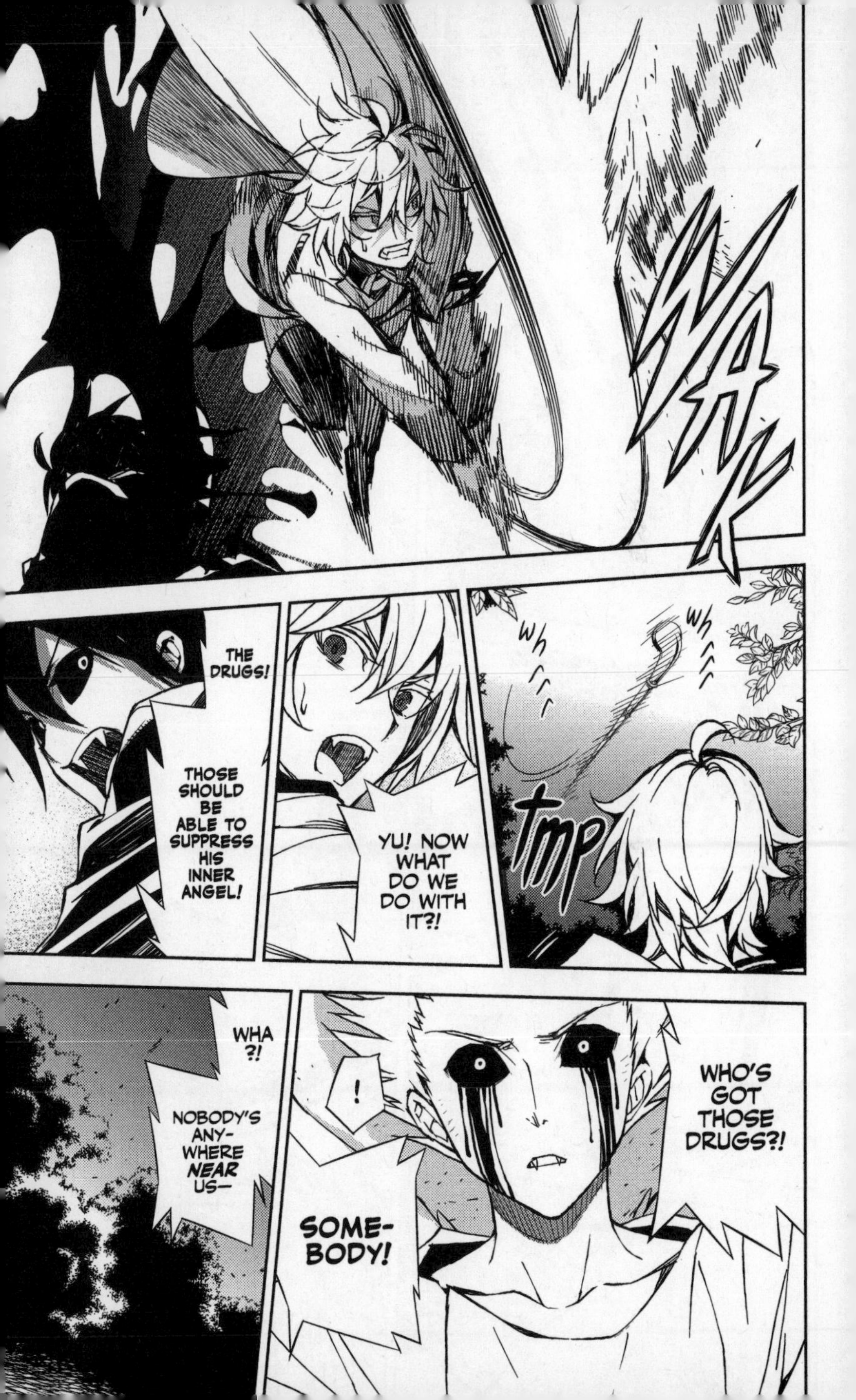
WHAK
wh
wh
tmp
YU! NOW WHAT DO WE DO WITH IT?!
THE DRUGS!
THOSE SHOULD BE ABLE TO SUPPRESS HIS INNER ANGEL!
WHO'S GOT THOSE DRUGS?!
!
SOME-BODY!
WHA?!
NOBODY'S ANY-WHERE *NEAR* US—

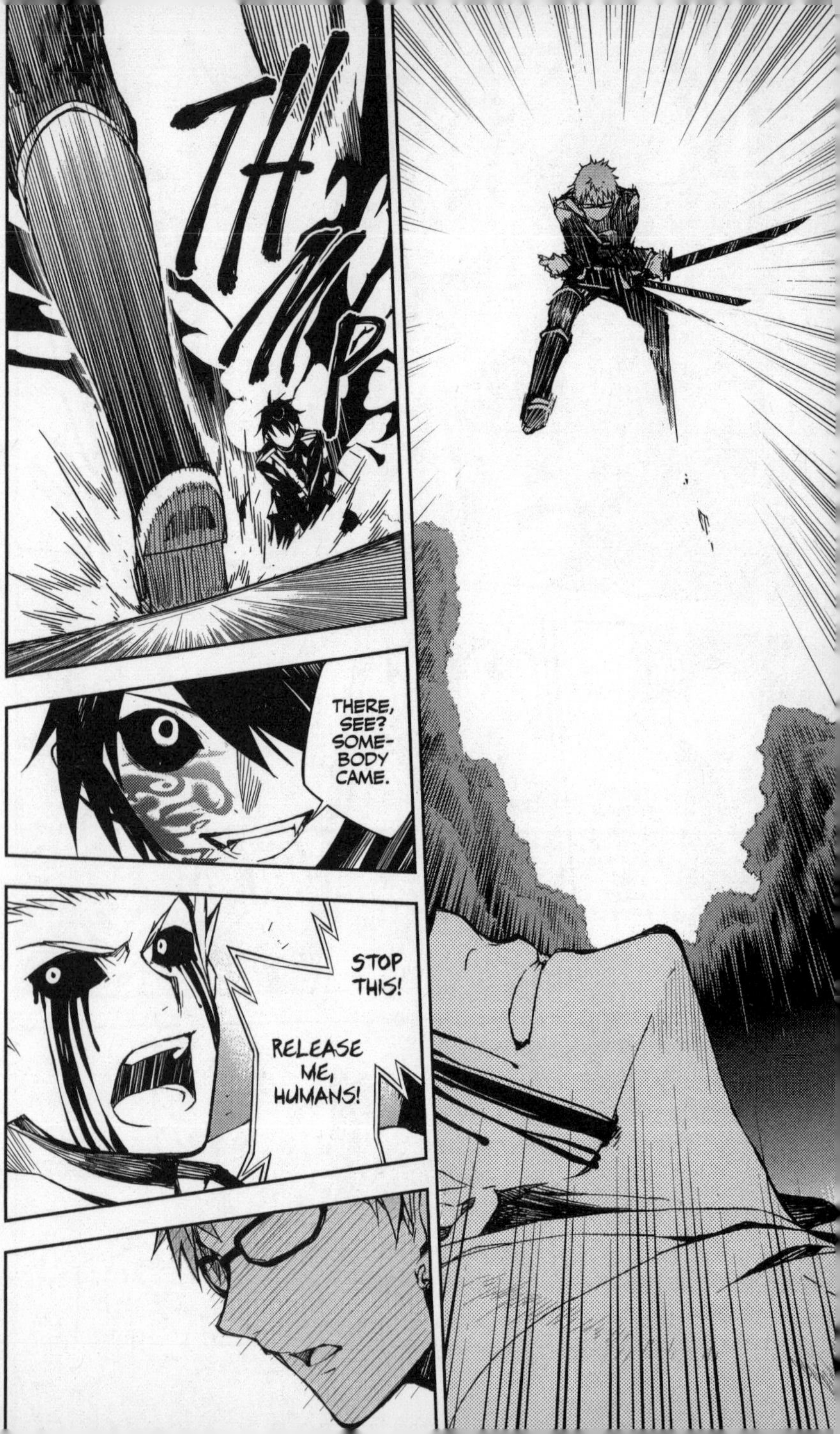
THUMP
THERE, SEE? SOME-BODY CAME.
STOP THIS!
RELEASE ME, HUMANS!

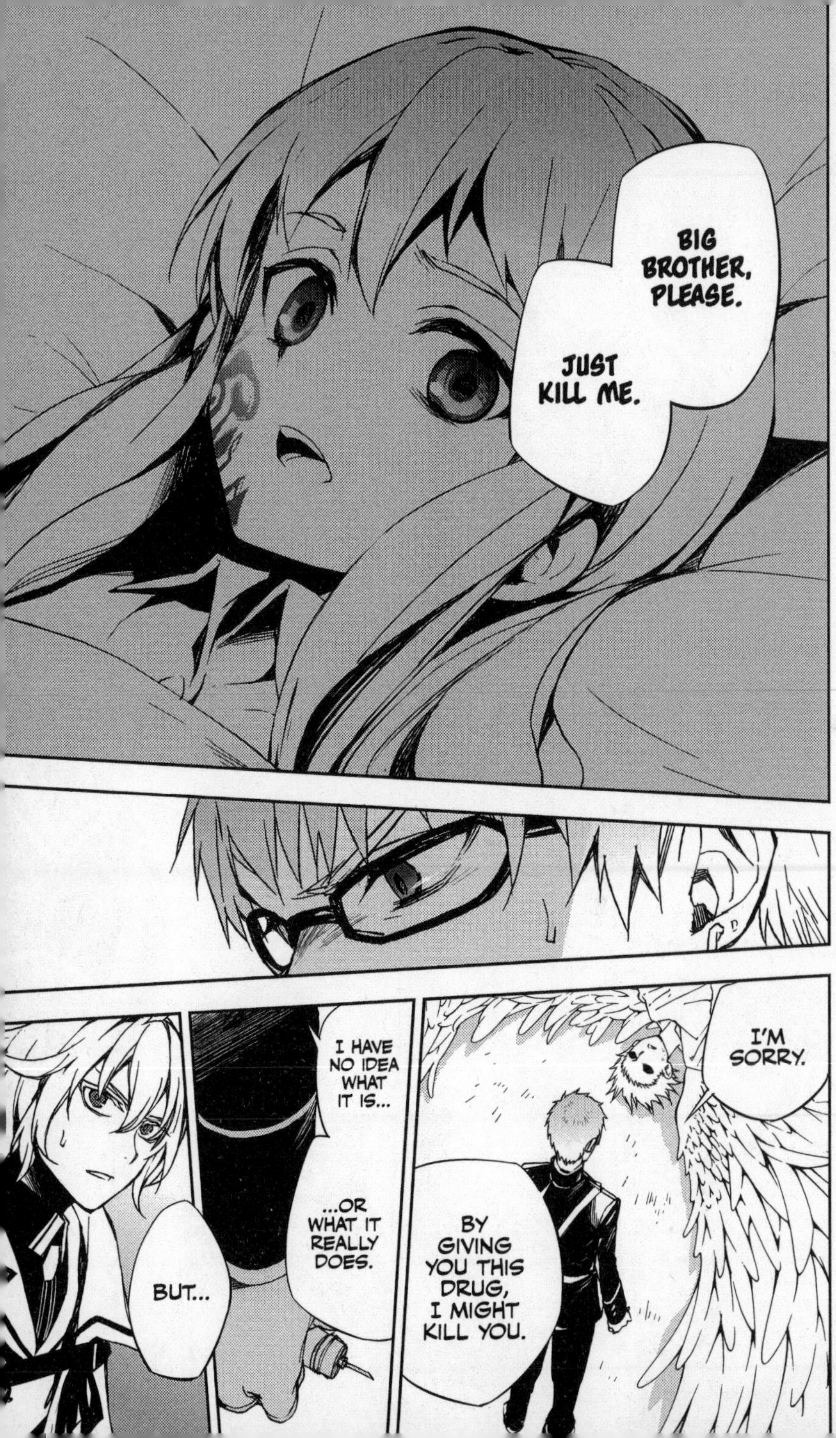
BIG BROTHER, PLEASE.
JUST KILL ME.
I'M SORRY.
BY GIVING YOU THIS DRUG, I MIGHT KILL YOU.
I HAVE NO IDEA WHAT IT IS...
...OR WHAT IT REALLY DOES.
BUT...

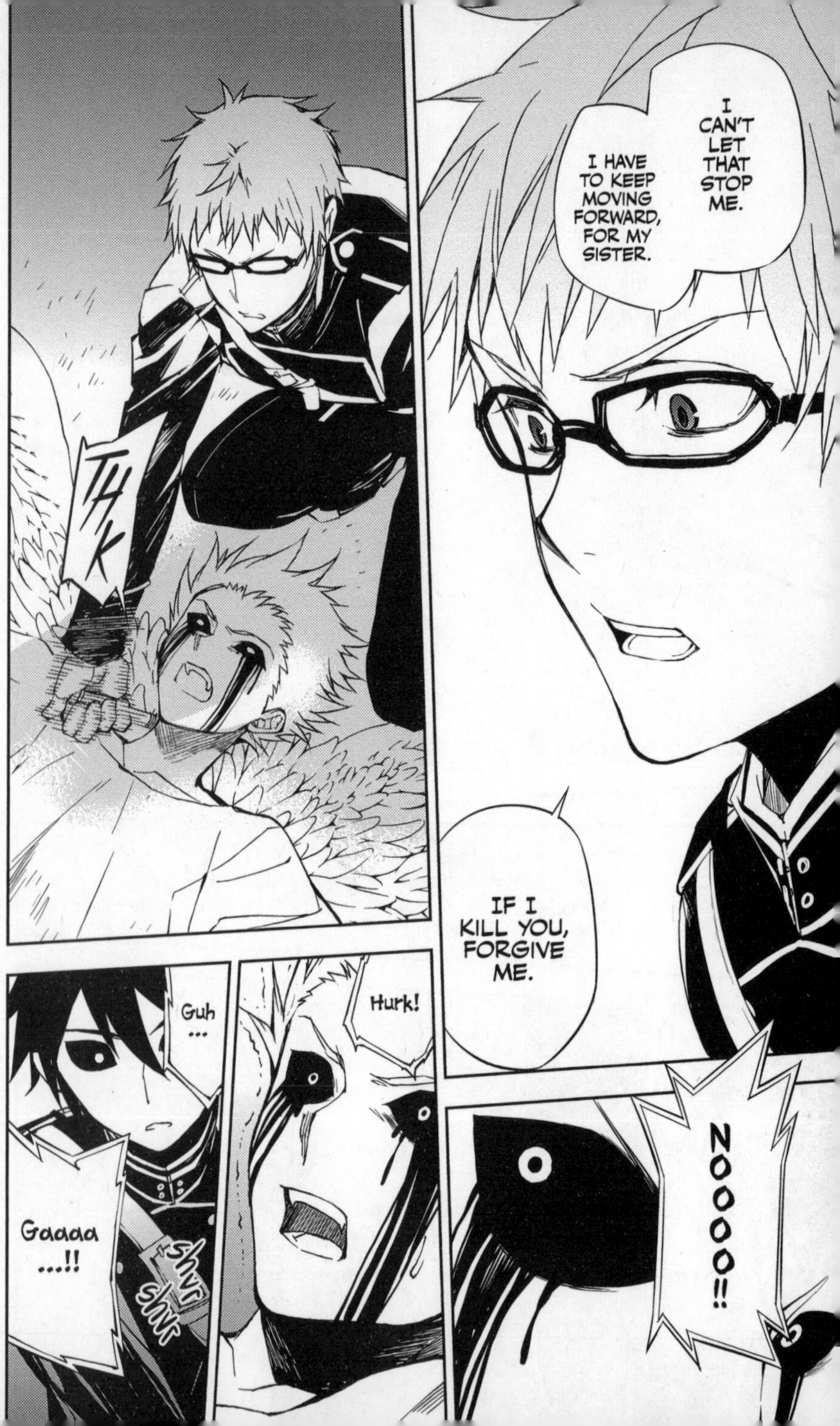
I CAN'T LET THAT STOP ME.
I HAVE TO KEEP MOVING FORWARD, FOR MY SISTER.
IF I KILL YOU, FORGIVE ME.
THK
NOOOO!!
Hurk!
Guh ...
Gaaaa ...!!
shvr shvr

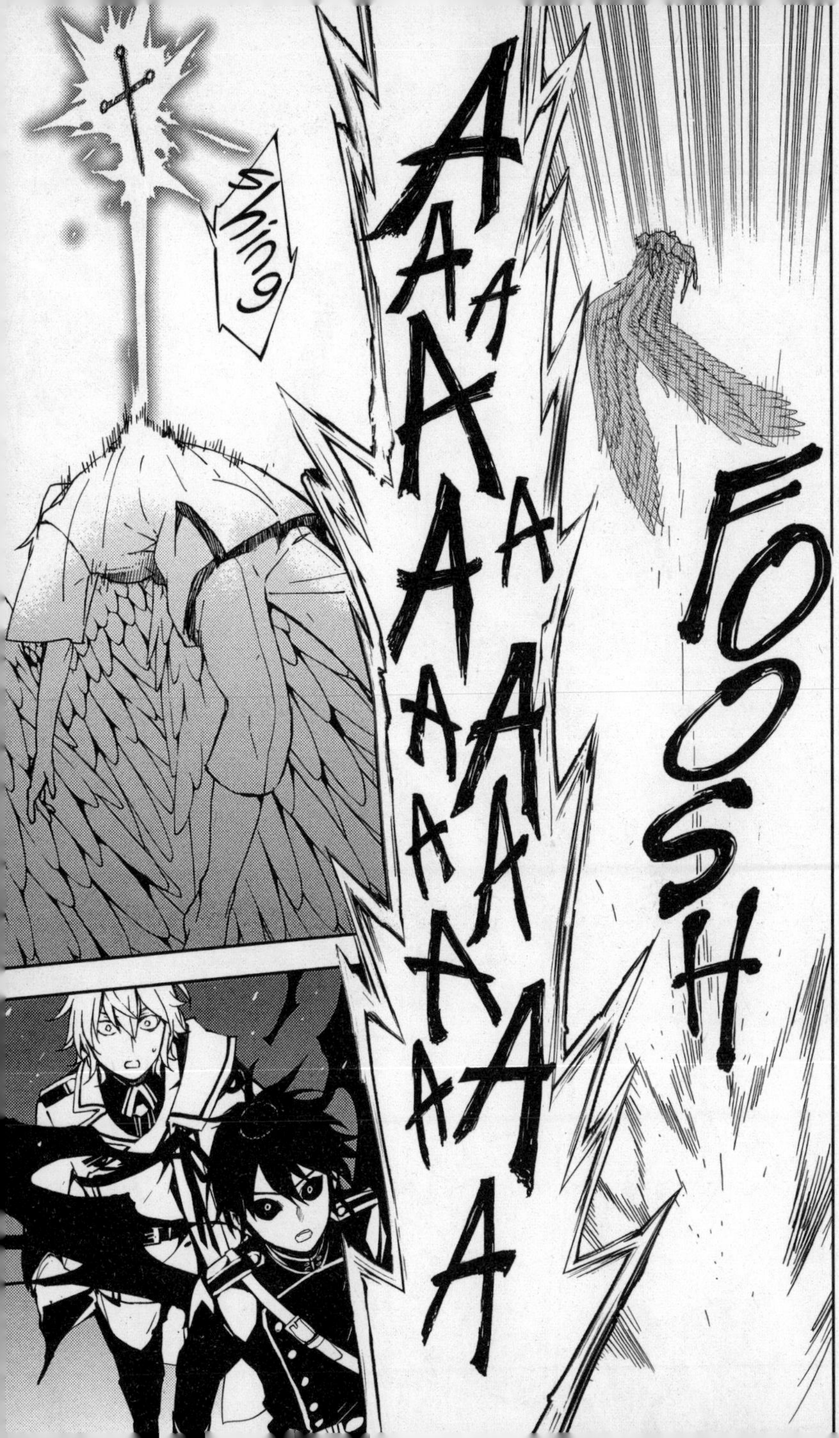
FOOSH
AAAAAAAAAAAAAAA
Shing

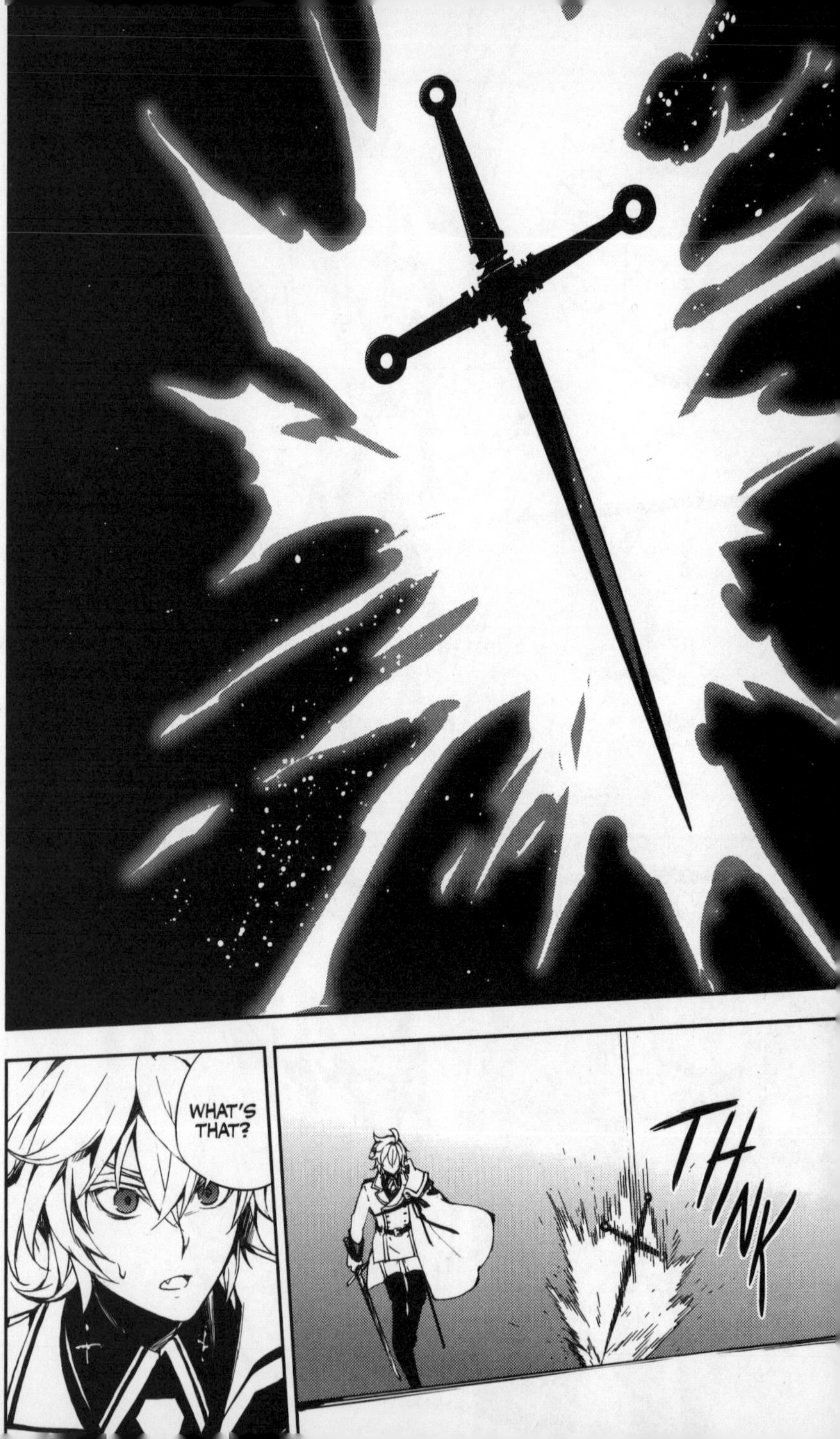
THINK
WHAT'S THAT?

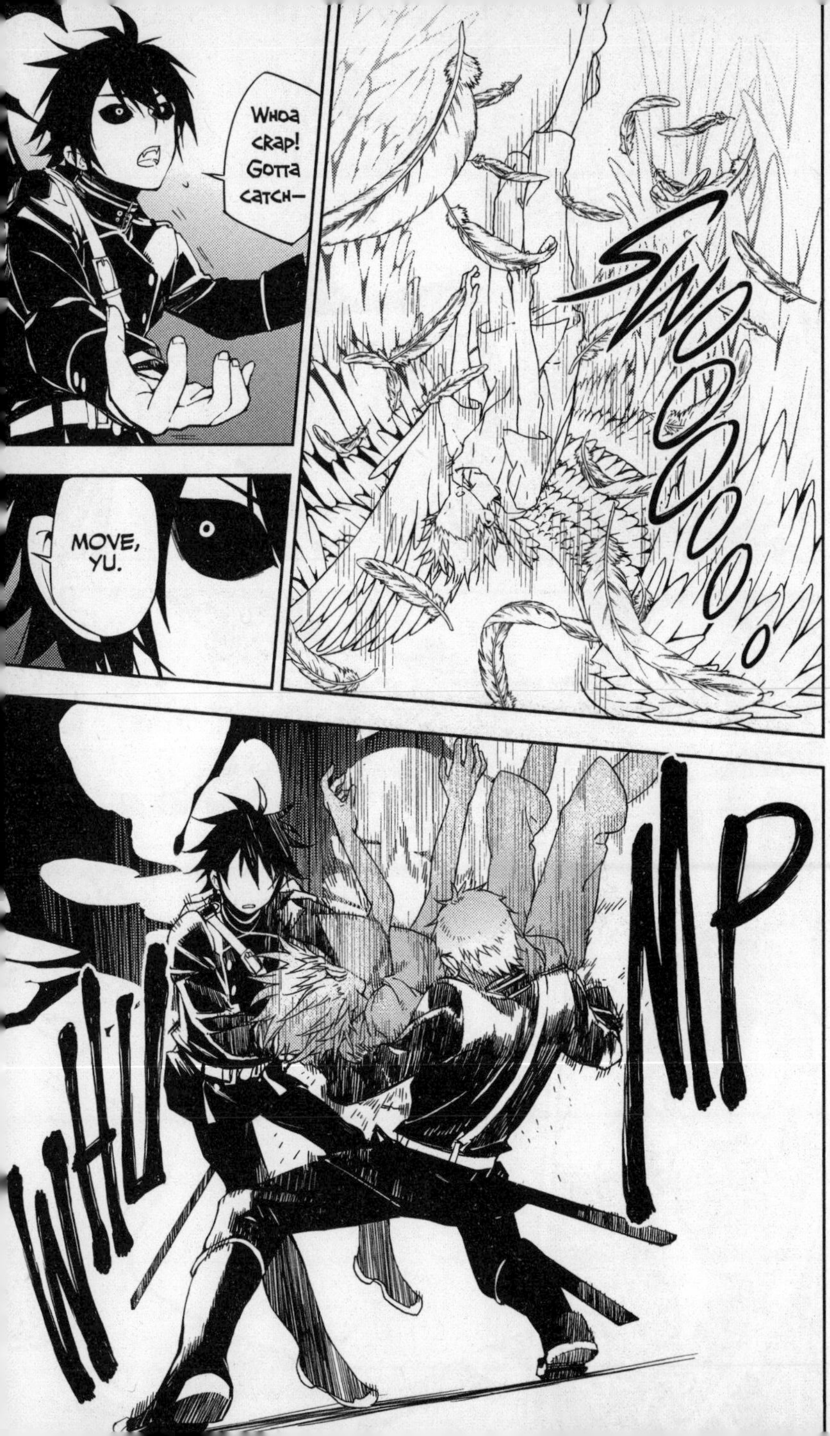
SWOOOOOO
Whoa crap! Gotta catch—
MOVE, YU.
WHUMP

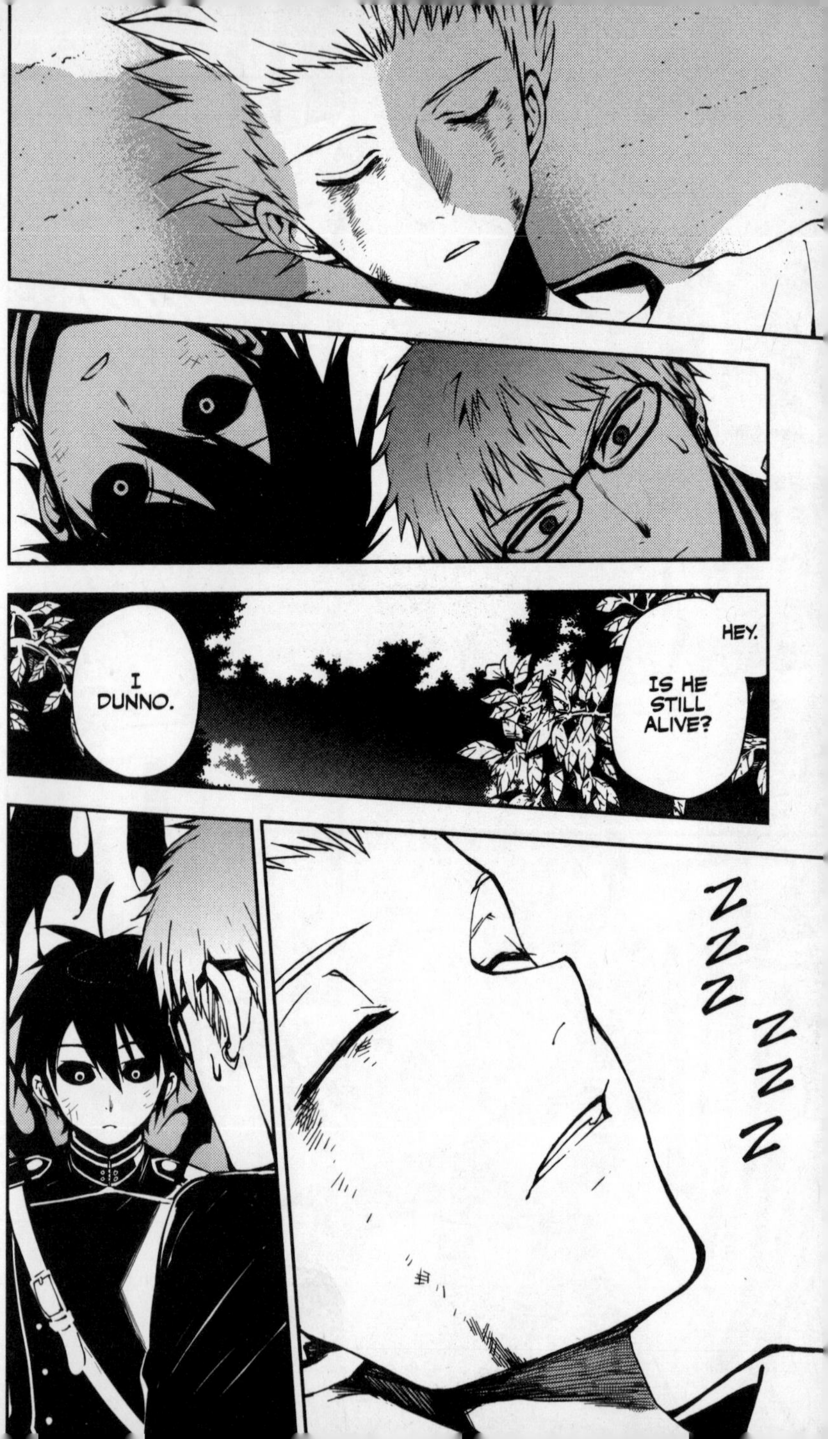
HEY.
IS HE STILL ALIVE?
I DUNNO.
ZZZ ZZZ

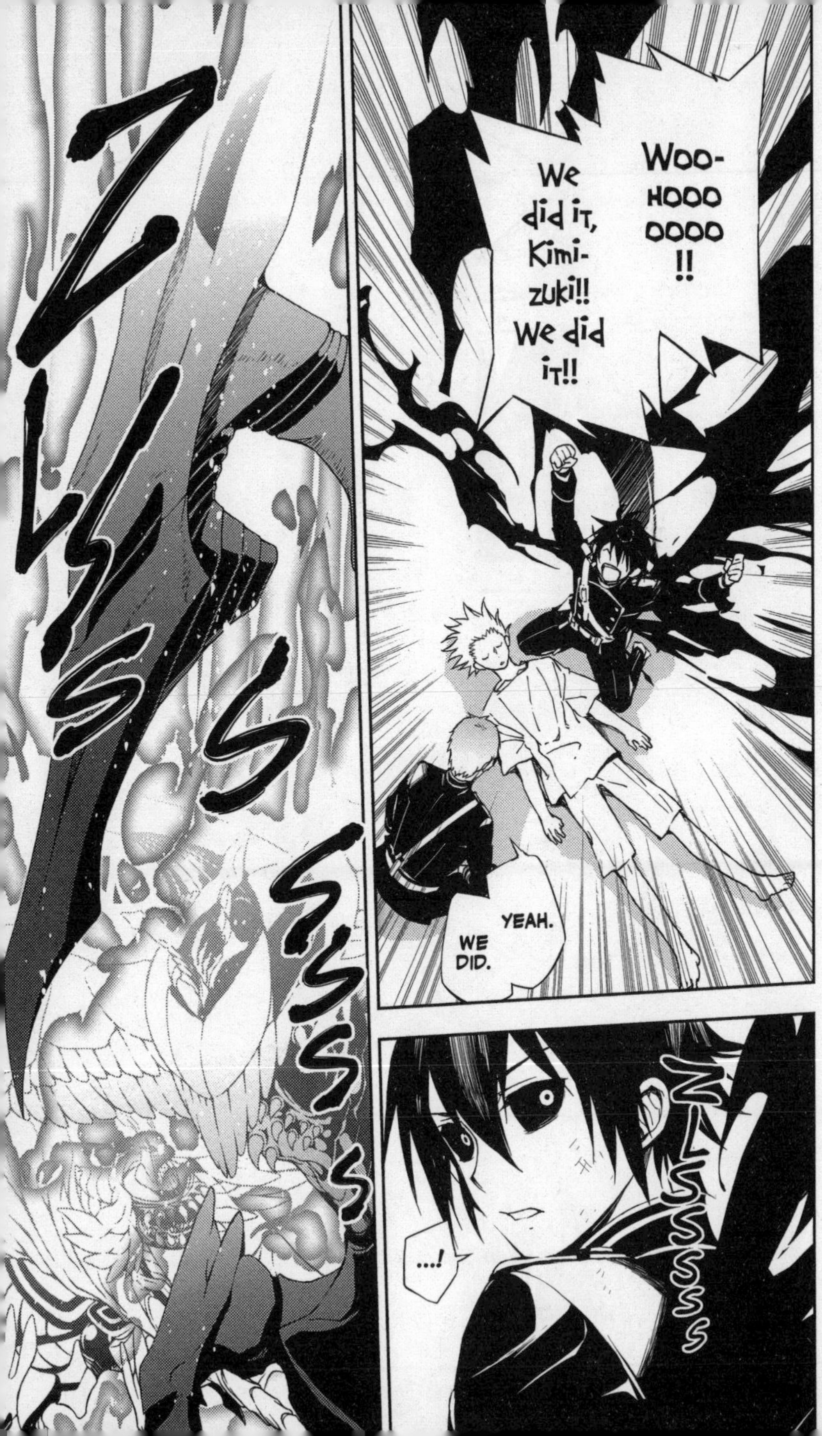
WOO-HOOOOOOO!!
We did it, Kimi-zuki!! We did it!!
YEAH.
WE DID.
...!
ZZSSSSSS
ZZSSS
SSSSS

Seraph of the End

VAMPIRE REIGN

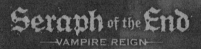

Ikebukuro, Tokyo The Sunshine 60 Building

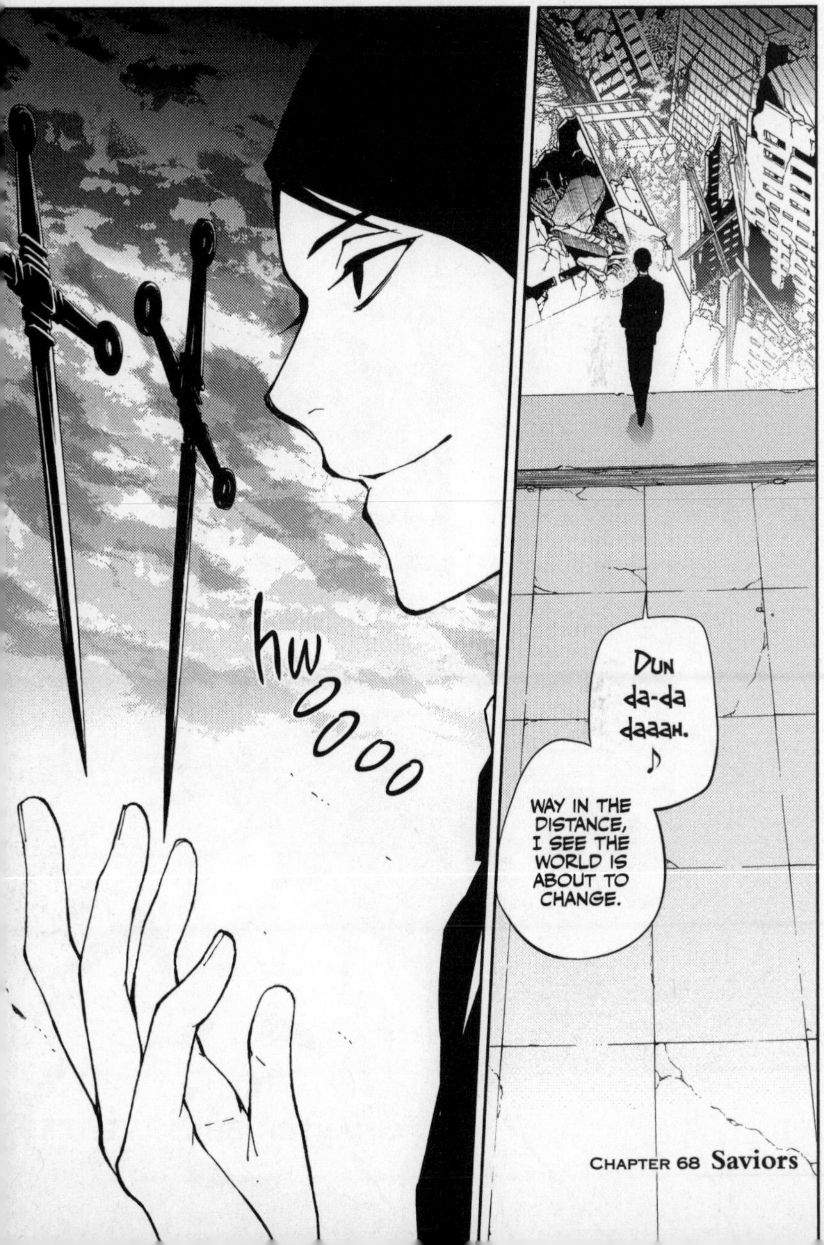
DUN da-da daaah. ♪
WAY IN THE DISTANCE, I SEE THE WORLD IS ABOUT TO CHANGE.
hwoooooo

CHAPTER 68 Saviors

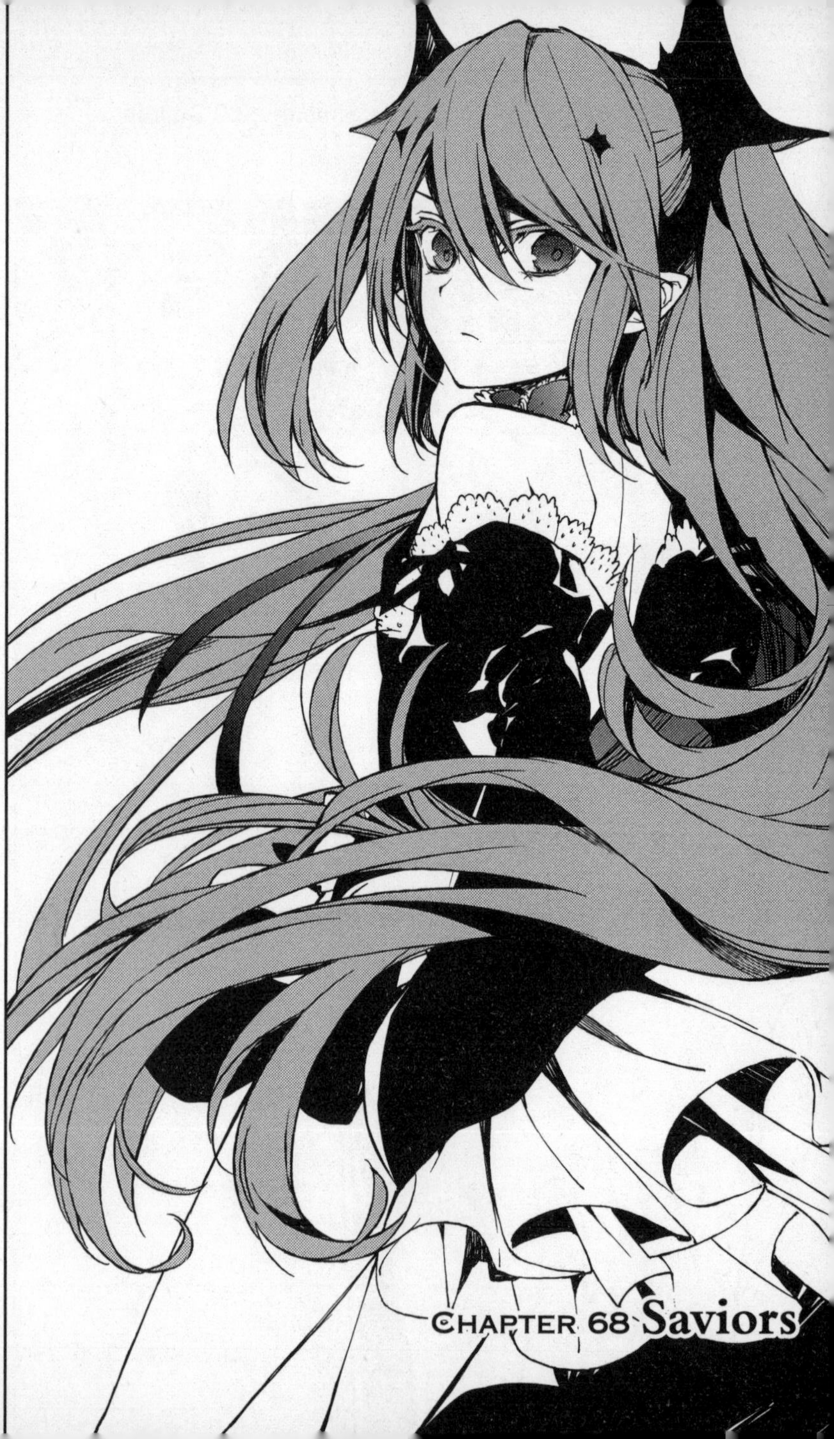

Chapter 68 Saviors

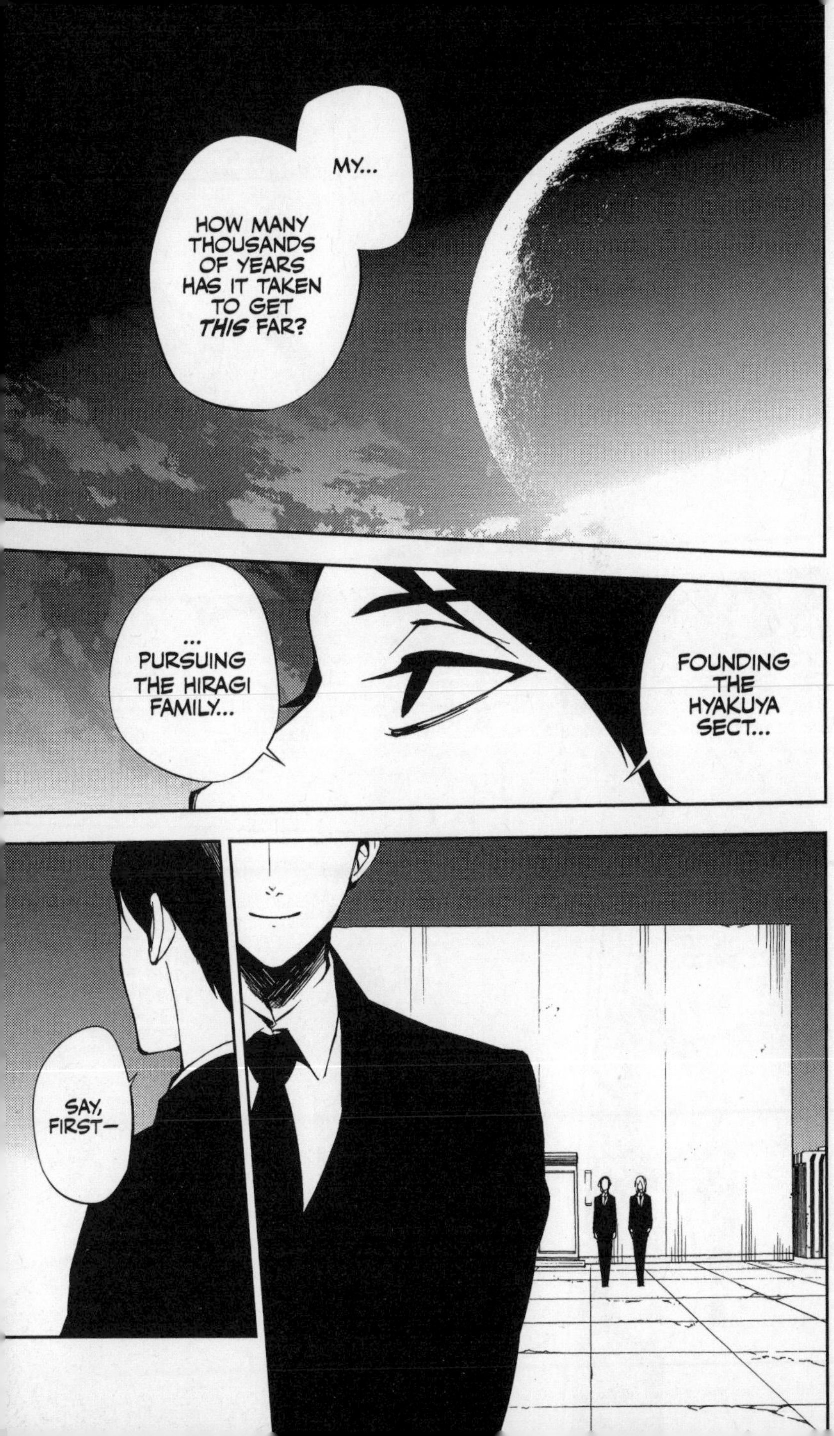
MY...
HOW MANY THOUSANDS OF YEARS HAS IT TAKEN TO GET *THIS* FAR?
FOUNDING THE HYAKUYA SECT...
... PURSUING THE HIRAGI FAMILY...
SAY, FIRST—

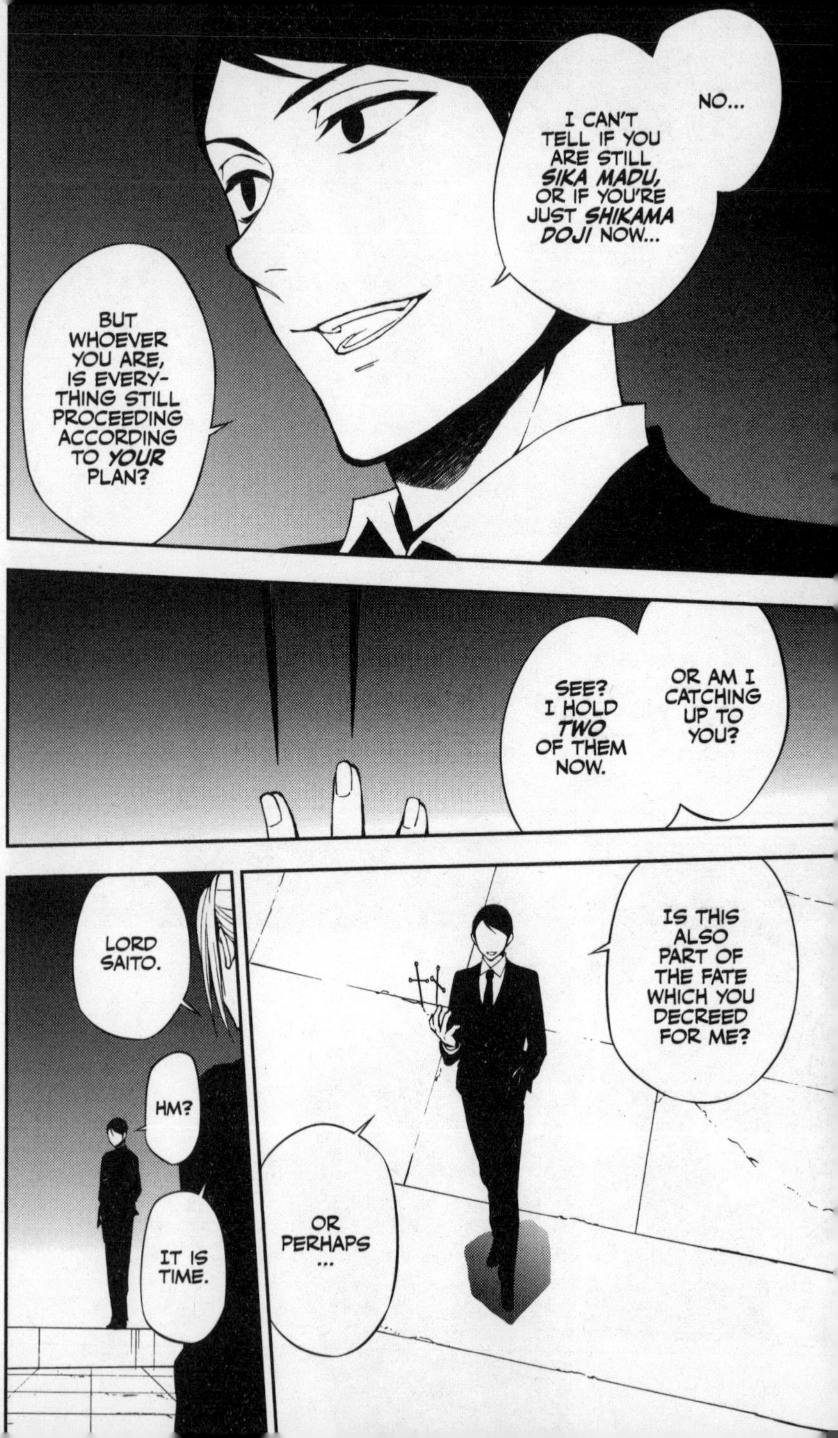
NO...
I CAN'T TELL IF YOU ARE STILL SIKA MADU, OR IF YOU'RE JUST SHIKAMA DOJI NOW...
BUT WHOEVER YOU ARE, IS EVERY-THING STILL PROCEEDING ACCORDING TO YOUR PLAN?
OR AM I CATCHING UP TO YOU?
SEE? I HOLD TWO OF THEM NOW.
IS THIS ALSO PART OF THE FATE WHICH YOU DECREED FOR ME?
OR PERHAPS ...
LORD SAITO.
HM?
IT IS TIME.

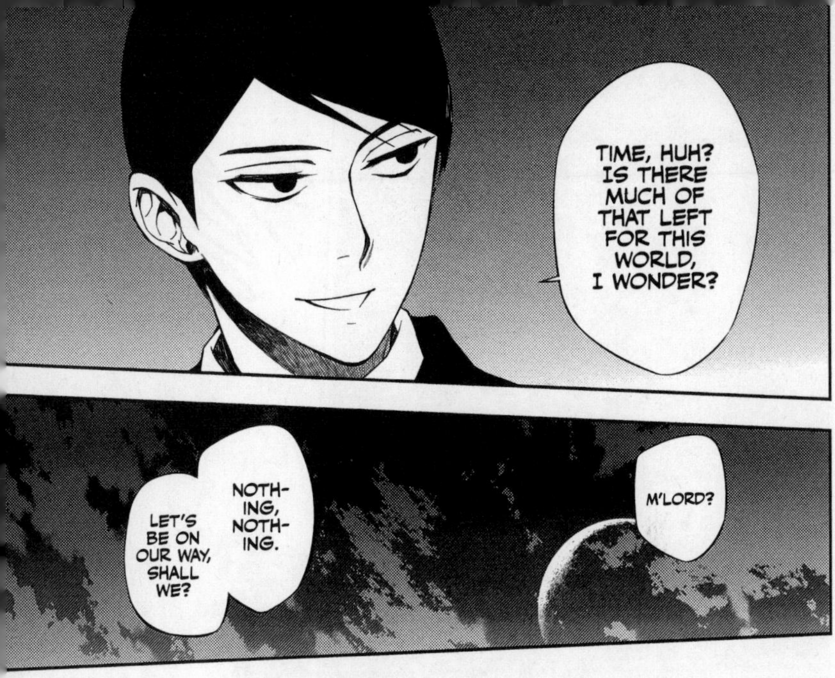
TIME, HUH? IS THERE MUCH OF THAT LEFT FOR THIS WORLD, I WONDER?
M'LORD?
NOTHING, NOTHING.
LET'S BE ON OUR WAY, SHALL WE?

Nagoya, Guren Ichinose's Lab

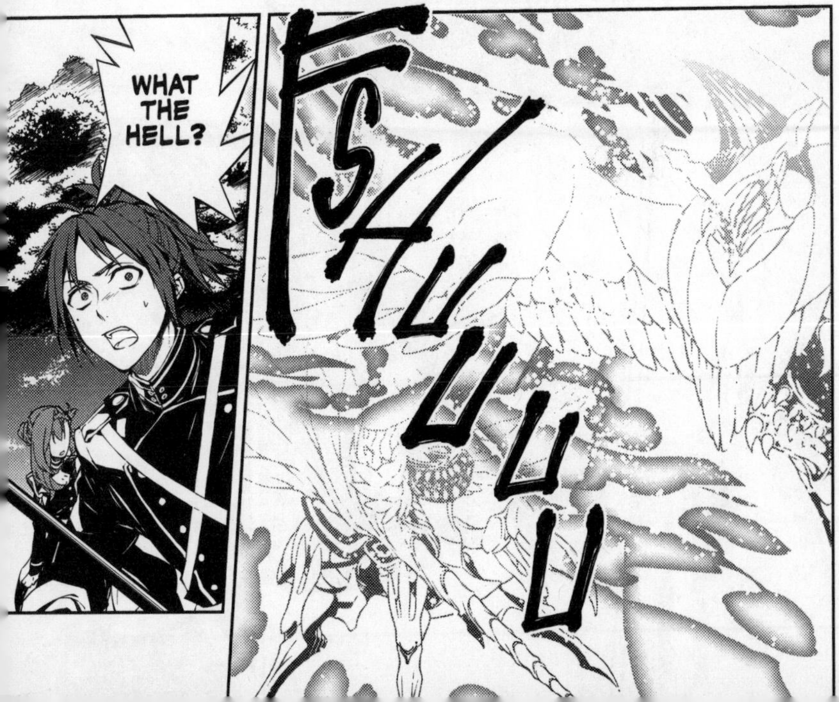
FSHUUUU
WHAT THE HELL?

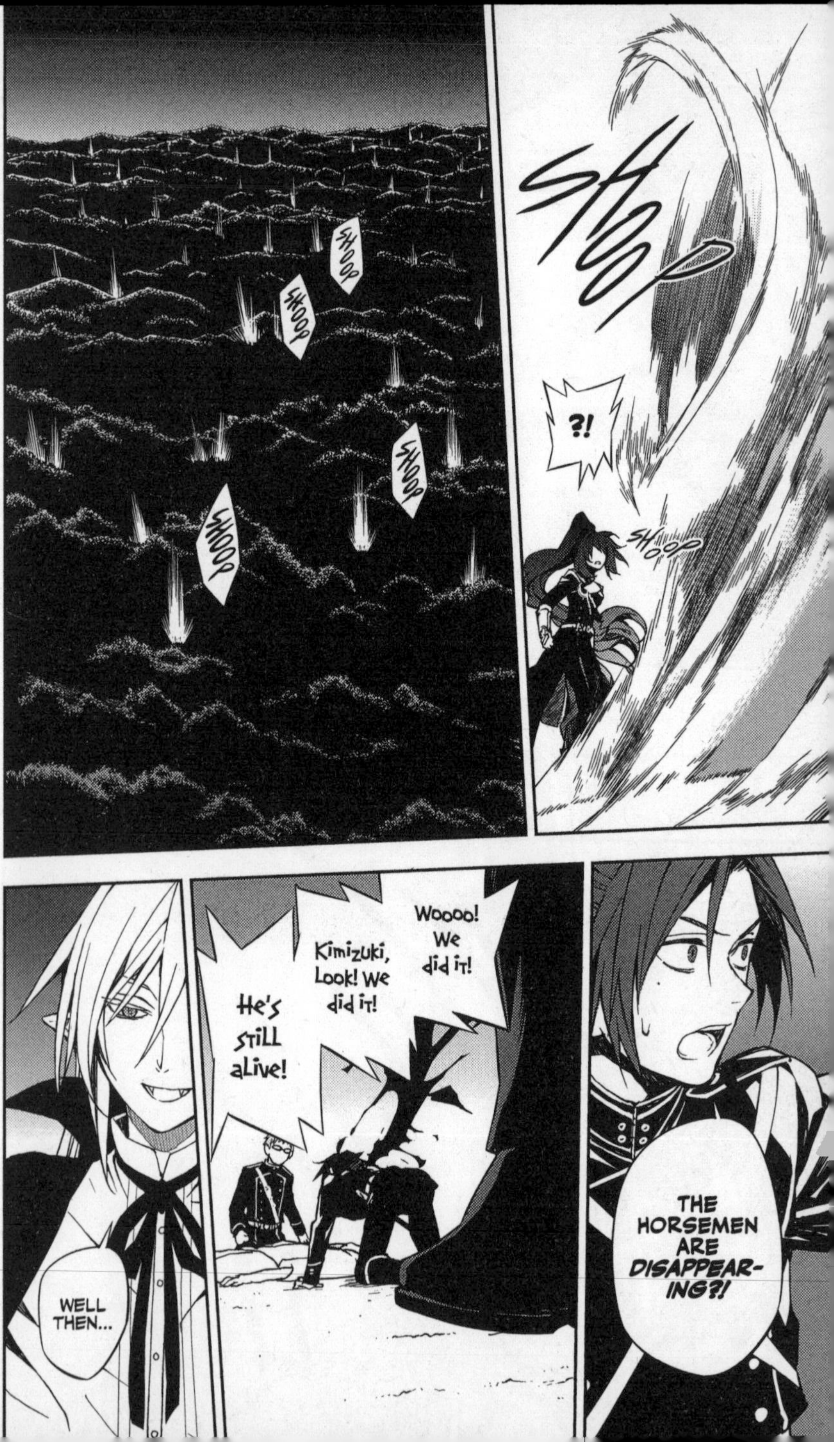
SHOOP
?!
SHOOP
SHOOP
SHOOP
SHOOP
SHOOP
THE HORSEMEN ARE DISAPPEARING?!
Woooo! We did it!
Kimizuki, Look! we did it!
He's still alive!
WELL THEN...

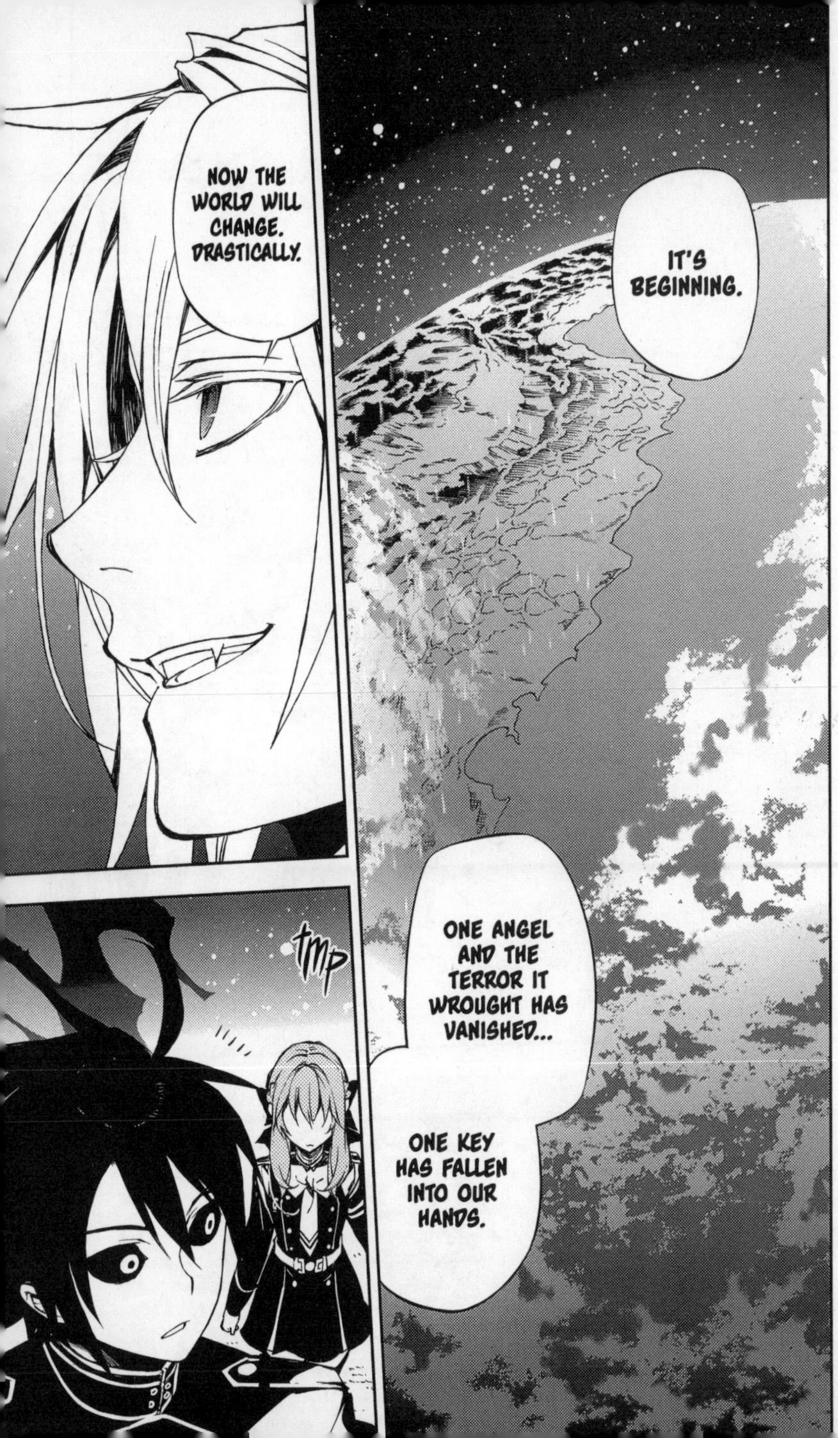
IT'S BEGINNING.
ONE ANGEL AND THE TERROR IT WROUGHT HAS VANISHED...
ONE KEY HAS FALLEN INTO OUR HANDS.
NOW THE WORLD WILL CHANGE. DRASTICALLY.
tmp

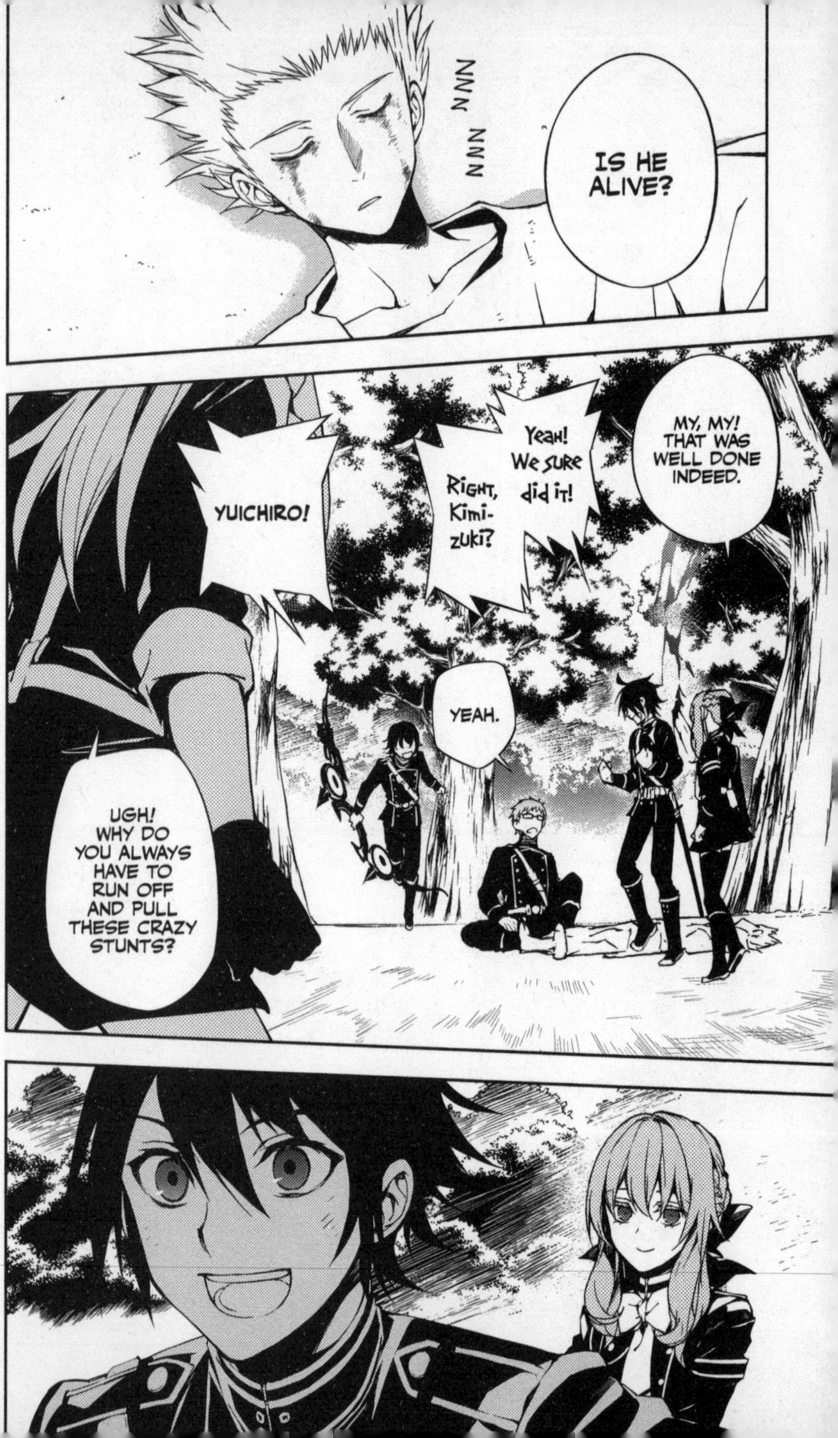
IS HE ALIVE?
NNN NNN
MY, MY! THAT WAS WELL DONE INDEED.
Yeah! We sure did it!
Right, Kimi-zuki?
YUICHIRO!
YEAH.
UGH! WHY DO YOU ALWAYS HAVE TO RUN OFF AND PULL THESE CRAZY STUNTS?

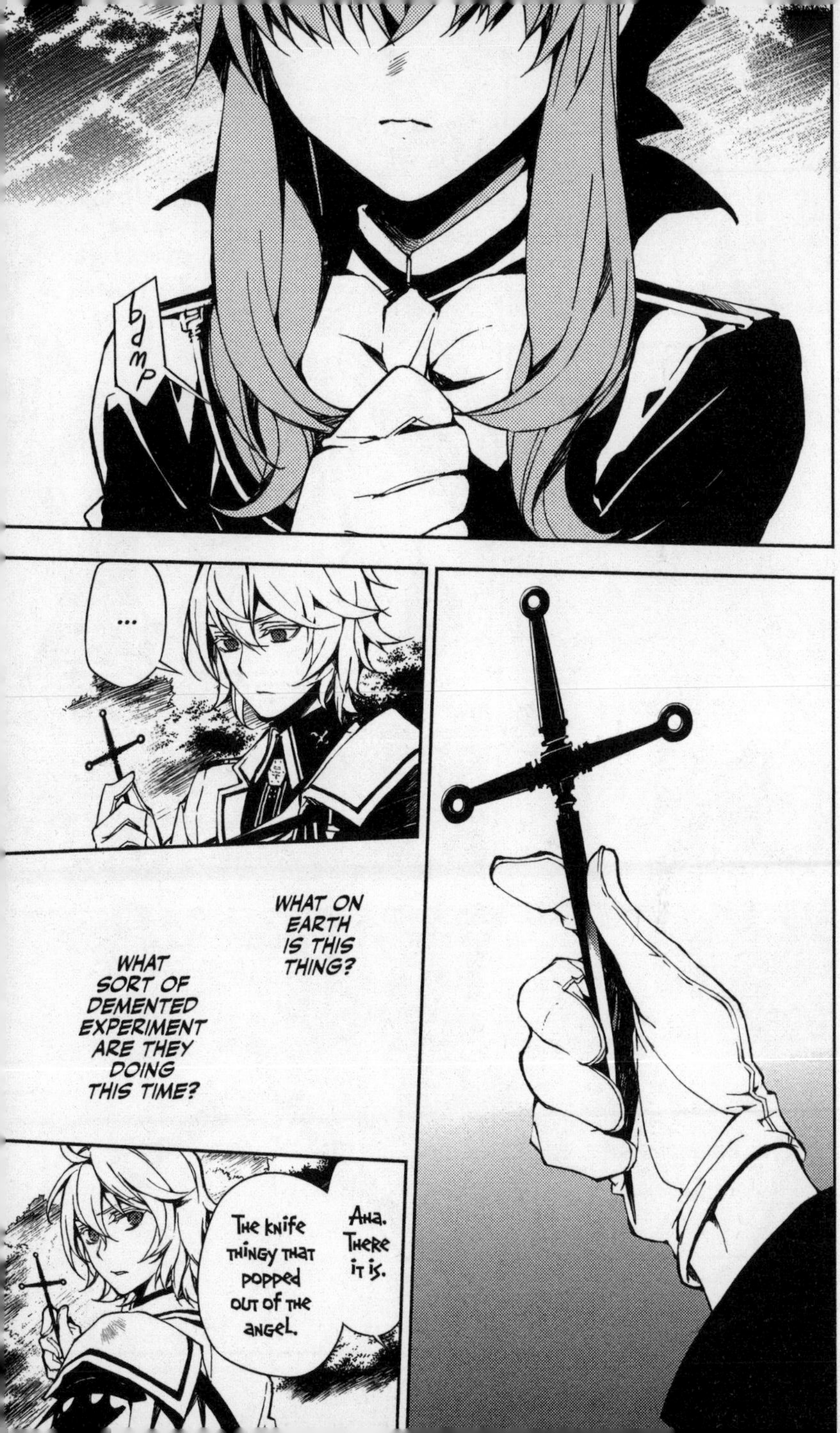
bdmp
...
WHAT ON EARTH IS THIS THING?
WHAT SORT OF DEMENTED EXPERIMENT ARE THEY DOING THIS TIME?
Aha. There it is.
The knife thingy that popped out of the angel.

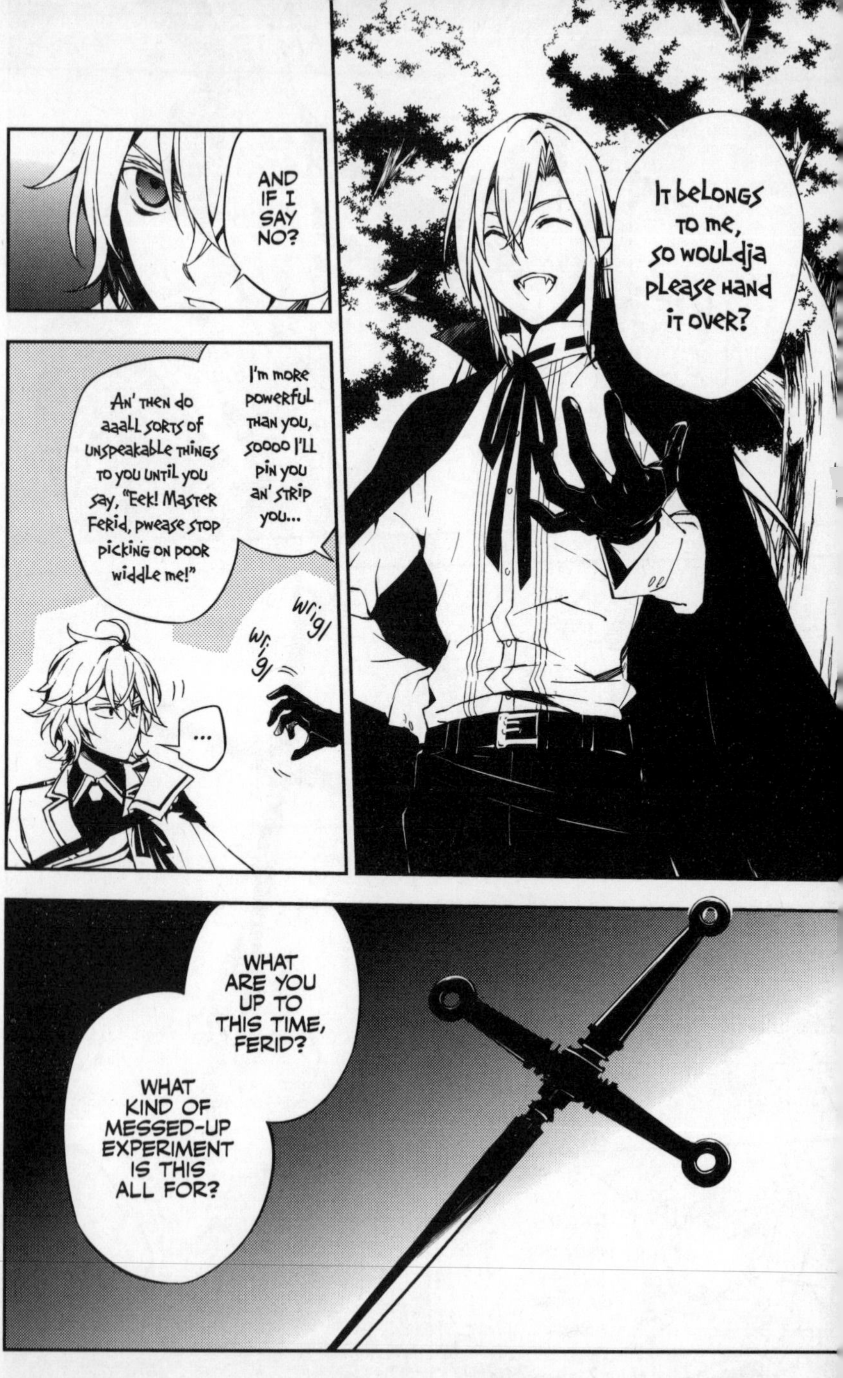
It belongs to me, so wouldja please hand it over?
AND IF I SAY NO?
I'm more powerful than you, soooo I'll pin you an' strip you...
An' then do aaall sorts of unspeakable things to you until you say, "Eek! Master Ferid, pwease stop picking on poor widdle me!"
wrigl
wrigl
...
WHAT ARE YOU UP TO THIS TIME, FERID?
WHAT KIND OF MESSED-UP EXPERIMENT IS THIS ALL FOR?

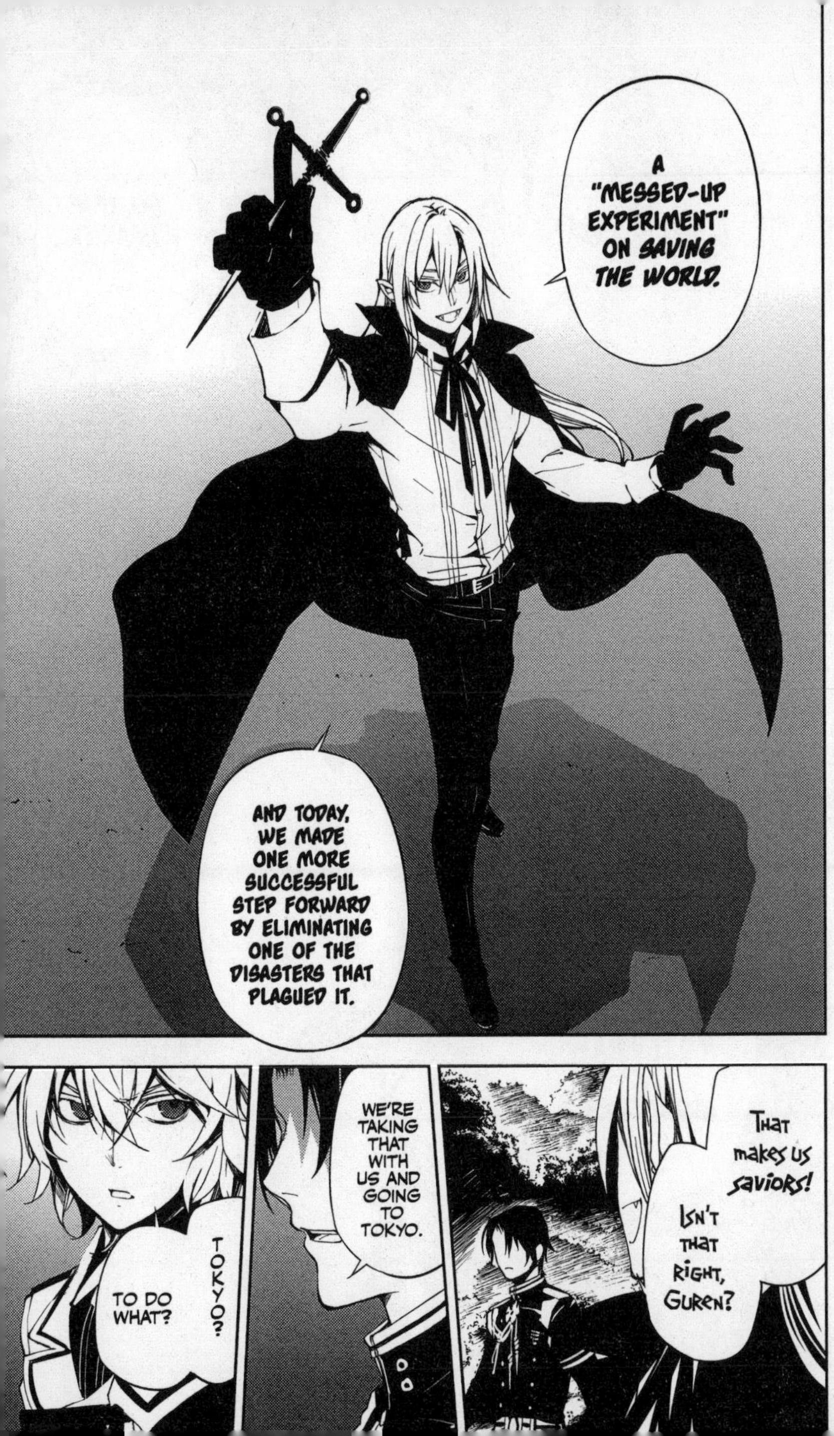
A "MESSED-UP EXPERIMENT" ON SAVING THE WORLD.
AND TODAY, WE MADE ONE MORE SUCCESSFUL STEP FORWARD BY ELIMINATING ONE OF THE DISASTERS THAT PLAGUED IT.
That makes us saviors!
Isn't that right, Guren?
WE'RE TAKING THAT WITH US AND GOING TO TOKYO.
TOKYO?
TO DO WHAT?

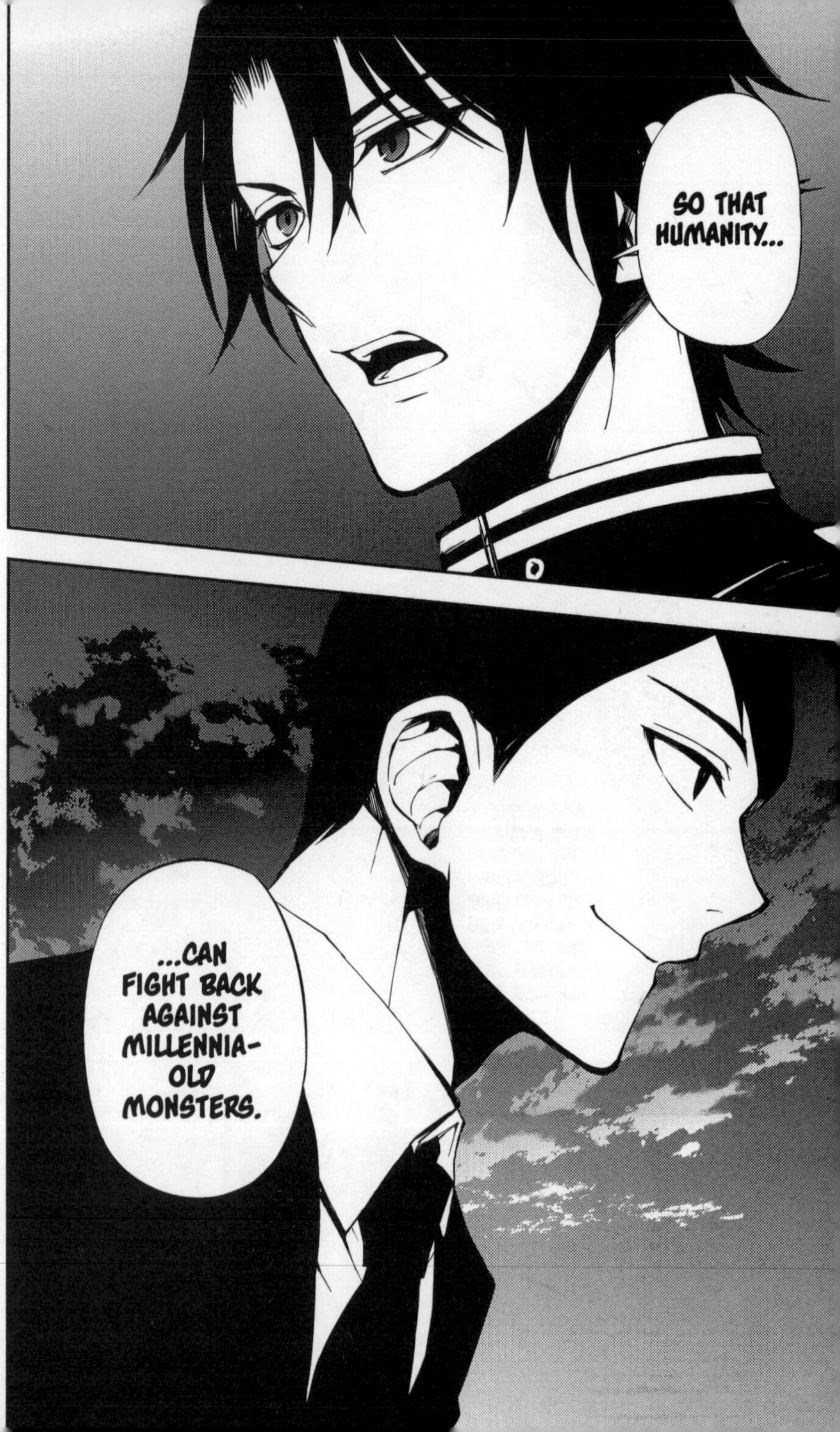
SO THAT HUMANITY...
...CAN FIGHT BACK AGAINST MILLENNIA-OLD MONSTERS.

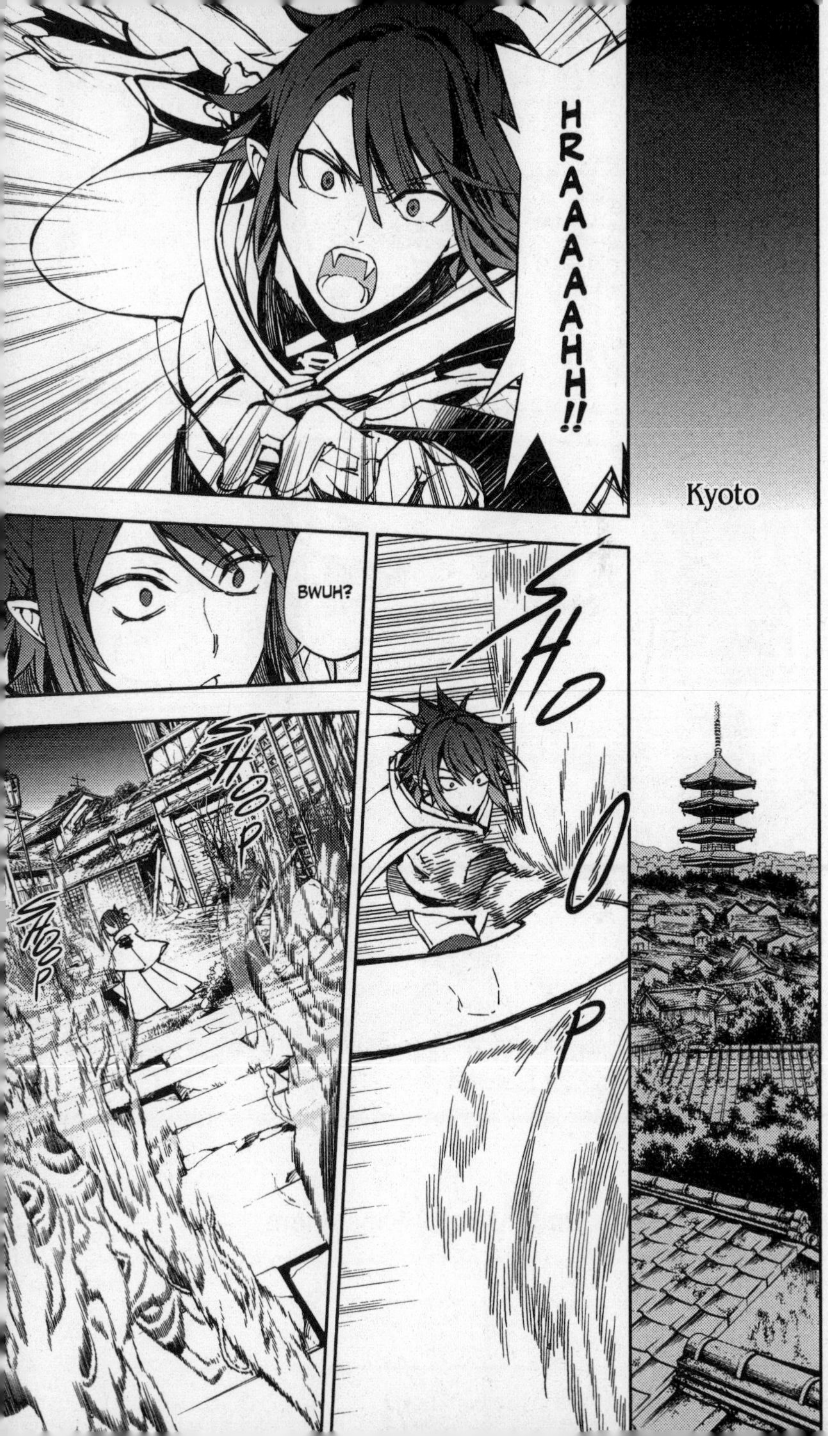
Kyoto
HRAAAAAAHH!!
SHOOP
BWUH?
SHOOP
SHOOP

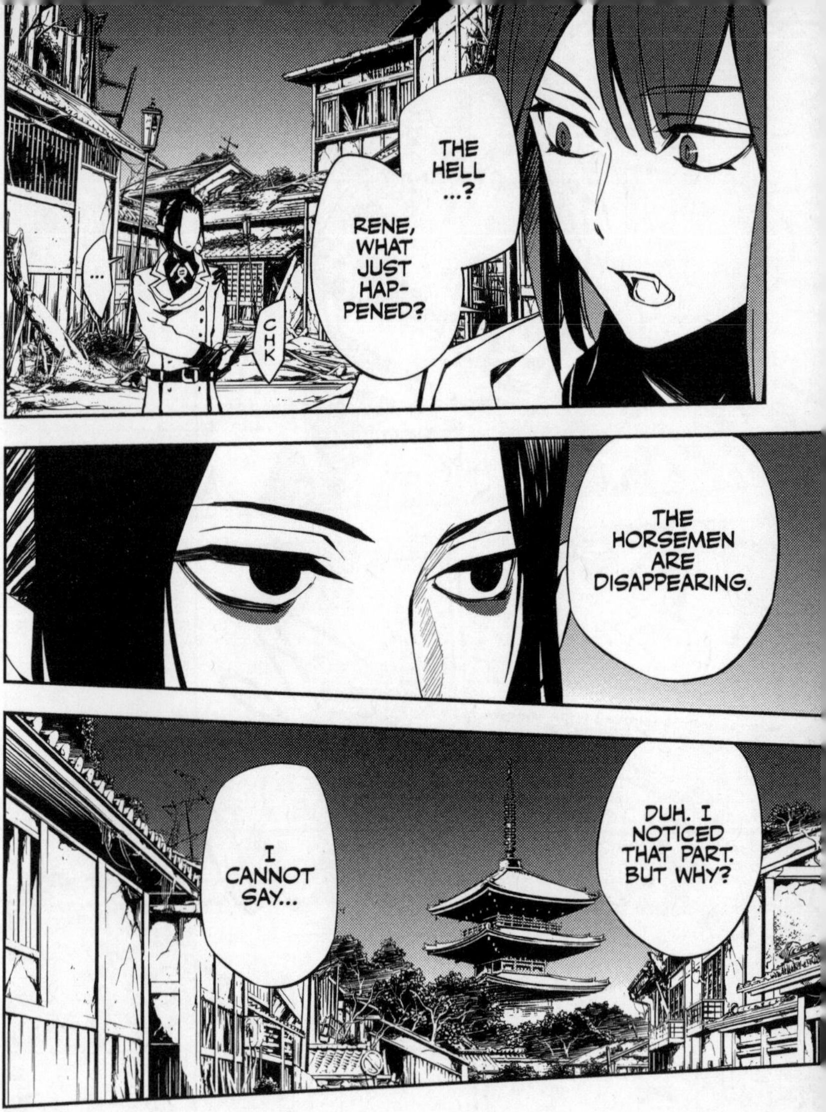
THE HELL ...?
RENE, WHAT JUST HAP-PENED?
CHK
...
THE HORSEMEN ARE DISAPPEARING.
DUH. I NOTICED THAT PART. BUT WHY?
I CANNOT SAY...

Under Kyoto, Sanguinem

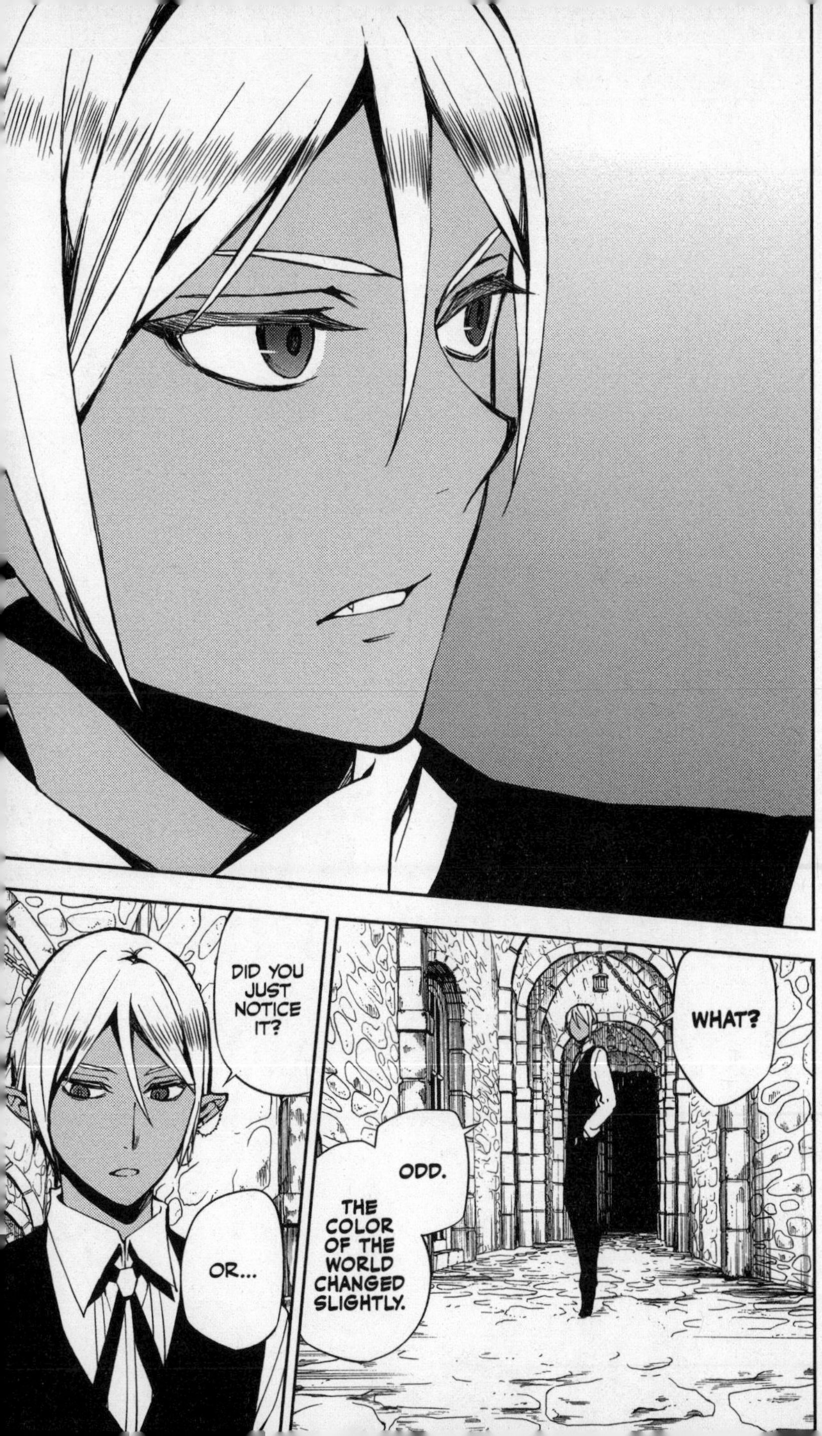
WHAT?
ODD.
THE COLOR OF THE WORLD CHANGED SLIGHTLY.
DID YOU JUST NOTICE IT?
OR...

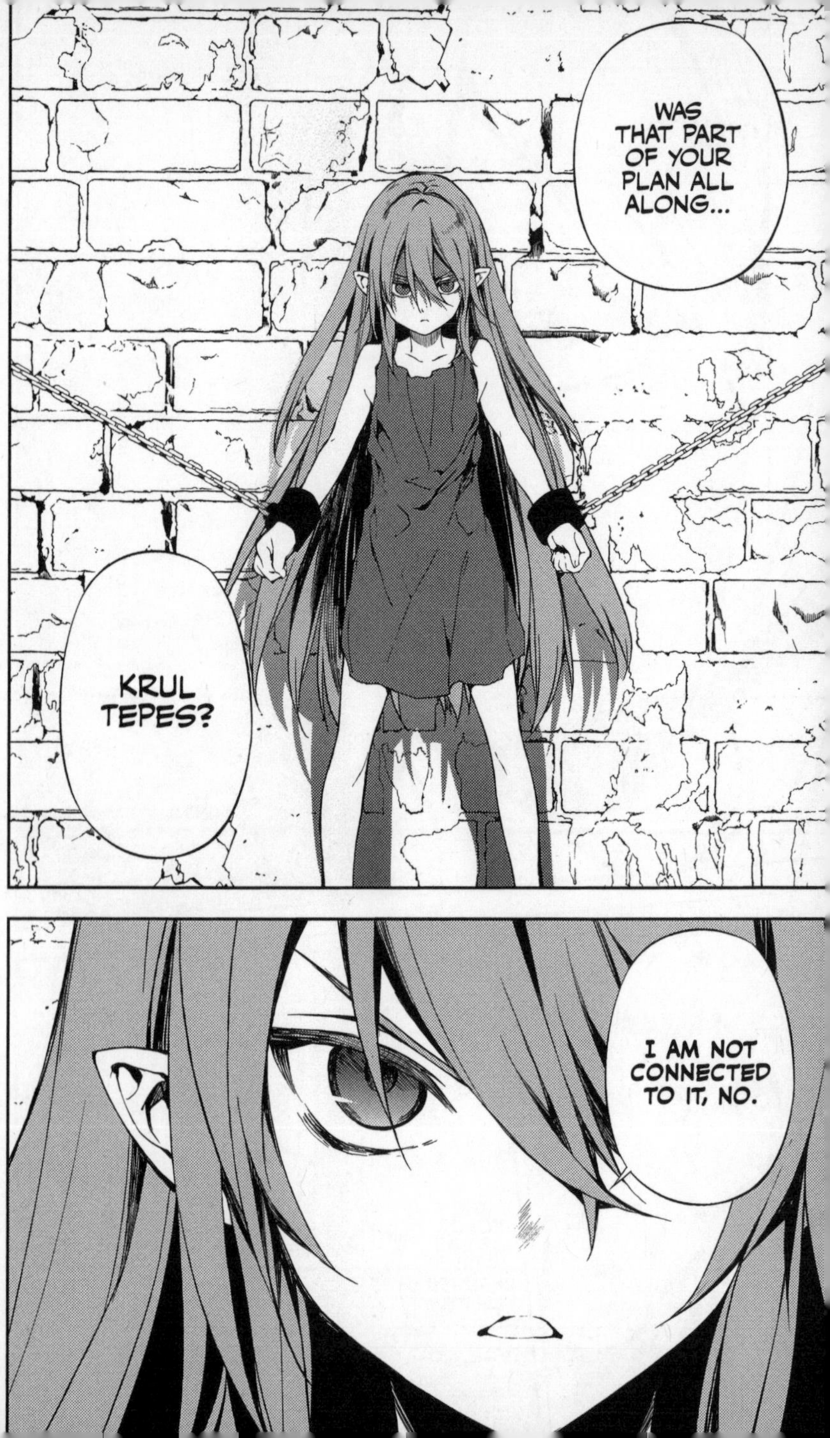
WAS THAT PART OF YOUR PLAN ALL ALONG...
KRUL TEPES?
I AM NOT CONNECTED TO IT, NO.

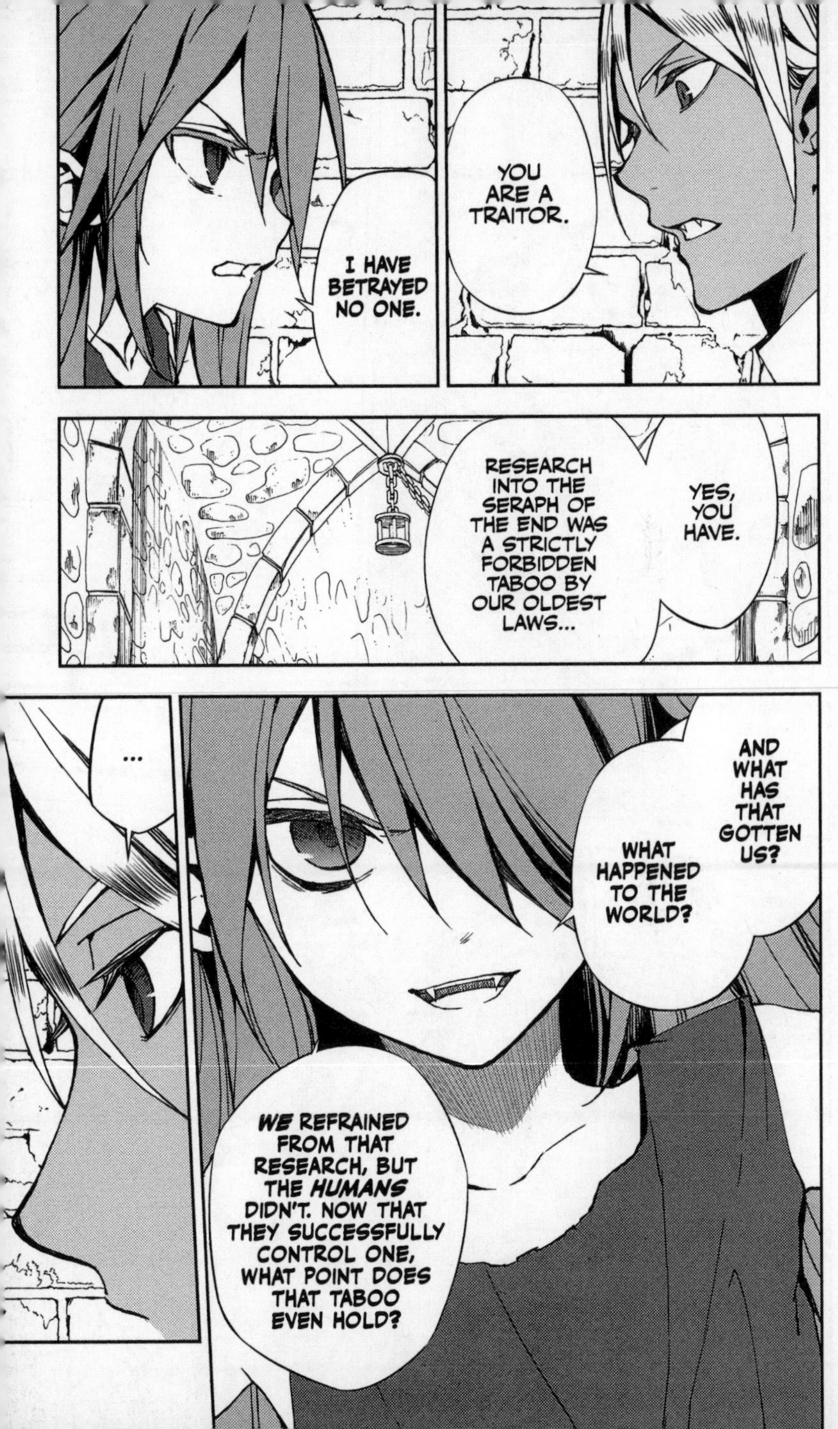
YOU ARE A TRAITOR.
I HAVE BETRAYED NO ONE.
YES, YOU HAVE.
RESEARCH INTO THE SERAPH OF THE END WAS A STRICTLY FORBIDDEN TABOO BY OUR OLDEST LAWS...
AND WHAT HAS THAT GOTTEN US?
WHAT HAPPENED TO THE WORLD?
WE REFRAINED FROM THAT RESEARCH, BUT THE *HUMANS* DIDN'T. NOW THAT THEY SUCCESSFULLY CONTROL ONE, WHAT POINT DOES THAT TABOO EVEN HOLD?
...

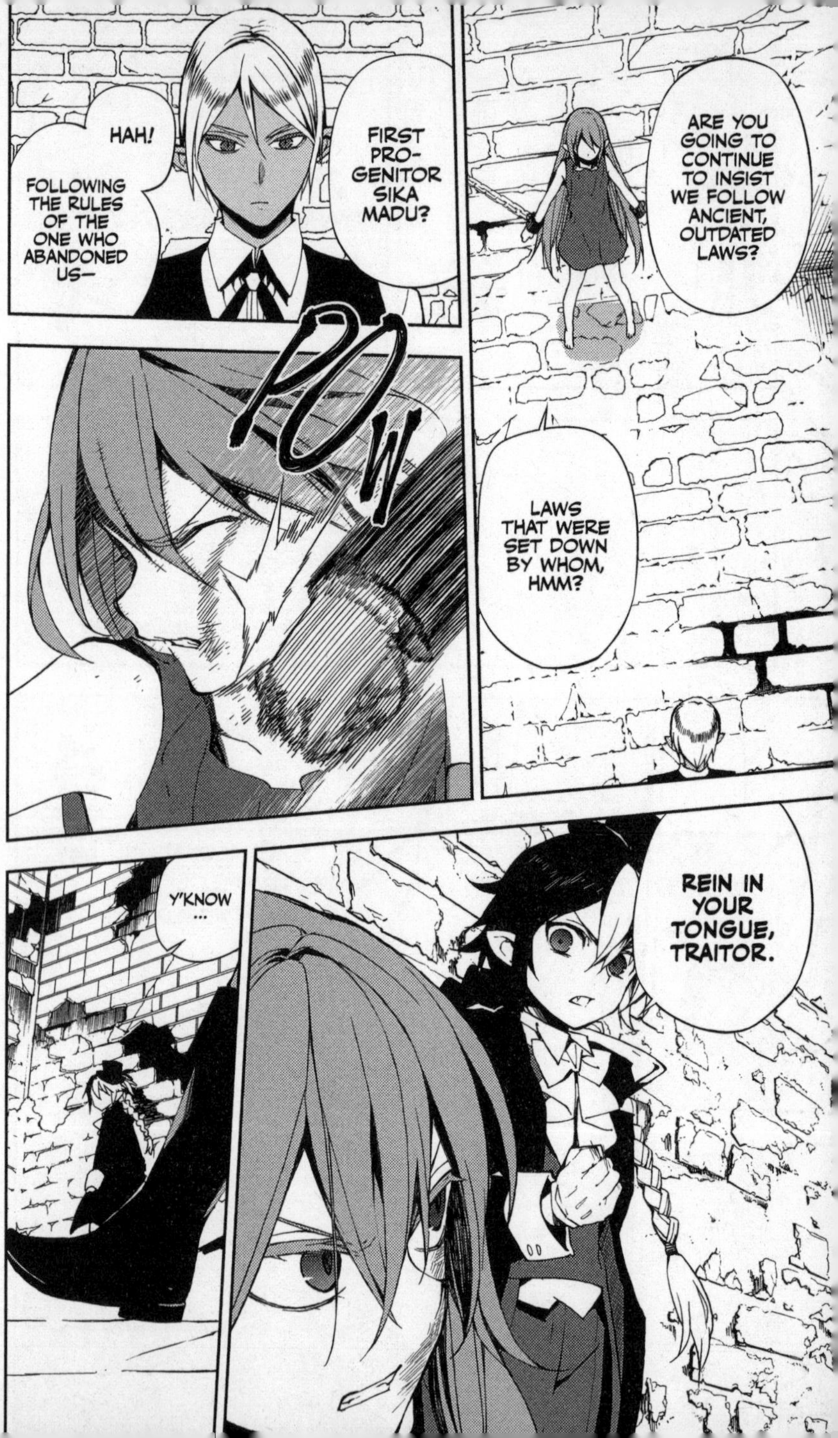

ARE YOU GOING TO CONTINUE TO INSIST WE FOLLOW ANCIENT, OUTDATED LAWS?
LAWS THAT WERE SET DOWN BY WHOM, HMM?
FIRST PRO-GENITOR SIKA MADU?
HAH!
FOLLOWING THE RULES OF THE ONE WHO ABANDONED US—
POW
REIN IN YOUR TONGUE, TRAITOR.
Y'KNOW ...

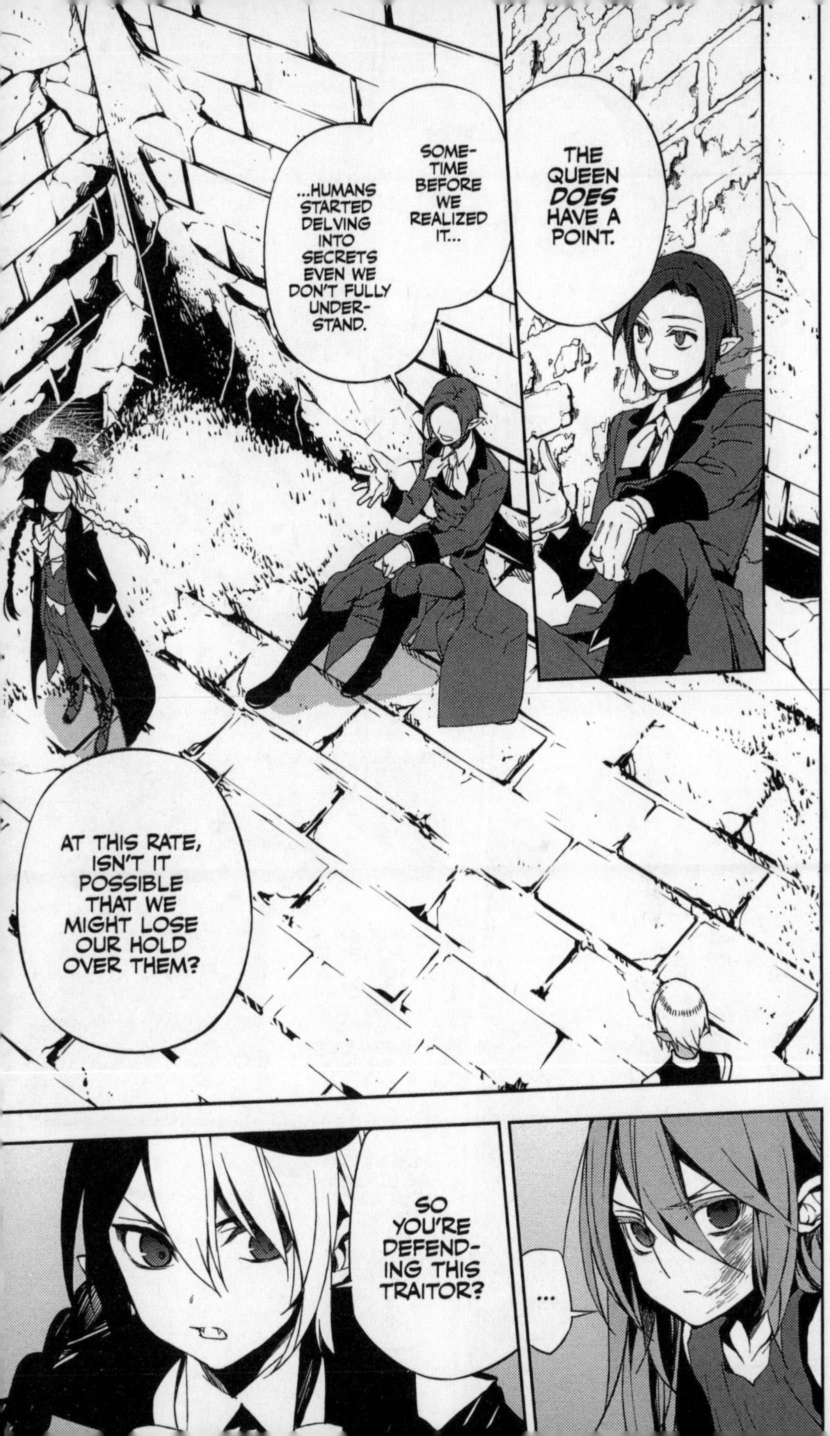
THE QUEEN *DOES* HAVE A POINT.
SOME-TIME BEFORE WE REALIZED IT...
...HUMANS STARTED DELVING INTO SECRETS EVEN WE DON'T FULLY UNDER-STAND.
AT THIS RATE, ISN'T IT POSSIBLE THAT WE MIGHT LOSE OUR HOLD OVER THEM?
...
SO YOU'RE DEFEND-ING THIS TRAITOR?

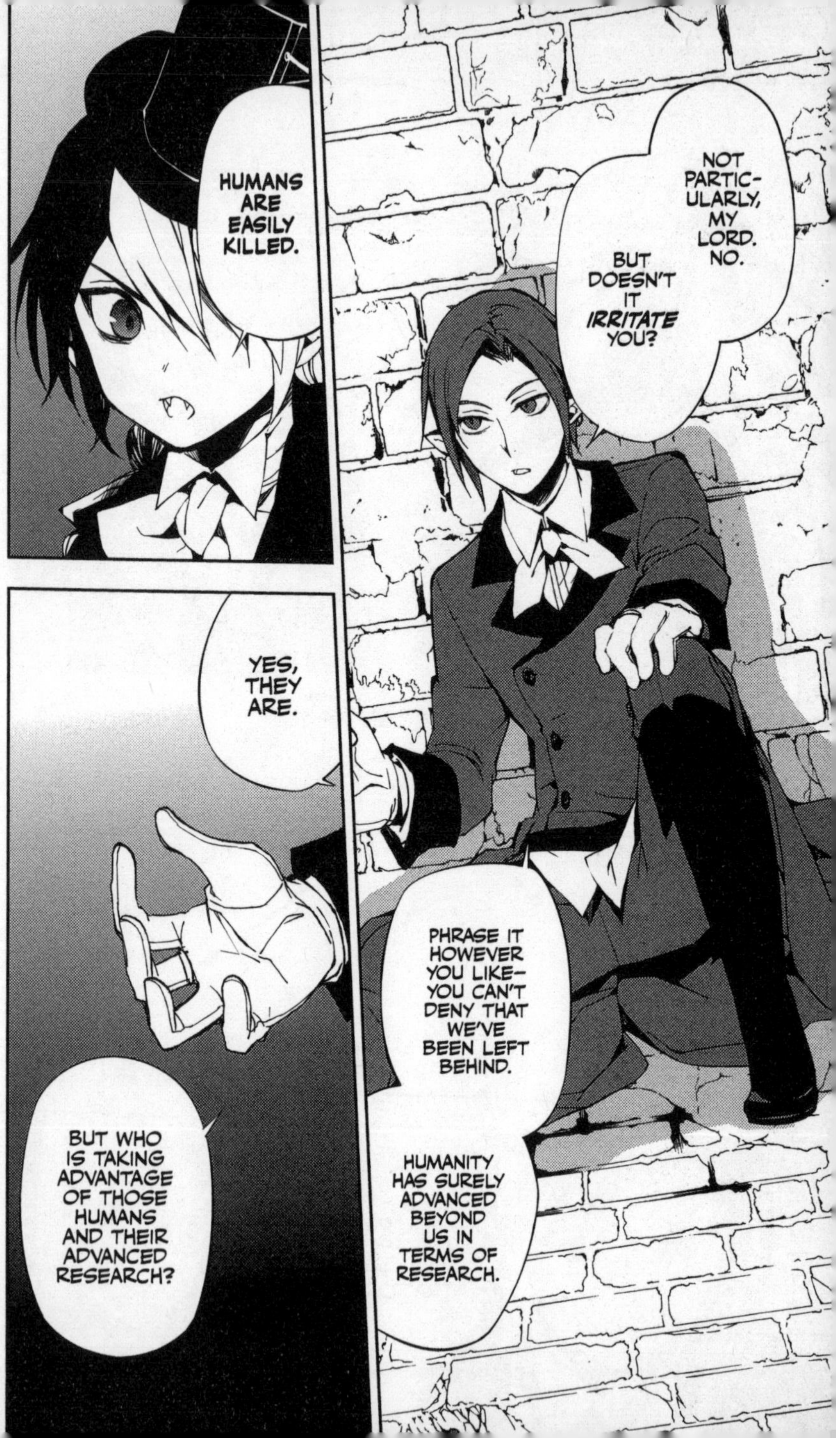
NOT PARTICULARLY, MY LORD. NO.
BUT DOESN'T IT *IRRITATE* YOU?
PHRASE IT HOWEVER YOU LIKE— YOU CAN'T DENY THAT WE'VE BEEN LEFT BEHIND.
HUMANITY HAS SURELY ADVANCED BEYOND US IN TERMS OF RESEARCH.
HUMANS ARE EASILY KILLED.
YES, THEY ARE.
BUT WHO IS TAKING ADVANTAGE OF THOSE HUMANS AND THEIR ADVANCED RESEARCH?

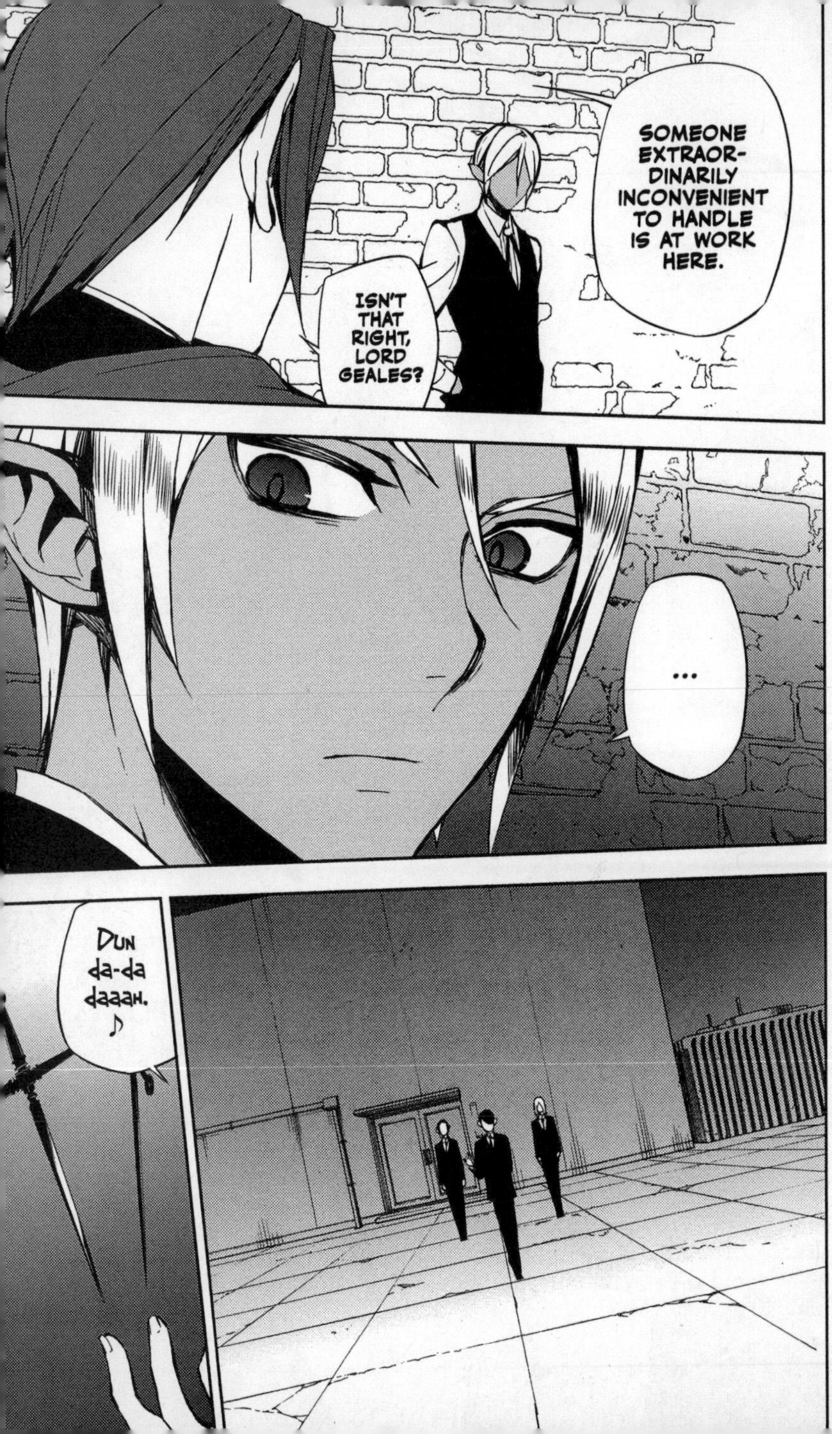
SOMEONE EXTRAOR-DINARILY INCONVENIENT TO HANDLE IS AT WORK HERE.
ISN'T THAT RIGHT, LORD GEALES?
...
Dun da-da daaah. ♪

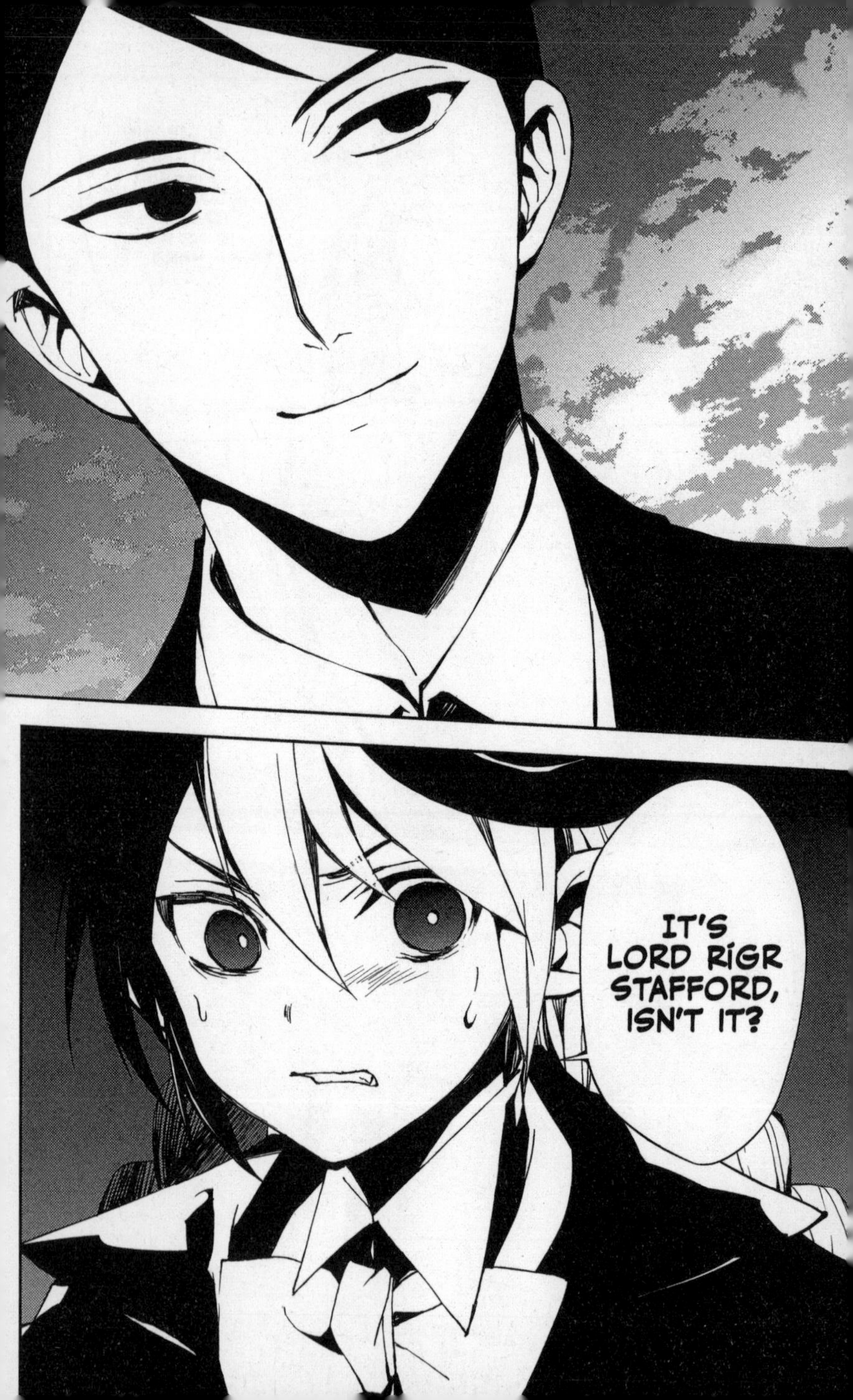
IT'S LORD RIGR STAFFORD, ISN'T IT?

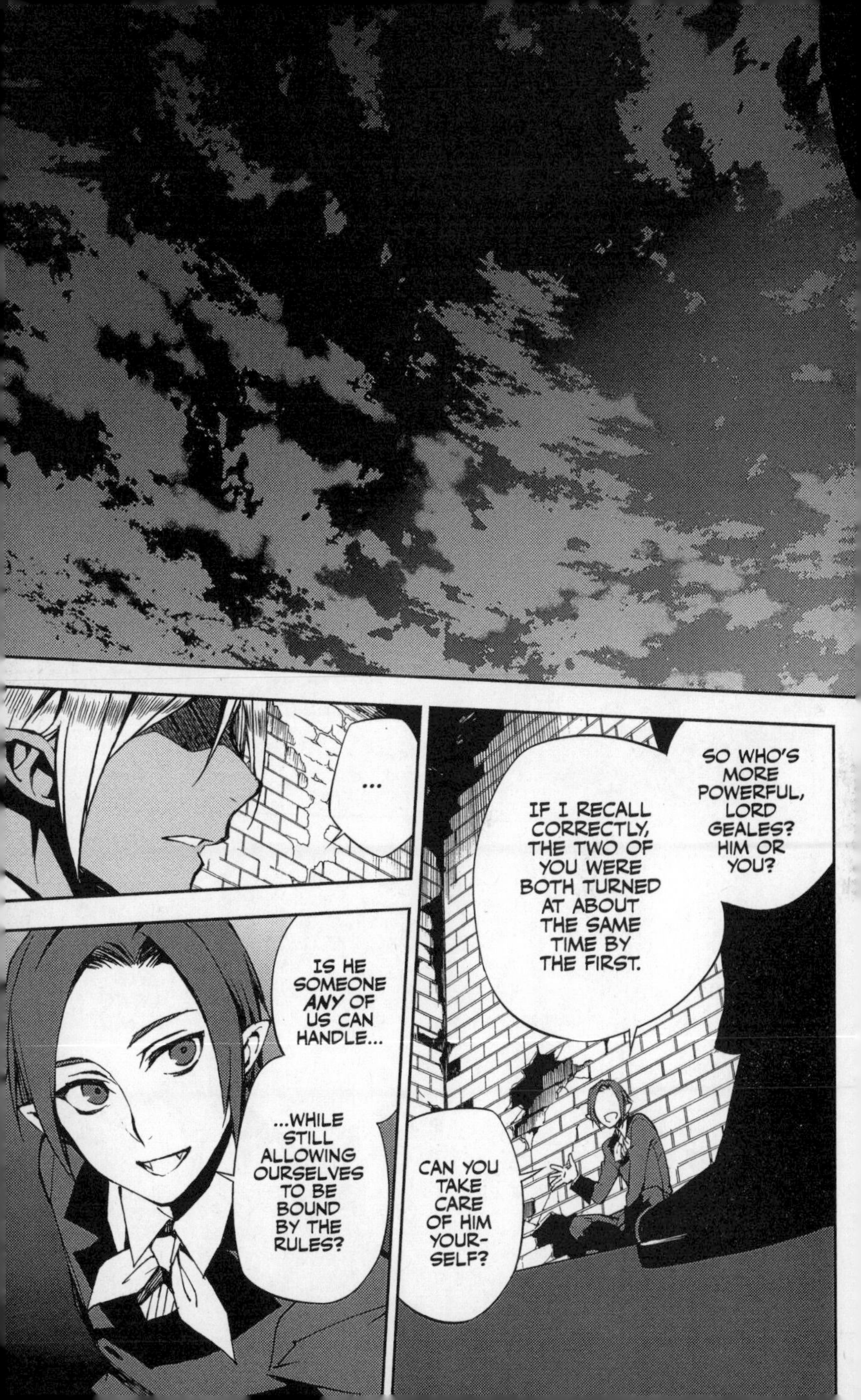
SO WHO'S MORE POWERFUL, LORD GEALES? HIM OR YOU?
IF I RECALL CORRECTLY, THE TWO OF YOU WERE BOTH TURNED AT ABOUT THE SAME TIME BY THE FIRST.
CAN YOU TAKE CARE OF HIM YOURSELF?
...
IS HE SOMEONE *ANY* OF US CAN HANDLE...
...WHILE STILL ALLOWING OURSELVES TO BE BOUND BY THE RULES?

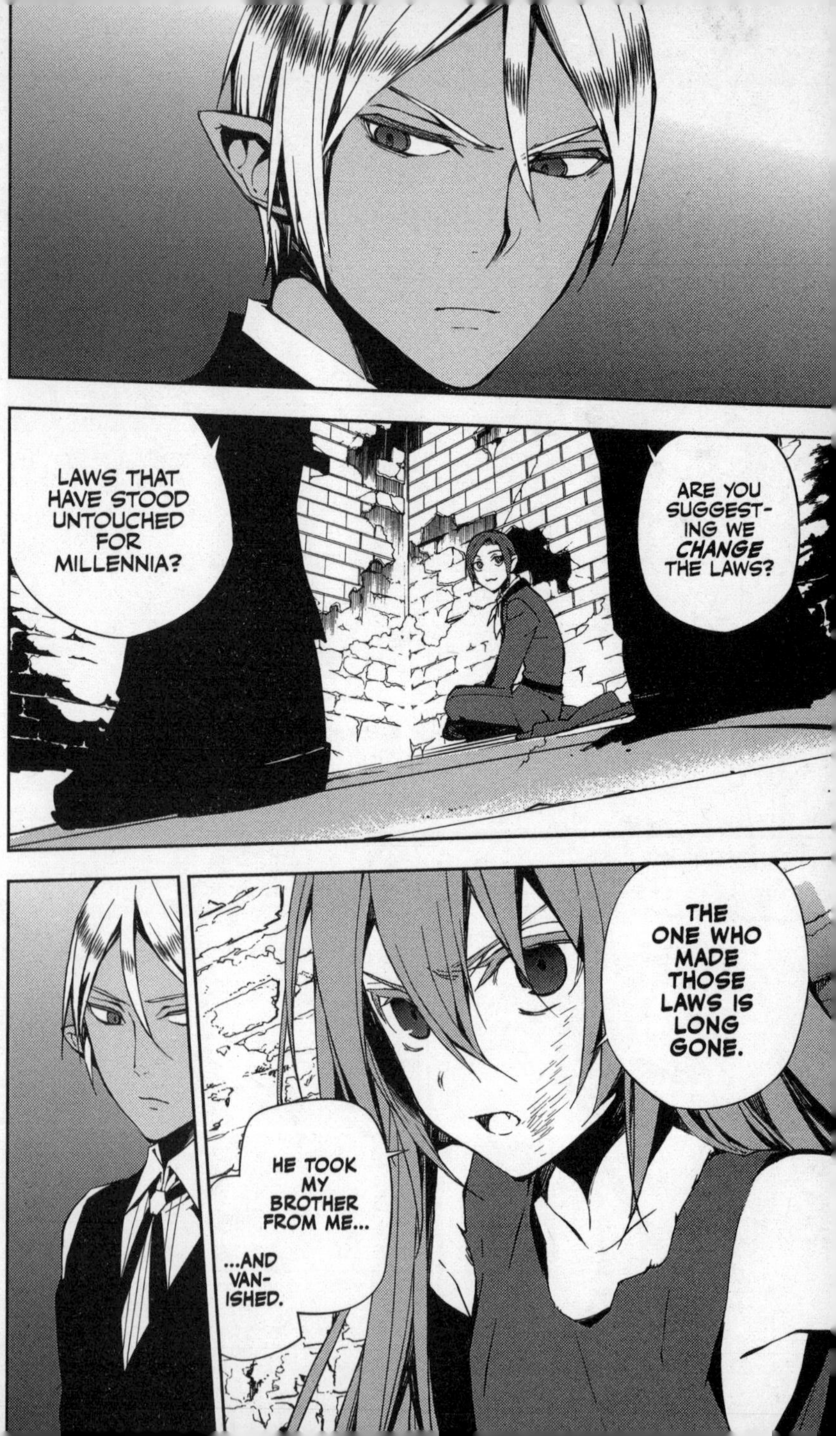

ARE YOU SUGGEST-ING WE *CHANGE* THE LAWS?
LAWS THAT HAVE STOOD UNTOUCHED FOR MILLENNIA?
THE ONE WHO MADE THOSE LAWS IS LONG GONE.
HE TOOK MY BROTHER FROM ME...
...AND VAN-ISHED.

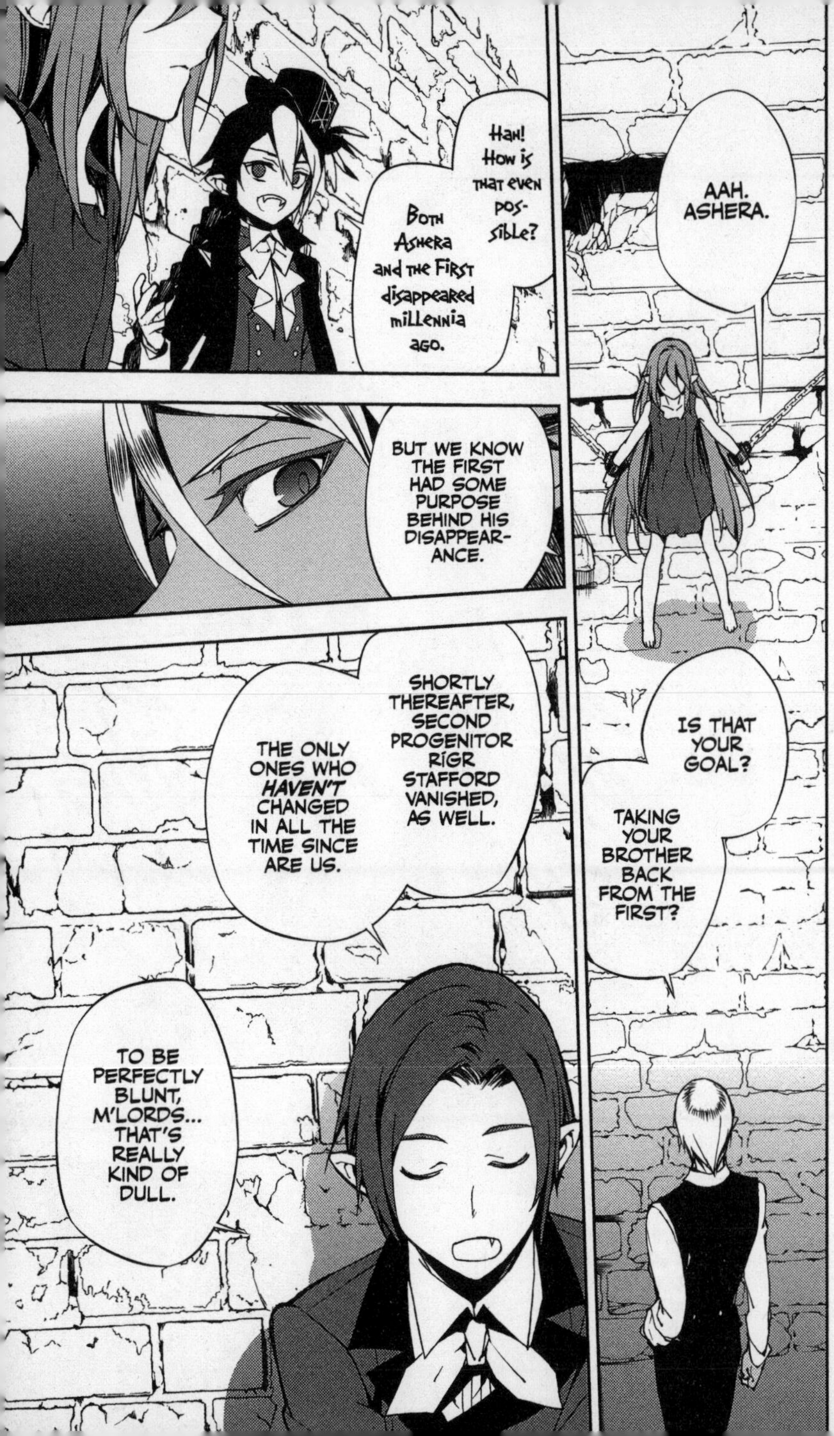
AAH. ASHERA.
IS THAT YOUR GOAL?
TAKING YOUR BROTHER BACK FROM THE FIRST?
HAH! HOW IS THAT EVEN POSSIBLE?
BOTH ASHERA AND THE FIRST DISAPPEARED MILLENNIA AGO.
BUT WE KNOW THE FIRST HAD SOME PURPOSE BEHIND HIS DISAPPEARANCE.
SHORTLY THEREAFTER, SECOND PROGENITOR RIGR STAFFORD VANISHED, AS WELL.
THE ONLY ONES WHO *HAVEN'T* CHANGED IN ALL THE TIME SINCE ARE US.
TO BE PERFECTLY BLUNT, M'LORDS... THAT'S REALLY KIND OF DULL.

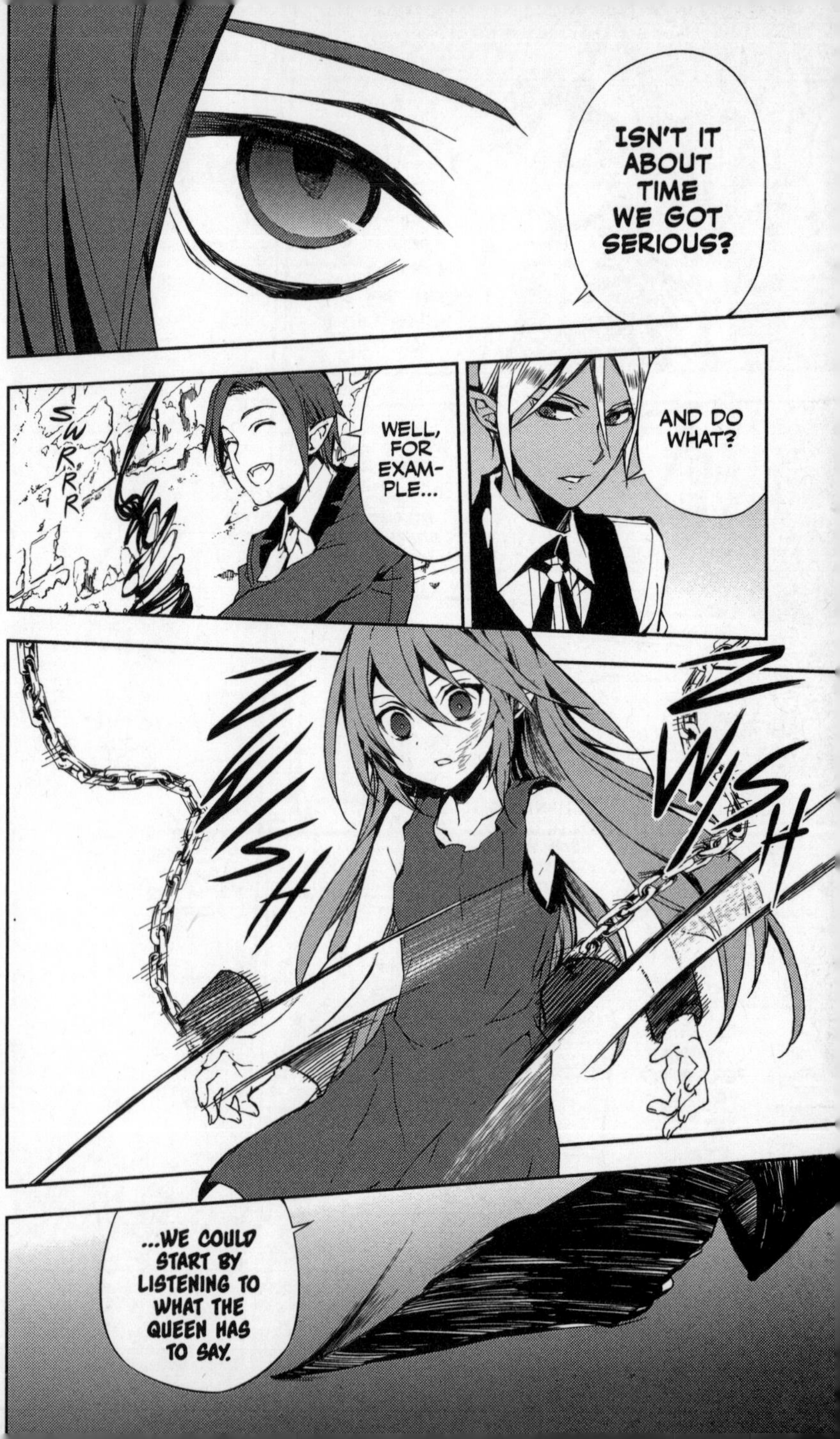
ISN'T IT ABOUT TIME WE GOT SERIOUS?
AND DO WHAT?
WELL, FOR EXAM-PLE...
SWRRR
ZWISH!
ZWISH
...WE COULD START BY LISTENING TO WHAT THE QUEEN HAS TO SAY.

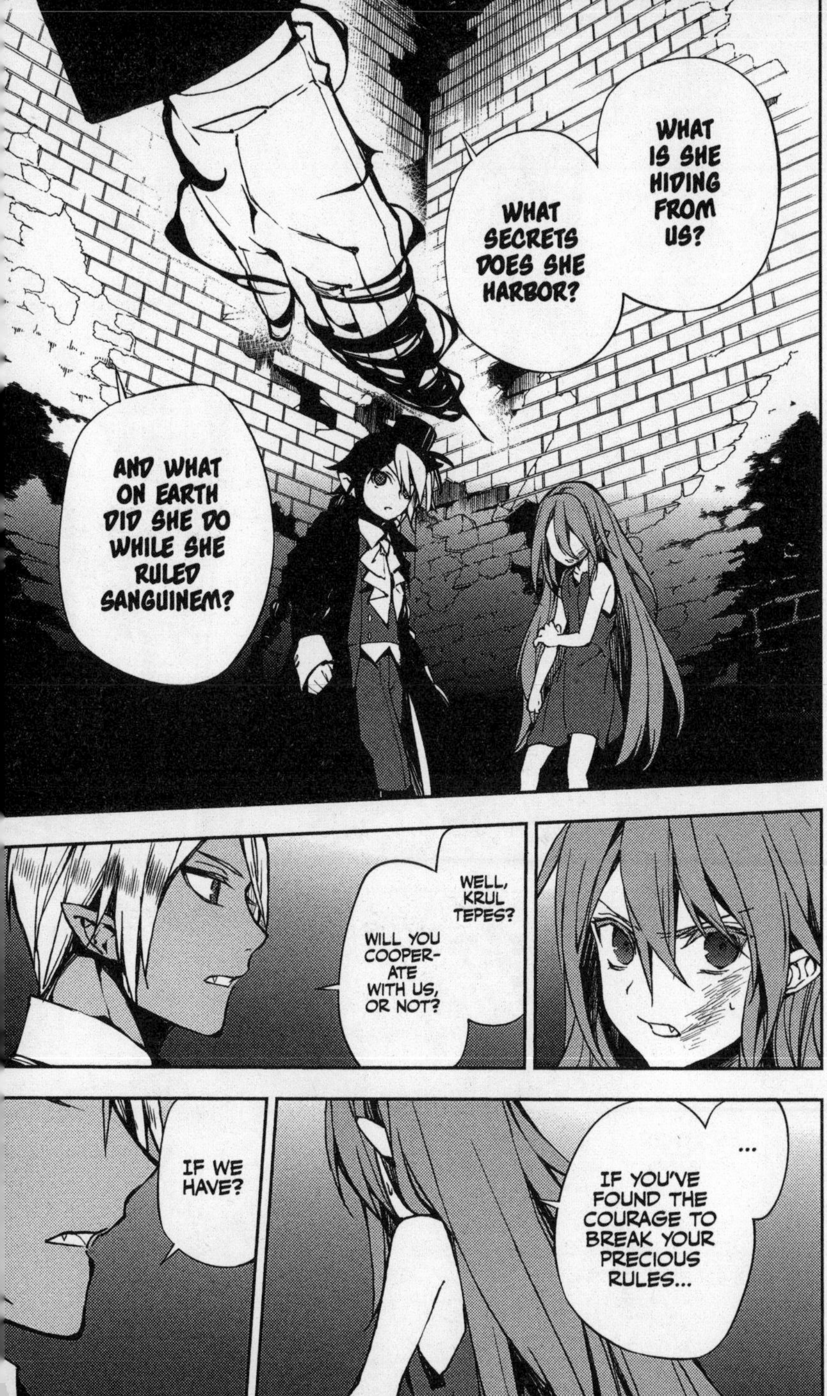
WHAT IS SHE HIDING FROM US?
WHAT SECRETS DOES SHE HARBOR?
AND WHAT ON EARTH DID SHE DO WHILE SHE RULED SANGUINEM?
WELL, KRUL TEPES?
WILL YOU COOPER-ATE WITH US, OR NOT?
...
IF YOU'VE FOUND THE COURAGE TO BREAK YOUR PRECIOUS RULES...
IF WE HAVE?

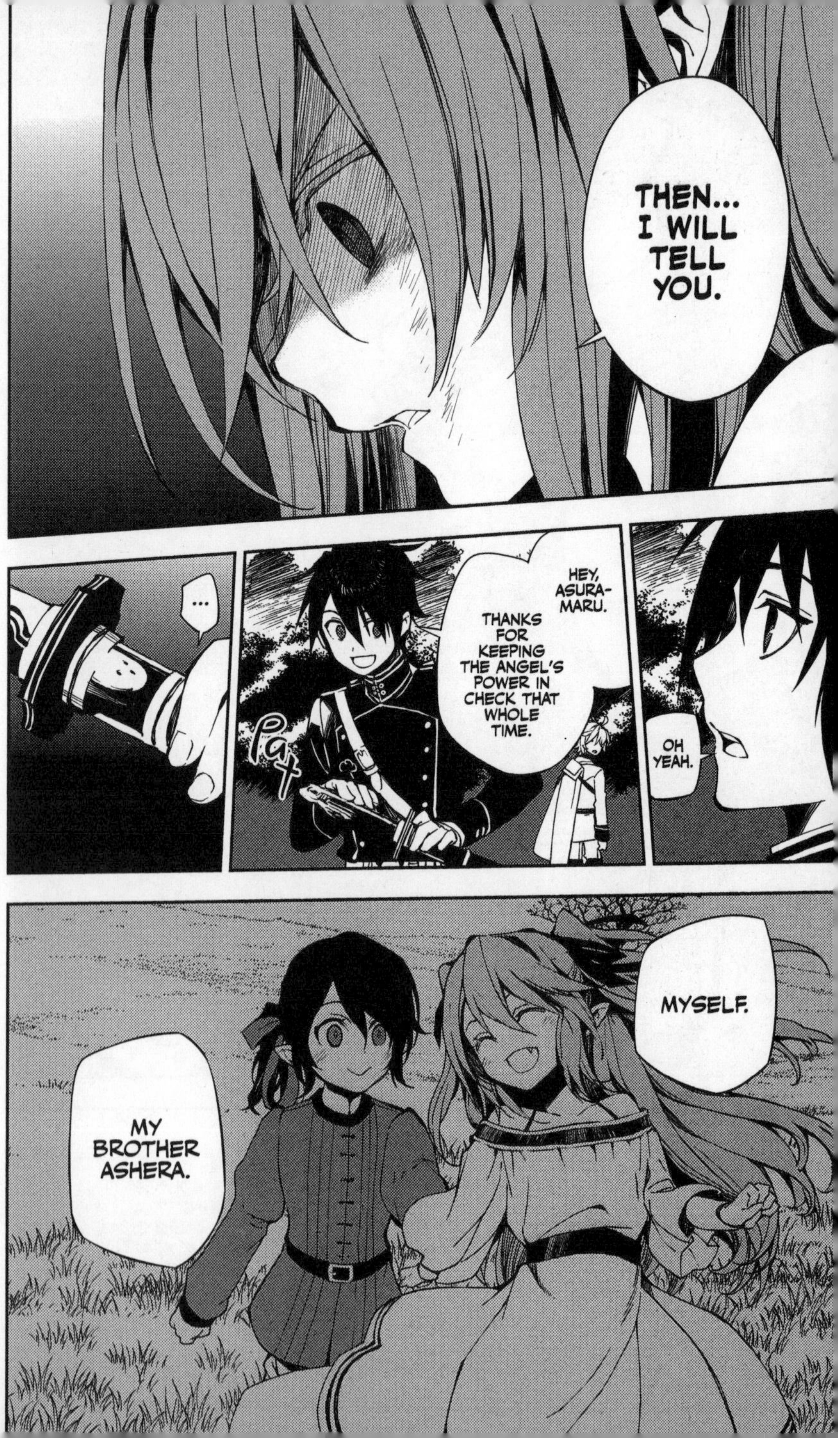
THEN... I WILL TELL YOU.
OH YEAH.
HEY, ASURA-MARU.
THANKS FOR KEEPING THE ANGEL'S POWER IN CHECK THAT WHOLE TIME.
Pat
...
MYSELF.
MY BROTHER ASHERA.

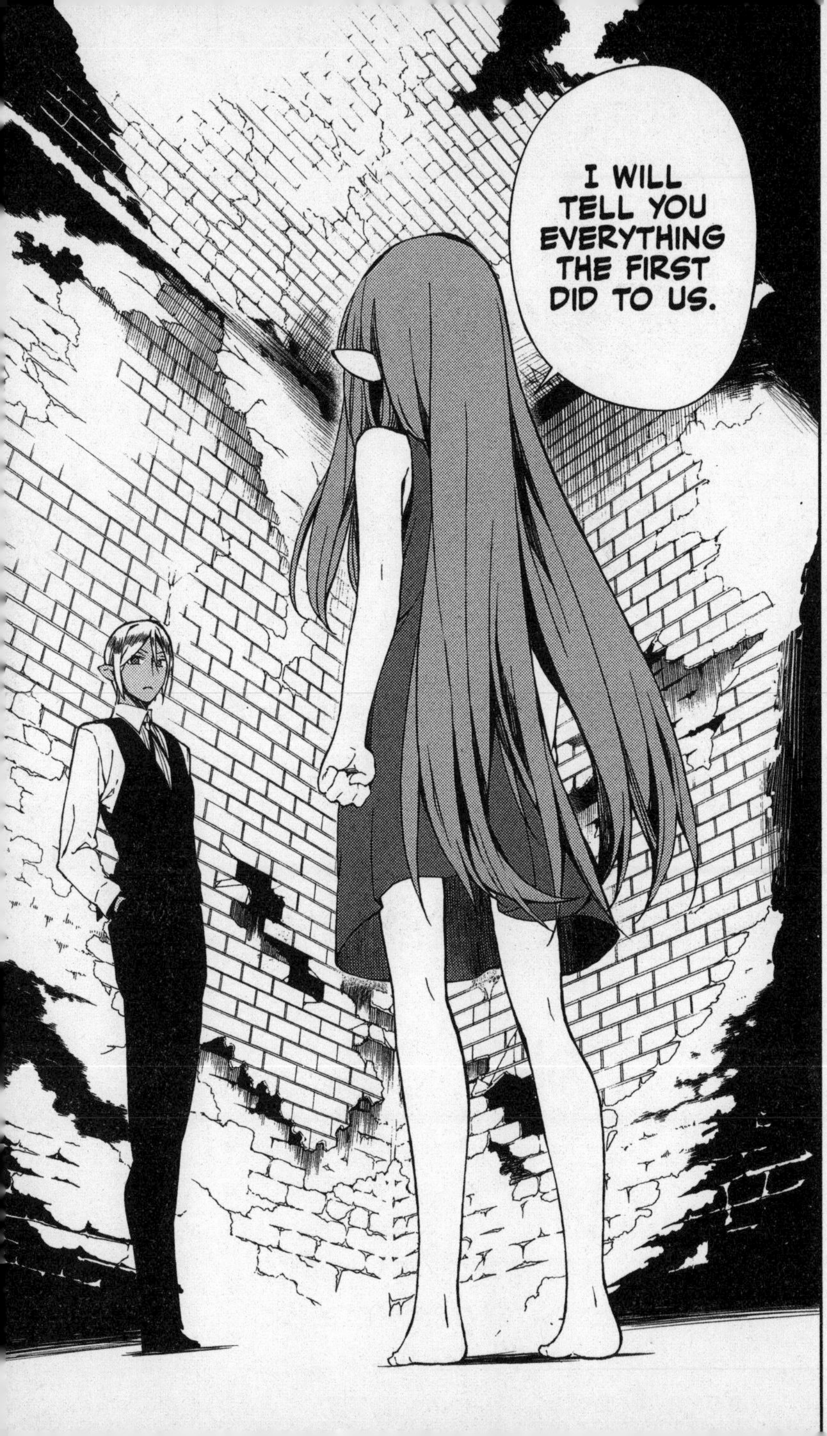
I WILL TELL YOU EVERYTHING THE FIRST DID TO US.

Seraph of the End

VAMPIRE REIGN

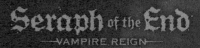

Chapter 69
The Day the Sun Was Lost

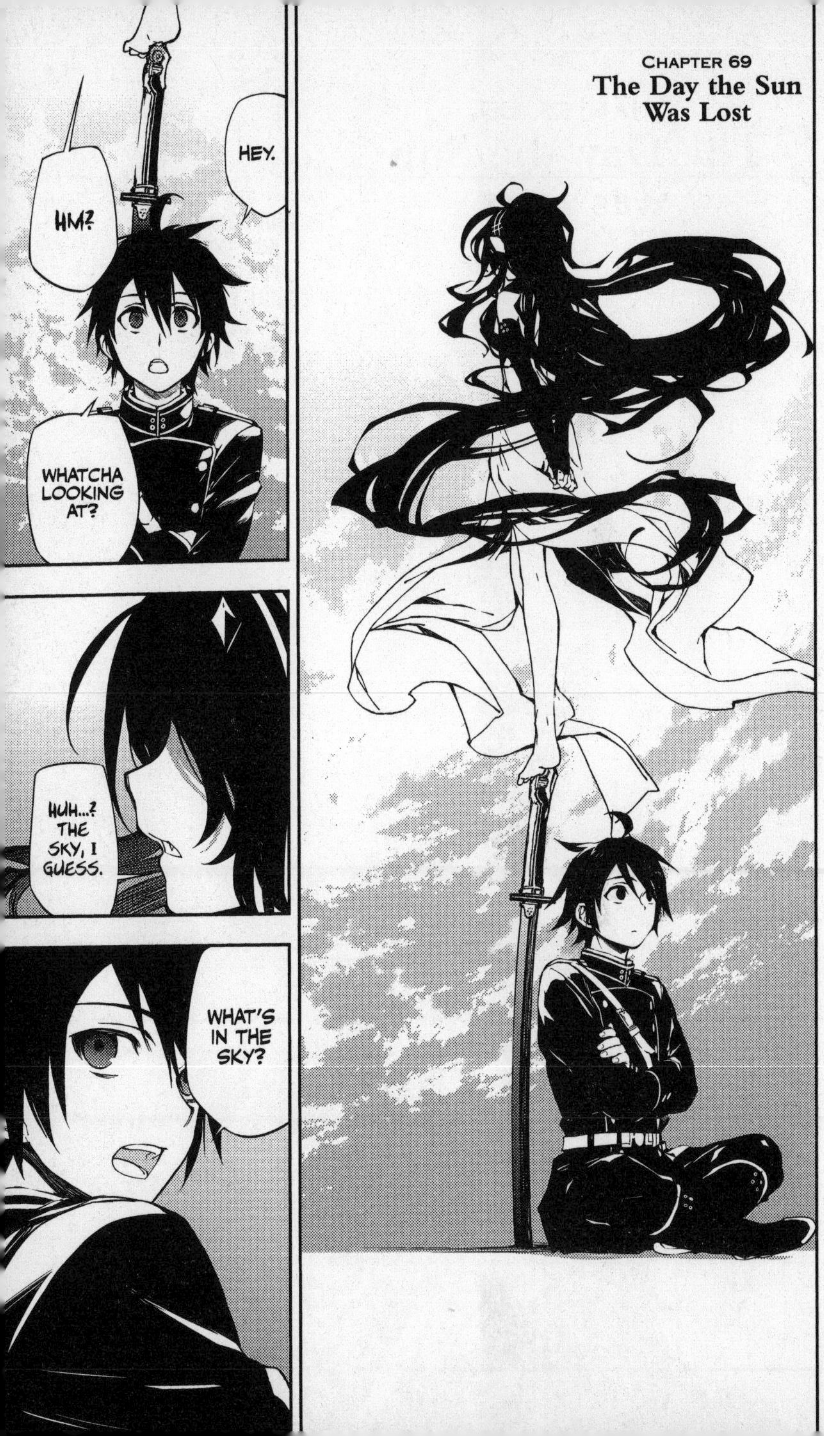
HEY.
HM?
WHATCHA LOOKING AT?
HUH...? THE SKY, I GUESS.
WHAT'S IN THE SKY?

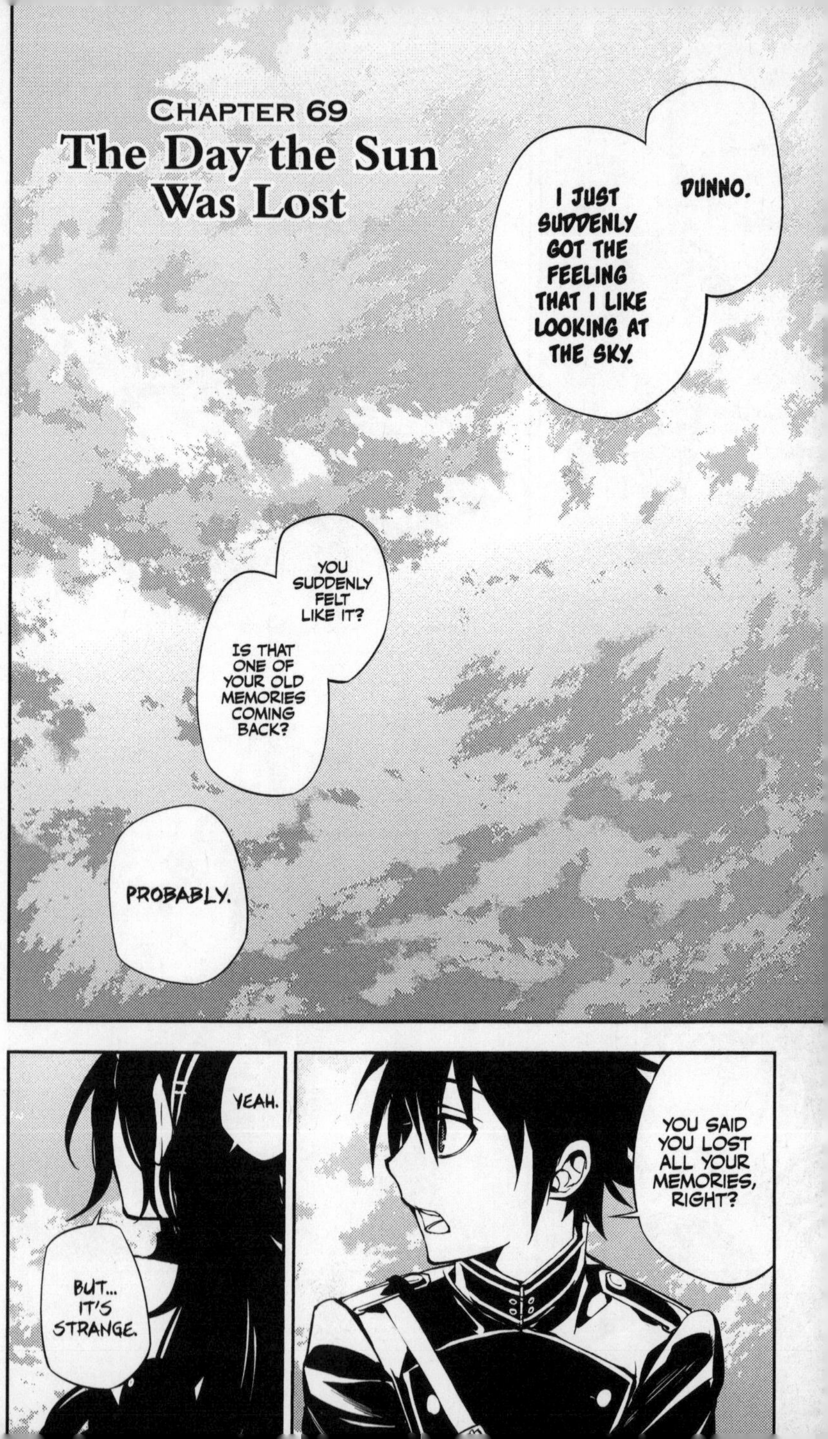
CHAPTER 69
The Day the Sun Was Lost
DUNNO.
I JUST SUDDENLY GOT THE FEELING THAT I LIKE LOOKING AT THE SKY.
YOU SUDDENLY FELT LIKE IT?
IS THAT ONE OF YOUR OLD MEMORIES COMING BACK?
PROBABLY.
YOU SAID YOU LOST ALL YOUR MEMORIES, RIGHT?
YEAH.
BUT... IT'S STRANGE.

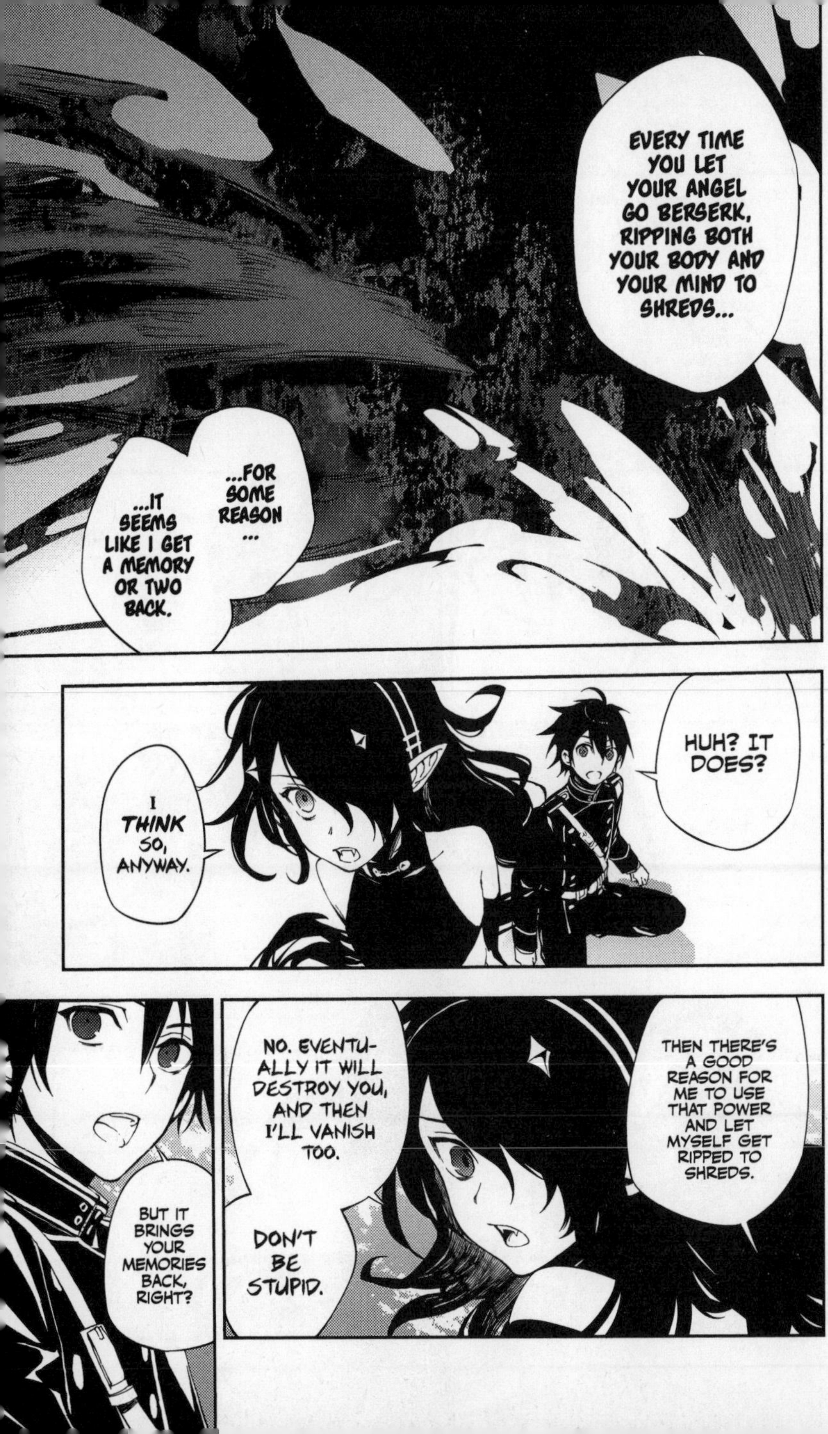
EVERY TIME YOU LET YOUR ANGEL GO BERSERK, RIPPING BOTH YOUR BODY AND YOUR MIND TO SHREDS...
...FOR SOME REASON...
...IT SEEMS LIKE I GET A MEMORY OR TWO BACK.
HUH? IT DOES?
I THINK SO, ANYWAY.
THEN THERE'S A GOOD REASON FOR ME TO USE THAT POWER AND LET MYSELF GET RIPPED TO SHREDS.
NO. EVENTUALLY IT WILL DESTROY YOU, AND THEN I'LL VANISH TOO.
DON'T BE STUPID.
BUT IT BRINGS YOUR MEMORIES BACK, RIGHT?

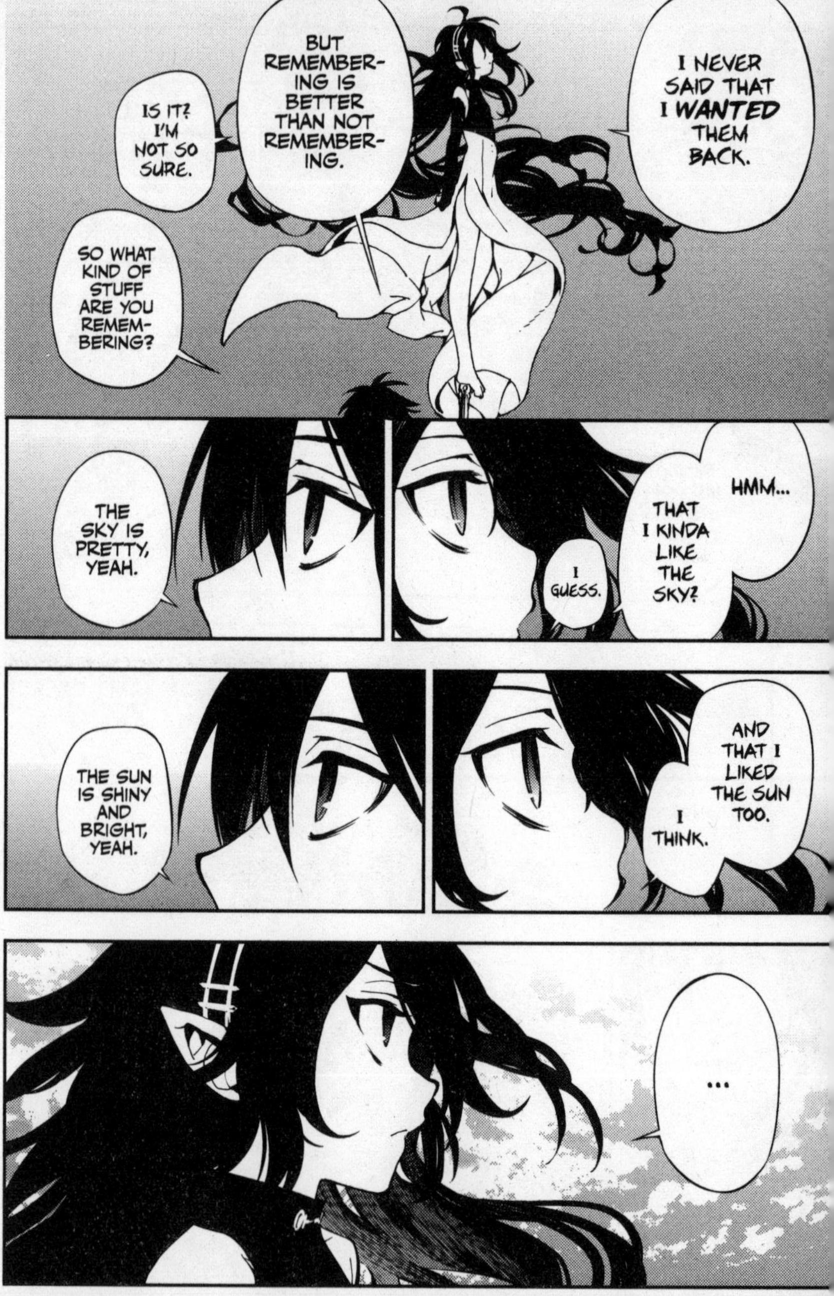
I NEVER SAID THAT I WANTED THEM BACK.
BUT REMEMBERING IS BETTER THAN NOT REMEMBERING.
IS IT? I'M NOT SO SURE.
SO WHAT KIND OF STUFF ARE YOU REMEMBERING?
HMM... THAT I KINDA LIKE THE SKY?
I GUESS.
THE SKY IS PRETTY, YEAH.
AND THAT I LIKED THE SUN TOO.
I THINK.
THE SUN IS SHINY AND BRIGHT, YEAH.
...

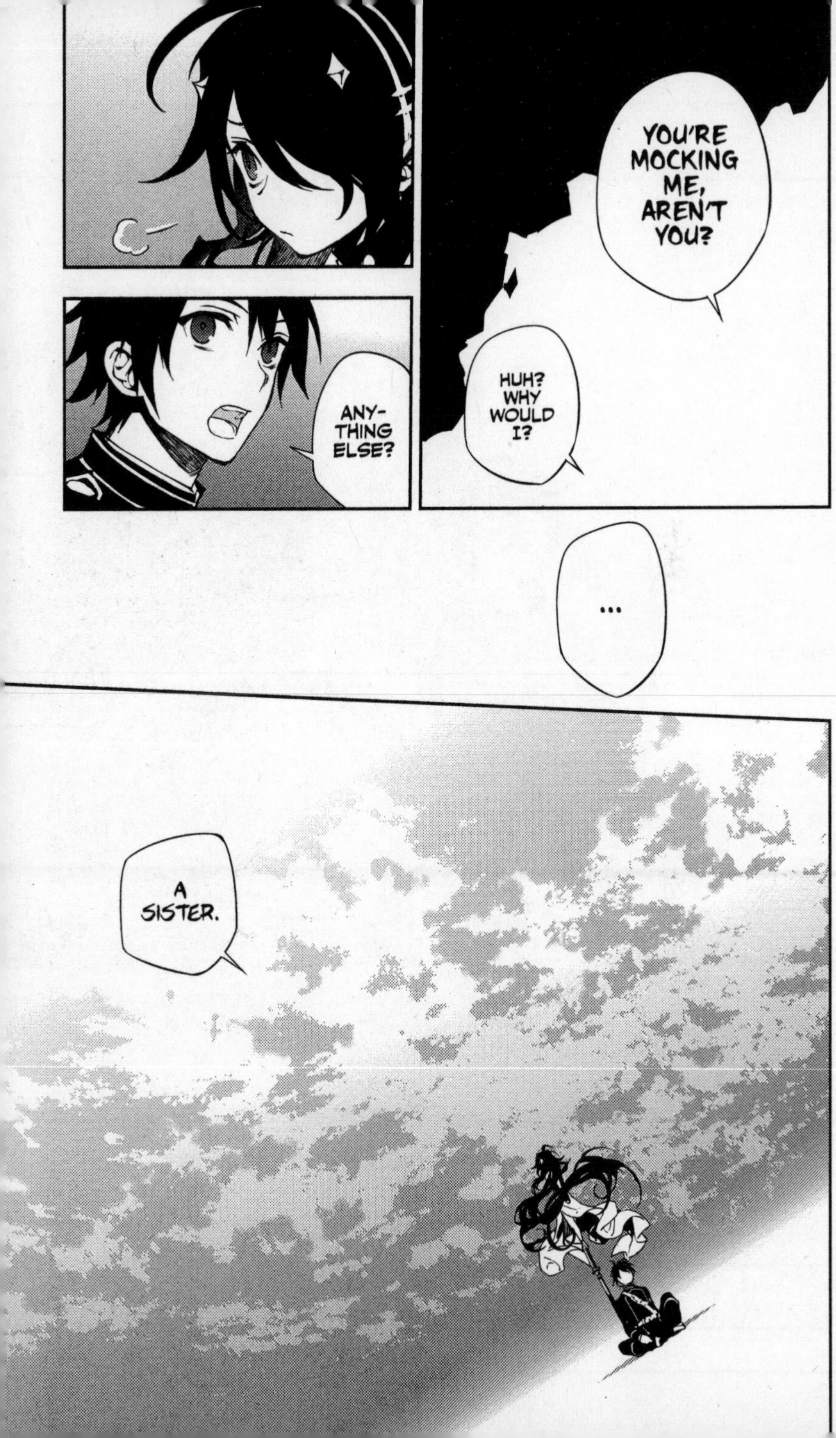
YOU'RE MOCKING ME, AREN'T YOU?
HUH? WHY WOULD I?
ANY-THING ELSE?
...
A SISTER.

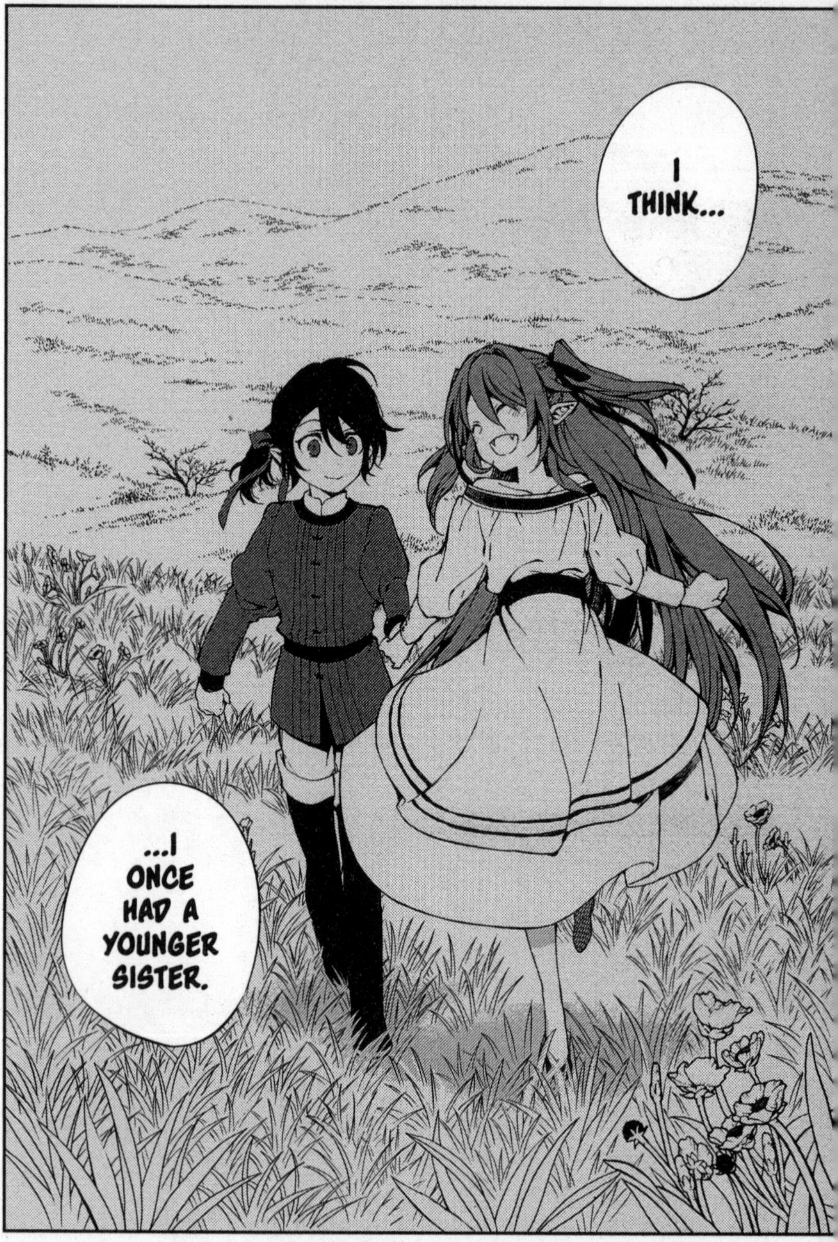
I THINK...
...I ONCE HAD A YOUNGER SISTER.

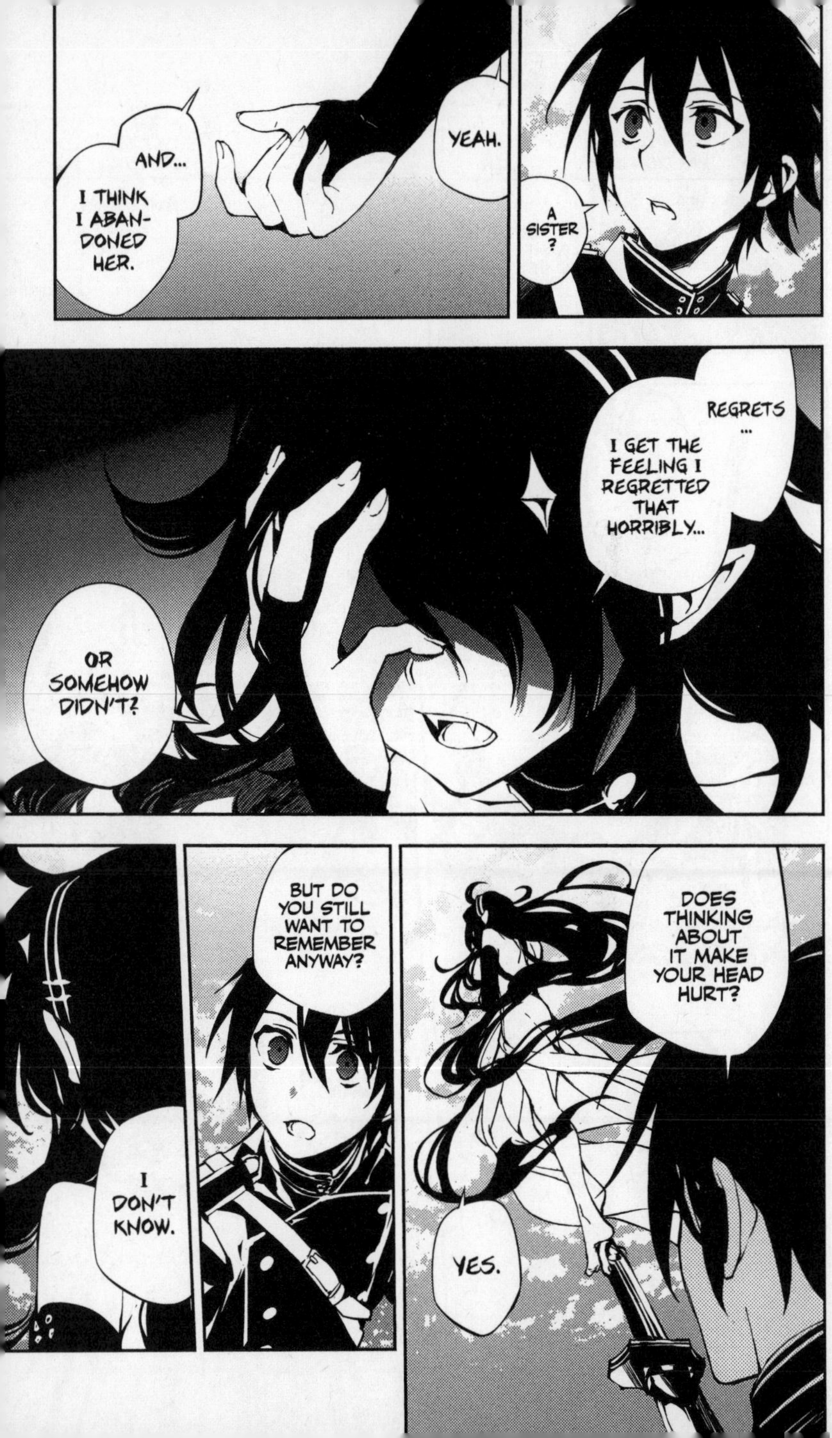
A SISTER?
YEAH.
AND... I THINK I ABANDONED HER.
REGRETS... I GET THE FEELING I REGRETTED THAT HORRIBLY...
OR SOMEHOW DIDN'T?
DOES THINKING ABOUT IT MAKE YOUR HEAD HURT?
YES.
BUT DO YOU STILL WANT TO REMEMBER ANYWAY?
I DON'T KNOW.

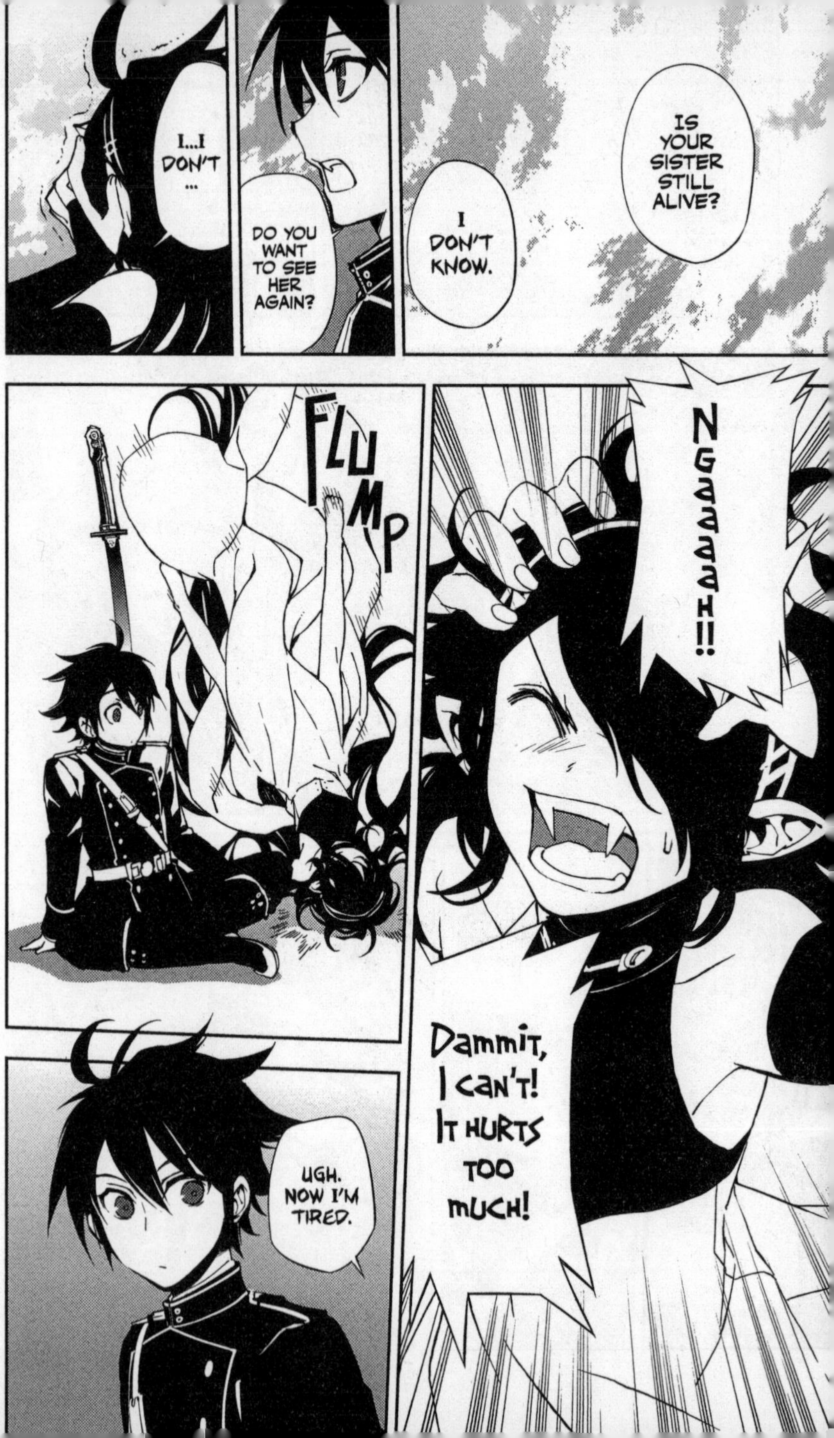
IS YOUR SISTER STILL ALIVE?
I DON'T KNOW.
DO YOU WANT TO SEE HER AGAIN?
I...I DON'T ...
NGAAAAAH!!
Dammit, I can't! It hurts too much!
FLUMP
UGH. NOW I'M TIRED.

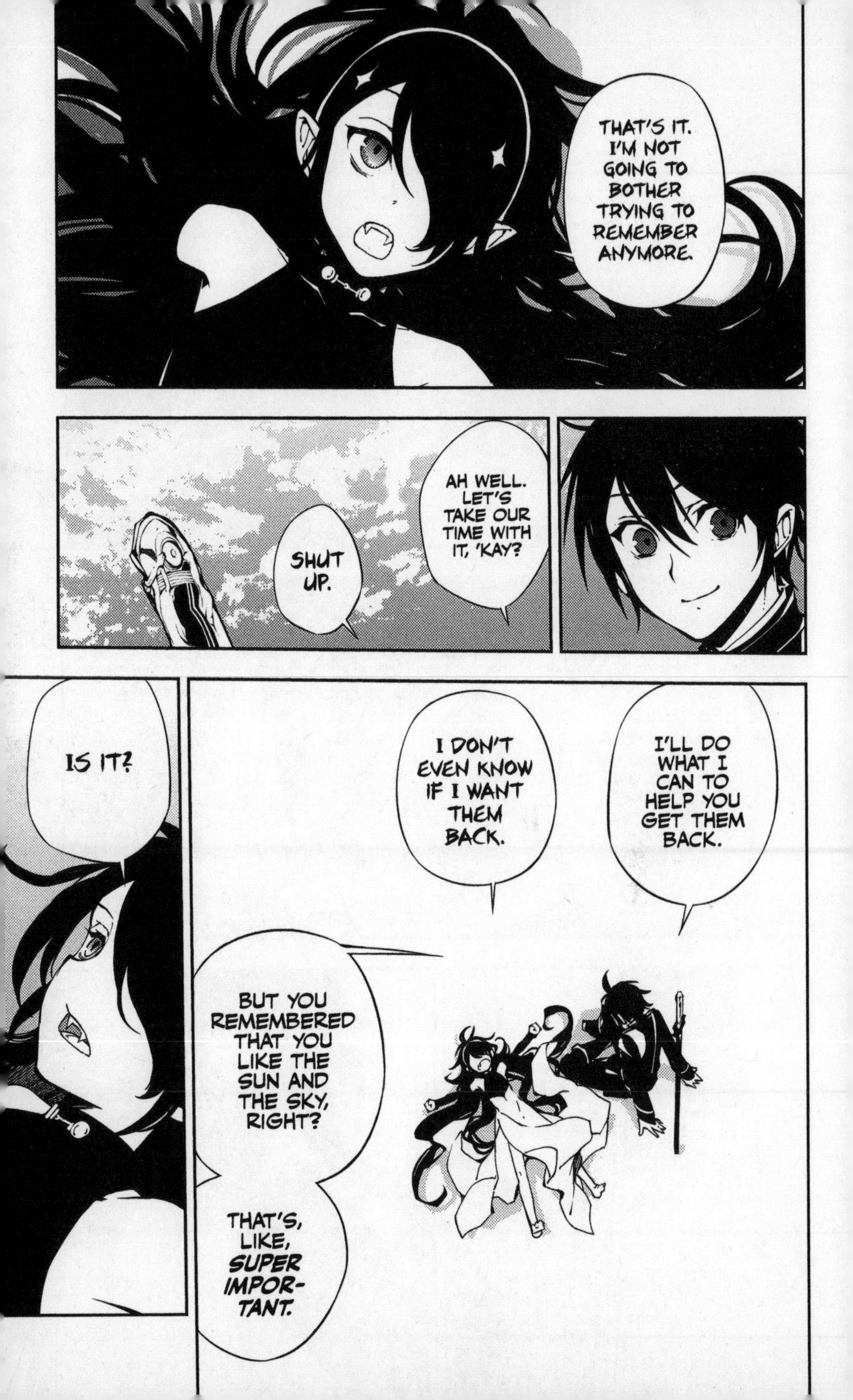
THAT'S IT. I'M NOT GOING TO BOTHER TRYING TO REMEMBER ANYMORE.
AH WELL. LET'S TAKE OUR TIME WITH IT, 'KAY?
SHUT UP.
I'LL DO WHAT I CAN TO HELP YOU GET THEM BACK.
I DON'T EVEN KNOW IF I WANT THEM BACK.
BUT YOU REMEMBERED THAT YOU LIKE THE SUN AND THE SKY, RIGHT?
THAT'S, LIKE, *SUPER IMPORTANT.*
IS IT?

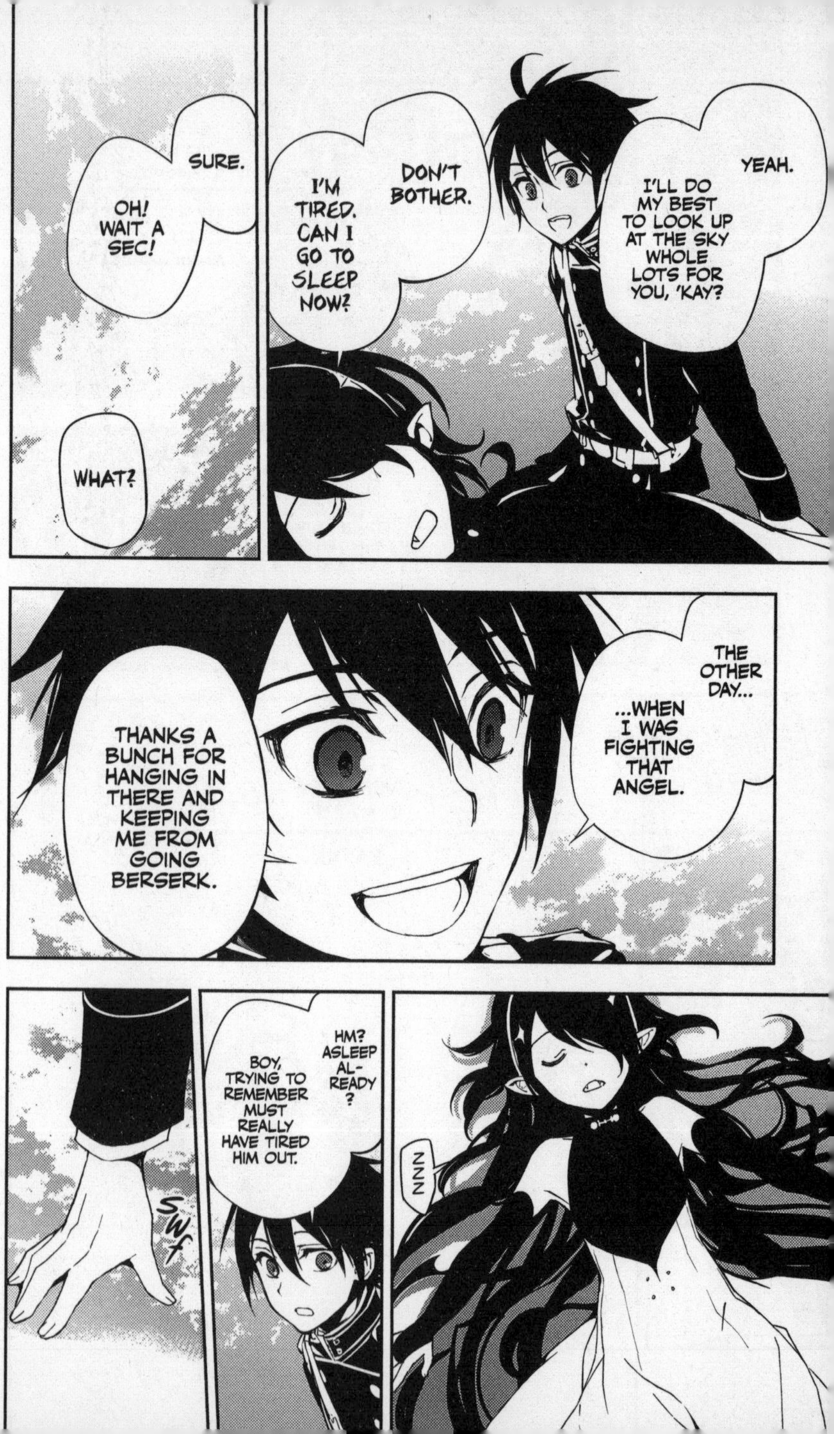

YEAH.
I'LL DO MY BEST TO LOOK UP AT THE SKY WHOLE LOTS FOR YOU, 'KAY?
DON'T BOTHER.
I'M TIRED. CAN I GO TO SLEEP NOW?
SURE.
OH! WAIT A SEC!
WHAT?
THE OTHER DAY...
...WHEN I WAS FIGHTING THAT ANGEL.
THANKS A BUNCH FOR HANGING IN THERE AND KEEPING ME FROM GOING BERSERK.
ZZZ
HM? ASLEEP AL-READY?
BOY, TRYING TO REMEMBER MUST REALLY HAVE TIRED HIM OUT.
SWF

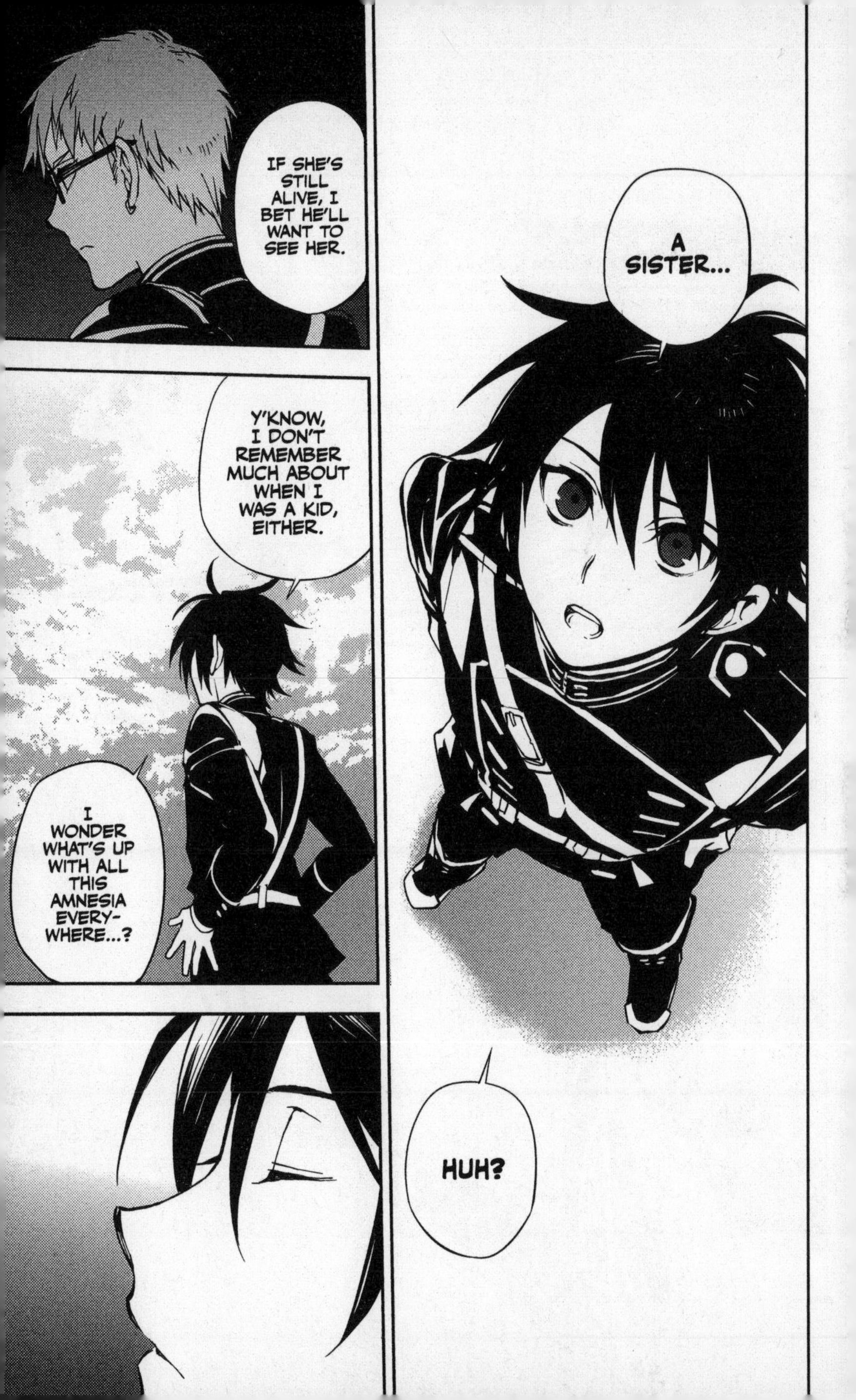
A SISTER...
HUH?
IF SHE'S STILL ALIVE, I BET HE'LL WANT TO SEE HER.
Y'KNOW, I DON'T REMEMBER MUCH ABOUT WHEN I WAS A KID, EITHER.
I WONDER WHAT'S UP WITH ALL THIS AMNESIA EVERY-WHERE...?

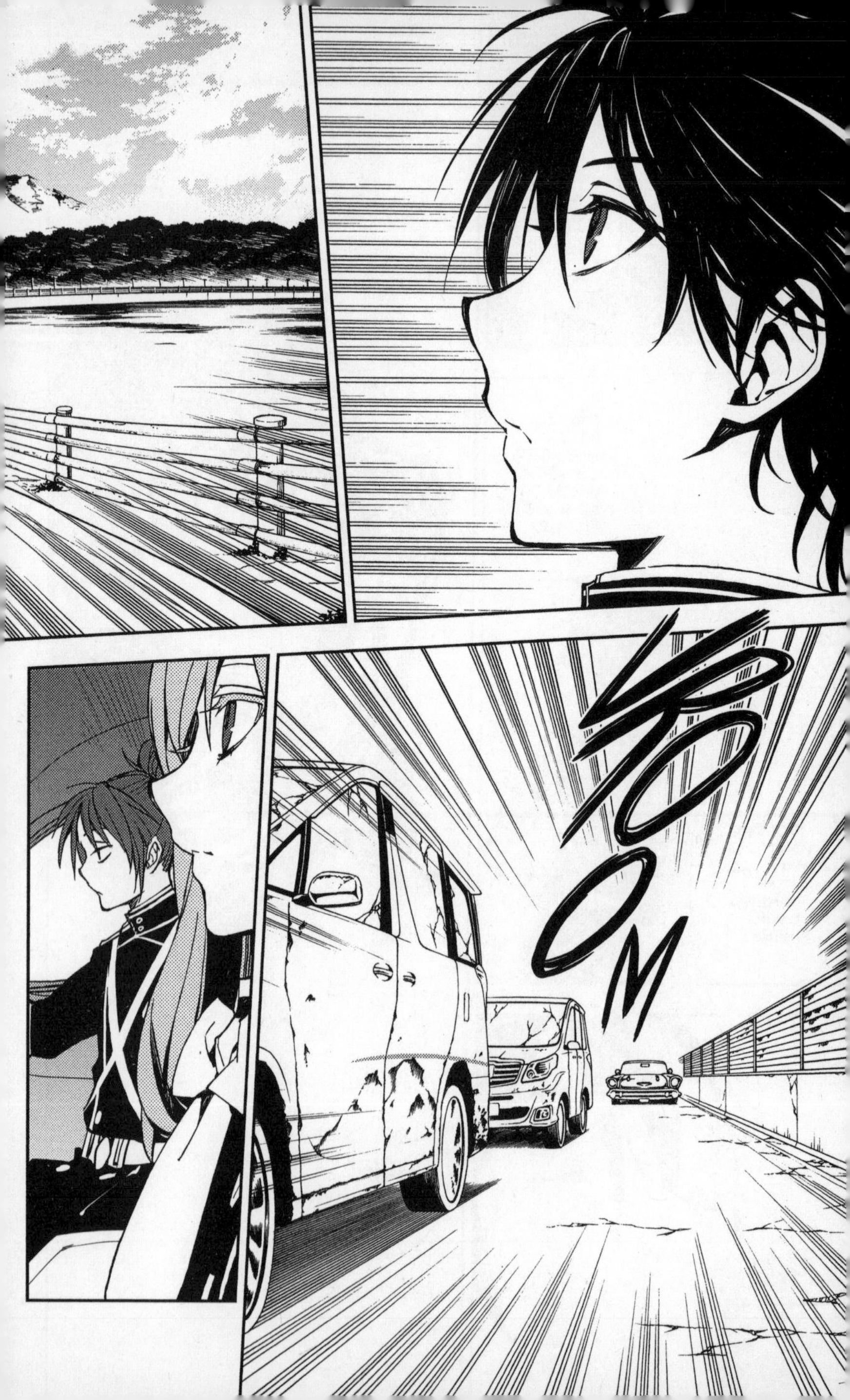
VROOOM

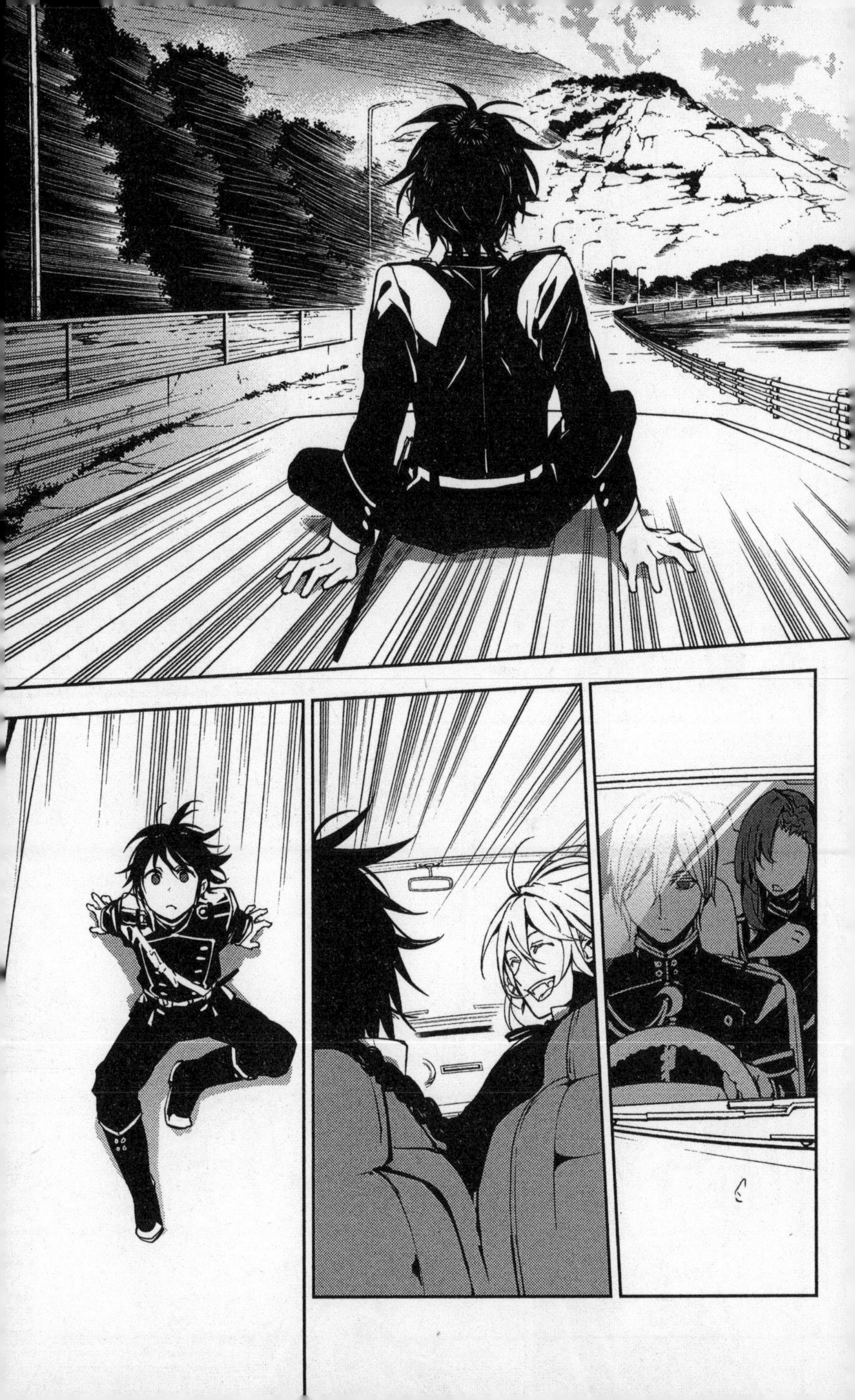

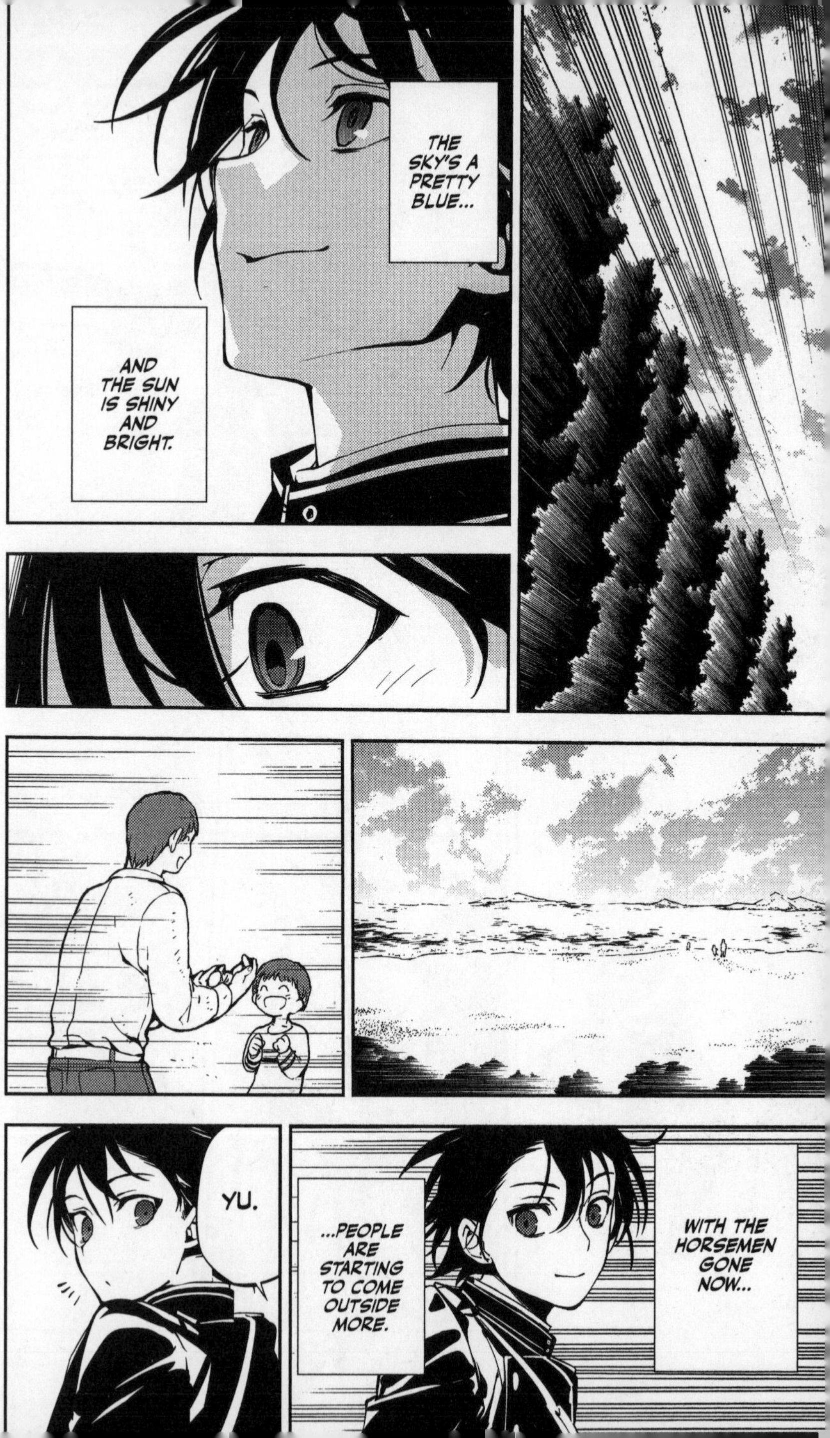
THE SKY'S A PRETTY BLUE...
AND THE SUN IS SHINY AND BRIGHT.
WITH THE HORSEMEN GONE NOW...
...PEOPLE ARE STARTING TO COME OUTSIDE MORE.
YU.

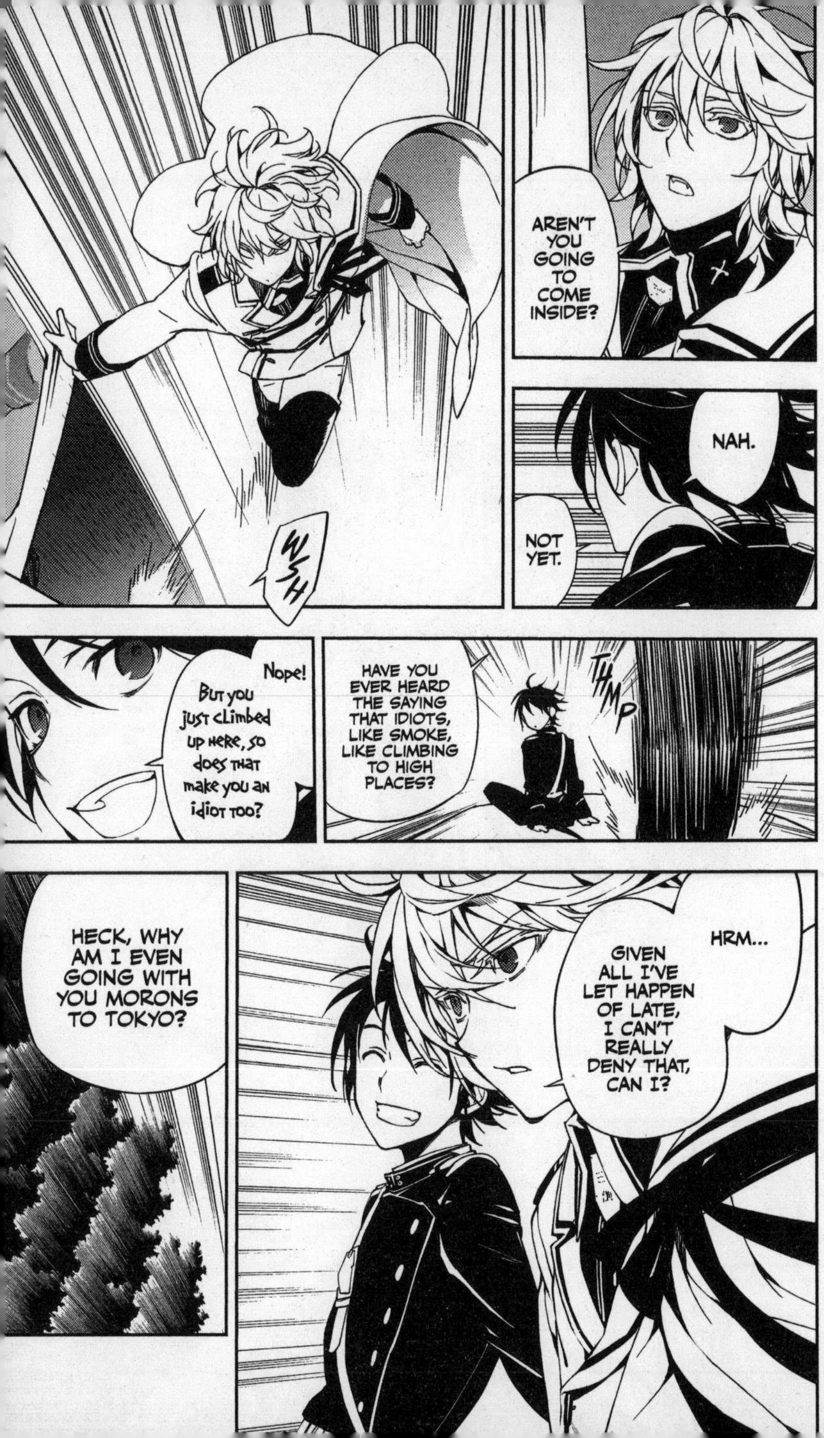
AREN'T YOU GOING TO COME INSIDE?
NAH.
NOT YET.
WSH
THMP
HAVE YOU EVER HEARD THE SAYING THAT IDIOTS, LIKE SMOKE, LIKE CLIMBING TO HIGH PLACES?
Nope!
But you just climbed up here, so does that make you an idiot too?
HRM...
GIVEN ALL I'VE LET HAPPEN OF LATE, I CAN'T REALLY DENY THAT, CAN I?
HECK, WHY AM I EVEN GOING WITH YOU MORONS TO TOKYO?

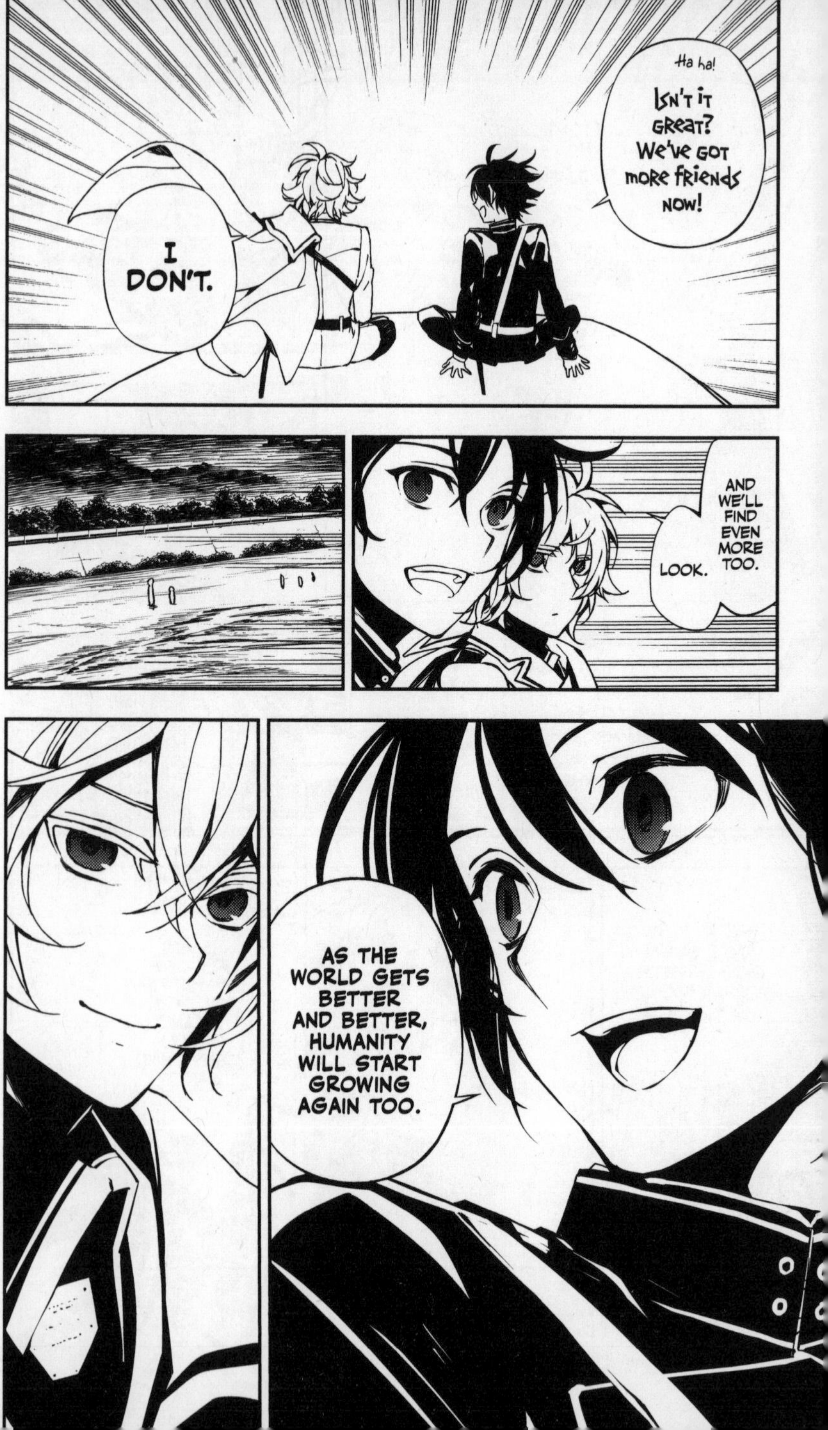
Ha ha!
Isn't it great? We've got more friends now!
I DON'T.
LOOK.
AND WE'LL FIND EVEN MORE TOO.
AS THE WORLD GETS BETTER AND BETTER, HUMANITY WILL START GROWING AGAIN TOO.

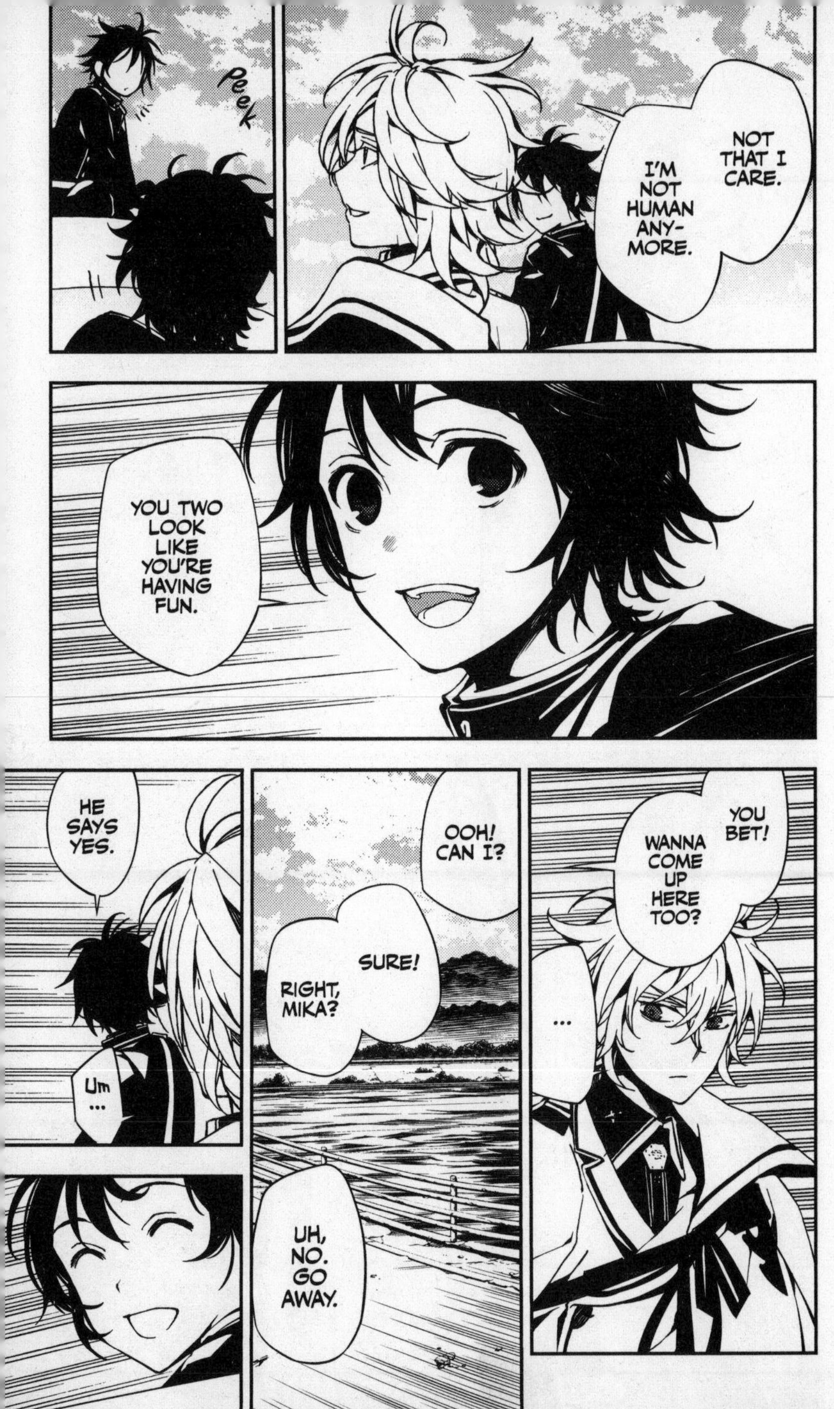
NOT THAT I CARE.
I'M NOT HUMAN ANYMORE.
Peek
YOU TWO LOOK LIKE YOU'RE HAVING FUN.
YOU BET!
WANNA COME UP HERE TOO?
...
OOH! CAN I?
SURE!
RIGHT, MIKA?
UH, NO. GO AWAY.
HE SAYS YES.
Um...

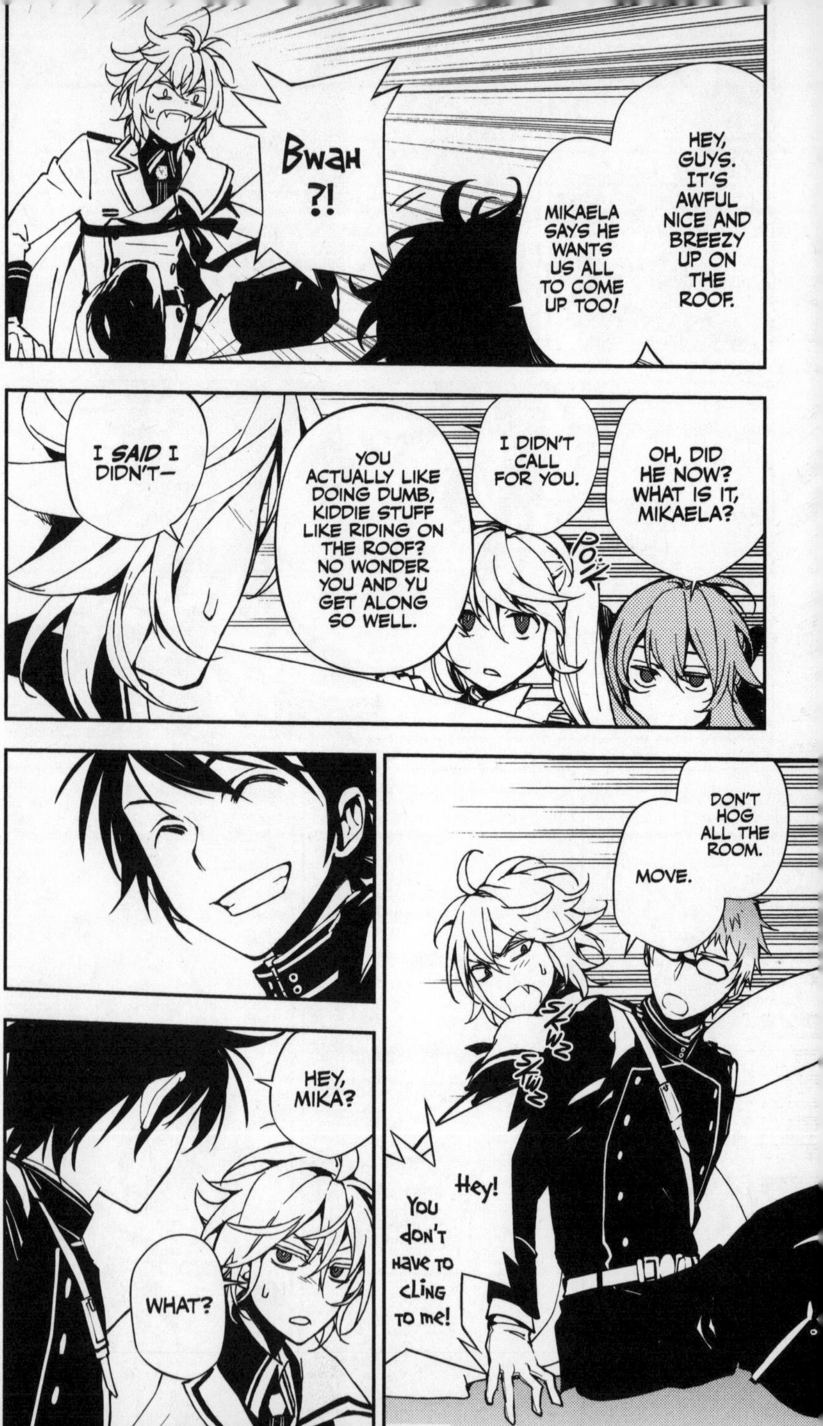
HEY, GUYS. IT'S AWFUL NICE AND BREEZY UP ON THE ROOF.
MIKAELA SAYS HE WANTS US ALL TO COME UP TOO!
Bwah ?!
OH, DID HE NOW? WHAT IS IT, MIKAELA?
I DIDN'T CALL FOR YOU.
POIK
YOU ACTUALLY LIKE DOING DUMB, KIDDIE STUFF LIKE RIDING ON THE ROOF? NO WONDER YOU AND YU GET ALONG SO WELL.
I SAID I DIDN'T—
DON'T HOG ALL THE ROOM.
MOVE.
SKWZ SKWZ
Hey!
You don't have to cling to me!
HEY, MIKA?
WHAT?

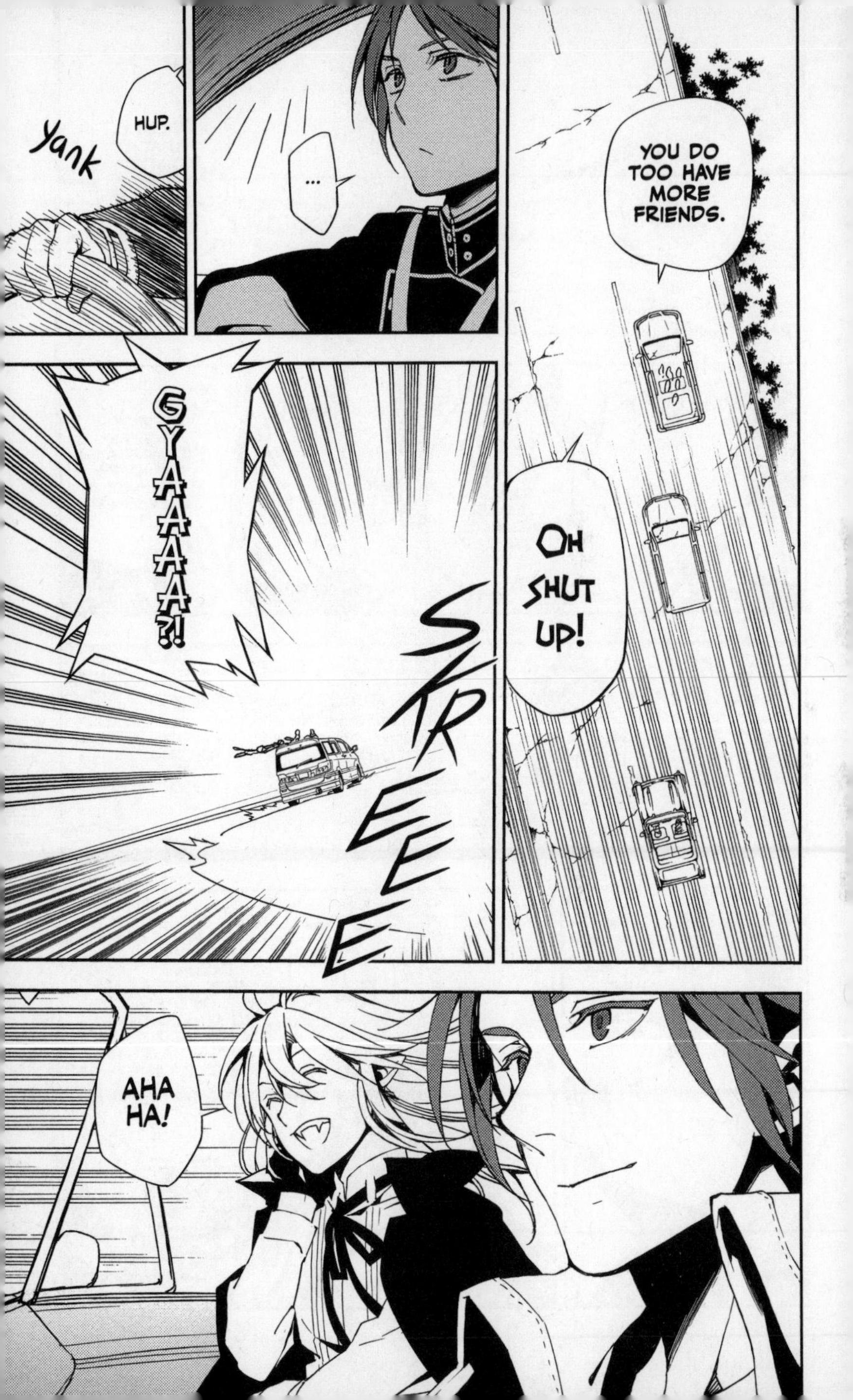

YOU DO TOO HAVE MORE FRIENDS.
OH SHUT UP!
...
HUP.
yank
GYAAAAA?!
SKREEEE
AHA HA!

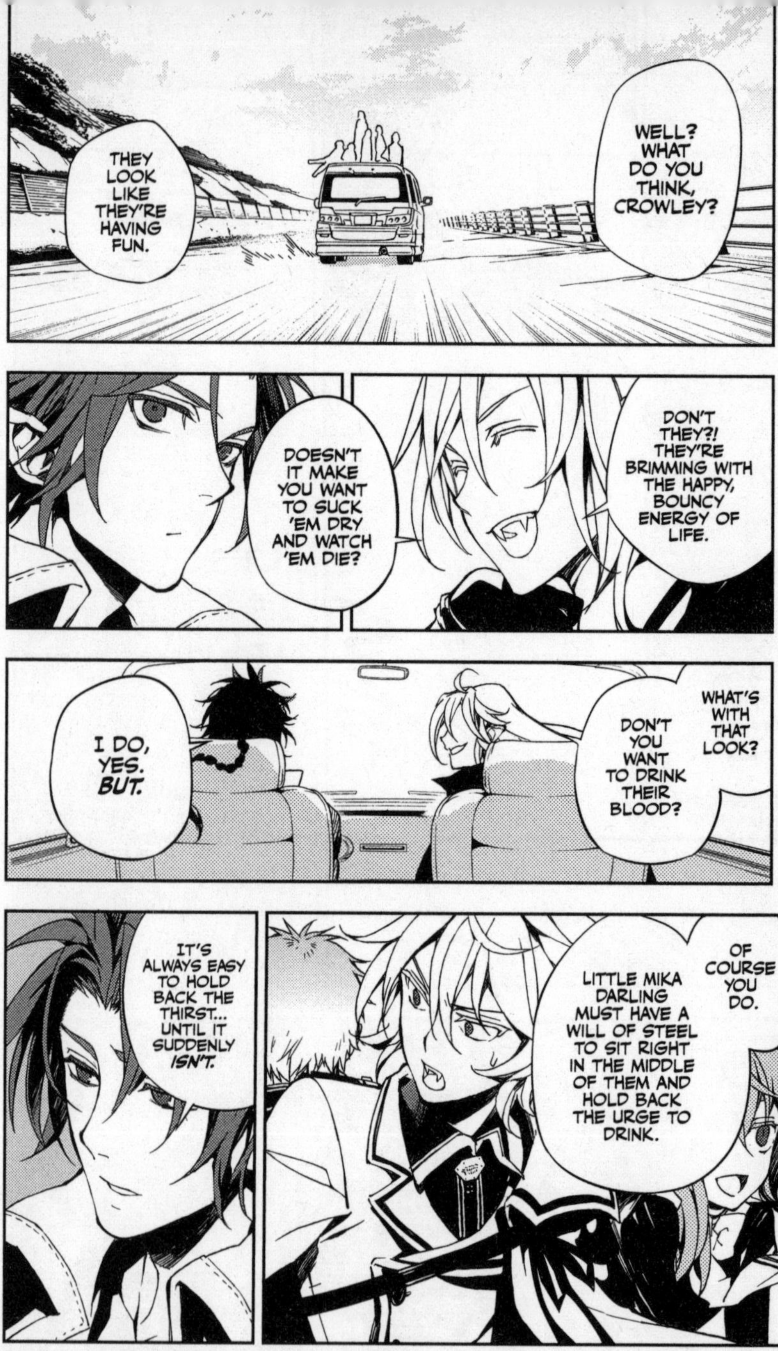
WELL? WHAT DO YOU THINK, CROWLEY?
THEY LOOK LIKE THEY'RE HAVING FUN.
DON'T THEY?! THEY'RE BRIMMING WITH THE HAPPY, BOUNCY ENERGY OF LIFE.
DOESN'T IT MAKE YOU WANT TO SUCK 'EM DRY AND WATCH 'EM DIE?
WHAT'S WITH THAT LOOK?
DON'T YOU WANT TO DRINK THEIR BLOOD?
I DO, YES. *BUT.*
OF COURSE YOU DO.
LITTLE MIKA DARLING MUST HAVE A WILL OF STEEL TO SIT RIGHT IN THE MIDDLE OF THEM AND HOLD BACK THE URGE TO DRINK.
IT'S ALWAYS EASY TO HOLD BACK THE THIRST... UNTIL IT SUDDENLY *ISN'T.*

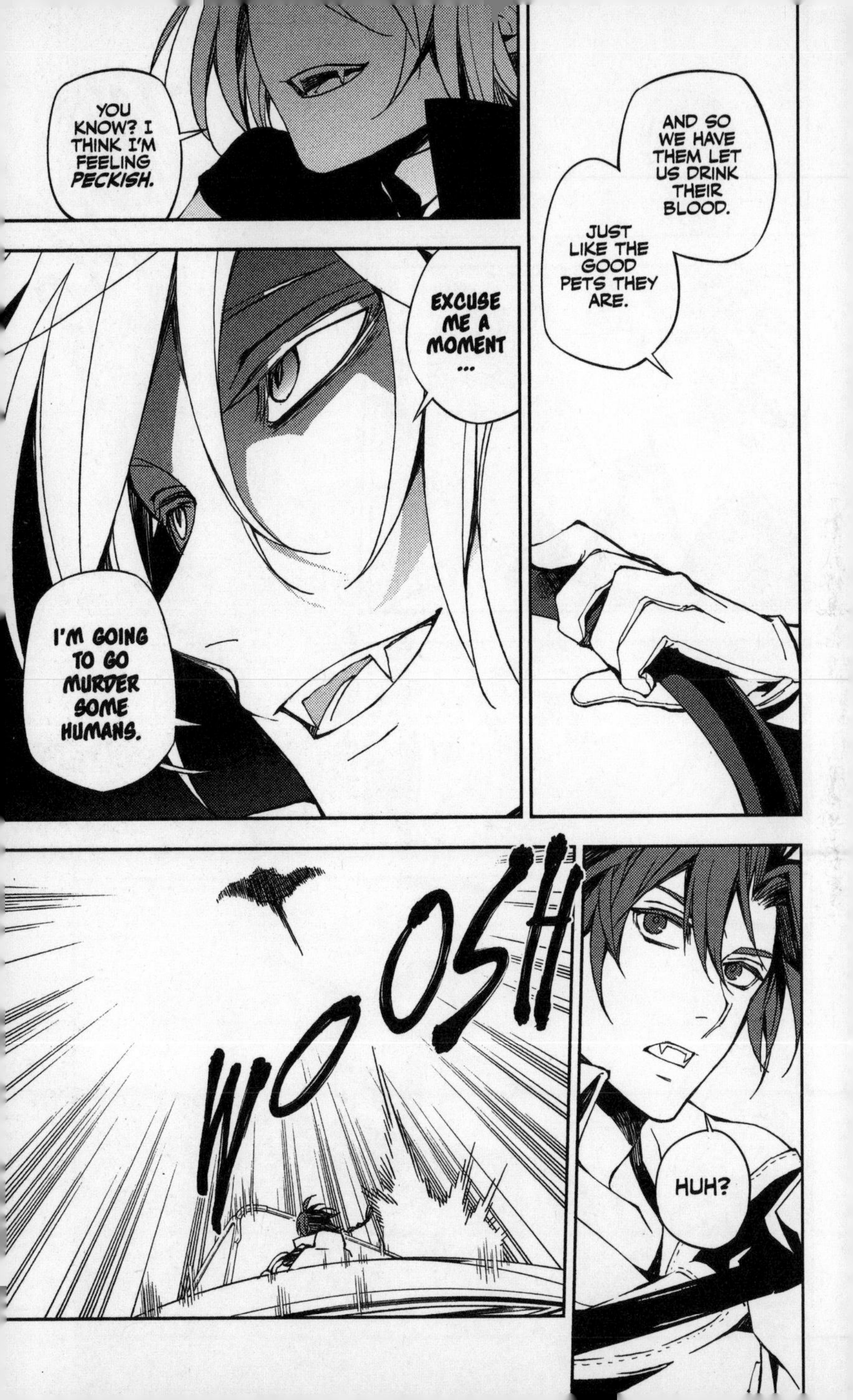
AND SO WE HAVE THEM LET US DRINK THEIR BLOOD.
JUST LIKE THE GOOD PETS THEY ARE.
YOU KNOW? I THINK I'M FEELING *PECKISH.*
EXCUSE ME A MOMENT ...
I'M GOING TO GO MURDER SOME HUMANS.
HUH?
WOOSH

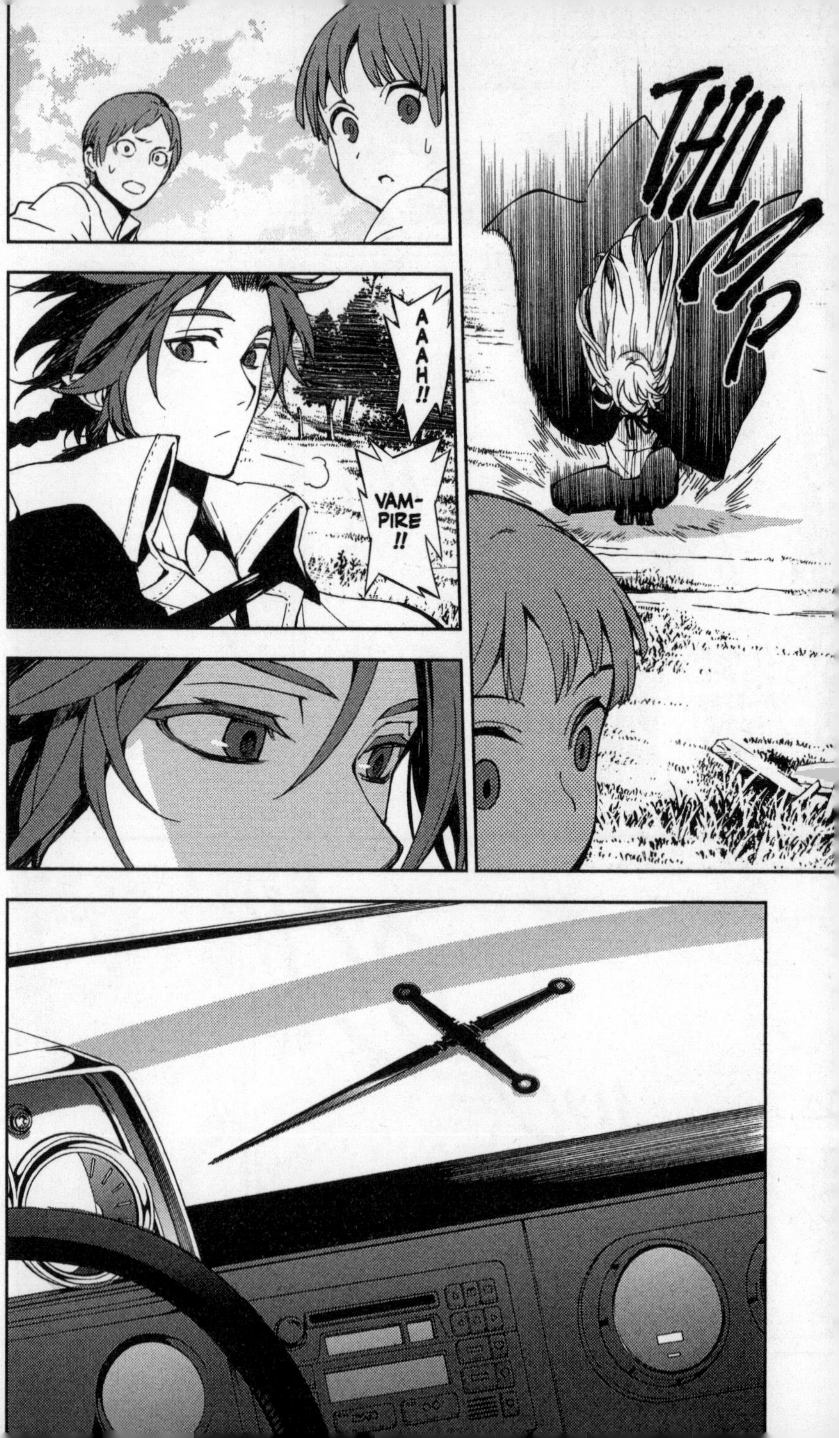
THUMP
AAAAH!!
VAM-PIRE!!

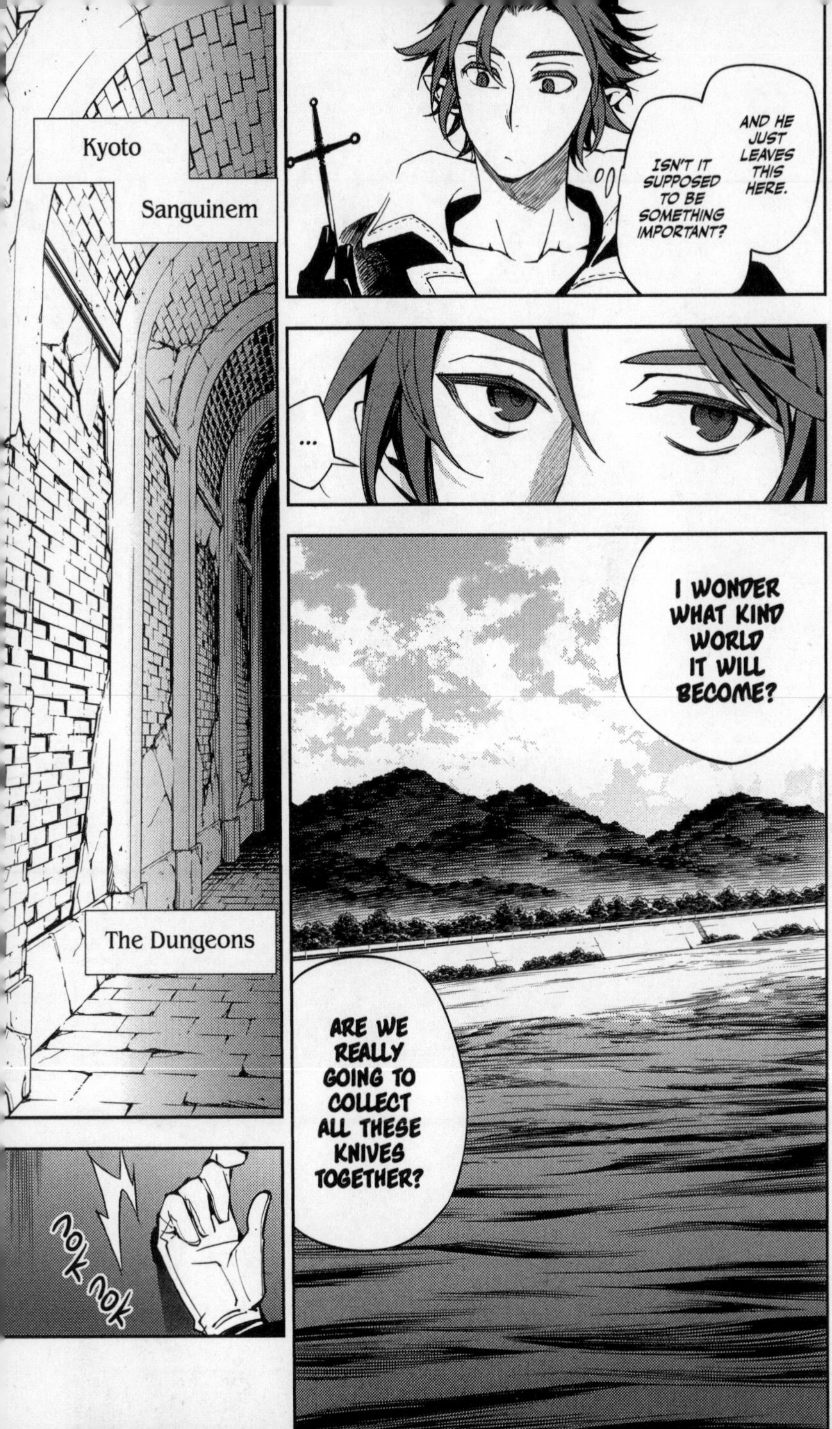
AND HE JUST LEAVES THIS HERE.
ISN'T IT SUPPOSED TO BE SOMETHING IMPORTANT?
...
I WONDER WHAT KIND WORLD IT WILL BECOME?
ARE WE REALLY GOING TO COLLECT ALL THESE KNIVES TOGETHER?
Kyoto
Sanguinem
The Dungeons
nok nok

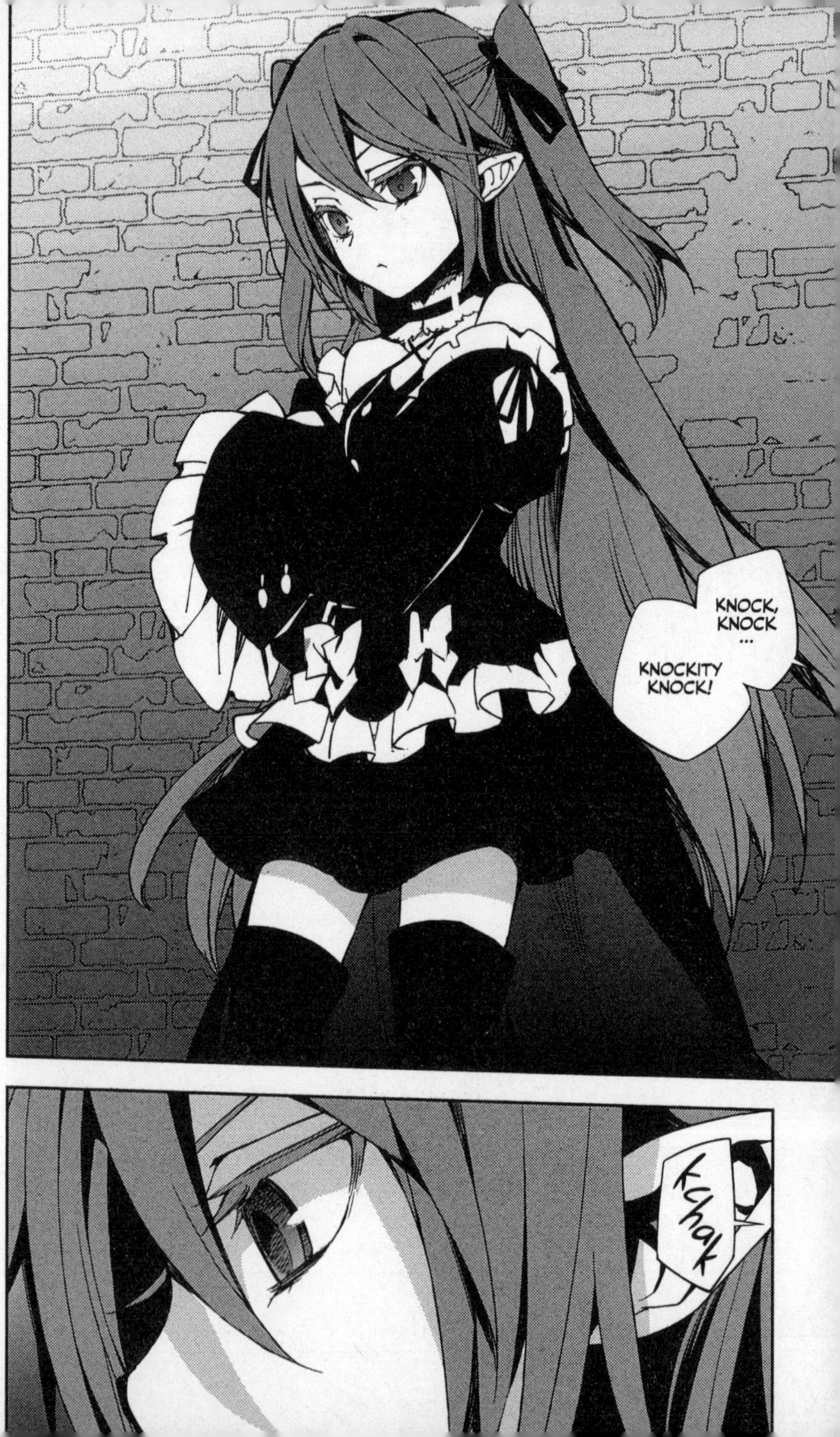
KNOCK, KNOCK ...
KNOCKITY KNOCK!
KCHAK

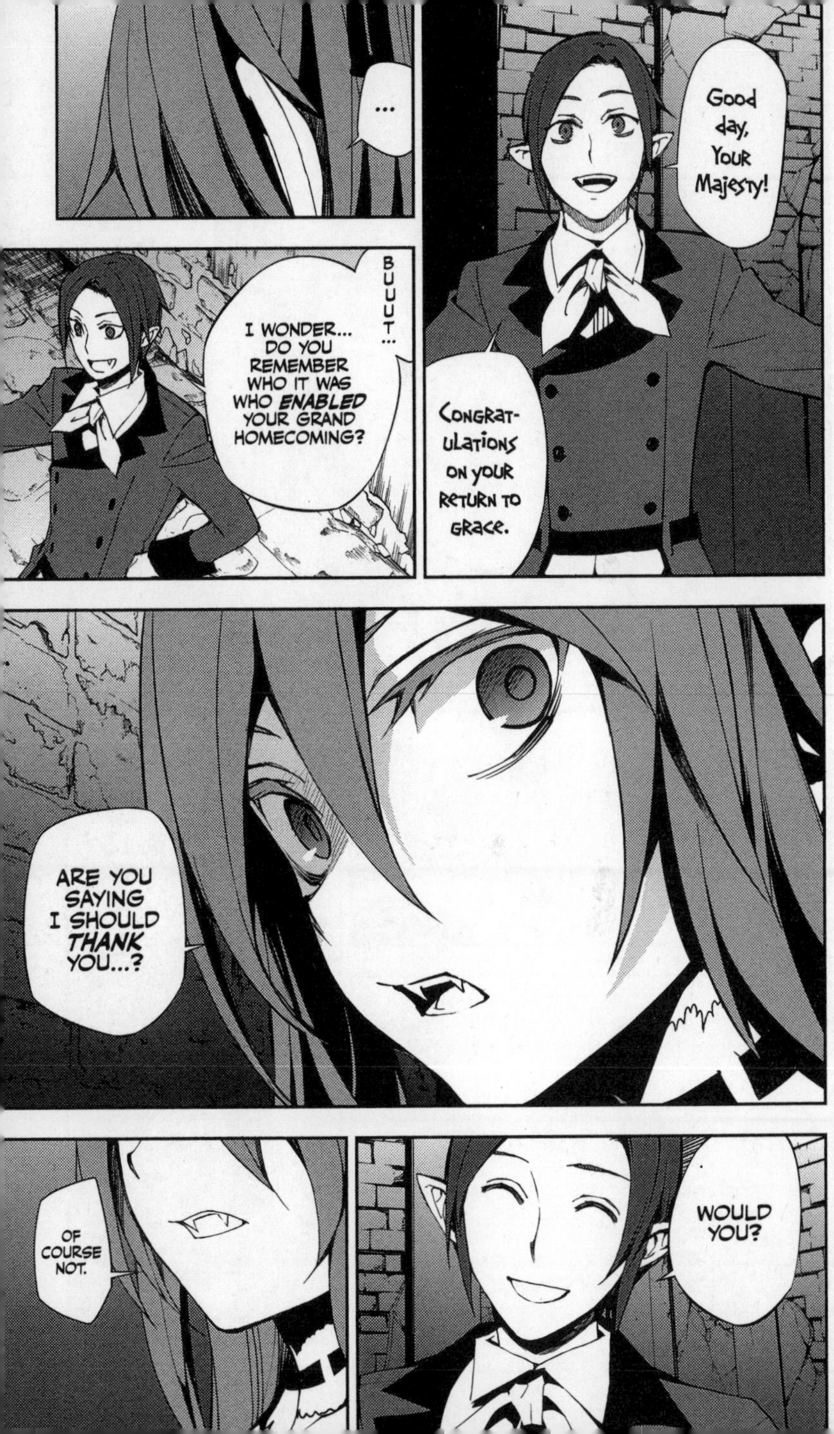
Good day, Your Majesty!
Congratulations on your return to grace.
...
BUUUT...
I WONDER... DO YOU REMEMBER WHO IT WAS WHO ENABLED YOUR GRAND HOMECOMING?
ARE YOU SAYING I SHOULD THANK YOU...?
WOULD YOU?
OF COURSE NOT.

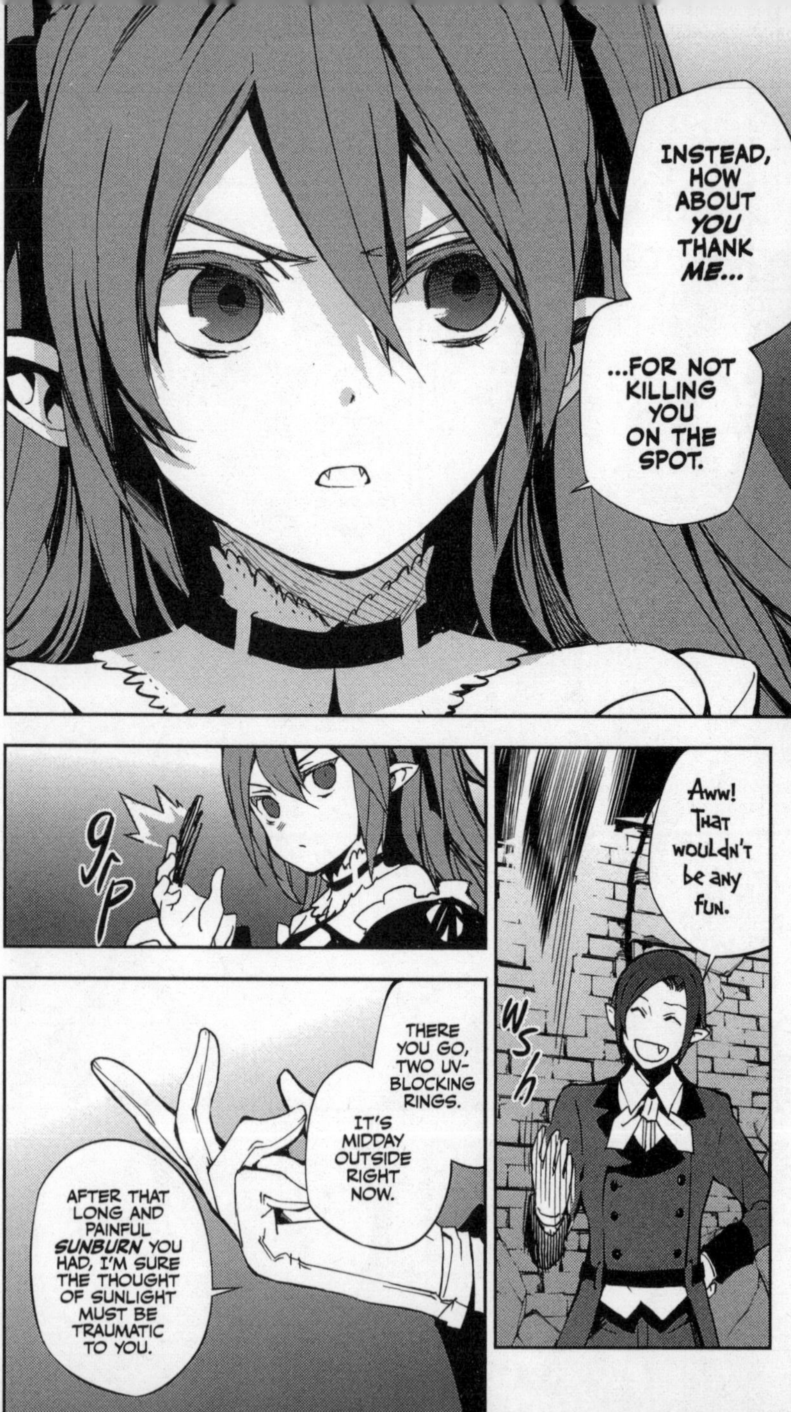
INSTEAD, HOW ABOUT *YOU* THANK *ME*...
...FOR NOT KILLING YOU ON THE SPOT.
Aww! That wouldn't be any fun.
WSH
GRIP
THERE YOU GO, TWO UV-BLOCKING RINGS.
IT'S MIDDAY OUTSIDE RIGHT NOW.
AFTER THAT LONG AND PAINFUL ***SUNBURN*** YOU HAD, I'M SURE THE THOUGHT OF SUNLIGHT MUST BE TRAUMATIC TO YOU.

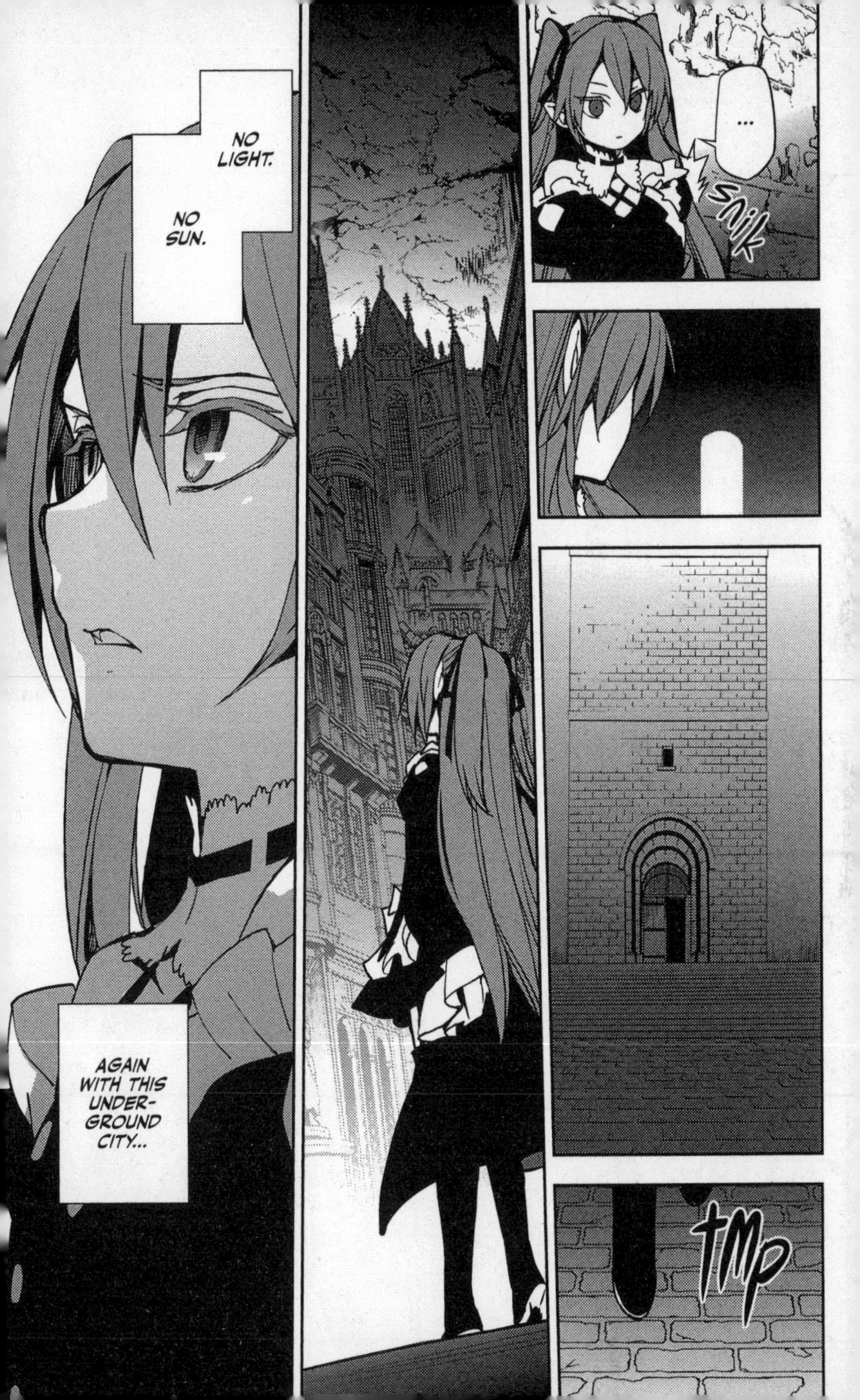
...
SNIK
TMP
NO LIGHT.
NO SUN.
AGAIN WITH THIS UNDER-GROUND CITY...

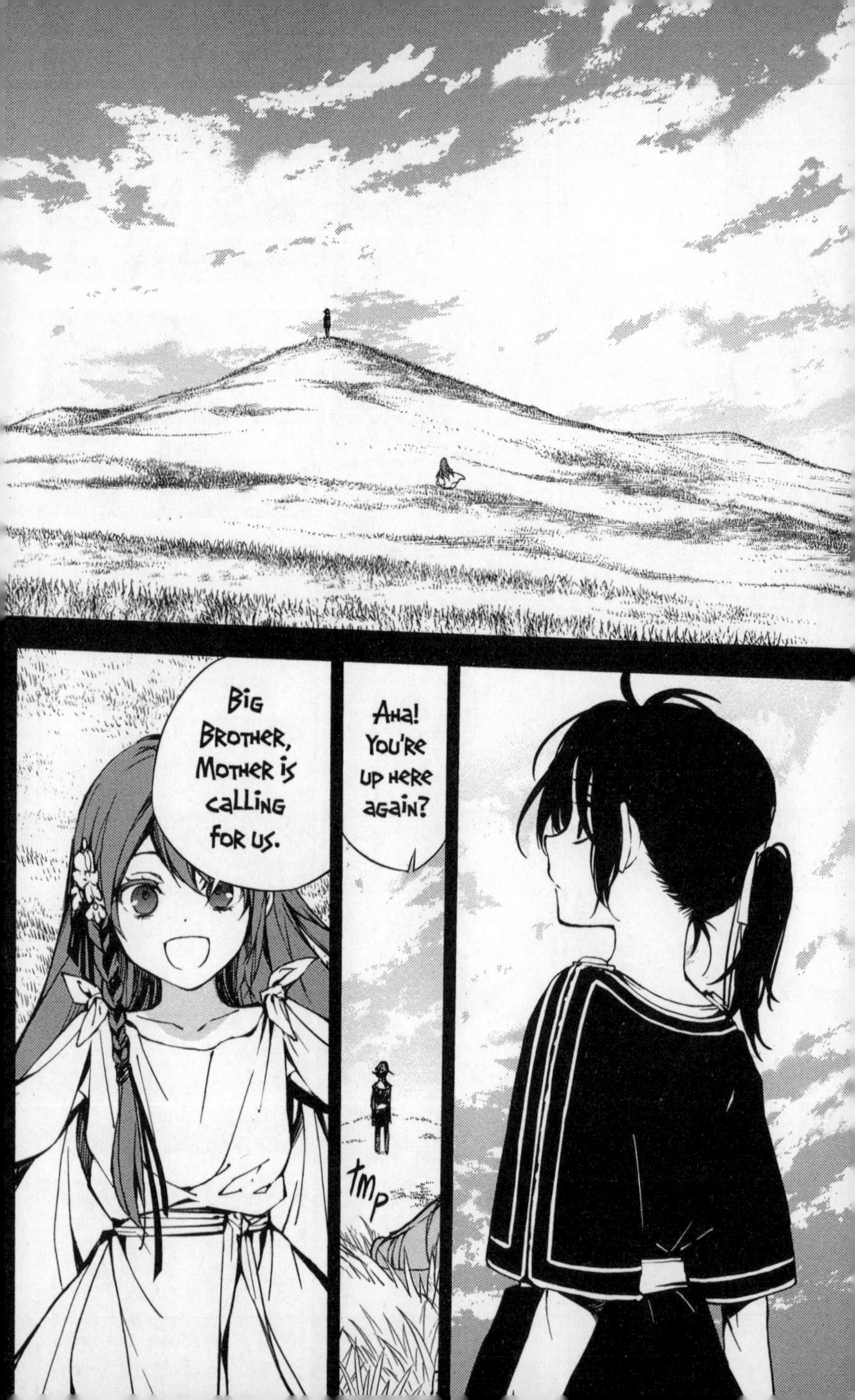
Aha! You're up here again?
tmp
Big Brother, Mother is calling for us.

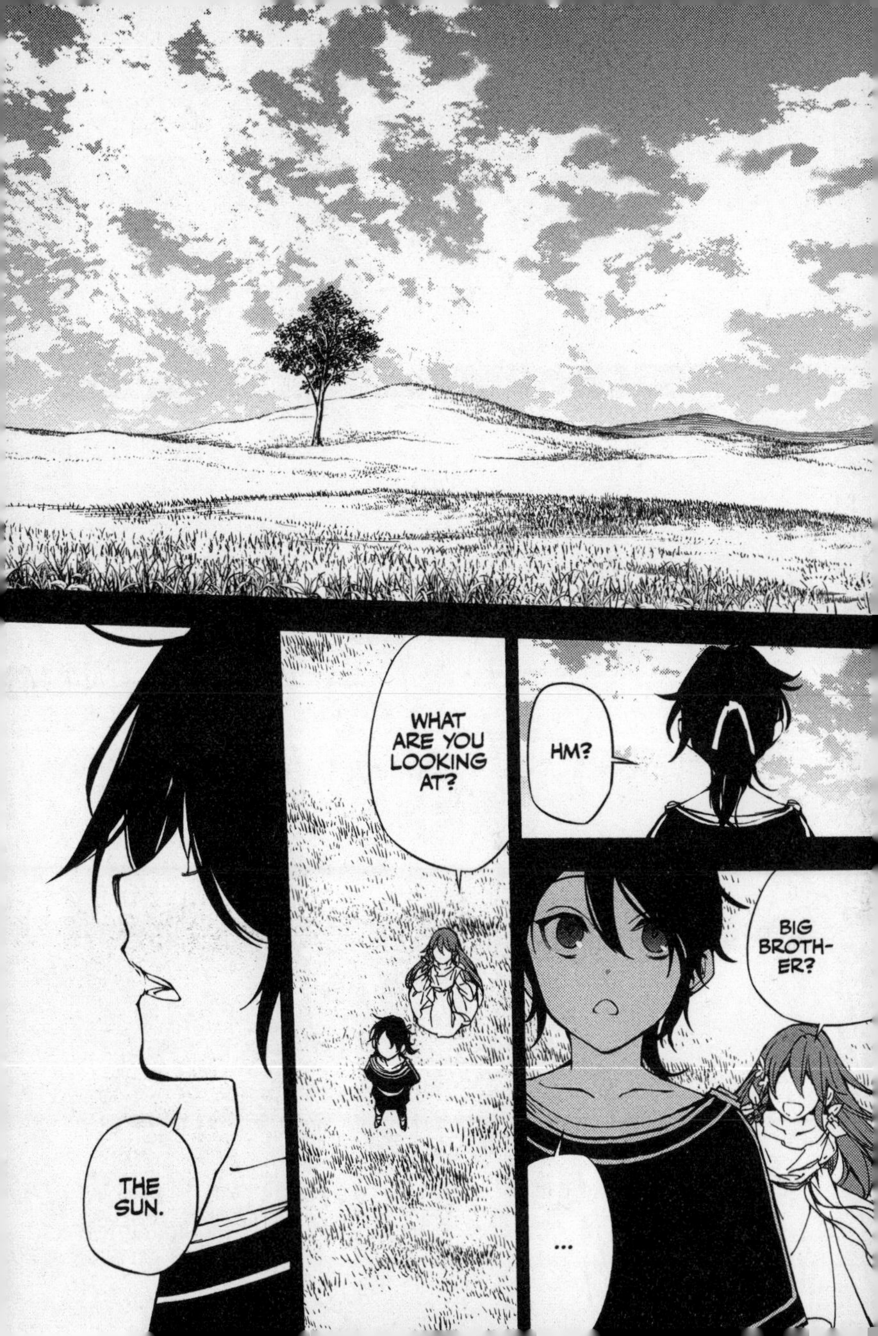
HM?
BIG BROTH-ER?
...
WHAT ARE YOU LOOKING AT?
THE SUN.

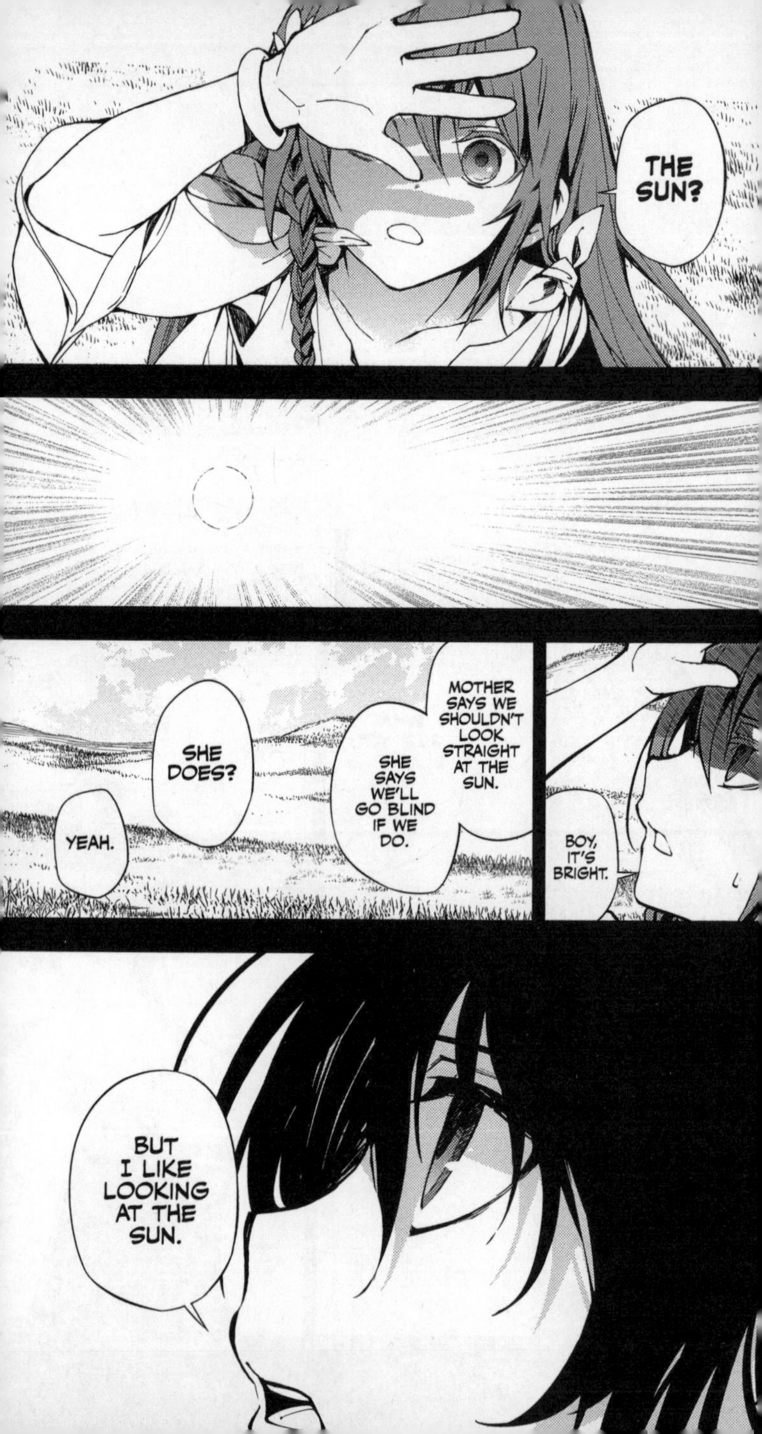
THE SUN?
BOY, IT'S BRIGHT.
MOTHER SAYS WE SHOULDN'T LOOK STRAIGHT AT THE SUN.
SHE SAYS WE'LL GO BLIND IF WE DO.
SHE DOES?
YEAH.
BUT I LIKE LOOKING AT THE SUN.

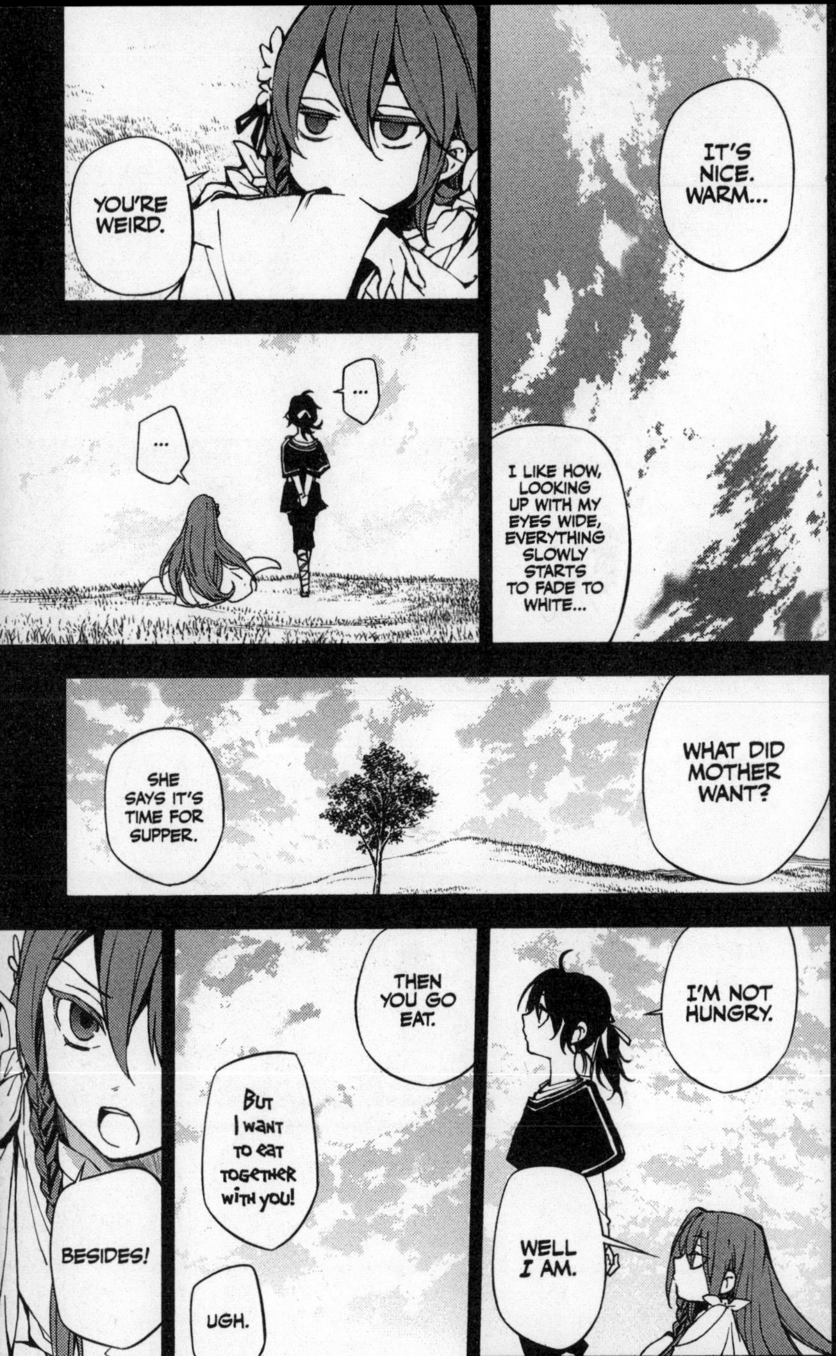
IT'S NICE. WARM...
I LIKE HOW, LOOKING UP WITH MY EYES WIDE, EVERYTHING SLOWLY STARTS TO FADE TO WHITE...
YOU'RE WEIRD.
...
...
WHAT DID MOTHER WANT?
SHE SAYS IT'S TIME FOR SUPPER.
I'M NOT HUNGRY.
WELL I AM.
THEN YOU GO EAT.
But I want to eat together with you!
UGH.
BESIDES!

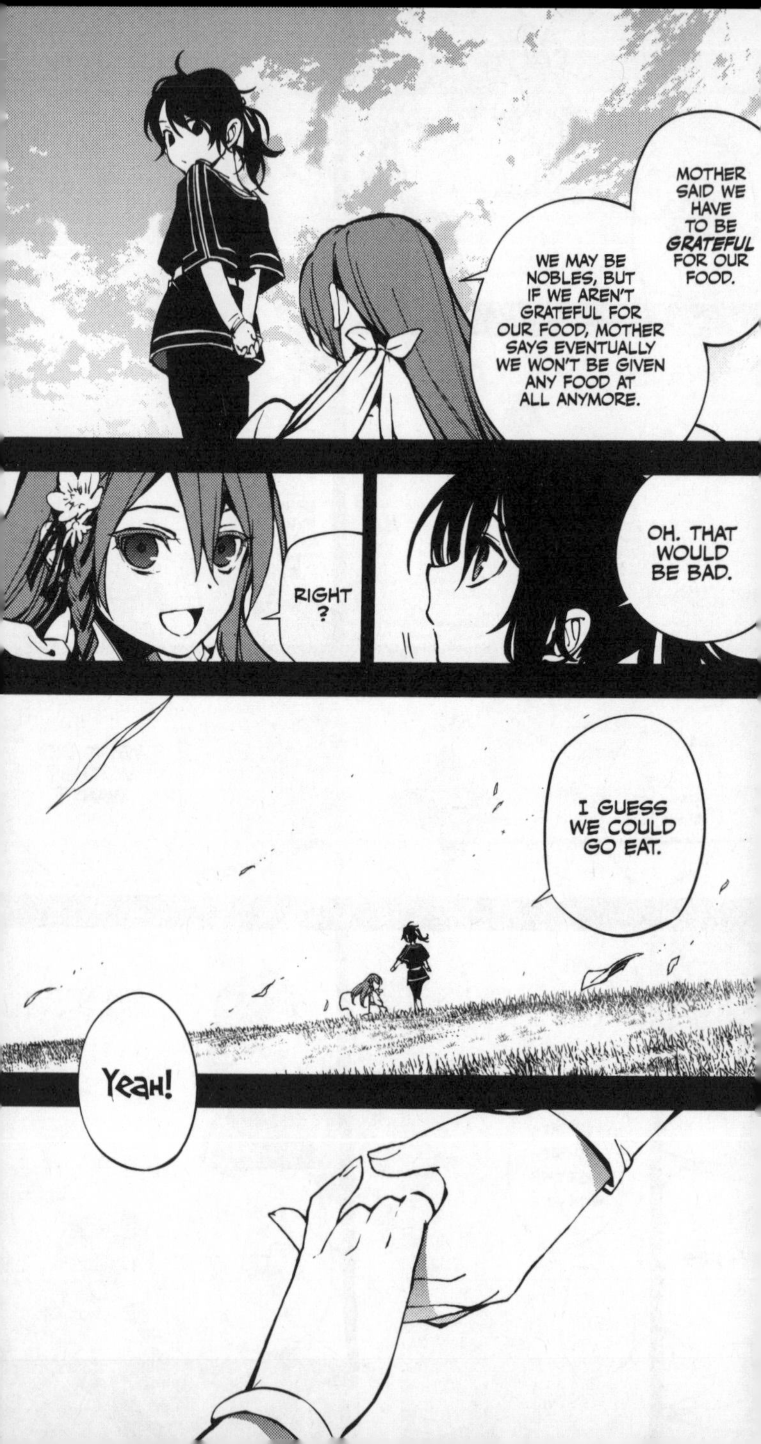
MOTHER SAID WE HAVE TO BE **GRATEFUL** FOR OUR FOOD.
WE MAY BE NOBLES, BUT IF WE AREN'T GRATEFUL FOR OUR FOOD, MOTHER SAYS EVENTUALLY WE WON'T BE GIVEN ANY FOOD AT ALL ANYMORE.
OH. THAT WOULD BE BAD.
RIGHT?
I GUESS WE COULD GO EAT.
Yeah!

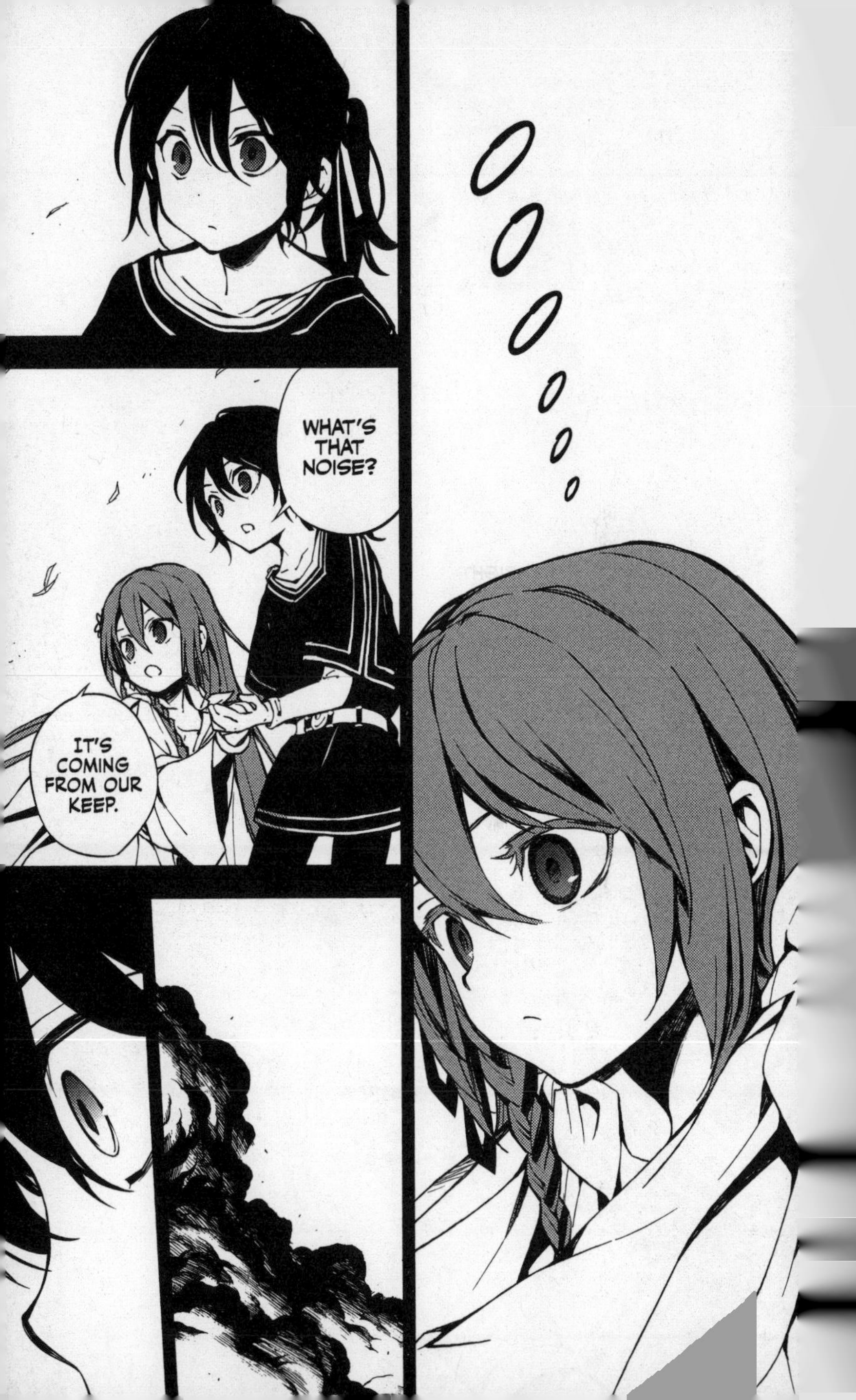
WHAT'S THAT NOISE?
IT'S COMING FROM OUR KEEP.

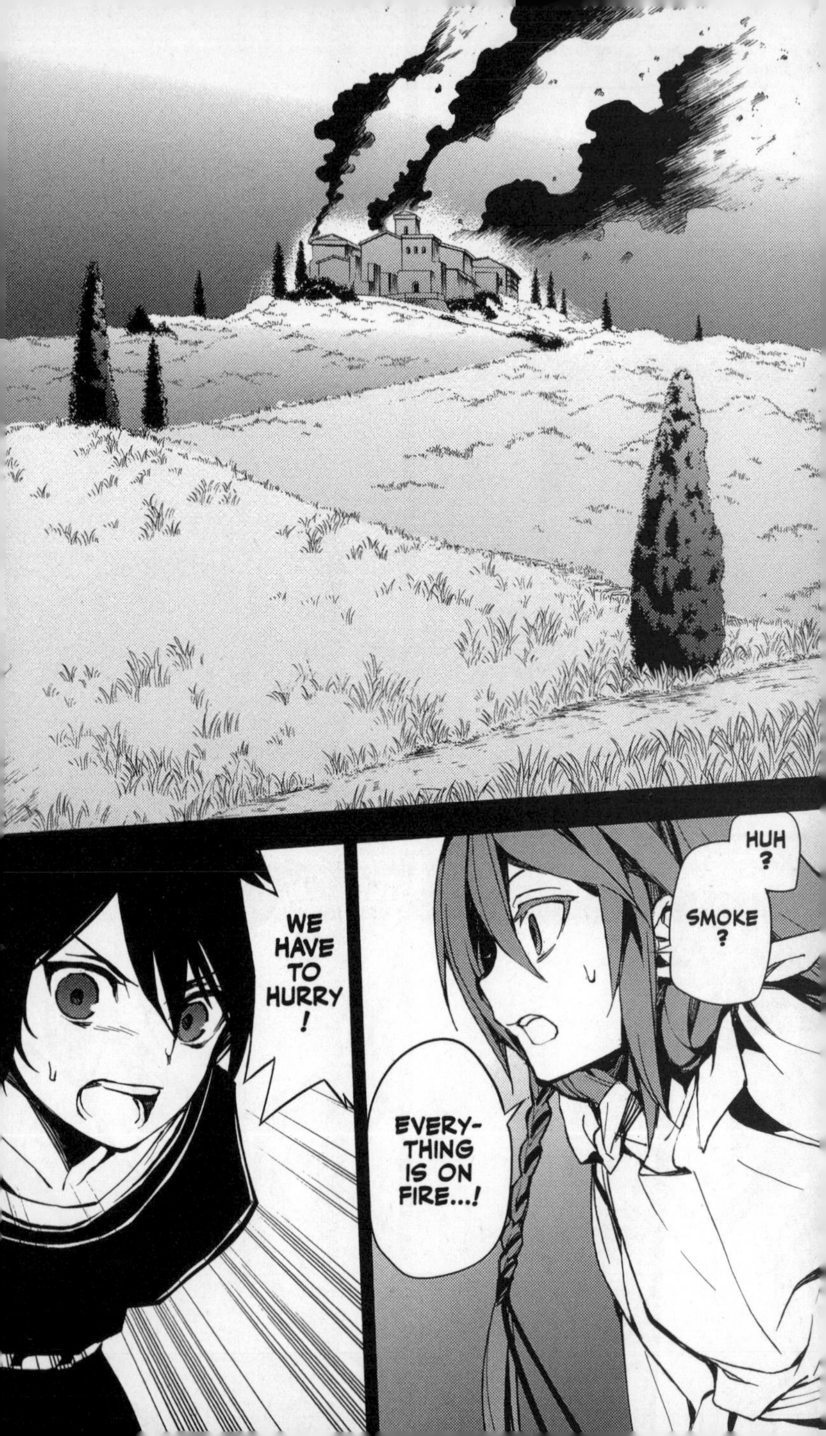
HUH?
SMOKE?
EVERYTHING IS ON FIRE...!
WE HAVE TO HURRY!

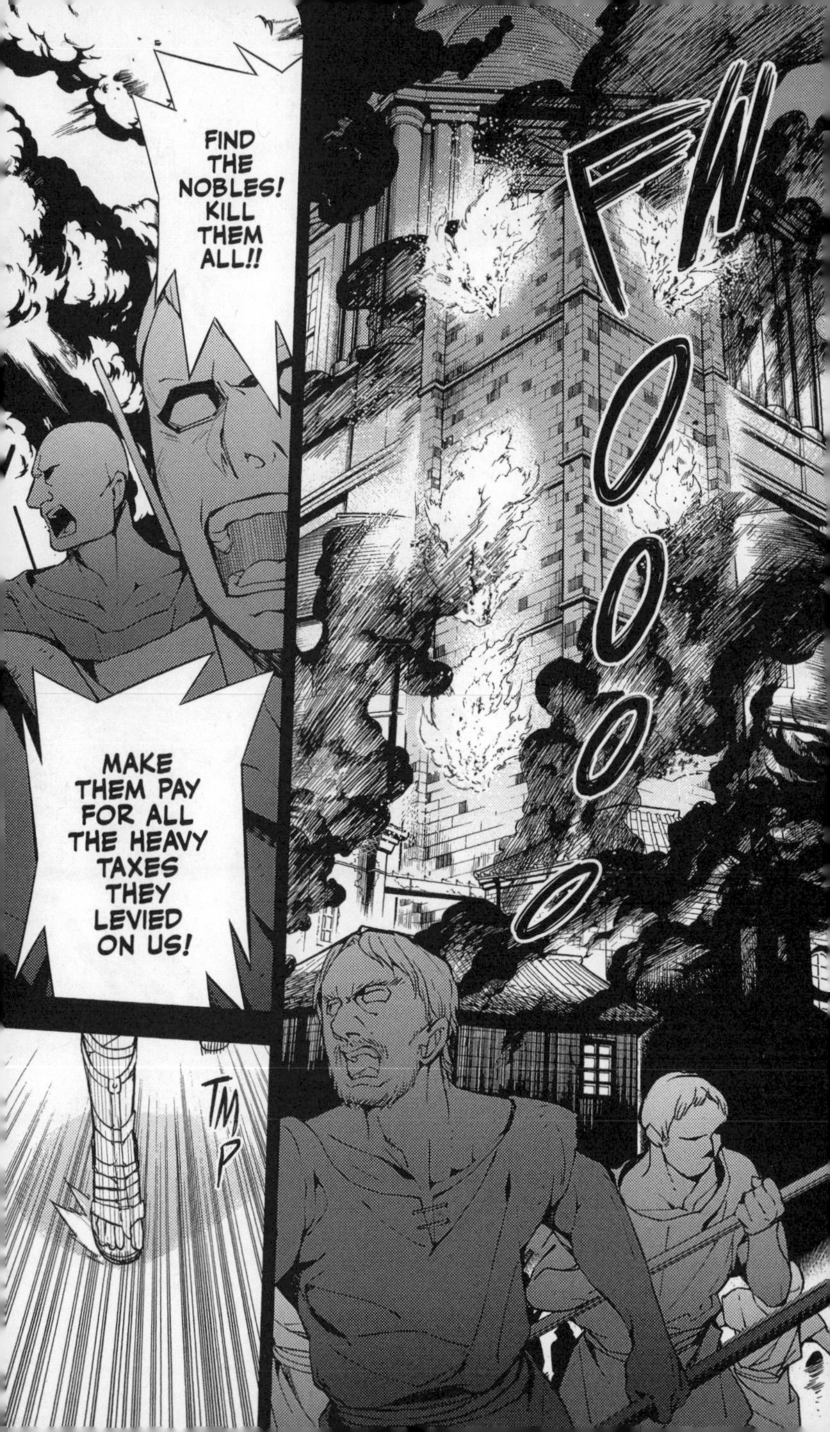
FWOOOO
FIND THE NOBLES! KILL THEM ALL!!
MAKE THEM PAY FOR ALL THE HEAVY TAXES THEY LEVIED ON US!
TMP

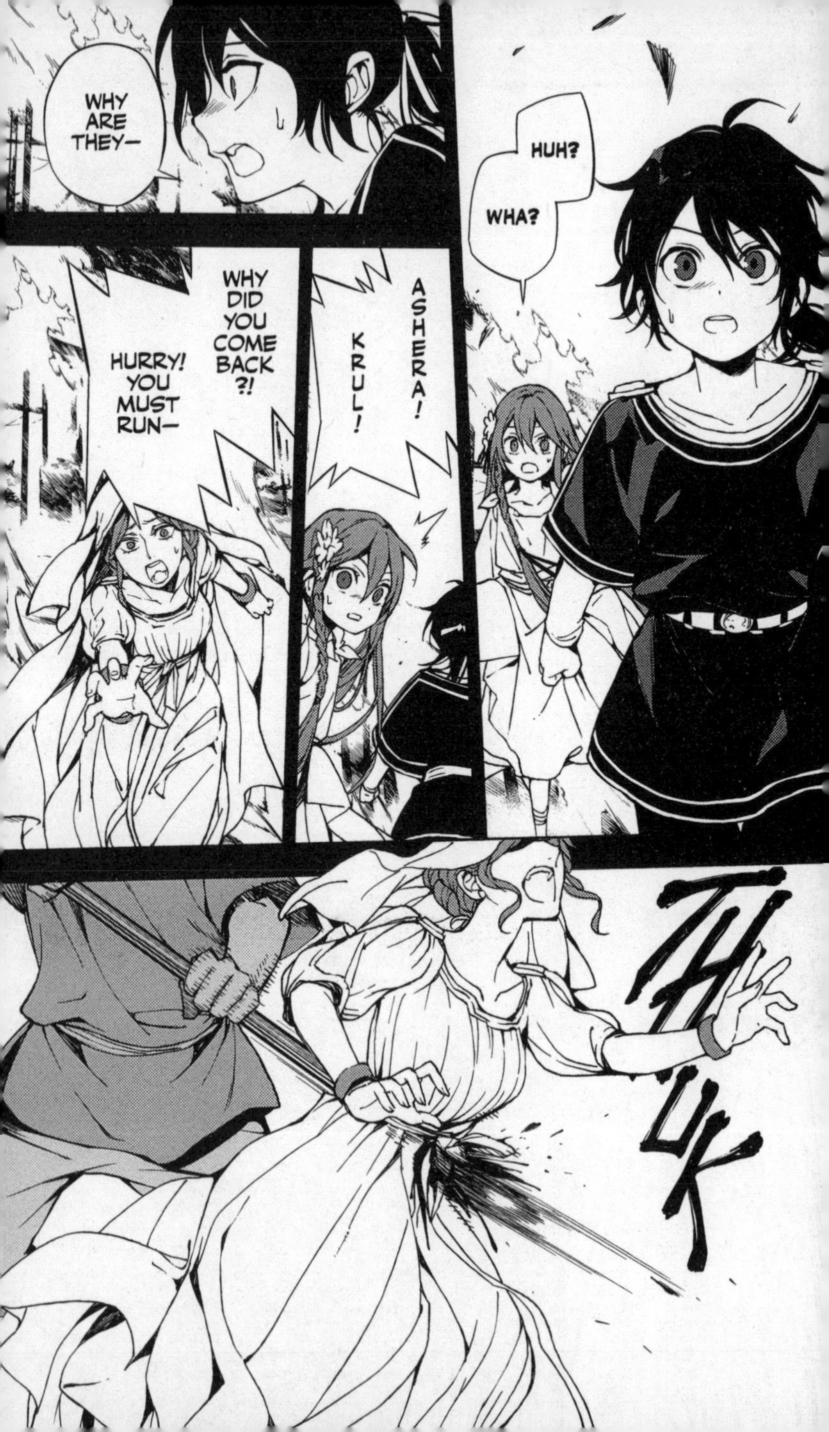
HUH?
WHA?
WHY ARE THEY—
ASHERA!
KRUL!
WHY DID YOU COME BACK?!
HURRY! YOU MUST RUN—
THUK

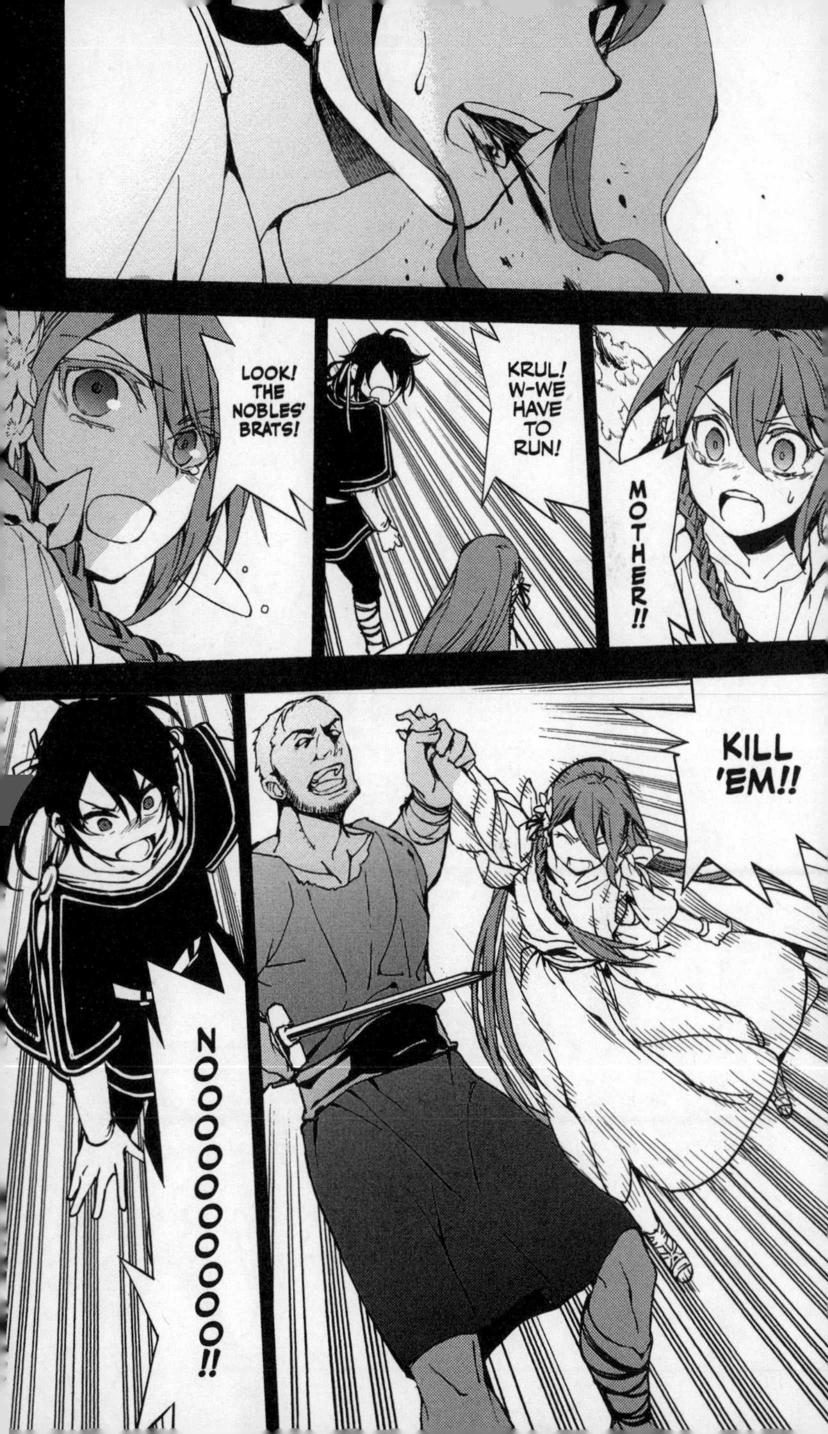
MOTHER!!
KRUL! W-WE HAVE TO RUN!
LOOK! THE NOBLES' BRATS!
KILL 'EM!!
NOOOOOOOOOOOOOOO!!

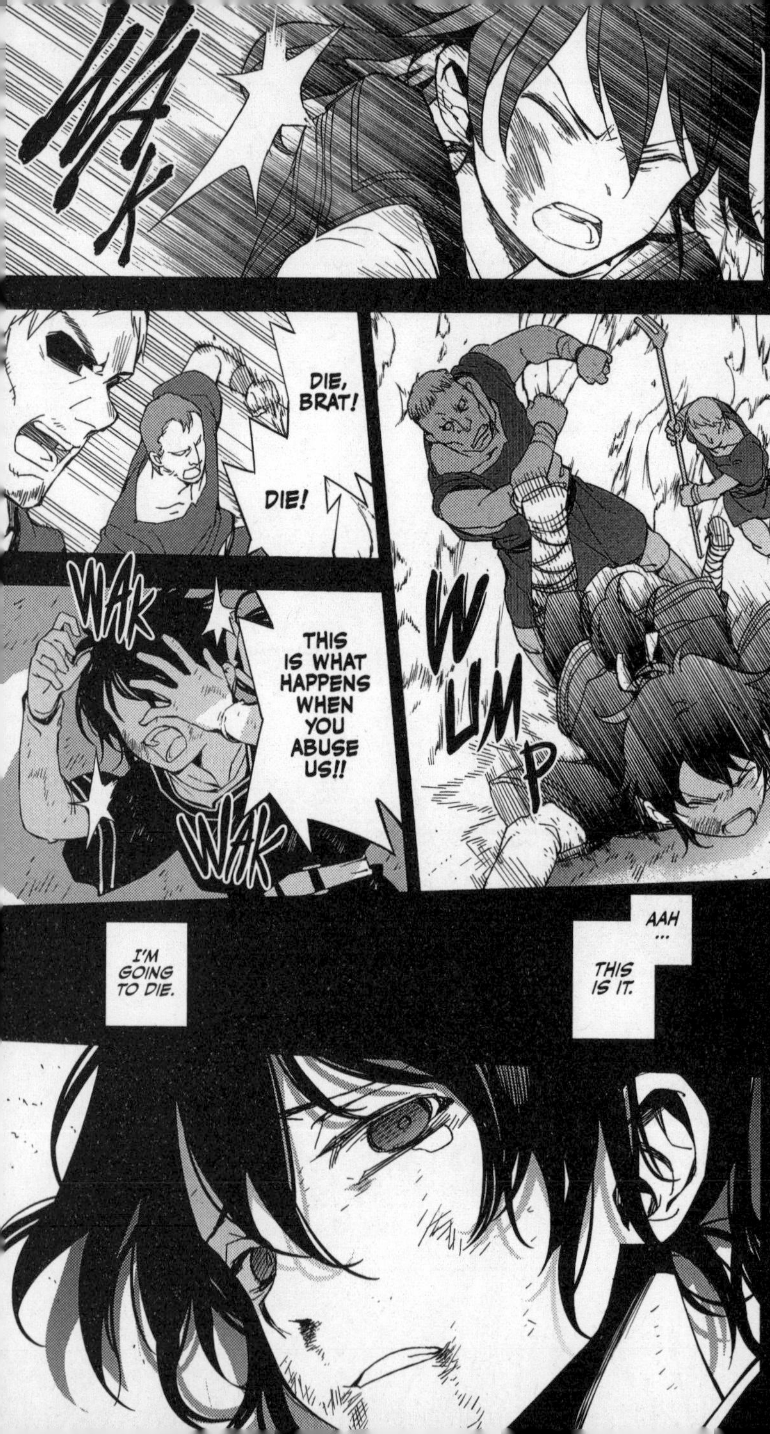
WAK
WUMP
DIE, BRAT!
DIE!
WAK
THIS IS WHAT HAPPENS WHEN YOU ABUSE US!!
WAK
AAH...
THIS IS IT.
I'M GOING TO DIE.

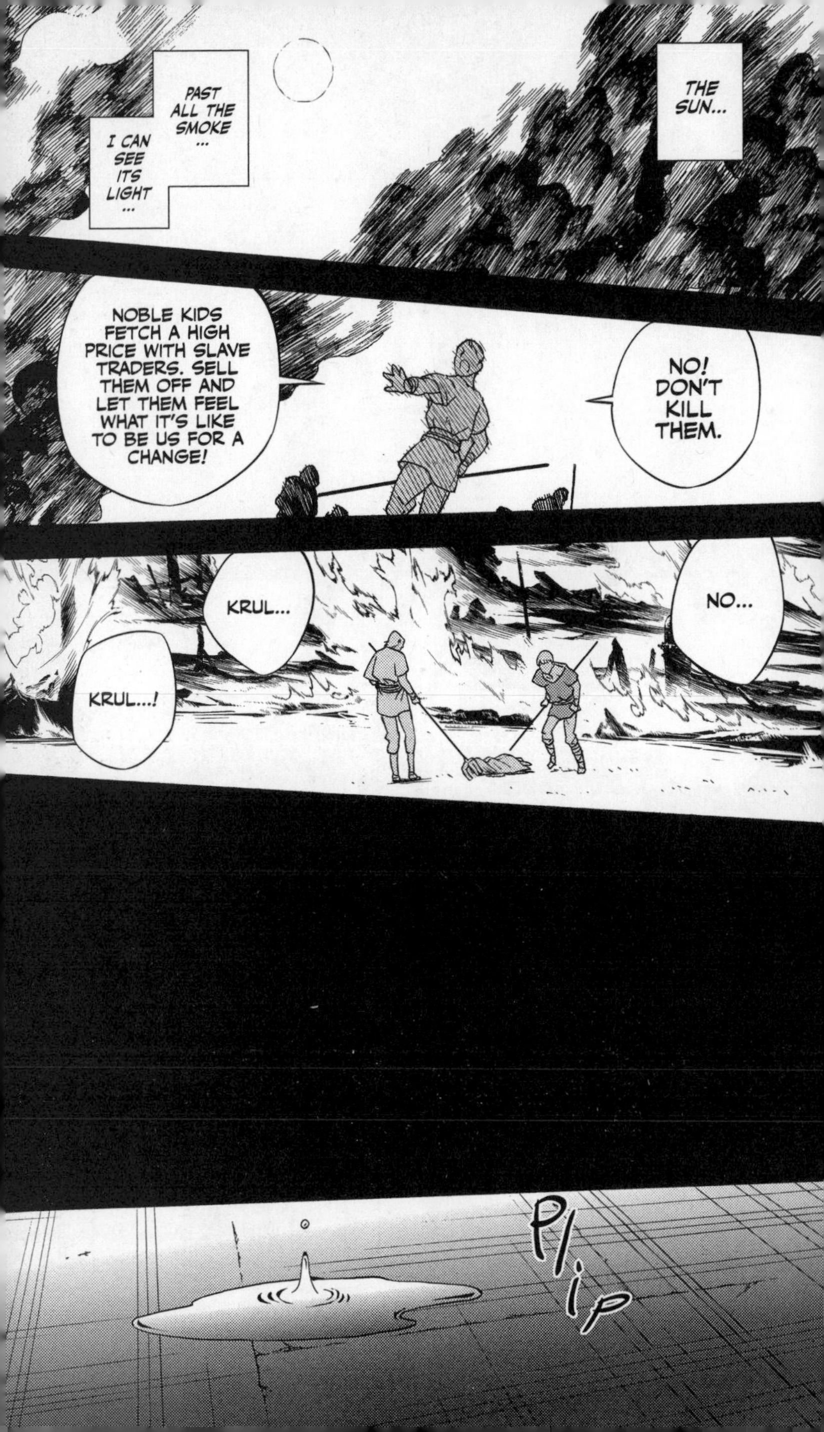
THE SUN...
PAST ALL THE SMOKE...
I CAN SEE ITS LIGHT...
NO! DON'T KILL THEM.
NOBLE KIDS FETCH A HIGH PRICE WITH SLAVE TRADERS. SELL THEM OFF AND LET THEM FEEL WHAT IT'S LIKE TO BE US FOR A CHANGE!
NO...
KRUL...
KRUL...!
Plip

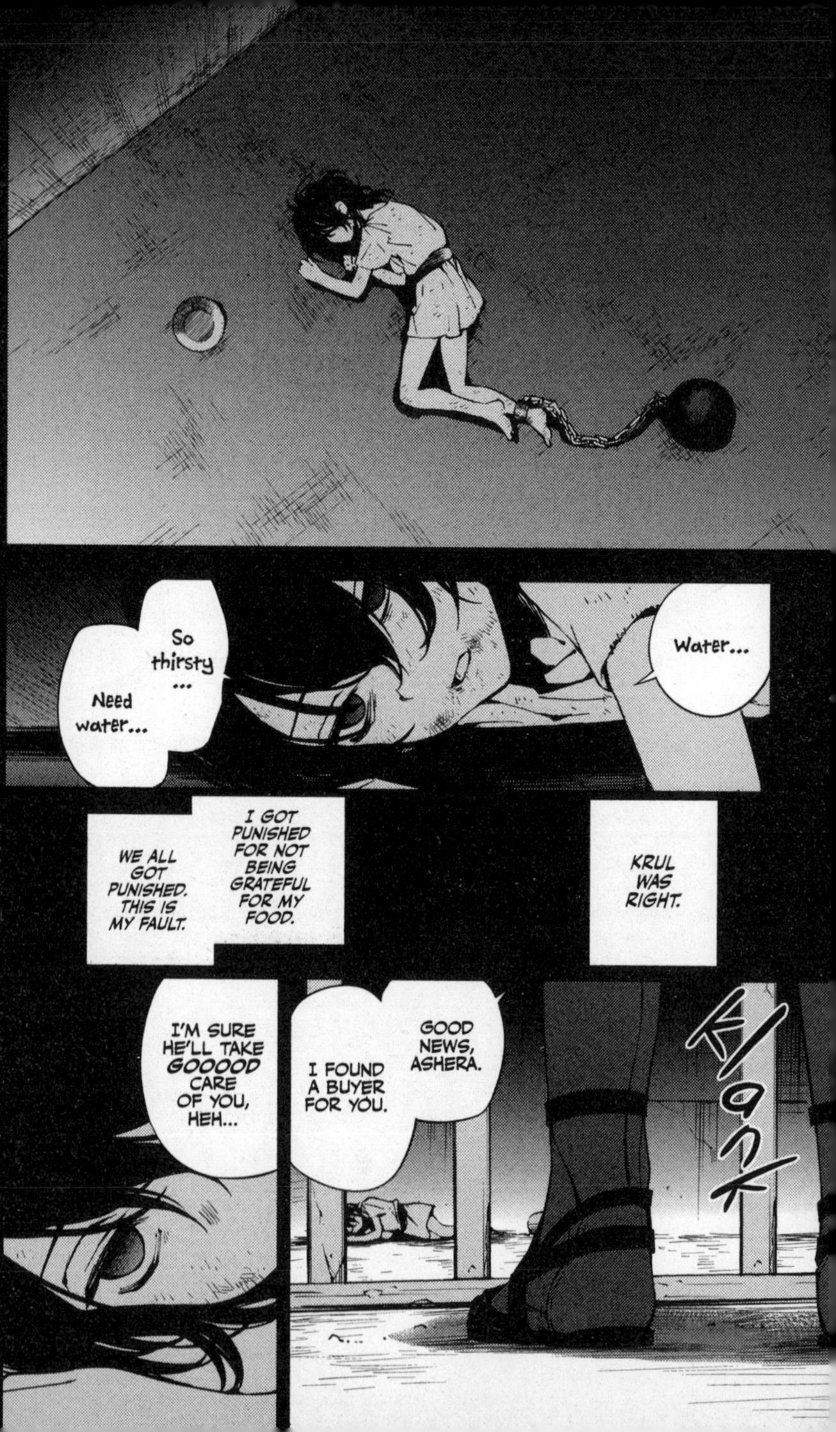
Water...
So thirsty...
Need water...
KRUL WAS RIGHT.
I GOT PUNISHED FOR NOT BEING GRATEFUL FOR MY FOOD.
WE ALL GOT PUNISHED. THIS IS MY FAULT.
klank
GOOD NEWS, ASHERA.
I FOUND A BUYER FOR YOU.
I'M SURE HE'LL TAKE GOOOOD CARE OF YOU, HEH...

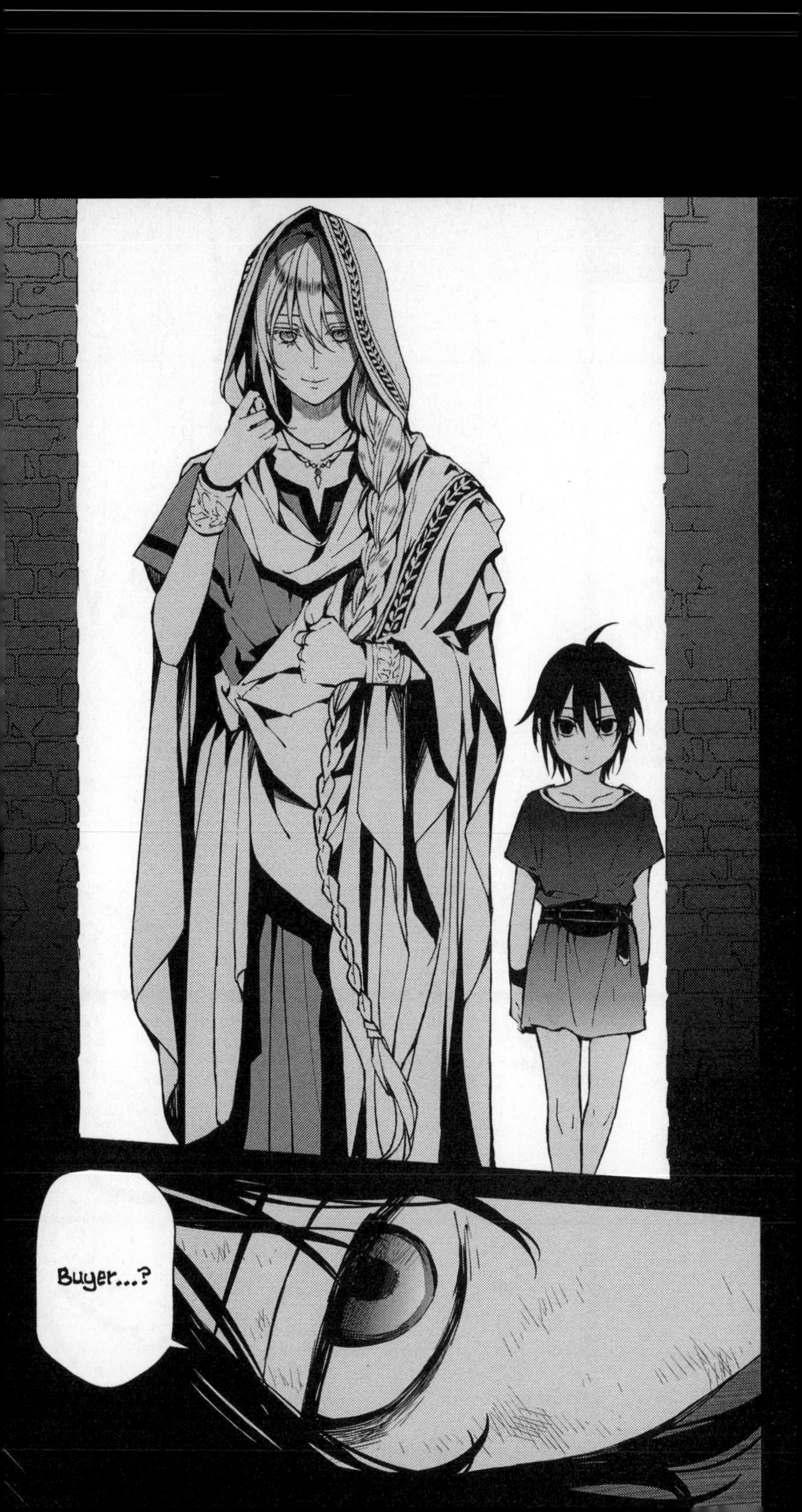
Buyer...?

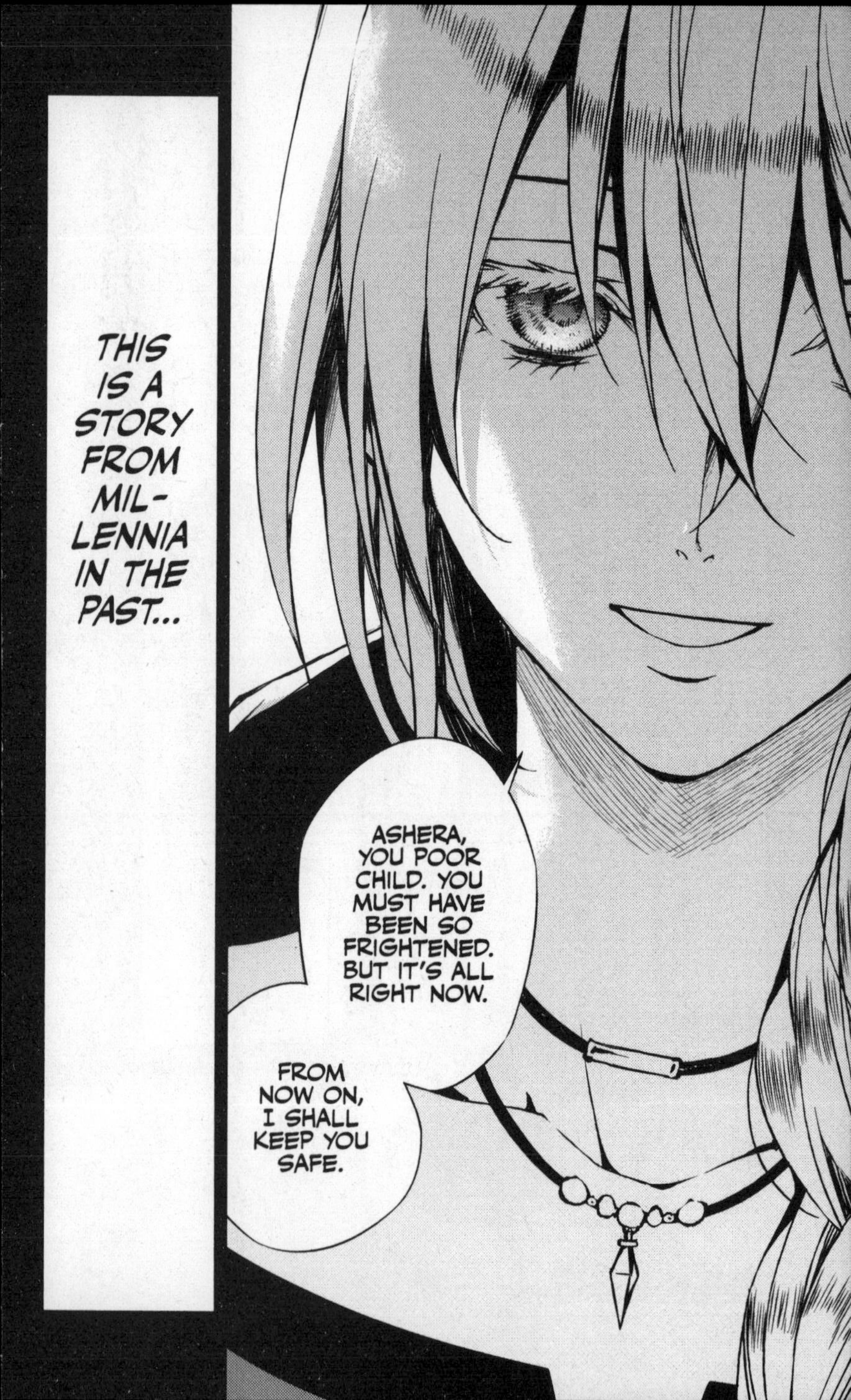
ASHERA, YOU POOR CHILD. YOU MUST HAVE BEEN SO FRIGHTENED. BUT IT'S ALL RIGHT NOW.
FROM NOW ON, I SHALL KEEP YOU SAFE.
THIS IS A STORY FROM MIL-LENNIA IN THE PAST...

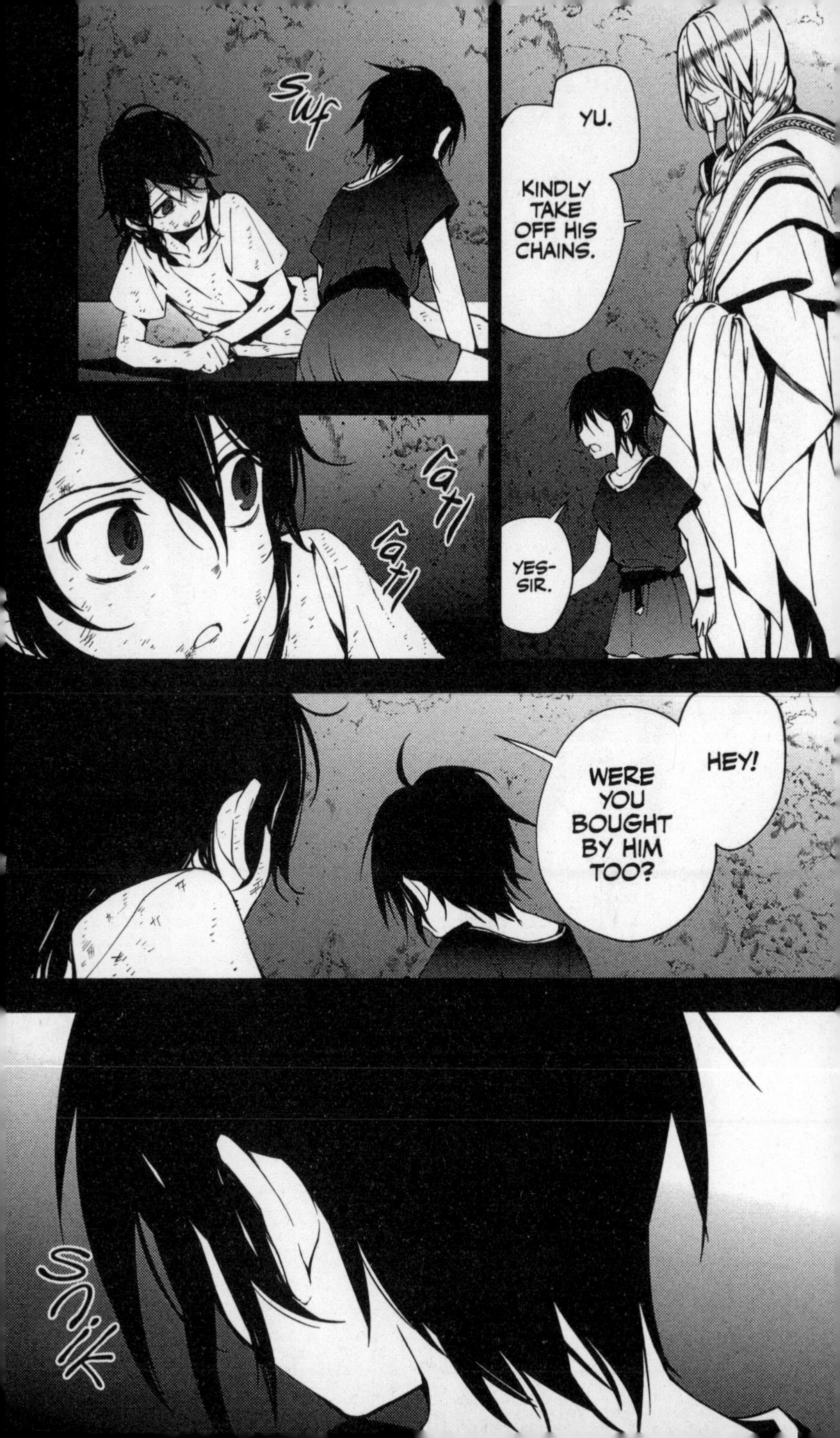
YU.
KINDLY TAKE OFF HIS CHAINS.
YES-SIR.
SWF
RATL
RATL
HEY!
WERE YOU BOUGHT BY HIM TOO?
SNIK

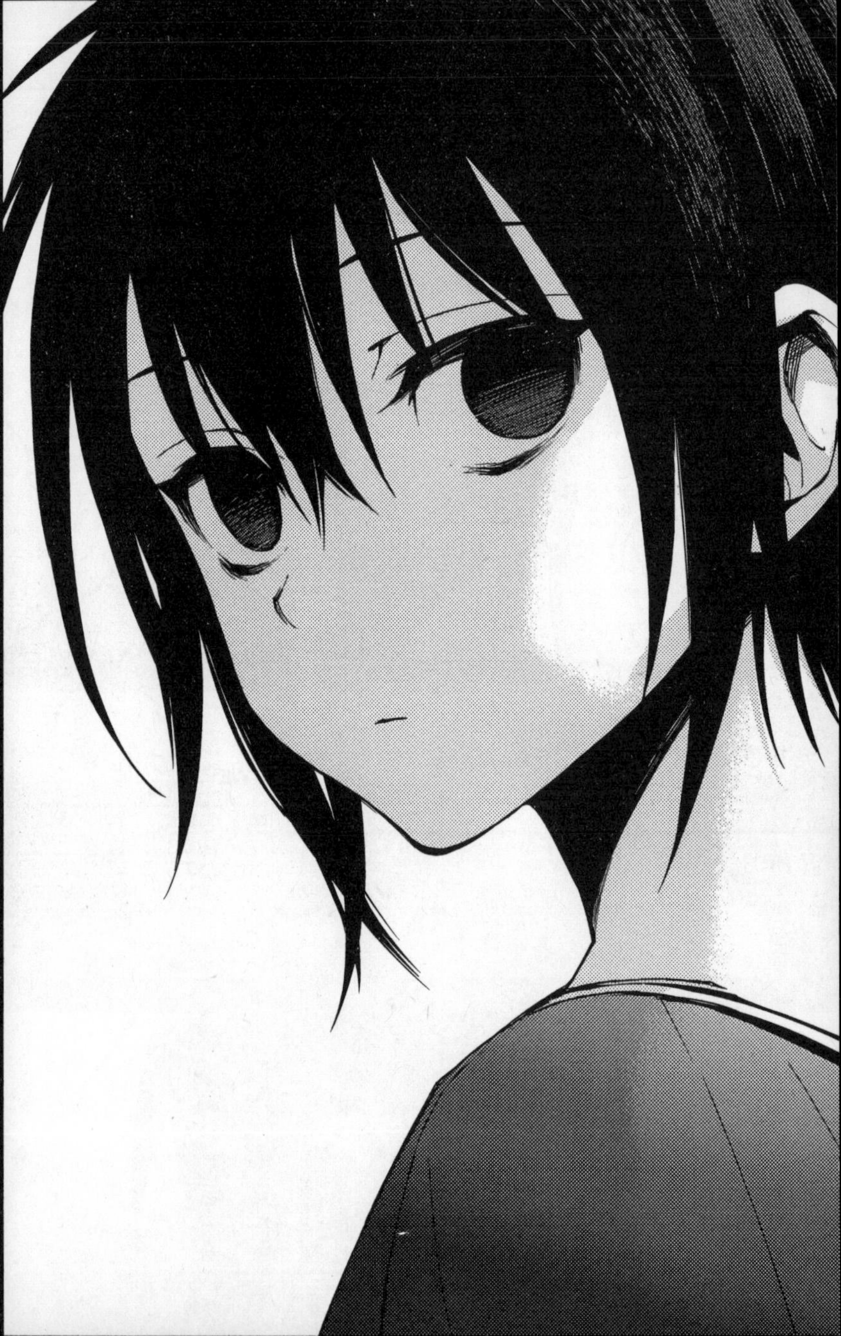

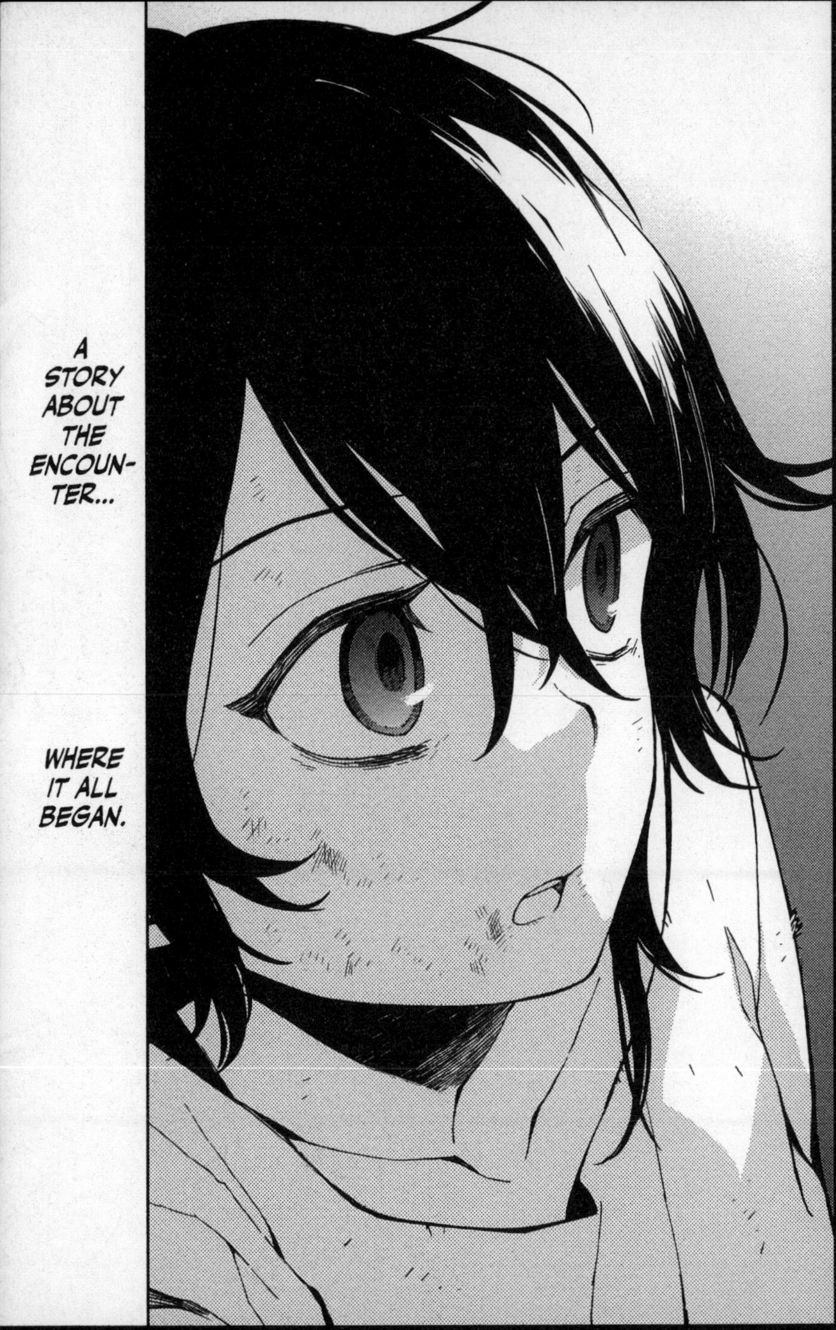
A STORY ABOUT THE ENCOUN-TER...
WHERE IT ALL BEGAN.

Seraph of the End: Vampire Reign 17 / END

Seraph of the End
VAMPIRE REIGN

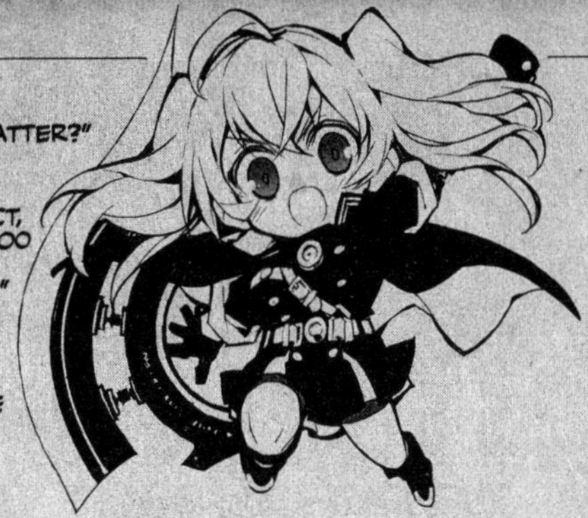

MITSUBA: "SIGH..."

SHINOA: "IS SOMETHING THE MATTER?"

MITSUBA: "SIIIIIIIIGH..."

SHINOA: "GOODNESS, WHY THE ACT, MITSU. YOU HAVE MUCH TOO LARGE A BUST TO HAVE ANY PRESSING WORRIES."

MITSUBA: "HEY. QUIT IMPLYING THAT A BIGGER BUST MEANS LESS BRAINS. BODY PARTS DON'T DETERMINE WHAT KIND OF WORRIES A PERSON HAS."

SHINOA: "OH MY! SO THERE IS SOMETHING YOU ARE WORRYING ABOUT?"

MITSUBA: "OF COURSE THERE IS! EVERYONE HAS THINGS THEY WORRY ABOUT."

SHINOA: "WELL I MOST CERTAINLY DON'T, AS I HAVE THE BIGGEST BUSTLINE OF THEM ALL."

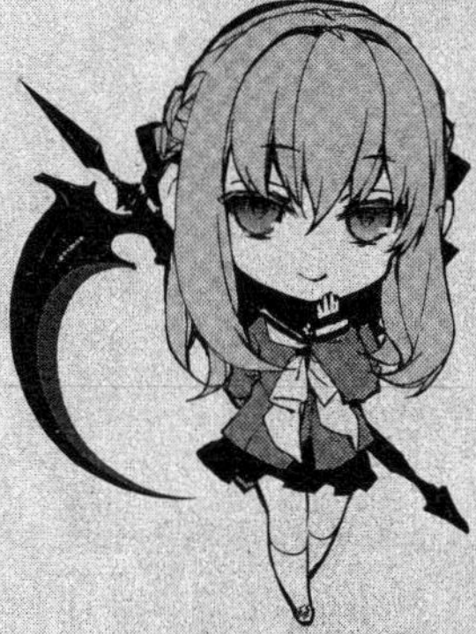

MITSUBA: "..."

SHINOA: "ACTUALLY, IT'S BECAUSE I HAVE LESS BRAINS THAN ANYONE!"

MITSUBA: "..."

SHINOA: "MITSU."

MITSUBA: "HM?"

SHINOA: "THIS IS THE PART WHERE YOU SAY SOMETHING WITTY IN RESPONSE."

MITSUBA: "AH. I NOTICED YOU'RE REALLY CONCERNED ABOUT YOUR BUSTLINE."

SHINOA: "SIGH..."

MITSUBA: "SIGH..."

SHINOA: "SIGH..."

YU: "WHAT'S WITH ALL THE SIGHING OVER HERE?"

SHINOA: "WE ARE GRAPPLING WITH GREAT AND WEIGHTY CONCERNS NO IDIOT COULD EVER COMPREHEND."

YU: "HEY! WHO'RE YOU CALLING AN IDIOT?"

SHINOA: "ISN'T THAT RIGHT, MITSU."

MITSUBA: "YEP. THAT'S RIGHT."

YU: "C'MON, IF THERE'S ANYTHING THAT'S BUGGING YOU, TELL ME. I'LL LISTEN. CAN'T GUARANTEE I'LL BE ABLE TO DO ANYTHING ABOUT IT, THOUGH."

SHINOA: "WOULD YOU PLEASE STOP WITH THE SEXUAL HARASSMENT? IT'S DISGRACEFUL."

YU: "WAH?"

MITSUBA: "NOT THAT SHINOA AND I ARE WORRIED ABOUT EVEN REMOTELY THE SAME THING."

SHINOA: "OH? WE AREN'T?"

MITSUBA: "NOPE. MINE DON'T NEED TO BE ANY BIGGER."

SHINOA: "OH, OUCH! BURN!"

YU: "HUH? WHAT IS IT YOU WANT TO BE BIGGER?"

SHINOA: "IT ISN'T SO MUCH "BIGGER" AS "TALLER." I WOULD LIKE TO BE TALLER."

YU: "OH, YOUR HEIGHT? YEAH, I CAN UNDERSTAND THAT. I WANNA BE TALLER TOO."

SHINOA: "HM? YOU LET SUCH THINGS BOTHER YOU TOO, YUICHIRO?"

YU: "YEAH. I MEAN, I'M 16 NOW. I'M STARTING TO WORRY THAT I'VE STOPPED GROWING. IF I HAVE, THEN I'M STUCK WITH THAT STUPID GUREN LOOKING DOWN ON ME FOR THE REST OF MY LIFE! HE'S WAY TOO TALL, Y'KNOW?"

SHINOA: "VERY TRUE."

YU: "WHEN HE LOOKS AT ME, EVERY TIME HE'S GOT THIS "WELL AREN'T YOU THE SHORT, STUPID IDIOT" LOOK ON HIS FACE. SEE? HE GETS THIS EXACT LOOK ON HIS FACE."

SHINOA: "OH, THAT IS VERY ACCURATE. THE LT. COLONEL IS QUITE THE TWISTED INDIVIDUAL, AFTER ALL."

YU: "HE LOOKS JUST LIKE THIS. SEE? SEE?"

SHINOA: "OH YES. JUST LIKE THAT."

GUREN: "YO, SHRIMPY AND SHORTY."

YU: "DIE!!"

SHINOA: "DIE!!"

GUREN: "DO THAT AGAIN AND I'LL LOOK AT YOU JUST LIKE THIS. SO HAH."

YU: "I'M GONNA KILL YOU!!"

SHINOA: "ALL THAT ASIDE... HEY, MITSU?"

MITSUBA: "HM?"

SHINOA: "WHAT WAS IT YOU WERE SO CONCERNED ABOUT AGAIN?"

MITSUBA: "I WOULDN'T SAY I'M 'CONCERNED' ABOUT IT, REALLY. IT ISN'T THAT BIG A THING."

YU: "WHAT IS IT?"

MITSUBA: "THERE'S ONE THING I HAVEN'T EATEN AT ALL SINCE THE CATASTROPHE HAPPENED, AND ALL OF A SUDDEN I GOT A WEIRD HANKERING FOR IT."

SHINOA: "OH? WHAT IS IT?"

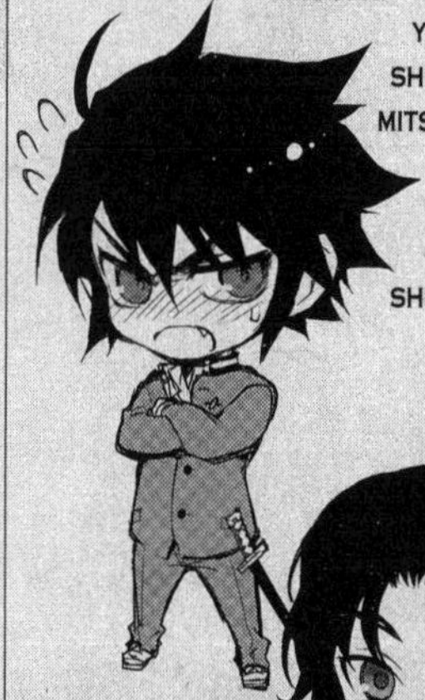

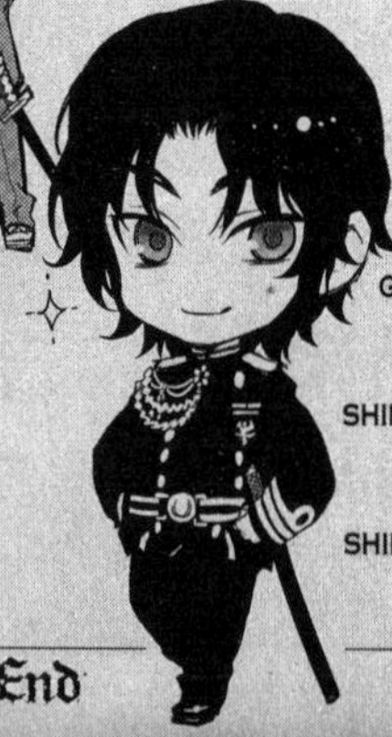

MITSUBA: "GARIGARI-KUN ICE POPS."

YU: "HUH? WHAT'RE THOSE?"

SHINOA: "YES, WHAT ARE THOSE?"

MITSUBA: "WHAT, YOU TWO HAVE NEVER HEARD OF GARIGARI-KUN ICE POPS? SERIOUSLY? SIGH..."

YU: "WELL, SEE, I KINDA DON'T REALLY HAVE TOO CLEAR A MEMORY OF ANYTHING THAT HAPPENED BEFORE THE CATASTROPHE..."

SHINOA: "PERSONALLY, I SPENT MY ENTIRE LIFE BEFORE THE WORLD ENDED LIVING UNDER A ROCK. I DIDN'T SEE OR SPEAK WITH ANYONE AT ALL."

GUREN: "I TOTALLY GET WHERE YOU'RE COMING FROM, MITSUBA. IT'S THE END OF SUMMER AND EVERYTHING."

MITSUBA: "YOU KNOW ABOUT THAT, LT. COLONEL? REALLY?"

GUREN: "REALLY."

MITSUBA: "I COULD REALLY GO FOR ONE OF THOSE POPSICLES RIGHT NOW. SIGH..."

GUREN: "ME TOO. SIGH..."

YU: "HEY, UH, SHINOA? WHAT DO YOU THINK ABOUT THAT?"

SHINOA: "I THINK THE LT. COLONEL WISHES HIS BUSTLINE WAS LARGER TOO."

YU: "HUH? WHAT DO YOU MEAN?"

SHINOA: "SIGH..."

YU: NO, SERIOUSLY. WHAT DO YOU MEAN?"

AFTERWORD

HELLO. I'M TAKAYA KAGAMI.

A NEW VOLUME IS OUT YET AGAIN.

I HOPE YOU ARE ALL DOING WELL. FOR THE FIRST TIME IN A WHILE, I DECIDED I'D DO A CHARACTER MINI-SKIT THAT WAS ALL DUMB LAUGHS, WITH NO SUBTLE CONNECTION TO ANY OF THE LARGER PLOT POINTS OF THE MAIN STORY. IN CONTRAST, THE MAIN STORY IN THIS VOLUME DIGS EVER DEEPER INTO THE MYSTERIOUS CORE OF THE PLOT.

THE FIRST PROGENITOR.
SAITO.
KRUL.
URD AND LEST KARR.

HOW WILL YU AND MIKA AND THEIR FRIENDS DEAL WITH THESE MONSTERS WHO HAVE LIVED AND PLOTTED FOR MIND-BOGGLING LENGTHS OF TIME? HOW HAVE THEY ALREADY BEEN CONNECTED? ALL WILL BE LAID BARE SOON. I'M GETTING READY TO START REELING IN ALL THE LITTLE HINTS AND STORY THREADS I'VE PAINSTAKINGLY PLANTED HERE AND THERE ACROSS THE WHOLE STORY. I HOPE YOU'LL STICK AROUND FOR THE RIDE!

IN OTHER NEWS, THE MANGA VERSION OF *SERAPH OF THE END: GUREN ICHINOSE: CATASTROPHE AT 16* IS STILL ONGOING IN *MONTHLY SHONEN MAGAZINE*. YOU CAN FIND SOME OF MY FAVORITE SCENES OVER THERE, LIKE WHEN GUREN AND SHINYA HAVE A LIFE-AND-DEATH MOTORCYCLE CHASE WITH VAMPIRES. IF YOU HAVEN'T LOOKED INTO WHY THE WORLD ENDED IN THE LIGHT NOVELS, I HOPE YOU'LL GO OVER AND CHECK IT OUT IN THE MANGA VERSION!

I'D BE HONORED IF YOU CONTINUE TO KEEP UP WITH THIS STORY.

SEE YOU NEXT TIME!

—TAKAYA KAGAMI

A brilliant sketch of Yuichiro by the author!

TAKAYA KAGAMI is a prolific light novelist whose works include the action and fantasy series *The Legend of the Legendary Heroes*, which has been adapted into manga, anime and a video game. His previous series, *A Dark Rabbit Has Seven Lives*, also spawned a manga and anime series.

66 Before I knew it, autumn has arrived. I've been so busy lately that it feels like I've barely had the time to flail in panic before a whole year went by. The only thing that hasn't changed is that I still love potato chips and curry. I hope you enjoy the new volume. 99

YAMATO YAMAMOTO, born 1983, is an artist and illustrator whose works include the *Kure-nai* manga and the light novels *Kure-nai*, *9S -Nine S-* and *Denpa Teki na Kanojo*. Both *Denpa Teki na Kanojo* and *Kure-nai* have been adapted into anime.

66 This volume we get a little glimpse at Krul's and Asuramaru's past. The mystery around Yu's too. The way things go, you wind up very curious about the other vampires' pasts by the end. 99

DAISUKE FURUYA previously assisted Yamato Yamamoto with storyboards for *Kure-nai*.

Seraph of the End

VAMPIRE REIGN

VOLUME 17
SHONEN JUMP MANGA EDITION

STORY BY TAKAYA KAGAMI
ART BY YAMATO YAMAMOTO
STORYBOARDS BY DAISUKE FURUYA

TRANSLATION Adrienne Beck
TOUCH-UP ART & LETTERING Sabrina Heep
DESIGN Shawn Carrico
EDITOR Marlene First

Printed in the U.S.A.

Published by VIZ Media, LLC
P.O. Box 77010
San Francisco, CA 94107

10 9 8 7 6 5 4 3 2 1
First printing, June 2019

VIZ MEDIA
viz.com

SHONEN JUMP
shonenjump.com

RATED T+ OLDER TEEN
ratings.viz.com

PARENTAL ADVISORY
SERAPH OF THE END is rated T+ for Older Teen and is recommended for ages 16 and up. This volume contains violence and some adult themes.

Twin Star Exorcists
ONMYOJI
STORY AND ART BY Yoshiaki Sukeno
The action-packed romantic comedy
from the creator of Good Luck Girl!
Rokuro dreams of becoming anything but an exorcist!
Then mysterious Benio turns up. The pair are dubbed the
"Twin Star Exorcists" and learn they are fated to marry...
Can Rokuro escape both fates?
SHONEN JUMP
viz media
www.viz.com
RATED T FOR TEEN
ratings.viz.com
SOUSEI NO ONMYOJI © 2013 by Yoshiaki Sukeno /SHUEISHA Inc.

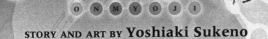

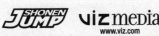

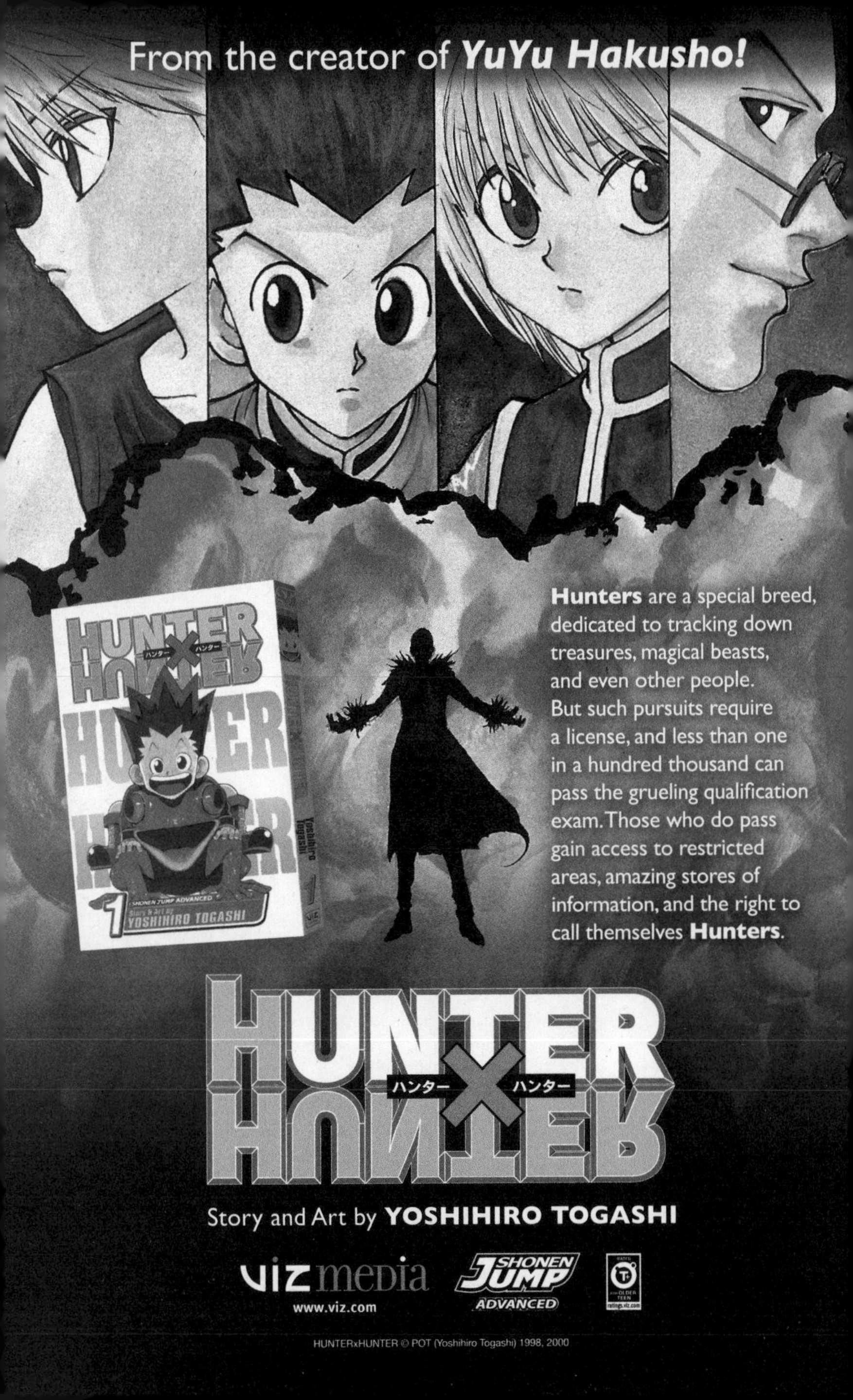
From the creator of YuYu Hakusho!
HUNTER × HUNTER ハンター ハンター
1 SHONEN JUMP ADVANCED Story & Art by YOSHIHIRO TOGASHI
Hunters are a special breed, dedicated to tracking down treasures, magical beasts, and even other people. But such pursuits require a license, and less than one in a hundred thousand can pass the grueling qualification exam. Those who do pass gain access to restricted areas, amazing stores of information, and the right to call themselves Hunters.
HUNTER × HUNTER ハンター ハンター
Story and Art by YOSHIHIRO TOGASHI
VIZ media
www.viz.com
SHONEN JUMP ADVANCED
RATED T+ FOR OLDER TEEN ratings.viz.com
HUNTERxHUNTER © POT (Yoshihiro Togashi) 1998, 2000

YOU'RE READING THE **WRONG WAY!**

SERAPH OF THE END reads from right to left, starting in the upper-right corner. Japanese is read from right to left, meaning that action, sound effects, and word-balloon order are completely reversed from English order.

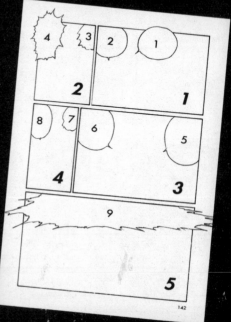

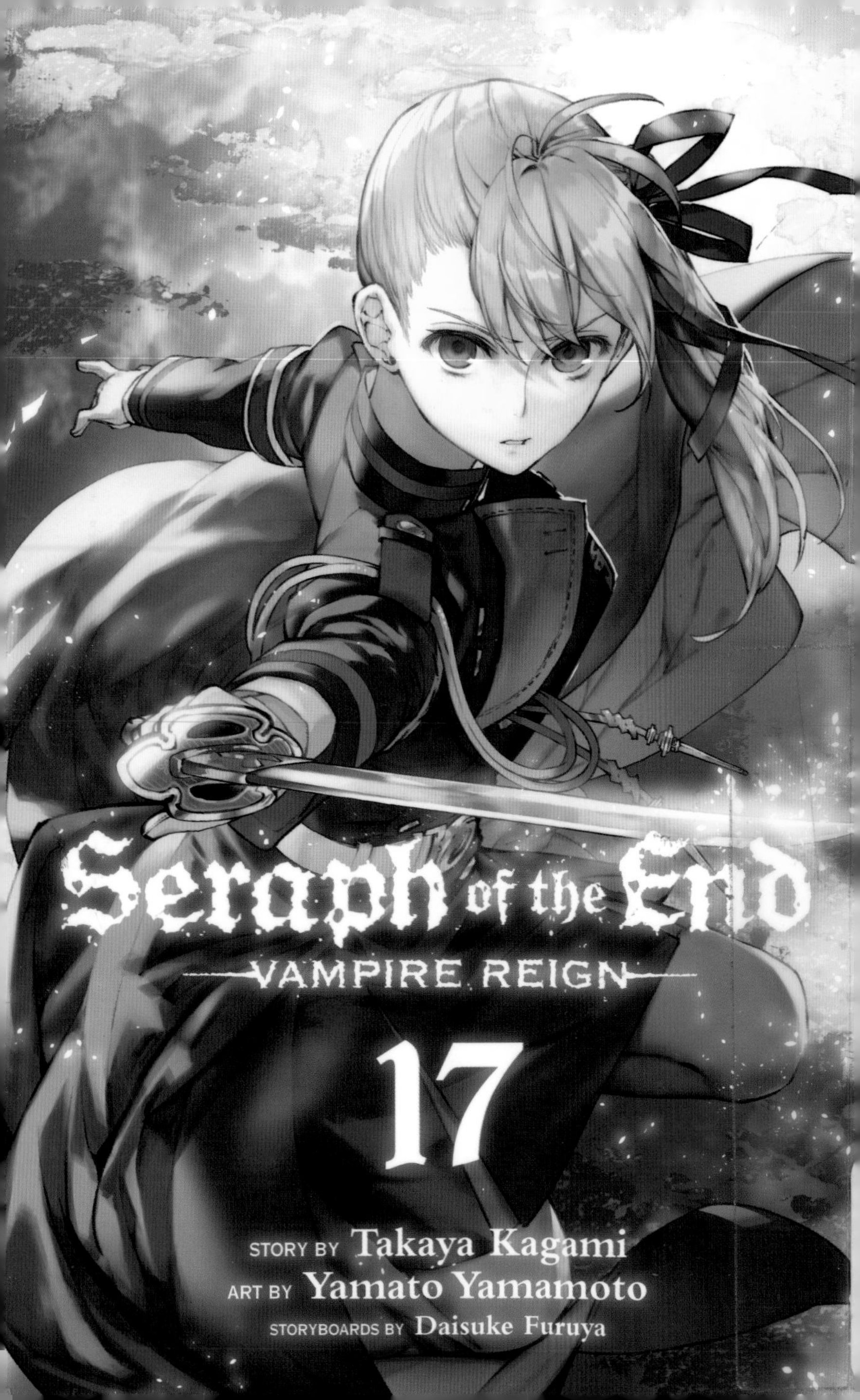
Seraph of the End
VAMPIRE REIGN
17
STORY BY Takaya Kagami
ART BY Yamato Yamamoto
STORYBOARDS BY Daisuke Furuya